Global Culture and Sport Series

Series Editors
Stephen Wagg
Carnegie School Of Sport
Leeds Beckett University
Leeds, UK

David Andrews
School of Public Health
University of Maryland
College Park, MD, USA

Series Editors: Stephen Wagg, Leeds Beckett University, UK, and David Andrews, University of Maryland, USA.

The Global Culture and Sport series aims to contribute to and advance the debate about sport and globalization by engaging with various aspects of sport culture as a vehicle for critically excavating the tensions between the global and the local, transformation and tradition and sameness and difference. With studies ranging from snowboarding bodies, the globalization of rugby and the Olympics, to sport and migration, issues of racism and gender, and sport in the Arab world, this series showcases the range of exciting, pioneering research being developed in the field of sport sociology.

More information about this series at
https://link.springer.com/bookseries/15008

Augustine E. Ayuk
Editor

Football (Soccer) in Africa

Origins, Contributions, and Contradictions

Editor
Augustine E. Ayuk
Clayton State University
Morrow, GA, USA

ISSN 2662-3404 ISSN 2662-3412 (electronic)
Global Culture and Sport Series
ISBN 978-3-030-94865-8 ISBN 978-3-030-94866-5 (eBook)
https://doi.org/10.1007/978-3-030-94866-5

© The Editor(s) (if applicable) and The Author(s), under exclusive licence to Springer Nature Switzerland AG 2022
This work is subject to copyright. All rights are solely and exclusively licensed by the Publisher, whether the whole or part of the material is concerned, specifically the rights of translation, reprinting, reuse of illustrations, recitation, broadcasting, reproduction on microfilms or in any other physical way, and transmission or information storage and retrieval, electronic adaptation, computer software, or by similar or dissimilar methodology now known or hereafter developed.
The use of general descriptive names, registered names, trademarks, service marks, etc. in this publication does not imply, even in the absence of a specific statement, that such names are exempt from the relevant protective laws and regulations and therefore free for general use.
The publisher, the authors and the editors are safe to assume that the advice and information in this book are believed to be true and accurate at the date of publication. Neither the publisher nor the authors or the editors give a warranty, expressed or implied, with respect to the material contained herein or for any errors or omissions that may have been made. The publisher remains neutral with regard to jurisdictional claims in published maps and institutional affiliations.

Cover illustration: Kyle Marcano / Augustine E. Ayuk

This Palgrave Macmillan imprint is published by the registered company Springer Nature Switzerland AG.
The registered company address is: Gewerbestrasse 11, 6330 Cham, Switzerland

Acknowledgments

I am particularly grateful to all contributors to this volume for their patience and commitment to completing this project despite the many hiccups we encountered along the way. I am indebted to Stephen Wagg and David Andrews (Series Editors) for their invaluable advice, support, and guidance and from the proposal through the production of the volume. I owe a debt of gratitude to Sharla Plant, editor, for her quick responses to my inquiries and who made this process less stressful. My sincere appreciation also go to Raghupathy Kalyanaraman, Project Coordinator for Springer Nature, for his prompt response to my emails and his timely feedback.

My family has been my most important source of support in this journey. I want to give special thanks to my wife, Esther O. Ayuk, who has been very supportive of this undertaking, and her incredible patience in listening to testimonies and praises from strangers about the life of a footballer she never knew. My sons, Ebai and Nyenty were "pillars" in the midfield and defense during their playing days in high school and college. My daughter, Bessem, who was fast, strong, and difficult to stop when she played for a local YMCA team. I want to express my sincere thanks to my childhood friend, Obi Tabot Tabe, who reminded me all the time, especially when I traveled to Yaoundé for the Junior National Team selection, "not to forget our plans to go to America."

I dedicate this work to all my former teammates, friends, fans, and supporters of Customs Football Club of Mamfe and Cammark Social Club of Mamfe, whose endless support and encouragement was instrumental in inspiring me and contributed to my selection in the Cameroon Junior

National Team. Special appreciation goes to Mr. Matthew Munang, former President of Cammark Social Club of Mamfe, and my former boss, at the National Produce Marketing Board (NPMB). Mr. Munang's dedication to further football in Mamfe and Manyu Division was his way of giving back to the community and he did so without reservation. I am equally indebted to our dynamic team manager, Mr. Eyong Joe, for his selflessness and commitment to promoting football in Manyu Division, Mamfe town, and the Southwest province.

I have been especially fortunate to work with an exceptional team of colleagues in the College of Arts Sciences, at Clayton State University, particularly in the Department of Social Sciences for the collegial milieu of their incredible support through the years.

I am grateful to Mr. Kyle Marcano, Center for Instructional Development at Clayton State University, for designing the cover page of this book and making many timely revisions as needed.

I would like to extend my sincere gratitude to Mr. Njomo Kevin, Sports Commentator of Radio Buea, whose " voice behind the microphone" transformed football in the Southwest Province, when I was an active player. Despite his numerous commitments, he always found time to share his extensive knowledge and recollection of football in Cameroon, particularly in the Southwest region. His commentaries and analysis impelled national team coaches to travel to the Southwest, to observe, and select players like me and other deserving talents to the Junior National Team.

My success in football with Customs Mamfe and Cammark Mamfe would not have been possible without a resilient cast of players. The list is too long to mention everyone by name; however, some of these individuals deserve mention: Eyong Martin (Esele), Emoh Edward, Essambe Robert, Eyong Paul, Arreyngang Walter, Joseph Tanyi, Tabi Fred, Ekpombang Maurice, Daniel Orock (The Rock), Atiabet Thomas, Takor Daniel, Etchu Takor, Etchu Abaunaw, Egbe Sunday, Agbor Fidelis, and Yetna Jacques. Special thanks also go to my friend and the former captain of Electsport Limbe, Gregg Tataw, for his invaluable advice during and after our playing days and for helping me with recollections of episodes in the Southwest Division Two League.

Contents

1 Introduction: Football (Soccer) in Africa: Origins, Contributions, and Contradictions   1
Augustine E. Ayuk

2 FIFA and Football Development in Africa   25
Njororai Wycliffe W. Simiyu

3 The Confederation of African Football (CAF): Origins, Accomplishments, and Challenges   55
Peter Ajongwa Ngwafu and Augustine E. Ayuk

4 Football in Cameroon, Best of Times, Worst of Times: Exploring the Paradox of Africa's Venerable Football Nation   77
Augustine E. Ayuk

5 Historicizing Football Nigeria: Disciplinary, Governmentality, and Resistance Within Football Labor's Struggle   103
Chuka Onwumechili

6 Football in DR Congo: A Critical Account of "Congolese Football"   125
Tamba Nlandu

7   Football in Egypt: Between Joy and Politics   147
    Hala Thabet

8   The History and Development of Football in Ghana   165
    Kwame B. Dankwa

9   The Politics of Soccer Management in Kenya: The Rise
    and Decline of a Popular Sport   189
    Wanjala S. Nasong'o

10 Soccer in Senegal: National Identity, Commercialization,
    and Acquisition of Wealth   213
    Tamba E. M'bayo

11 Contradictions and Inconsistencies Facing the South
    African Football Association and the Premier Soccer
    League   231
    David L. Bogopa

12 The Origins, Status, Contributions and Contradictions of
    Association Football in Uganda   253
    Njororai Wycliffe W. Simiyu

13 Vicious Cycle: Cameroon(ization) and/or
    Foreign(ization) of the Indomitable Lions' Head
    Coaching   275
    Alain Lawo-Sukam

14 Conclusion   299
    Augustine E. Ayuk

Index   305

NOTES ON CONTRIBUTORS

Augustine E. Ayuk is Professor of Political Science at Clayton State University. His areas of interest include American Government, International Relations, Comparative Politics, and Politics of Africa. Ayuk holds his bachelor's and master's degrees from Georgia College and State University, and PhD in Political Science from Clark Atlanta University. He previously taught at Kennesaw State University and the University of West Georgia. He is co-editor of The African Civil Service: Fifty Years after Independence, with Case Studies from Cameroon, Ghana, Kenya, and Nigeria (January 2016). His book chapters include: "The Roots of Stability and Instability in Cameroon." Post-Colonial Cameroon: Politics, Economy, and Society (2018). "Africa's Debt Burden and the HIPC Initiative: Cameroon, from Contemporary Africa: Challenges and Opportunities Challenges to Opportunity." Contemporary Africa: Challenges and Opportunities (Palgrave Macmillan (2014)). "The Struggle Against Endemic Corruption in Post-Independence Africa: Cameroon, is 'Kondengui' the Answer?" Routledge, Encyclopedia of African Studies, (2020). "Privatization in Developing Countries: A Comparative Examination of Cameroon and Costa Rica." *Georgia Political Science Association* (online Journal, Proceedings), 2010. He has also chaired numerous panels and presented papers at many international and US academic conferences.

Ayuk is serving a second term as a member of the Faculty Senate at Clayton State University. In 2014, Ayuk served as Director of the Southeast Model African Union (SEMAU). In 2018, Ayuk was a nominee for Clayton State University's College of Arts and Sciences Teacher of the Year, and Clayton State University Presidential Making Things Better

ix

nominee. Ayuk was a member of Cameroon's Junior National Football team selection-1985. He coached Youth soccer in Georgia, the USA for four years and won eleven championships.

David L. Bogopa He is an academic in the Department of Sociology and Anthropology at the Nelson Mandela University based in the School of Social Sciences. He is an anthropologist with an undergraduate degree in Anthropology and Sociology, an Honours Degree in Anthropology and Master of Arts in Anthropology. He also holds a Master of Arts in Development Studies as well as a PhD in Anthropology. He is a former Pan African Anthropological Association President (2003–2005) and he is a co-founder of World Council of Anthropological Association which was established in Brazil (2004) and he is an Advisory Board member in World Council of Anthropological Association. He is a deputy chairperson of the Eastern Cape Geographical Name Change in South Africa. He also serves in the editorial board of Indo-Pacific Journal of Phenomenology. His work was published in various scholarly accredited journals, namely: Indo-Pacific Journal of Phenomenology, Acta Criminologica Journal, Indilinga Journal of Indigenous Knowledge Systems, and other journals. He is the sole author of the book entitled "Shebeen Culture in South Africa" and he has a book chapter in the book entitled "Global Perspective on Physical Education. He also has chapters published in other scholarly books. He has over the years successfully supervised more than twenty master's students in Anthropology, Development Studies and Sociology.

Kwame B. Dankwa is Professor of Political Science at the Department of History, Political Science, and Interdisciplinary Studies at Albany State University (ASU), Albany, Georgia, where he has taught courses in International Relations, History of Political Thought, International Political Economy, State and Local Government, and Comparative Government. His research interests are in the areas of United State Congress, state and local government, as well as social justice and politics in transitional societies. He received his PhD in Political Science from Clark-Atlanta University (with areas of interest including Political Philosophy, International Relations and African Politics, and Public Administration) in 1999 and joined Albany State University in January 2001. During his professional career at ASU, he has presented papers at several academic conferences, contributed book chapters and published articles in professional journals. He initiated the Model United Nations Club at Albany State University, where he succeeded in preparing students to the annual Model UN Conferences in New York for the 2002, 2003, and 2004 sessions. He is the coordinator of Albany State University's Southeast Model African Union (SEMAU) group.

Alain Lawo-Sukam is Associate Professor of Hispanic and Africana Studies at Texas A&M University in College Station. His area of interest include Hispanic Studies with a specialty in Afro-Hispanic literature and culture. He is the author of Hacia una poética afro-colombiana: el caso del Pacífico (2010), Sueño con África. Dream of Africa. Rêve d'Afrique (2013) and Mange-Mil y otros relatos. He has published numerous articles in national and international peer reviewed journals. He is a member of several editorial boards and has served as manuscript reviewer for many national and international journals. He is a recipient of numerous grants and awards; among the most recent are the 2015–2016 AFS College-Level Distinguished Achievement Award for Teaching and the Hispanic Studies Research Enhancement and High Impact Research Grants. He was elected for five years as a member of the Executive Committee of the Modern Language Association, where he served as Secretary and Chair of the African Division.

Tamba E. M'bayo is Associate Professor of History at West Virginia University, where he teaches both graduate and undergraduate courses in African history. His first book was on Muslim interpreters in colonial Senegal, a product of his research interest in the colonial and post-colonial history of French West Africa. His research for his second monograph focuses on Sierra Leone, his country of origin, and traces its long history of epidemic episodes from 1787 to the Ebola outbreak of 2013–2015.

Wanjala S. Nasong'o is Professor of International Studies and former chair of the department at Rhodes College in Memphis, Tennessee. Professor Nasong'o received his BA and MA degrees from the University of Nairobi, Kenya, and his PhD in Public and International Affairs from Northeastern University in Boston. Professor Nasong'o previously taught at the University of Tennessee, Knoxville, University of Nairobi, Kenya and Kenyatta University, Kenya. He is author, editor, and co-editor of numerous peer-reviewed books and articles in refereed journals. Wanjala has been honored with the Rhodes College's Clarence Day Award for Outstanding Research and Creative Activity, and the Ali Mazrui Award for Research and Scholarly Excellence from the University of Texas at Austin. Professor Nasong'o was also awarded a Diaspora Visiting Professor Fellowship by the Council for the Development of Social Science Research in Africa. In 2020, Nasong'o was named Carnegie African Diaspora Fellow, tenable at Egerton University, Njoro, Kenya.

Peter Ajongwa Ngwafu is a Professor of Political Science and Public Administration & Director of the Master of Public Administration Program at Albany State University, Albany, Georgia, where he has taught courses in Organizational Theory &Bureaucratic Behavior, Public Policy, Human Resources Management, Labor-Management Relations and Public Management. His research interests are in the areas of development administration, diversity management, social justice, and politics in transitional societies. He has also taught upper-level Political Science courses in International Relations, American Government & Politics and African Politics. He received his PhD in Political Science from Clark-Atlanta University (with areas of interest including in Public Administration, American Government& Politics, International Relations and African Politics), in 1999 and joined Albany State University in August 2000. During his professional career at ASU, he has contributed numerous book chapters and published several articles in professional journals. He has also served on the Network of Schools of Public Policy, Affairs &Administration's Commission for Peer Review &Accreditation (COPRA) 2017–2020.

Tamba Nlandu is an associate professor in the Department of Philosophy, John Carroll University, University Heights, Ohio, USA. He has always been a soccer fan who grew up in Kinshasa, Democratic Republic of the Congo (formerly Zaire), one of the world's largest soccer-crazy cities. Over the years, he has coached club, middle school, and high school soccer. He has been a USSF (United States Soccer Federation) and NFHS (National Federation of State High School Associations) certified referee since 2001. He has taught courses in philosophy and ethics of sport, introduction to philosophy, American philosophy, African philosophy, business ethics, and contemporary ethical problems. His published articles include (1) "On the Concept of Fair Competition Prevalent in Today's European Soccer Leagues," *Sport, Ethics and Philosophy: Official Journal of the British Philosophy of Sport Association*, Vol. 12, No. 2, May 2018, 162–176, (2) "On Some Philosophical Foundations of the Disappointing Performances of the African Soccer Teams in World Competitions," *Sport, Ethics and Philosophy*, Vol. 11, No. 2, May 2017, 192–206, (3) "The Fallacies of the Assumptions behind the Arguments for Goal-line Technology in Soccer," *Sport, Ethics, and Philosophy*, Vol. 6, No. 4, 2012, 451–66, (4) "One Play Cannot Be Known to Win or Lose a Game: A Fallibilist Account of Game,"

Sport, Ethics and Philosophy, Vol. 5, Number 1, February 2011, 21–33, (5) "Play Until the Whistle Blows: Sportsmanship as the Outcome of Thirdness," *Journal of the Philosophy of Sport*, 35 (2008): 73–89, (6) "On Habit and Consciousness: A Peircean Critique of William James's Conception of Habit," *Streams of William James*, Vol. 6, Issue 3, Fall 2004, 25–29, (7) "Charles S. Peirce on the Foundations of Philosophy and Culture," *International Studies in Philosophy*, Vol. 34, No. 1, 2002, 143–173, and (8) "The Fallacy of Universalism: The Nature and Status of African Philosophy Revisited," *International Studies in Philosophy*, Vol. 33, No. 1, 2001, 83–104.

Chuka Onwumechili is Professor of Strategic, Legal, and Management Communication (SLMC) at Howard University in Washington, DC (USA). He edits the *Howard Journal of Communications* and is member of the executive board of ex-Enugu Rangers FC Players Association, USA. Onwumechili is author or co-editor of over ten books, book chapters, and several peer-reviewed academic journal articles. He hosts a blog on Nigerian football and owns a database on the Nigerian national team. His most recent book (with Gerard Akindes) is *Identity and Nation in African Football: Fans, Community, and Clubs* and a recent journal article (with Koren Bedeau) is 'Analysis of FIFA's Attempt at Image Repair' in the *Communication and Sport* journal. He has sports articles published in *Soccer and Society, Critical African Studies, International Journal of Sport Communication*, and *International Journal of the History of Sport*. Chuka has also written sports articles for *The Conversation*, an online publication integrating academic research with journalistic writing. He also helps former international players write their memoirs. A recent memoir is by Nigeria's former international Francis Moniedafe titled *Moniedafe: My Life and Gloray Years of Bendel Insurance FC*. Onwumechili is married to Adora and has three children.

Njororai Wycliffe W. Simiyu is Professor of Kinesiology at The University of Texas at Tyler, Texas, USA. He holds a PhD in Physical Education and Sport from Kenyatta University, Kenya and has a research focus on race and sport, international soccer, track and field, sport labor migration, physical activity and health, performance sport, sociology of sport, pedagogy, and leadership in Kinesiology.

He has taught at universities in Kenya (Egerton and Kenyatta University), Uganda (Kyambogo), and USA (Wiley and University of

Texas, Tyler (UTTYLER)). He has 36 years of teaching experience, 30 of which are at a university. He joined Texas Association of Health, Physical Education, Recreation and Dance (TAHPERD) and Society of Health and Physical Educators (SHAPE) in 2011. He volunteers in TAHPERD serving on the College Committee and serving on a nominating committee for the Vice President for the College Section.

He has previously served as president of the US-based Kenya Scholars and Studies Association (KESSA) (2017–2020) and as President of faculty Senate at The University of Texas at Tyler, Texas, USA. He has published over 120 peer-reviewed articles, book chapters and proceedings. He has presented papers at many US and international conferences. He has also been invited to deliver keynote speeches at both local and international conferences on various themes pertaining to Physical Education and Sport. He frequently writes opinion pieces for The Conversation on various aspects of sport in Africa.

Hala Thabet is Associate Professor of Political Science. She has over 15 years' experience in research and teaching in both Cairo University, Egypt and Zayed University, the UAE.

She was the assistant director of the Centre for African Future Studies, Cairo, since 1996, and a board member of the African Association of Political Science (AAPS), based in Pretoria, South Africa. Thabet is the chair of the department of International Studies and Social Sciences AUH and DXB, Zayed University, the UAE, and is an executive board member of the International Political Science Association (IPSA), based in Canada, Research Committee 44 on Security, Conflict and Democratization.

Dr. Thabet has published many book chapters, articles, and books in both Arabic and English. Her research focuses on African Issues, Conflict management, State building, terrorism, and fundamental groups. Her most recent publications include: Thabet, Hala, "COVID-19 and the Road to Authoritarian Rule in Ethiopia", in: Steven Ratuva, Hamdy A. Hassan, Radomir Compel (Editors): Risks, Identity and Conflict: Theoretical Perspectives and Case Studies, 2021, Palgrave Macmillan.

Abbreviations

AAFA	Accra Amateur Football Association
AFA	African Football Association
AFCON	African Cup of Nations
AFLU	Association de Football de Lubumbashi
AWCON	Africa Women's Cup of Nations
BBC	British Broadcasting Corporation
CAF	Confederation of African Football
CDC	Cameroon Development Corporation
CECAFA	Confederation of East and Central African Football Associations
CEO	Chief Executive Officer
CHAN	African Nations Championship
CHM	Chandibai Himathmal Mansukihani College
CNU	Cameroon National Union
CONCACAF	Confederation of North, Central American, and Caribbean Association of Football
CONMEBOL	South American Football Confederation
COS	Central Organization of Sports
COSAFA	Confederation of Southern African Football Federation
FECAFOOT	Fédération Camerounaise de Football
FIFA	Fédération Internationale de Football Association
FKF	Football Kenya Federation
FKL	Football Kenya Limited
GAFA	Ghana Amateur Football Association
GCA	Ghana Coaches Association
GRA	Ghana Referees Association
IOC	International Olympic Committee
ISL	International Sport Leisure

KCCA	Kampala City Authority
KFA	Kenya Football Association
KSA	Kadji Sports Academy
LTC	Lagos Town City
MTN	Mobile Telephone Network
NAM	Non-Aligned Movement
NFF	Nigerian Football Federation
OAU	Organization of African Unity
ONCAV	Organism Nationale de Coordination des Activités des Vacances
P&T	Post and Telecommunications
PSG	Paris Saint Germain
PWD	Public Works Department
SAFA	South African Football Association
SONARA	Société National De Faffinage
SONEL	National Electricity Company
UBL	Ugandan Big League
UEFA	Union of European Football Association
UFA	Uganda Football Association
UGCAF	United Gold Coast Amateur Football Association
WASF	West African Soccer Federation
WWC	Women World Cup

LIST OF FIGURES

Fig. 4.1　Map of Cameroon showing the ten administrative territories, including the English-speaking areas of the northwest and southwest regions　80
Fig. 4.2　Cameroon Junior National team selection (1985)　97
Fig. 4.3　My time in the Junior National team (1985)　98

List of Tables

Table 2.1	The FIFA presidents, 1904–present	29
Table 2.2	FIFA's growth since 1904 and Africa's emergence	30
Table 4.1	Composition of the national team: foreign, domestic, and regional disposition	86
Table 9.1	List of Kenya's soccer chairmen	204
Table 9.2	Kenya national team coaches	207
Table 11.1	SAFA Executive Committee	241
Table 11.2	PSL executive committee	241
Table 11.3	PSL teams, owners, coaching staffs, and province	242
Table 11.4	SAFA teams	242
Table 11.5	SAFA competitions	242

CHAPTER 1

Introduction: Football (Soccer) in Africa: Origins, Contributions, and Contradictions

Augustine E. Ayuk

INTRODUCTION

Football (soccer) is the most popular sport in the world, a game that arouses the type of hot-tempered passions not experienced in other sports. Like other sporting activities in Africa, football, however, strives for status, the assertion of identity, the maintenance of power in one form or another, and the indoctrination of youth into the culture of their elders.[1] Giulianotti[2] maintains that football "is one of the great cultural institutions, like education and the mass media, which shapes and cements national identities

[1] Baker, William J. and James A. Mangan, eds., *Sport in Africa: Essays in Social History*, New York: Africana, 1987.
[2] Richard Giulianotti, *Football: A Sociology of the Global Game*, Cambridge, UK: Polity Press, 1999.

A. E. Ayuk (✉)
Clayton State University, Morrow, GA, USA
e-mail: Augustineayuk@clayton.edu

© The Author(s), under exclusive license to Springer Nature Switzerland AG 2022
A. E. Ayuk (ed.), *Football (Soccer) in Africa*, Global Culture and Sport Series, https://doi.org/10.1007/978-3-030-94866-5_1

throughout the world." Tamir Bar-On points out that "in countries that face stark economic and political problems, from extreme poverty to a 'war on drugs,' football [soccer] acts as the great societal equalizer, as it provides popular expressions of celebration and pride for the national team victories."[3]

Through the years, success in football in Africa and many developing countries has been viewed as a major yardstick to a country's "greatness." Whether this viewpoint is an illusion or real, some African countries and their respective regimes have capitalized on football's success to wield their diverse peoples and regions together, as well as avert political turmoil. Africa's participation in international football has added a new aestheticization to the game, which has captured and excited fans beyond the geographical margins of the continent. The exposure and popularity of some footballers such as George Weah of Liberia played an immeasurable role in his successful run as a presidential candidate and his eventual victory to becoming the 25th president of Liberia in 2018. Achievement in football has contributed to the success of some former footballers who have become successful entrepreneurs like Samuel Eto'o, Didier Drogba, Michael Essien, and John Obi Mikhel.

The purpose of this book is to provide a basis for understanding the political, economic, social, and cultural contexts in which Europeans introduced football in their former colonies and to undrape the exuberance and the despondencies of football in colonial Africa, assessing the transformation of the game in the postcolonial era.

We will explore football in the post-independence period, highlighting the accomplishments and challenges experienced by African states participating in football. Throughout the book, contributors will focus on the ways political leaders in Africa have tried sometimes unsuccessfully to exploit football to achieve both domestic and foreign policy goals by linking themselves closely to and exploiting to their advantage the successes of their respective national football teams. On the domestic front, for example, contributors will probe how many African leaders have used football as a subterfuge to unite their diverse ethnic, linguistic, and religious populations, as well as using the game as a ploy to prolong their stay in power. Furthermore, contributors will examine critical issues that continue to impede football's development and growth in the continent, including

[3] Bar-On, T., *The World Through Soccer: The Cultural Impact of a Global Sport*, New York: Rowman & Littlefield, 2014.

endemic corruption, racism, tribalism, undue interference by politicians and bureaucrats in football matters, poor/sub-standard infrastructure, poor medical care, and the death of footballers, migration of footballers, foot drain, and failures by many football federations to pay their players' participation bonuses.

Each chapter follows a common format, beginning with a historical overview of the introduction and development of football in each country, accompanied by an examination of the role of football in the formation of national, class, and ethnic identity, as well as the impact of football on both domestic and international affairs.

This volume takes inspiration from previous works, yet it contemporarily distinguishes itself from other books on African football in scope and focus. Many of the other volumes treat football as an after-thought or a footnote when discussing sports in general. This volume focuses on some of the most recent and important changes that have taken place in the landscape of African football. For example, the number of teams in the African Cup of Nations (AFCON) has increased from sixteen to twenty-four in 2019. In addition, new technology (such as the Video Assistant Referee—VAR) is used in the game, after much resistance and debate. The Indomitable Lions of Cameroon won their fifth (AFCON) title in 2017. This volume also tackles an important problem facing many African footballers "death on the football field."

According to author and historian Peter Alegi,[4] football (soccer) was introduced and popularized in Africa by European imperialism, particularly involving the British, French, and other European powers. The first football match in the continent was in South Africa, in 1862, played by Europeans. The French introduced the football in Algeria in the nineteenth century, followed by dispersion of the game to other former French colonies. With the establishment of FIFA in 1904, Egypt became the first African country to participate in the World Cup competition in 1934. However, it took thirty-six years before another African country, Zaire (the Democratic Republic of the Congo), earned a berth to participate in the World Cup tournament. George Weah of Liberia became the first African player to be recognized as FIFA's World Player of the Year in 1995. Similarly, Roger Milla of Cameroon thus far remains the oldest

---

[4] Alegi, Peter. African Soccerscapes: How a Continent Changed the World's Game. Ohio: Ohio University Press, 2010.

player in the world to score goals in two consecutive World Cup tournaments.

The popularization of football in Africa gained momentum in the 1920s and 1930s, as missionaries, traders, soldiers, and the expansion of railways into the interiors of Africa increased. Depetris-Chauvin and Durante argue that although football continues to play a key role in nation building, in Africa, paradoxically, the game has inadvertently amplified unpleasant display of iniquities such as racism, ultra-nationalism, sexism, and tribalism and contributed to football conflicts between two countries,[5] like in the case of Egypt and Algeria.

Peter Alegi contends that Africans were instrumental in democratizing football, which was exclusively in the hands of Europeans and South Americans until the 1960s. He maintains that as many African countries gained their independence and affiliated with the Fédération Internationale de Football Association (FIFA), a football governing body, they contributed to altering FIFA's character.[6] Independent African states, Alegi notes, pressured FIFA to impose sanctions on apartheid South Africa. This move by the African states and their allies resulted in the exclusion of South Africa under apartheid regime from participating in FIFA-organized football activities for three decades.

Using the United Nation's Human Development Index (HDI) and other Western yardsticks of social, economic, and cultural indexes to evaluate Africa's socio-economic accomplishments vis-à-vis other regions of the world, one would agree with Paul Darby's argument that "the vast majority of African countries remain firmly rooted at the pedestal of the world order of nation-states."[7] However, in the world of football, Africa is emerging as a "force to be reckoned with," and its presence and accomplishments in this arena have slowly been recognized by the football world. For example, in the 1982 FIFA World Cup tournament in Spain, Africa's two-torch bearers, Algeria and Cameroon, challenged the assumption that Africa is a tangential football continent. Remarkably, Algeria defeated "mighty" West Germany and Chile in the first round of the tournament, while Cameroon fearlessly drew all its three matches against Poland, Peru,

---

[5] Depetris-Chauvin and Ruben Durante. "One Team, One Nation: Football, Ethnic Identity, and Conflict in Africa", Afro Barometer, Working Paper No. 177, 2017.

[6] P. Alegi, Peter. African Soccerscapes: How a Continent Changed the World's Game. Ohio: Ohio University Press, 2010.

[7] Paul Darby, Africa Football and FIFA: Politics, Colonialism and Resistance, London: Frank Class Publishers, 2002.

and eventual cup winners Italy. Despite their outstanding performances, both countries could not advance to the second round of the tournaments.

African football, however, has experienced a seismic shift from 1990, following Cameroon's victory over reigning FIFA World Cup holders, Argentina, and advancing to the quarterfinals of the tournament. This victory and the jubilation that ensued reverberated throughout the world, but more so in Africa. Similarly, Nigeria's success in winning the men's Olympic gold medal in football at the 1996 Summer Olympics in Atlanta, Georgia, followed by Cameroon's victory of the men's gold medal at the Olympic tournament held in Sydney, Australia, in 2000 confirmed that Africa's place in world football was not an accident. Both accomplishments by Cameroon and Nigeria would be summed up by Armstrong and Giulianotti as "a continental rather than a national success and marked the competitive arrival of African football on the world stage."[8] Cameroon's success in advancing to the quarterfinals in the FIFA World Cup tournament in 1990 has been replicated by other African countries, including Senegal in 2002 and Ghana in 2010. Success in football has opened new opportunities for obscured countries in the continent to achieve global pre-eminence, and it demonstrates how the game has contributed to transforming the lives and livelihoods of African footballers locally and globally.

In analyzing football in the continent, three major power blocs that constitute the Confederation of African Football will be interrogated, including (1) The Arabophobe bloc, made up of the Arab/Maghreb countries of North Africa; (2) The Anglophone bloc, made up of some of the west, south, and eastern bloc countries; and (3) The Francophone bloc, made up of some countries in the west and central African regions.

THE CONFEDERATION OF AFRICAN FOOTBALL (CAF)

The Confederation of African Football (CAF) was founded in 1957 by the only independent countries in Africa at the time—Egypt, Ethiopia, South Africa, and Sudan. The founding of CAF was "crucial in a political sense in that it lent considerable weight to the use of the game as a tool for asserting African and Pan-African identity and represented a highly visible podium for mediating that identity both through Africa and on a global

---

[8] Garry Armstrong, and Richard Giulianotti, *Football in Africa: Conflict, Conciliation and Community*, New York: Palgrave Macmillan, 2004.

basis. The hosting of the first African Cup of Nations tournament by Sudan in 1957, which was won by Egypt, further awakened national consciousness throughout the continent."[9] The association was also successful in exhorting FIFA to increase the number of African teams participating in the FIFA World Cup tournaments. Today, five African teams represent the continent instead of one in 1970 or 1974. Additionally, the association has encouraged and supported female participation in football in Africa. In 1991, Nigeria represented Africa in the inaugural FIFA Women's World Cup tournament in China. Unfortunately, CAF has not been able to allocate sufficient resources to serve and promote female football abroad.

In 2019, CAF embraced new technology to enhance the game. The Video Assistant Referee (VAR) was used in the quarterfinals of AFCON 2019. The association also increased the number of teams for the AFCON 2019 tournament, from sixteen to twenty-four.

Despite these accomplishments, CAF and its affiliate associations face many challenges, which have tarnished the credibility of CAF, including chronic corruption and favoritism perpetuated by administrators and referees. The example of the former CAF president, Ahmad Ahmad, accused of abusing his office and mishandling of funds was removed from his position and initially banned for five years by FIFA because of corruption and mismanagement of funds. In Africa, however, the problem has been exacerbated by poverty, lack of transparency, and the "win at all costs" mindset. Many football federation officials view the national teams as a "cash cow," where monies designated for players end up in the pockets of bureaucrats and their friends. Referees are often bribed to favor one team against another, while ticket salesmen and women print duplicate tickets to enrich themselves.

FIFA AND AFRICAN FOOTBALL, THE RIFT: DOMINANCE AND DEFIANCE

Paul Darby[10] argues that football has historically been thought of as a reservoir of cultural imperialism in Africa, as well as a source of resistance against the game's governing body, FIFA, whose primary focus was on European football. As we stated before, Europeans introduced the game

[9] P. Darby, "Culture, Sports Society", Taylor and Francis, Vol. 3, No. 1 (Spring 2000), 61–67.
[10] Ibid.

in Africa, and the governing body's attitude toward Africa was based on a Eurocentric predisposition rooted in inequality. Peter Alegi[11] maintains that European condescending attitudes toward African and Asian associations made headway in the Extraordinary Congress in 1953 when FIFA officials excluded Africans and Asians from the "corridors of power" by refusing to recognize their organizations. Although the game brought unity and solidarity to the continent, this was not the case with South Africa under the apartheid regime. Alegi (2010) further argues that "Africans democratized world football by helping to change the character of world football's governing body, FIFA." Alegi adds that Africans' resolve for FIFA to sanction apartheid South Africa paid off on September 26, 1961, when the organization banned South Africa from participating in the beautiful game until the collapse of the apartheid regime in 1990.

WOMEN AND FOOTBALL IN AFRICA

Women and girls' football in Africa is still in its infancy compared to other regions of the world. Certainly, not much scholarship has been devoted to this subject; hence, only a few contributors will navigate women and girls' football in their country of focus.

Women and girls in Africa have not benefited from many of society's opportunities granted to their male counterparts. Women and girls in many countries in Africa are deprived of opportunities to participate in societal affairs based on some esoteric rules and norms.

Women and girls from religiously conservative countries are prohibited from educational opportunities and are forbidden from participating in what "society" believes to be masculine activities such as playing football.

According to liberal feminist scholars and advocates, socialization and stereotyping, which starts at birth and continues for life, have an upper hand in discouraging women and girls from participating in "masculine" activities, including football. According to Scraton,[12] women and girls are socialized into feminine sporting activities such as netball, handball, gymnastics, volleyball, and so on and into a female physicality, while boys are socialized into masculine sports such as football, rugby, or cricket and into

[11] Alegi, Peter. African Soccerscapes: How a Continent Changed the World's Game. Ohio: Ohio University Press, 2010.
[12] S. Scraton, Shaping Up to Womanhood: Gender and Girls' Physical Education, Buckingham, UK: Open University Press, 1992.

a male physicality. In many cultures in Africa and other developing countries, "a woman's place is in the kitchen," and participation of women and girls in sports, especially football, has been seen as "the presence of women in a man's world."[13] There are copious myths in Africa that discourage women and girls from participating in football. A familiar sociocultural myth is that girls who participate in football may lose their virginity and that those women who engage in the game are bisexuals.[14] These myths are present in the English-speaking sector of Cameroonian society.

Other myths in society are that women and girls who play football cannot bear children, hence will not be able to get married. Mean provides a persuasive reason why many women and girls refuse to participate in football, arguing that "women who are actively involved in football as participants are viewed as having failed in the feminine duties, and, symbolically, had 'become' men."[15] Without a doubt, this lucidity forces many women and girls to keep off football and serves as a discouragement to those who play the game (ibid.). Digest (1998), however, counters that a lack of economic power, facilities, and even time—especially for women and girls due to their other gender roles—is a huge barrier that blocks women and girls from participating in football. Crompton argues that participating in any sporting activity requires some financial input; therefore, a child from a poor family, especially a girl is less likely to participate in sport, particularly football, compared to one from a more affluent background.[16]

Most women and girls in Africa engage in many other sports like track and field, netball/basketball, and volleyball, but not in football. George Godia argues that the key issue that has hindered the development of female football in Africa is that "many people hold the view that women should not take part in strenuous physical activities because they might lose their beauty by appearing masculine. They find it difficult that women have to wear tracksuits and even shorts to participate in football."[17]

---

[13] N. Kiouvulu, "Ratings of Gender Appropriateness of Sports Participation," Sex Roles: A Journal of Research, Vol. 33, No. 7–8 (1995): 543–557.

[14] K. Bailey, K., The Girls Are the Ones with the Pointy Nail, London: CAN Althouse Press, 1999.

[15] L. Mean, "Identity and Discursive Practice: Doing Gender on the Football Pitch," Discourse and Society, 12(6), (2001): 789–815.

[16] Crompton, J.L., "Economic Impact Analysis of Sports Facilities and Events: Eleven Sources of Misapplication," Journal of Sport Management, 9(1), 1995: 14–35.

[17] Godia, G., "Sport in Kenya," in *Sport in Asia and Africa: A Comparative Handbook*, edited by Eric A. Wagner, New York: Greenwood Press, 1989.

Saavadra contends that women's football in Africa is not given much attention relative to the men's game.[18] Women's football in Africa, however, kicked off in 1991, with the establishment of the Africa Women's Cup of Nations. Although the game has gained a stronghold in two countries, Nigeria and South Africa, today, more than a dozen other African countries have women's football leagues or national teams. According to Saavadra, other African countries such as Senegal, Ghana, Cameroon, Equatorial Guinea, Mali, Zambia, Algeria, and Kenya are actively participating in football tournaments, even in the continent, but have not been successful in challenging Nigeria in the Total Women Africa Cup of Nations tournament.[19]

In the 2019 FIFA Women's World Cup tournament, Cameroon and Nigeria advanced to the knock-out stage of the tournament, a major accomplishment for late contestants in the game. The outcry for equal pay for women's football after the women's tournament in 2019 has forced many African football federations to commit their governments and the private sector to be as supportive of the women's game as their male counterparts. Stereotypes about women and girls who play football are slowly waning, and this has led to increased participation of women and girls playing football at both the club and national team levels.

Racism and Tribalism

Footballers of African lineage, playing their craft in Europe, Asia, and the Americas, have faced vitriolic racist chants, dog whistles, and threats from fans of their opposing teams. Black players born in European countries have not escaped this cruel and vicious abuse on the field or on social media, which has become the modern-day launch missile of racism. It raises a key question: what is behind this outburst of racist attacks on the field and on the Internet that has so tarnished the reputation of the beautiful game? Some examples of black players in established football leagues who have suffered this humiliating experience include Kevin-Prince Boateng, Samuel Eto'o Fils, Raheem Sterling, Virgil van Dijk, Marcus Rashford, Romelu Lukaku, Yaya Touré, Gervinho, and Chris Samba. In 2007, for example, Samuel Eto'o, then of FC Barcelona, took

---

[18] Saavedra, Martha. "Football Feminine-Development of the African Game: Senegal, Nigeria, and South Africa." Soccer and Society 4, Nos. 2–3 (2003): 225–253.
[19] Ibid.

extraordinary actions against this scourge by walking out of a game against their opponents Real Zaragoza.

Paradoxically, this problem is not only prevalent in Europe, the Americas, and Asia. In Africa, teams from sub-Saharan regions have encountered the same racist chants when they play in the Maghreb regions of North Africa. This was the case when Cameroon played against host nation Egypt, in Cairo, in the final of the African Cup of Nations tournament in 1986, and Cameroon's players were taunted by fans of the home team. Tribalism is another incurable cancer in African football, especially in the national team selection. Most countries in Africa are multiethnic, and the selection of players in the national team is based on ethnic preferences. The decision in many countries to choose players of the national team based primarily on ethnic/regional affiliation continues to pose major problems for many countries in Africa.

Tragedies

The lives of many footballers throughout the world have ended abruptly while playing the game they love. In Africa, the number of players who have collapsed and died either on the field or en route to the hospital, while representing their national teams, local clubs, or foreign clubs, is terrifying. Many of these deaths are due to heart failure, lightning strikes, or food poisoning. In 1998, for example, eleven players from a local team in the Democratic Republic of Congo were struck and killed by lightning. Inexplicably, their opponents left the pitch safe and unscathed. In France in 2003, during the FIFA Confederations Cup semi-finals between Cameroon and Colombia, Cameroon's midfielder Marc-Vivien Foé collapsed and was pronounced dead en route to the hospital.

The major cause of death for many footballers is cardiac arrest, which has ignited debate and raised new questions of what accounts for this high number of casualties in individuals who are purportedly physically fit. Is it genetics or a failure to properly diagnose these players by the medical personnel of the national teams or clubs? What have football federations such as FIFA and CAF done to solve this problem? Besides physical death, a handful of African players face another mishap after their glory days on the pitch come to an end. Many African players do not plan adequately during their primes or for life after football. Hence, some of these players become so poor that they are not able to afford a place to live, food to eat, or proper healthcare services. Some of these players become homeless, alcoholics, and die prematurely. Some examples in Cameroon include three heroes of the 1990 World Cup team: Louis-Paul M'Fédé, Benjamin Massing, and captain Stephen Tataw. Many African football federations and governments treat former national team players as dispensable merchandise once their playing days are over.

Football Migration

The migration of African footballers to Europe, the "Soccer Drain" or "Leg Drain," is yet another challenge African football faces. Murray contents that the trans-continental migration of African footballers to Europe is clearly one of the biggest problems afflicting the African game.[20] Paul Darby[21] argues that the expropriation of African players by wealthy European clubs can be interpreted as an "extension of economic imperialism of the colonial period and beyond, during which first world development has been sustained by. Since the 1980s, African countries have become nurseries or incubators for developing top-quality players who later migrate to Europe, Asia, and the Americas to play for top-flight football league clubs. This migration pattern no doubt has resulted in weak and unentertaining football in their respective countries. Similarly, the satellization of the beautiful game has negatively impacted African football clubs and national teams. The broadcast of top European football league matches on television has indirectly and negatively impacted football in the continent. Attendance at elite football league matches in most African countries, according to CAF (2010), is down forty-five to sixty-five percent, while international tournaments involving national teams have also seen significant drops in attendance as well as in the purchase of local club or national team memorabilia. The availability of and easy access to satellite television in homes and bars, broadcasting European league matches, is largely responsible for this decline in attendance and support for local clubs and national teams. Interestingly, most African football fans identify more with and support their favorite European club teams than their local or national teams. This behavior is akin to a colonial mindset wherein Africans regard what comes from Europe as superior compared to what comes from Africa.

---

[20] B. Murray B, Football: A History of the World Game. Aldershot: Scolar Press, 1995.
[21] P. Darby, "Culture, Sports Society", Taylor and Francis, Vol. 3, No. 1 (Spring 2000): 61–87.

Inconsistency in African Football

Inconsistency remains an idiosyncratic feature in most African national football teams. One of the many plausible reasons advanced for this lack of consistency in the performance by African national football teams is the high turnover ratio in the coach and his/her staff members. Indeed, the pressure from football fans and political operatives in Africa in pursuit of quick and positive results often leads to impetuous dismissal of coaches who have not had the time to understand the players and implement their strategy for success. In some cases, coaches, who have been successful, have equally been sidelined by bureaucrats or refused to extend their contracts for political and other reasons. Some notable examples from a few African countries will corroborate our assertion. Cameroon's poor performances in post-the 1990 World Cup are symptomatic of other African national teams. After the incredible success of the Indomitable Lions with Russian coach Valeri Nepomniachi in the 1990 World Cup, Cameroon's football federation and officials in government were not able to or willing to retain or cajole the coach to continue with the national team. Instead, the federation hired a mediocre and an inexperienced coach, Henri Michel from France, to chaperone the Lions. His inexperience and poor management skills were a calamity to the Lions and millions of devoted fans throughout the world.

The same is true with the Teranga Lions of Senegal, who became the second African country to reach the quarterfinals of the FIFA World Cup tournament, after defeating cup holders France. Like Cameroon, the post-World Cup performance of the Teranga Lions was disappointing, as Senegal failed to qualify for the World Cup in 2006 after her stellar performance in the 2002 World Cup in Japan/South Korea.

South Africa was the first nation in Africa to host a FIFA World Cup tournament. The Black Stars of Ghana reached the quarterfinals of the FIFA World Cup, on home soil in Africa, but lost to Uruguay, hence, unable to reach the semi-finals. Like Cameroon and Senegal before them, Ghana's post-World Cup performance in Brazil in 2014 was disappointing to say the least, as the Black Stars recorded one point out of a possible total of nine in the group stage, the same as what Cameroon did in their post-World Cup performance in the USA in 1994.

These three cases demonstrate why African national teams have not been consistent in their performances after major victories on the international stage. Thus far, it appears as if the quarterfinals in the FIFA World Cup tournament has become Africa's new football apex.

THEORETICAL PERSPECTIVES

The introduction, development, and diffusion of football in Africa are best be understood when we analyze the game using different theoretical perspectives. Scholars and researchers have utilized constructs such as colonialism, neocolonialism, dependency theory, and World System theory, to explain colonial legacies and postcolonial strategies, and how these perpetuate uneven power relationship and exploitation of the colonies.[22] Colonization has historically been linked with early European acquisition, domination, and occupation of many countries in Africa, Asia, and the Americas. Europeans used education in facilitating and imposing power and control on colonial governments. This coerced external control of the political, economic, and cultural domain is often described as "classical colonial" model. However, contemporary scholars on this subject also describe another phenomenon which they call "internal colonialism," whereby certain groups of people are dominated and oppressed within their own country/territory because of their religion, ethnicity, or language.

In this volume, most contributors utilize and reference Immanuel Wallerstein's World System theory (WST) in analyzing and explaining football in Africa.

The World System theory (WST) is "an approach, an analytical tool for studying reality."[23] The theory helps us understand the role African football plays in national development. Wallerstein developed a three-tier hierarchy of countries/regions, which includes the core, periphery, and the semi-periphery. At the center of this theory is the notion of the "Core and Periphery," with the core exploiting the periphery.[24] In Africa, football is

---

[22] John Bale and Joe Sang, 'Out of Africa: The "Development" of Kenyan Athletics, Talent Migration and the Global Sports System', in Bale, J, and Maguire, J. (eds), The Global Sports Arena: Athletic Talent Migration in an Interdependent World (London: Frank Cass Publishers, 1994.

[23] Eckhardt, I., "Immanuel Wallerstein's World-Systems Analysis: An Introduction," *Central European Review of International Affairs*, 2005/2006, 25–95.

[24] Terlouw, C.P., "The Elusive Semiperiphery: A Critical Examination of the Concept of Semiperiphery," *International Journal of Comparative Sociology*, XXXIV 1–2 (1993): 87–99.

prominent in the core centers or metropolitan areas—the political and economic capitals at the expense of the rural areas.

The World System model theorizes that some countries/regions benefit in a world economic system, while other countries and regions are exploited. Accordingly, the core countries/regions are the dominant entities in the world capitalist system because they control capital and technology and serve as the cultural centers, which attract intellectuals and artists. The core exploits the peripheral countries/regions, which generally serve as suppliers of labor and materials to core countries or regions. Similarly, semi-peripheral countries/regions exploit peripheral countries just as core countries/regions do.

Dependency theory is an approach developed by Argentinian economist Raúl Prebisch to explain the unequal relationship between advanced and developing economies. Prebisch argued that underdeveloped countries offer cheap raw materials and cheap labor on the world market, and the advanced economies transform these raw materials to finished goods and sell them to peripheral countries at much higher prices. Elements of Africa's over-dependence on the West—including their coaches, marketing, financial assistance, and football gears to African national teams, especially during international tournaments like the FIFA World Cup, African Cup of Nations, and the Olympic Games—prevent Africa from developing.

Dependency or underdevelopment theory has been employed repeatedly to emphasize the subordination of less developed economies within the international capitalist system. According to Scott[25] when applied to football, this theory holds that the success of European professional football league clubs is linked to the underdevelopment of football in the global south, including Africa. Former Confederation of African Football (CAF) president, Issa Hayatou (2007), acknowledges that "the importation of African footballers by European clubs is exploitative and smells of economic imperialism." This theory has become especially handy in unmasking inequality in power relations and in revealing the unequal distribution of resources and the practice of discriminatory laws that favor rich European countries at the expense of African countries.[26] Walter Rodney (1972, 111) argues that Africa has not developed because of

[25] Scott, C.-G., *African Footballers in Sweden: Race, Immigration, and Integration in the Age of Globalization*, New York: Palgrave Macmillan, 2014.
[26] Lunga, V.B., "Postcolonial Theory: A language for a Critique of Globalization?" in *Perspectives on Global Development and Technology*, 7 (2008): 191–199.

subordination and dependence on Europeans. I submit that the exodus of Africa's best footballers to European football clubs is synonymous with the shipping of Africa's mineral resources or abled-bodied men and women during the slave trade period to Europe. The migration of these players has contributed to the growth of football in Europe and the advancement of European economies. Meanwhile, as European clubs have continued to benefit because of this exodus of African football talents, it has undermined the growth of football in the continent.

Besides, football continues to pave the way for upward mobility for thousands of men, women, and girls throughout the world and provide entertainment to billions of fans. Nonetheless, the game continues to exhibit contradictory roles in the cultures and societies of many countries in Africa. On the one hand, football serves as a glue, unifying diverse ethnic, cultural, linguistic, and religious groups, and at the same time, it has been used as a tool of exclusion based on the aforementioned factors in many countries in Africa.

Chapter Synopsis

The chapters in this volume will examine football in Africa from the colonial to the post-independence period. Contributors will probe the ways African leaders have exploited football to develop national identities as well as prolong their stay in power and the games' impact in Africa during the colonial era and post-independence period.

Chapter 2: FIFA and Football Development in Africa

In this chapter, the author sets out to discuss the relationship between FIFA and African football and how that relationship has influenced the development of the sport to date. To analyze this relationship, the chapter draws upon the discourse on globalization and development. Some of the key constructs used in the analysis of the relationship between FIFA and African football include the notions of the World System theory, imperialism, dependency paradigm, and globalization. The author argues that the development of African football on the playing field especially in the 1980s and 1990s led to an erroneous prediction by noted commentators that the name of an African nation would soon appear on the World Cup trophy.

Chapter 3: *The Confederation of African Football (CAF): Origins, Accomplishments, and Challenges*

This chapter explores the origins and operations of Africa's principal football governing body, The Confederation of African Football (CAF), which was formally established on February 8, 1957, by representatives from Egypt, Ethiopia, Sudan, and South Africa. The chapter examines the extent to which politics and corruption have impacted CAF's leadership to effectively manage football in Africa and offers suggestions for improved governance under its new leadership. Finally, the chapter concludes with a perspective view of what the confederation portends for contemporary African soccer and how it can be improved to reflect the quality and continued enthusiasm that the confederation seeks to infuse into African soccer in the future.

Chapter 4: *Football in Cameroon, Best of Times, Worst of Times: Exploring the Paradox of Africa's Venerable Football Nation*

This chapter explores football culture in Cameroon, where origins, nationalism, power, passion, and lifestyles intersect. The author examines football in different segments in Cameroon, beginning with introduction of the game by the French. This is followed by an examination and analysis of football in the French and English sectors of Cameroon, proffering reasons why football developed more rapidly in the French territory, but less so in the English sector of the country. Furthermore, the author discusses and offers reasons why Cameroon lost in the 1972 African Cup of Nations tournament, focusing especially on the role tribalism played in the loss. Similarly, the author examines the reasons for Cameroon's precipitous rise in football at the continental and international stage, starting with its 1982 FIFA World Cup debut. The chapter also provides reasons why Cameroon is regarded as the "king" of football in Africa, focusing on the country's successes in continental and international football. Conversely, the author underscores many of the challenges that encumber football in the country, including tribalism, corruption, and mismanagement by football federation officials, interference by politicians in football matters, and failure to pay players their participation bonuses, poor and inadequate football infrastructure.

1 INTRODUCTION: FOOTBALL (SOCCER) IN AFRICA: ORIGINS... 17

Chapter 5: Historicizing Football Nigeria: Disciplinary, Governmentality, and Resistance Within Football Labor's Struggle

This chapter focuses on the relationship between elite football administrators within the Nigerian Football Federation (NFF) and labor (footballers) in Nigeria. The author maintains that this struggle has thwarted the progress of the game in the country, resulting in what he describes as an "oppressive situation in which football labor finds itself in Nigeria, limiting, slow, and at times aborting Nigeria's quest for sustained high performance in football."

The author utilizes the approach of critical thinking theorists such as Michel Foucault and Antonio Gramsi to illustrate the continued struggle between football bureaucrats who possess power and labor (players) in the country.

The author analyses the football struggle in Nigeria concerning three epochs, the early 1950s, 1960s to early 1980s, and then from the late 1980s to the present. The chapter highlights the many challenges that have plagued Nigerian other African football nations in the continent. Some key take-away from the chapter includes a critique of the structure of football in Nigeria, instruments of subjugation, and oppression utilized by elite football administrators against labor.

Chapter 6: Football in DR Congo: A Critical Account of "Congolese Football"

This chapter investigates football in the Democratic Republic of the Congo. The author argues that among the giants of African football, the Democratic Republic of Congo (DRC) has had, since its first participation in continental and world competitions, its moments of glory and demise. The author maintains that the paradox of Congolese football is epitomized by its success during times of political dictatorship, winning two African Cup of Nations (1968 and 1974) under the Mobutu regime, and its decline during times of democratic trials, failing to either qualify for or advance beyond the group stage of CAF and FIFA competitions. The author maintains that without any doubt, the DRC has always been blessed with both human and natural resources. However, in football, like many other spheres of Congolese life, these resources have tended to be mismanaged or squandered. As a result, fame without fortune appears to be the norm for Congolese football players loyal to their homeland.

Chapter 7: Football in Egypt: Between Joy and Politics

This chapter analyzes football and politics in the land of the Pharaohs. The author examines the history of football in Egypt and highlights the political role played by football in Egyptian political history since its introduction under the British occupation. Football, the beautiful game, is for many supporters a source of joy and happiness and an escape from social and economic challenges. Yet, the relationship between football and politics has long been close. The author argues that football managers, players, and even workers in sports media have all welcomed the intervention of political leaders in the game, who use football for their personal purposes. It discusses the relationship between football and social and political changes and how the major achievements of Egyptian football were used to raise the spirit of national pride and to glorify the political regime.

Chapter 8: The History and Development of Football in Ghana

This chapter examines the development and progress of football in Ghana, once known as the Gold Coast. The author argues that the story of the origins, development, and organization of football in Ghana may not differ from those of other countries in Africa. What perhaps distinguishes Ghana's football experience from most African countries was the deliberate and calculated attempt to make the process, organization, and operation of football a powerful instrument to achieve pre-conceived political ends by an astute and ambitious political actor in his capacity as a founding father of a new nation and a progenitor of his concept of Pan-Africanism.

Chapter 9: The Politics of Soccer Management in Kenya: The Rise and Decline of a Popular Sport

This chapter seeks to explore and probe the mixed fortunes of the history of soccer in Kenya to account for the rise and decline of this popular sport in the country. The main argument of the chapter is that the decline of soccer in Kenya is a function of the politics of soccer management since the country gained independence in 1963. The chapter begins with a historical exploration of the introduction and development of soccer in

Kenya. It then evaluates the mixed fortunes of the sport in the country before focusing on the impact of the politics of soccer management. The chapter concludes with a delineation of remedial measures for reviving soccer in the country back to the competitive edge of its glorious past.

Chapter 10: Soccer: Competing Sports, National Pride, Spectatorship, and Wealth in Senegal

Chapter 10 argues that sports, in this case, soccer, offer a trajectory to understand better the subtleties of disparities in political, social, and economic capital that exist between various groups in Senegalese society. The chapter analyzes football in Senegal. The chapter maintains that Soccer is by far the most popular sport in Senegal. With a long history dating as far back as the early colonial period, Senegalese soccer reached its peak when the national team, Les Lions de la Teranga (The Lions of Hospitality), qualified for the FIFA World Cup of 2002 and defeated the former colonial power, France, in the opening match of the tournament hosted by South Korea and Japan. The chapter also points to the problems and challenges faced by much African football, including corruption.

Chapter 11: Contradictions and Inconsistencies Facing the South African Football Association and the Premier Soccer League

The focus of this chapter is on some of the challenges facing the South African Football Association (SAFA) and the South African Premier Soccer League (PSL). The focus is to highlight the gender inequalities in football in South Africa within the context of SAFA and PSL. Further, this chapter aims to contribute to the anthropology of soccer in South Africa. The Marxist Feminist theoretical framework is utilized to understand issues of gender inequality within football in South Africa. The chapter concludes by providing the recommendations with the view of resolving some of the issues raised.

Chapter 12: The Origins, Status, Contributions, and Contradictions of Association Football in Uganda

The chapter traces the origins and development of football in Uganda. The author maintains that missionaries from the United Kingdom were responsible for introducing and diffusing football, and other sports, in the country in 1897. The author argues that the opening of schools by the missionaries in Uganda was the most important strategy used to diffuse the game in the country, particularly among the local youths and the indigenous men. Furthermore, "the introduction of football, though a foreign sport, found a willing and enthusiastic African population whose athleticism perfectly fitted the new sport." Football's popularity has been used by political leaders to unite Ugandans and bridge the (north and south divide), as well as check and prevent political upheaval among the more than 40 ethnic groupings in the country.

Chapter 13: Vicious Cycle: Cameroon(ization) and/or Foreign(ization) of the Indomitable Lions' Head Coaching

The chapter examines and analyzes a burning issue concerning football in Africa, "foreign versus domestic football coaches." The author maintains that the development of football and athletic talent, in general, is dependent upon quality coaching. Using the Cameroon national football team as his main point of reference, the author argues that football authorities in Cameroon have hired dozens of head coaches who have been for the most part foreigners or Europeans. This study is not so much a defense for or advocating against the choice of foreign coaches over native managers, but to analyze the disproportionate imbalance between the few numbers of Cameroonian head coaches selected to lead the national team versus the high number of European coaches. While discussion on this issue focuses on results and following the normal procedure dictated by FIFA to choose the best head coach for the position, other stakeholders such as fans and player's advocates often cite a conflict of interest, egocentric agenda, or avoiding ethnic tensions among other reasons. Although the focus of this chapter is on football coaches in Cameroon, the debate on foreign versus domestic or local coaches is widespread throughout Africa and has resulted in intense protests and opposition in some African countries against expatriate football managers.

Chapter 14: Conclusion

In concluding the chapter, the author argues that despite the important breakthroughs, optimism, and successes by African football, most of the challenges that inhibit the game's development and growth have not been resolved. Corruption is still pervasive in the corridors of the Confederation of African Football and its affiliate associations, dependence on foreign entities for financial and material assistance has not faded away, and undue interference by government officials in football matters is still ubiquitous throughout the continent. The issue of participation bonuses for footballers remains unsettled, as well as migration of talented African footballers to Europe, the Americas, Asia, and the Middle east.

REFERENCES

Abrahamsen, R., "African Studies and the Postcolonial Challenge," *African Affairs*, 102, 407 (2003): 189–210.
Alegi, Peter, *African Soccerscapes: How a Continent Changed the World's Game*, Athens, OH: Ohio University Press, 2010a.
Alegi, Peter, Interview with National Public Radio (NPR) Host, Melissa, The History of Soccer in Africa, June 2010b.
Armstrong, G., and Giulianotti, R., *Football in Africa: Conflict, Conciliation and Community*, New York: Palgrave Macmillan, 2004.
Baker, William J., and Mangan, James A. (eds.), *Sport in Africa: Essays in Social History*, New York: Africana, 1987.
Baker, William J., and Mangan, James A. (eds.), *Sport in Africa*. Also K. Heinemann, "Sport in Developing Countries," in E.D. Dunning, J. Maguire, and R.E. Pearton (eds.), *The Sports Process*, Champaign: Human Kinetics, 1993, 144.
Bale, J., "Three Geographies of African Football Migration: Patterns, Problems and Postcoloniality," in *Football in Africa: Conflict, Conciliation and Community*, edited by G. Armstrong and R. Giulianotti, New York: Palgrave Macmillan, 2004.
Bar-On, T., *The World Through Soccer: The Cultural Impact of a Global Sport*, New York: Rowman & Littlefield, 2014.
Beuchot, M., *Hermenéutica Analóg Applicaciones en Amé Latina*, Bogata: El Búho, 2003.
Bloomfield, S., *Africa United: Soccer, Passion, Politics, and the First World Cup in Africa*, New York: Harper Perennial Publishers, 2010.
Bradley, M., "Blatter Takes Swipe at G-14 'Colonialists'," *Guardian*, December 18, 2003.
Darby, P., "Culture, Sports Society," *Taylor and Francis*, 3, No. 1 (Spring 2000): 61–87.
Depetris-Chauvin, E., and Durante, Ruben, "One Team, One Nation: Football, Ethnic Identity, and Conflict in Africa," Afro Barometer, Working Paper No. 177, 2017.
Dubois, L., *Soccer Empire: The World Cup and the Future Power of France*, Berkeley, CA: University of California Press, 2010.

Eckhardt, I., "Immanuel Wallerstein's World-Systems Analysis: An Introduction," *Central European Review of International Affairs*, 2005/2006, 25–95.
Galeano, E., "Soccer in Sun and Shadow," *Third World Quarterly*, 25, No. 7 (2004): 1337–1345.
Godia, G., "Sport in Kenya," in *Sport in Asia and Africa: A Comparative Handbook*, edited by Eric A. Wagner, New York: Greenwood Press, 1989.
Hamel, H., *African Football Magazine*, January 20, 2008.
Hawkey, I., *Feet of the Chameleon: The Story of African Football*, London: Portico Books, 2010.
Hayatou, I., The President of the Confederation of African Football (CAF), as cited by Paul Darby, "Out of Africa: The Exodus of Elite African Football Talent to Europe," *Working USA: The Journal of Labor and Society*, 10 (2007): 444–445.
Jarvier, G., and Maguire, J., *Sport and Leisure in Social Thought*, London: Routledge, 1994.
Karoney, C., Sports Reporter/Presenter, Africa (BBC), 2018.
Kassimeris, C., *European Football in Black and White: Tackling Racism in Football*, New York: Lexington Books, 2008.
Keim, M., "Apartheid, Struggle and Transformation in South African Sport and Education," *Nation Building at Play: Sport as a Tool for Social Integration in Post-Apartheid South Africa*, 4th ed., Oxford: Meyer & Meyer, 2003.
Lever, J., *Soccer Madness*, Chicago, IL: University of Chicago Press, 1983.
Lunga, V.B., "Postcolonial Theory: A Language for a Critique of Globalization?" *Perspectives on Global Development and Technology*, 7 (2008): 191–199.
Mackay, M., "Football the New Religion, Warn Brazilian Academics," *Christian Today*, http://www.christiantoday.com/article/football.the.new.religion.warn.brazilian.academics/6900.htm (May 11, 2011).
Majhoub, F., "African Cup of Nations," Balafon: Air Afrique on *Flight Magazine* (December/January 1995), 125–146.
Martin, P., "Colonialism, Youth, and Football in French Equatorial Africa," *International Journal of the History of Sport*, 8, No. 1 (1991): 56–71.
Mazrui, A., and Tidy, M., *Nationalism and the New States in Africa*, Heinemann, 1984.
Murray, B., *Football: A History of the World Game*. Aldershot: Scolar Press, 1995.
Nkrumah, K., *Axioms of Kwame Nkrumah: Freedom Fighters Edition*, Panaf Books Ltd., 1967.
Poli, R., "Africans' Status in the European Football Players' Labor Market," *Soccer & Society*, 7, No. 2–3 (2006): 283–284.
Rodney, W., *How Europe Underdeveloped Africa*, Washington, DC: Howard University Press, 1972.
Rossi, J.P., *The National Game: Baseball and American Culture*, Ivan R. Dee Publisher, 2000.

Saavedra, Martha, "Football Feminine-Development of the African Game: Senegal, Nigeria, and South Africa." *Soccer and Society*, 4, No. 2–3 (2003): 225–253.

Schraeder, P.J., and Endless, B., "The Media and Africa: The Portrayal of Africa in the *New York Times*," *Journal of Opinion*, 26, No. 2 (1998): 29–35.

Scott, C.-G., *African Footballers in Sweden: Race, Immigration, and Integration in the Age of Globalization*, New York: Palgrave Macmillan, 2014.

Strenk, A., *What Price Victory? The World of International Sports and Politics*, The Annals of the American Academy of Political and Social Science, Vol. 445, 1997.

Stuart, O., "The Lions Stir: Football in African Society," in *Giving the Game Away: Football, Politics, and Culture on Five Continents*, ed. Stephen Wagg, London: Leicester University Press, 1995.

Terlouw, C.P., "The Elusive Semiperiphery: A Critical Examination of the Concept of Semiperiphery," *International Journal of Comparative Sociology*, XXXIV, No. 1–2 (1993): 87–99.

CHAPTER 2

FIFA and Football Development in Africa

Njororai Wycliffe W. Simiyu

INTRODUCTION

The development of African football in the playing field especially in the 1980s and 1990s led to an overly optimistic prediction by noted commentators that the name of an African nation would soon appear on the World Cup trophy.[1] However, events of the last 22 years in the twenty-first century have not borne out this prediction. Indeed, Africa's participation in the World Cup has tended to reflect poorly on the status of the African game. One aspect of the development of the African game that reveals its contradictory nature is the consistently good performance at the age-group competitions yet similar performances at the senior level are rare, if any. For example, both Nigeria and Cameroon won the Olympic Football titles in 1996 and 2000, respectively. However, only three countries to date have made it to the quarterfinal stage of the World Cup including

[1] Murray, "The World's Game", 1996, 128.

N. W. W. Simiyu (✉)
University of Texas at Tyler, Tyler, TX, USA
e-mail: Wnjororai@uttyler.edu

© The Author(s), under exclusive license to Springer Nature Switzerland AG 2022
A. E. Ayuk (ed.), *Football (Soccer) in Africa*, Global Culture and Sport Series, https://doi.org/10.1007/978-3-030-94866-5_2

25

Cameroon in 1990, Senegal in 2002, and Ghana in 2010.[2] Additionally, the relationship between the Confederation Africaine de Football (CAF), which oversees all football-related matters on the African continent, and Fédération Internationale de Football Association (FIFA) has seen its share of controversy and persistent conflict.[3] This is because FIFA, which is responsible for overseeing and directing international football and has as its goal promoting global fraternity united in sport, has had a long history of European and South American dominance.[4] This dominance on the playing arena as well as in the administrative organs of the body marginalized other continents, particularly the African countries. FIFA, which for a long time was deeply Eurocentric in its core operations and function, was reluctant to accede to Africa's request for democratization of the game's global institutional and competition structures. According to Darby,[5] "The resultant thrusting, politicized, and at times, confrontational response which this has elicited from Africa, championed by the CAF, has in many ways, forged the contemporary visage of world football politics" (2). Despite these conflicts, FIFA has become truly transnational in scope and its activities represent an integral part of the global infrastructure that characterizes modern sport.[6]

This chapter sets out to discuss the relationship between FIFA and African football. It focuses on how that relationship has influenced the development of sport to date. This chapter will draw upon the discourse on globalization and development to explain the FIFA and CAF relationship. Some of the key constructs used in the analysis of the relationship between FIFA and African football include the notions of the world system theory, imperialism, inter-dependency paradigm, and globalization.

---

[2] Njororai, "East African Football", 2014a, 67–80, and "African Players Global Labor", 2014b, 71–90.
[3] Darby, "African Football and FIFA", 2002, pp. 236.
[4] Ibid.
[5] Ibid., 2.
[6] Darby, "Football, Colonial Doctrine and Indigenous Resistance", 2000a, 61–87.

African Football and Its Peripheral Status in the World System

The development of African football can be understood best when it is contextualized in the broader World Economic system. According to Immanuel Wallerstein's World System theory, a world system of commerce and communication started in the sixteenth century. This led to a number of political networks and connections across the globe that characterize the modern economy.[7] According to Wallerstein,[8] the world coheres around four interdependent sectors whose position vis-à-vis the global capitalist economy has been determined through combinations of colonial history and economic power. These four include the following:

a. The core including Northwest Europe, North America, and Japan.
b. Semi-periphery including Southern Europe and the Mediterranean region.
c. The periphery including South America, Eastern Europe, North Africa, and parts of Asia.
d. The external arena, which includes most sub-Saharan Africa, parts of Asia, and the Indian sub-continent and due to a combination of colonialism and transnational corporate activity, and it is classified as being peripheral.[9]

Thus, the world system theory divides the world into tri-modal system or Trinitarian structure consisting of the core, semi-periphery, and periphery.[10] The argument put forward via the world system theory is that the "world system and not nation states should be the primary, but not exclusive unit of social analysis."[11] According to Aniche and Ukaegbu,[12] the world system refers to the inter-regional and transnational division of labor, which divides the world into core countries, semi-periphery countries, and periphery countries. According to the world system theory,

---

[7] Aniche and Ukaegbu, "Structural dependence in Africa", 2016, and also see Darby, "African Football and FIFA", 2002, 236.
[8] Wallerstein, "The Modern World System", 1974.
[9] Darby, "Football, Colonial Doctrine and Indigenous Resistance", 2000a, 61–87. Wallerstein, 1974.
[10] Aniche and Ukaegbu, "Structural dependence in Africa", 2016.
[11] Ibid., 110.
[12] Ibid.

core countries focus on higher skill, capital-intensive production and the rest of the world focuses on low skill, labor-intensive production and extraction of raw materials. This kind of arrangement therefore constantly reinforces the dominance of the core countries as they continually mine the raw materials from the peripheral countries causing the latter to be dependent on the former. The only hope however lies in the fact that the system is dynamic as it can be influenced by technological changes leading to some countries either gaining or losing their status over time.

From a football perspective, the development of the game has closely mirrored the economic development of nations as per Wallerstein's theorization.[13] This world system has been used by Darby[14] to argue that international football has been developing since the late nineteenth and early twentieth century as characterized by a rapid increase in global playing contacts, institutional and political relationships and the growing economic significance of world football. This development of football and the interrelationships among regions has been influenced a great deal by political, historical, economic, and cultural factors, which affected the power and privileges within the FIFA family. This explains why Europe and South America had a solid head start in football establishment and development in both administrative structure and competitions. Unlike Africa, the European and South American countries have not only had a long tradition of football involvement but also the sport enjoys high status.[15] Additionally, their economies especially that of Europe has provided a solid foundation to support thriving football competitions and organizations. African football, which started off as a peripheral entity, has over the years asserted its voice to positively affect its position within FIFA's administrative and competition structures.[16]

FIFA Leadership and the Formation of CAF

People, who had unique perspectives regarding football in Africa, dominated the leadership of FIFA. These changing perspectives therefore played a key role in FIFA's working relationships with the African nations

---

[13] Wallerstein, "The Modern World System", 1974.
[14] Darby, "Football, Colonial Doctrine and Indigenous Resistance", 2000, 61–87.
[15] Darby, "Africa Football and FIFA", 2002, pp. 236.
[16] Alegi, "Soccerscapes", 2010.

Table 2.1 The FIFA presidents, 1904–present

Number	Name	Country and confederation	Reign
1	Robert Guerin	France, UEFA	1904–1906
2	Daniel Woolfall	England, UEFA	1906–1918
3	Jules Rimet	France, UEFA	1921–1954
4	Rodolfe Seeldrayers	Belgium, UEFA	1954–1955
5	Arthur Drewry	England, UEFA	1956–1961
6	Sir Stanley Rous	England, UEFA	1961–1974
7	Dr. João Havelange	Brazil, CONMEBOL	1974–1998
8	Joseph "Sepp" Blatter	Switzerland, UEFA	1998–2015
9	Issa Hayatou	Cameroon, CAF	2015–2016
10	Gianni Infantino	Switzerland, UEFA	2016–present

FIFA.com

and CAF. Since FIFA was founded in 1904, there have been ten presidents as shown in Table 2.1:

Table 2.1 shows that Europe has produced the majority of the presidents, and out of the 117 years of existence of FIFA, only 25 of those years have been in the hands of a non-European. Indeed, Africa as a region was not involved in the governance of FIFA up to 1954, as they were not represented on the decision-making organs of the organization. The leadership of FIFA was essentially a European affair.[17] In the initial stages, FIFA only consisted of European Associations up until 1909. The first members from overseas joined in the following order: South Africa in 1909/1910, Argentina and Chile in 1912, and the United States in 1913. This was the start of FIFA's intercontinental activities as enshrined in their objectives. The FIFA presidents that left an indelible mark at global level include Rimet of France, Rous of Great Britain, Havelange from Brazil, and the latter's protégé, Sepp Blatter from Switzerland. Indeed, in the words of Alan Tomlinson,[18] "The profiles, style and impact of these four football bureaucrats" (p. 56) provide the deepest insight into the evolution and relationship of African Football and FIFA. This is because the first 50 years of FIFA were devoted to the establishment of the foundations in terms of administrative structure, initiation of international competition in form of the World Cup and competition rules. In the subsequent period starting from about 1954, there was a mounting challenge to the status quo and

---

[17] Onwumechili, "CAF Identity", 2014, 202.
[18] Tomlinson, "FIFA and Men Who Made It", 2000, 55–71.

the need for implementation of changes to accommodate the global dynamics of the game. These changes were needed to accomplish the objectives that were clearly articulated in the statutes of the FIFA organization. According to the FIFA Statutes,[19] FIFA's objectives are as follows:

- To improve the game of football constantly and promote it globally in the light of its unifying, educational, cultural, and humanitarian values, particularly through youth and development programs;
- To organize its own international competitions;
- To draw up regulations and provisions and ensure their enforcement;
- To control every type of association football by taking appropriate steps to prevent infringements of the FIFA Statutes, regulations, or decisions of FIFA or of the Laws of the Game;
- To prevent all methods or practices which might jeopardize the integrity of matches or competitions or give rise to abuse of association football.

Table 2.2 shows that indeed FIFA has been remarkably successful in growing the game globally as demonstrated by the number of nations affiliated with it over the years.

Table 2.2 shows the growth in the membership of FIFA from 1904 to 2021. It is clear from the table that Africa's presence in the FIFA family only picked up after the 1960s and currently constitutes more than a quarter of all the member nations. This dramatic increase in the membership of

Table 2.2 FIFA's growth since 1904 and Africa's emergence

Confederation	1904	1925	1950	1975	1990	2005	2007	2021
UEFA	8	28	32	35	35+1	51	53	55 (26.07%)
CONMOBEL	0	6	9	10	10+1	10	10	10 (4.74%)
CONCACAF	0	3	12	22	27	35	35	35 (16.59%)
AFC	0	1	13	33	37+1	46	46	46 (21.80%)
CAF	0	1	1	35	48	53	53	54 (25.59%)
OCEANIA	0	0	1	4	8	12	11	11 (5.21%)
Total	8	39	68	139	167	207	208	211(100%)

FIFA.com

[19] FIFA.com.

FIFA by African countries came because of serious and sustained demands in line with the new wind of change that swept across the continent leading to political independence in the late 1950s and early 1960s. This collective expression of African solidarity and desire for independence became apparent even within the FIFA circles. Thus, it is undeniable that FIFA has become truly transnational in scope and its activities represent an integral part of the global infrastructure that characterizes modern sport.[20] FIFA's massive popularity is illustrated by the fact that it even has more affiliates than the United Nations, which implies that more people around the world pay more interest in the activities of the former rather than the latter. Indeed, for many African countries, it was a national priority to seek affiliation to FIFA immediately upon gaining independence. Since most countries only gained their independence after 1957, it is evident in Table 2.2 that more countries made their entry into FIFA global family within the last 60 years. Currently, CAF, which represents African countries, has the second highest number of affiliates, 54 (25.59%) out of the 211 members of FIFA. This increase in membership has come after a long and sustained pressure mounted by CAF to have more voices in the boardroom as well as the playing field at the global level. The early defining moment of mounting pressure was the boycott of the 1966 World Cup to have a direct entry into the World Cup finals. Since 1970, Africa has had increasing slots climaxing in 2010 when Africa not only hosted its 1st World Cup but also fielded six teams.[21]

Despite the new realization on the part of FIFA's leadership for broadening the opportunities to bring on board new members from Africa, Jules Rimet (1921–1954) remained reluctant to whole-heartedly embrace the change. Fortunately, several leaders, including Stanley Rous (1961–1974), the eventual president of FIFA, were among the advocates for the formation of Continental area Confederations to bring together national associations on each continent. Similarly, there was stiff resistance by the European members to allow African and Asia representation on the Executive Council. This reluctance prompted Ratklo Pleic, representing the Yugolsav Association to argue that "the basis of any organization should be the equality of rights and obligations for all members"[22] (32)

---

[20] Darby, "Africa Football and FIFA", 2002, pp. 236.
[21] Njororai, "Africa at Football World Cup", 2019a.
[22] Ibid., 32.

and that as things stood, the African and Asian members were not getting equal rights and obligations.

As a form of compromise between European and South American members of FIFA, Continental Confederations were formed to facilitate appointment of a representative to the FIFA executive committee. The marginalization of Africa and Asian countries in FIFA's corridors of power served to alert the members from these emerging constituencies on the essence, in Darby's[23] words, "to organize themselves into unified, coordinated confederations. Not only was this imperative in terms of the development of football on their own continents but it was also critical if their voice was to be heard within the governance of world football" (33). Thus in 1957, African Football Associations were able to formally constitute their continental confederation, namely, Confederation of African Football (CAF). The pioneer members of CAF included Egypt, Ethiopia, Sudan, and South Africa. After its formation, the first undertaking was to host the African Cup of Nations, bringing together the elite African teams to vie for Continental honors. Given that at the global level, the ultimate competition, the World Cup, had started in 1930, there was a need for consistent representation of Africa at the event. Therefore, once CAF had gained representation in FIFA's Executive Council, the next battle cry was to have direct and fair representation in the lucrative World Cup tournament.

However, before going into the struggle for more competition slots at the World Cup level, it is important to point out the ideology that drove FIFA's leadership. As pointed out earlier, the period preceding 1954 witnessed very minimal representation of Africa in FIFA corridors be it in the boardroom or on the competition field. This was the time too that most African countries were under colonial rule. Despite being under colonial rule, most African countries had already been introduced to the game and indeed had adopted it as their favorite pastime activity across the continent. It is intriguing to note that the introduction of football into various African communities was led by, among others, missionaries, civil servants, and soldiers.[24] Coincidentally, Jules Rimet is described by Tomlinson[25] as follows:

---

[23] Ibid., 33.
[24] See Njororai, "Colonial legacy and football Kenya", 2009, 866–882; 2014ab, 2016.
[25] Tomlinson, "FIFA and Men Who Made It", 2000, 55–71.

Rimet was Christian and a patriot. His love of God and nation united in his passion for football. He believed in the universality of the church and saw in football the chance to create a world-wide 'football family' wielded to Christian principles. Like his countryman, founder of the modern Olympics Baron Pierre de Coubertin, Rimet believed that sport could be a force for good—bringing people and nations together, promoting physical and moral progress, providing healthy pleasure and fun, and promoting friendship between races. For meritocratic reasons he promoted full-time professionalism. (57)

Looking at Rimet's personal outlook toward football and what he envisaged its role in the world is remarkably like the mission of Missionaries as they strove to promote Christianity alongside football in many parts of Africa. Football was therefore one of the key mediums for introducing Christianity to African communities. However, Rimet's undoing was lack of foresight in terms of the shrinking colonial sphere of influence and the emerging new nations angry at the colonizers and hungry for their own international identity that was best promoted through football. Again Tomlinson[26] captures Rimet's conservative principles that refused to evolve with the times:

> Despite his desire for FIFA to encourage a global family, Rimet found it difficult to overcome an innate European imperiousness. Rimet did not believe that the administration of world football should be based upon geographical or regional groupings, and the development of continental confederations and the empowerment of football confederations in Africa and in Asia was resisted. Rimet's consistent goal was to preserve FIFA as a unit, and he argued that 'decentralization will destroy FIFA, only direct membership will retain FIFA as one family'. (58)

Indeed, Rimet's views were consistent with the imperialistic European powers that were ruling and dominating various parts of the globe with Africa included. Despite this conservative outlook toward restructuring the game to accommodate new members, especially from Asia and Africa, South America had already formed a continental confederation as early as 1916 and indeed already had a continental tournament that started the same year. Europe followed with their own Union of European Football Associations in 1954. Thus, it appears contradictory that FIFA leaders

---

[26] Tomlinson, "FIFA and Men Who Made It", 2000, 55–71.

were preaching to their families without allowing their counterparts from Africa to sit at table with them! This Eurocentric ideological position did not acknowledge the existence of any separate organization other than a European-based one. Rimet's concept of the world football family was deeply rooted in an entrenched imperialistic ideology and colonial control that elicited collective resistance from an African constituency that was already politically charged and ready to free themselves from the yolk of foreign rule.

The rigid Eurocentric stance by FIFA's leadership had the advantage of pushing African Football Associations to coalesce together and therefore fruitfully brought about the formation of CAF in 1957. The formation of CAF was good for Africa as it was now possible to formally and effectively be represented on FIFA's Executive Committee as well as coordinating the development of the African game. Having secured a seat on the executive committee of FIFA in 1954, there was an urgent desire to organize the African game especially creating a continental structure to guide the growth of the game.[27] Thus, in February 1957, CAF was formally constituted in Khartoum, Sudan, with Abdelaziz Abdallah Salem of Egypt assuming the mantle of the presidency, while Fred Fell (South Africa), Ydnekatchew Tessema (Ethiopia), and Abdel Mohamed (Sudan) were nominated members of the executive committee.[28] The rationale for the formation of CAF included:

1. To develop football throughout Africa.
2. To introduce continent-wide competitions.
3. To promote the African game on the global stage.[29]

The formation of CAF was a major launching pad for the development and entrenchment of football as Africa's most popular sport.[30] Apart from the sporting accomplishment, the formation of CAF proved to be a shot in the arm as the game lent considerable weight to the political cause by asserting national identity and pan-African identity. The game provided a highly visible podium for advancing the political fight for political independence around the African countries and even at the global level. By

[27] Hawkey, "Feet of the Chameleon", 2009, 38.
[28] Versi, "Football in Africa", 1986, 9–10.
[29] Ibid.
[30] Versi, "Football in Africa", 1986.

CAF organizing and administering football across the continent, it gave visibility of the game to the rest of the world.[31] As a late entrant in the FIFA family, Africa offered massive hopes for the advancement of sport. Eric Batty, as cited by Murray,[32] even predicted in 1963 that the 1978 World Cup final would be a match-up between Egypt and Ghana as the two were excelling in CAF competitions as well as in Olympic soccer tournaments. This, of course, never came to be. However, Africa has since made an impact in the corridors of power. Their voting power has proved pivotal in earning recognition as well as in shaping the strategic priorities of FIFA as a democratic and progressive transnational organization as I will demonstrate in the next section.

SIR STANLEY ROUS, SOUTH AFRICA, AND AFRICAN REPRESENTATION AT THE WORLD CUP

Right from inception, CAF was confronted with the dual challenge of collaborating with Europe to advance the African game while at the same time resisting FIFA's overbearing nature over African affairs.[33] What transpired between CAF and FIFA was an expression of the differing power differentials of the protagonists with Africa being viewed as an inferior partner by a more self-perceived dominant European force that dominated FIFA's decision-making organs at the time. Significantly, CAF's leadership successfully resisted European dominance and overtures on issues affecting their African constituency, while gaining major strides in getting their voices heard regarding South Africa's apartheid policies, increased representation on the playing field, and in the choice of presidents for FIFA. One testing case for pan-African unity was the question of South Africa's exclusion from Olympic sport as well as from FIFA-sanctioned competitions. It was clear that Rous's support for the South African Football Association against the will of most of the African Football Associations posed a huge threat to his re-election plans as well as isolating him within the FIFA executive. Despite the fears of isolation and potential loss of his presidency, Rous strongly continued to support FASA and even encouraged them to bring to FIFA's attention alleged instances of discriminatory practices on the part of other African football associations as a

[31] Onwumechili, "CAF Identity", 2014, 201.
[32] Murray, "The World's Game", 1996, 128.
[33] Onwumechili, "CAF Identity", 2014, 202.

way of encouraging a sympathetic outlook to their problems.[34] João Havelange, who had been watching and keenly monitoring the developing relations between FIFA, FASA, and CAF during Stanley Rous's tenure of office, launched his bid for the FIFA presidency in 1971. His campaign throughout the third world and exposure to the sentiments of the South African Non-Racial Olympic Committee (NROC), in his capacity as a member of the IOC, had given Havelange an understanding of the centrality of South Africa's continued sporting isolation in the psyche of African politicians, sports administrators, and its general population.[35] As the 1974 election grew closer, it was clear that the South African question was going to be a crucial factor in the FIFA elections. Coincidentally, in 1972 FASA had approached Rous for approval to secure special dispensation from FIFA's Executive Committee to allow them to invite amateur select teams from England, Brazil, and West Germany to take part in, what FASA described as, a "multi-racial sports festival in March of 1973. In Rous' mind, this festival would achieve a general relaxation of the existing governmental policies in respect of sport. However, the event was a flop as invited countries, including England, western Germany, and Brazil withdrew as they realized that the event was merely aimed at appeasing international opinion and represented a major outlet for the 'aggrandizement of white supremacy."[36]

One key aspect about the withdrawal of teams from this festival was the fact that Havelange who, in his position as president of the Brazilian Football Federation, was responsible for sanctioning such actions orchestrated Brazil's retreat. This active role by Havelange in withdrawing the Brazilian team from the South African multinational sports festival provides an enlightening insight into the nature of his political campaign in Africa. This opportunity presented him with a chance to demonstrate his sympathetic attitude to CAF's position on South Africa in contrast to that held by Stanley Rous, who had unconstitutionally mobilized the FIFA executive to sanction the event. Havelange's political acumen was therefore brought into the limelight as he fully exploited Rous's problems with Africa's national football associations to secure their political support.[37]

---

[34] Darby, "Africa Football and FIFA", 2002, pp. 236.
[35] Ibid.
[36] Ramsamy, "South African Sports Isolation", New York Times, 11 December 1988.
[37] Darby, "Africa Football and FIFA", 2002, pp. 236.

However, CAF did not just wait passively for the South African issue to play itself out. The CAF president, Ydnekatchew Tessema, had indeed threatened that Mr. Havelange would lose the support of the African associations in his fight for the presidency of FIFA if he did not apply his influence to withdraw Brazil from the event. According to Darby,[38] the fact that Tessema was able to "threaten the withdrawal of African support for Havelange's presidential challenge illustrates that CAF not only had the confidence to assert itself within world football politics but also recognized the potential that its voting powers offered the African continent" (81).

Compared to the pre-1954 FIFA, this active role by CAF to exert influence on matters of football ushered in an era that saw African nations as big influencers on major political dispensations within the power struggle for the control of FIFA. For the African nations, Havelange became the means through which they were to achieve a realignment of the distribution of power and privilege within world football in ways that would more adequately reflect their interests. In return, Havelange sought to harness Africa's growing confidence as well as the antipathy between CAF and Stanley Rous over the South African issue in order to increase his appeal to FIFA's African constituents.[39] The Brazilian made his intentions for South Africa explicitly clear, professing that so long as he was in charge and apartheid still existed, South Africa could never be welcome into FIFA. Indeed, Havelange' s promise to exclude FASA from the world body was realized two years after he replaced Rous as FIFA president, when the Executive Committee, on the new president's prompting, expelled South Africa from its ranks until racial discrimination (apartheid) had ceased to exist in their club matches.[40]

FIFA, Havelange-Blatter, and the Development of African Football

João Havelange, while campaigning to become the president of FIFA, made it a priority to focus on the disenfranchised, emergent nations and how to bring them into the mainstream of the global FIFA family. His platform for the presidency therefore made it clear that he was going to

---

[38] Darby, "Africa Football and FIFA", 2002, pp. 236.
[39] Darby, "Africa Football and FIFA", 2002, pp. 236.
[40] Darby, "Africa Football and FIFA", 2002, pp. 236.

move football away from its western European roots and to open it up to newer constituencies in Africa, Asia, and the Americas. His pledge to increase World Cup final places from 16 to 24 demonstrated his desire to accommodate calls for a more equitable distribution of places for African and Asian countries. By 1974, Africa had only one representative to the World Cup finals. Even securing this one slot had taken a boycott of the 1966 World Cup for their voices to be heard. Thus, Havelange not only pledged to increase slots for the African continent, but also went further by pledging to establish an international academy committed to the development of standards and adequate infrastructures and proposed an international youth championship to be hosted regularly by developing nations. He also committed himself to cash subsidies for the construction of stadia, the provision of top-class coaching, and support for more club competitions throughout Africa and Asia.[41] These pledges and strategic initiatives for Havelange, therefore, endeared him to the African constituency, as well as other hitherto marginalized nations in Asia, the Americas, and Oceania. One major advantage that Havelange also had over Rous was the fact that he came from a developing country that had not only a long football culture, but also a diverse population with a huge presence of black players in the national team. The forging of political ties between Havelange and Africa was facilitated by the broader cultural connections of Brazil to African people and the shared game of football.

The 1974 FIFA elections and the ascendency of João Havelange into the presidency marked a turning point in the power relations in the organization as it marked the loosening grip of the Europeans on FIFA and the world game. All this emanated from Rous's political miscalculations, UEFA's complacency, and Havelange' s skillful messaging to the African continent, as well as the other nations in Asia, Americas, and Oceania.[42] According to Darby,[43] African votes were clearly the key in a result that signaled an "unparalleled transformation in the affairs of FIFA as the balance of power shifted from the northern hemisphere to the southern" (7).

Upon taking up the presidency, Havelange immediately set about fulfilling the expensive promises that he had made to the third world as part of his election strategy. True to his pledges, he mobilized resources from the corporate world including Adidas and Coca-Cola and immediately

---

[41] Tomlinson, "FIFA and Men Who Made It", 2000, 55–71.
[42] Darby, "Africa, FIFA Presidency and Football", 2003, 1–24.
[43] Ibid.

embarked on the practical realization of his manifesto. Some of the key development programs that were established in Africa and Asia included inauguration of two new world youth tournaments hosted regularly by developing countries, and steps were taken to increase the number of African and Asian nations taking part in the World Cup finals. In addition, FIFA's committee structures underwent democratization that allowed Africa an enhanced say in the governance of world football.[44] Thus, one can say with confidence that Havelange had an enormous impact on African soccer, and he played a huge part in moving the African game from the margins of world football to the center.

However, during Havelange's reign, many within FIFA's European constituency harbored deep resentments at how Havelange had facilitated the expansion and democratization of world football. For many European nations, Havelange's plans to develop the game in underdeveloped football regions were being pushed through at Europe's expense. They were particularly incensed with the tampering of the format of the World Cup finals to accommodate developing nations as well as his sympathetic response to their demands often made at FIFA Congress.[45] On the playing field, African teams had improved their credibility. World Cup representatives from Africa competed well in 1978, 1982, and 1986 and Cameroon made it to the quarterfinals in the 1990 edition losing to England in extra time. African teams also won medals at the Olympic soccer tournaments in 1992, 1996, and 2000. Indeed, African teams won or competed well in most age-group competitions. These performances showed that Africa was closing the gap between Europe and South America.

When Havelange announced that he was standing down on the eve of the 1998 elections, UEFA thought it was the opportune time to reclaim their mantle. However, just as in 1974, Havelange threw his weight behind his then Secretary-General, Sepp Blatter, to ascend to the presidency to the chagrin of UEFA and its President Lennart Johnson who was eying the position. According to Darby,[46] because almost a quarter of the nations' eligible vote at the FIFA congress is from Africa, the interests of Africa's football associations had to be incorporated in a central way into any European strategy aimed at reclaiming the FIFA presidency. Lennart Johnson strategized on earning the African vote in the first half of the

[44] Ibid.
[45] Darby, "Africa, FIFA Presidency and Football", 2003, 1–24.
[46] Ibid.

1990s by finding areas of common ground with CAF's president, Issa Hayatou, and worked toward a more amicable and cooperative relationship between Europe and Africa.

The substantive elements of the program of cooperation between UEFA and CAF that Johansson had set in motion were the vision proposals and the Meridian Project. The 1995 vision proposals were aimed at involving the confederations more actively in the administration of world football, and it appeared to herald a radical transformation in UEFA's attitude to the other continental bodies.[47] Following the initiative, UEFA explained that it now recognized the progress of all the continental confederations and considered them as equal partners, who should be appropriately involved in FIFA matters.[48] The Meridian Project, an accord between UEFA and CAF formally ratified on 30 January 1997, was built on the key principles of the vision documents in that it proclaimed that the notions of equal partnership and mutual respect should characterize Afro-European relations in world football. Crucially, the project involved the provision of financial, technical, and technological aid from UEFA to selected African football associations.[49] The publication of the vision proposals and the signing of the Meridian Project appeared to have ushered in a new era of friendship between both confederations. This collaborative initiative would mark a new era in the relationship between the African Football Confederation and UEFA as the African confederation enthusiastically welcomed the philosophy and material support that underpinned the Vision and Meridian initiatives. But whereas CAF's leadership felt the initiative was pivotal to the growth of the African game, others feared that European benevolence was based solely on recognition of the value of African votes in the succession battle.[50]

Given that Blatter was pledging to continue the legacy of Havelange and therefore FIFA's goodwill to Africa and other marginalized countries, it was not surprising that he won the elections. Havelange and his Secretary-General, Sepp Blatter, tore African representatives between supporting CAF's newfound, yet suspicious, partnership with UEFA and their demonstrated decent work in Africa. The good record and the need

---

[47] Sugden, Tomlinson, and Darby, "FIFA versus UEFA in World Football", 1998.
[48] Darby, "Africa, FIFA Presidency and Football", 2003, 1–24, and Darby, "Africa Football and FIFA", 2002, 139–140.
[49] Darby, 2002, 2003.
[50] Maradas, "Meaning of Meridian", 1999.

to sustain FIFA's partnership with Africa paid off for Blatter. During his first term of office, there were strong signs that the development of African football would benefit from Blatter's emergence as the man to lead FIFA into the twenty-first century. His support for Africa's bid for the 2006 World Cup hosting rights was unstinting, and he would have preferred South Africa to Germany's candidatures had he been given the opportunity to cast a deciding vote. Although his stance on the 2006 World Cup was of huge symbolic significance, his decision to finance football development in the game's underdeveloped regions through the GOAL project, launched in March 1999, represented the clearest manifestation of his commitment to the development of the African game.[51] By far the biggest slice of GOAL funds was to go to Asia, Africa, and the north and Central American regions. The overall aim of the GOAL project was to help bridge the gap between European and South American football, on the one hand, and the rest of the world, on the other hand.[52]

The FIFA president's efforts on behalf of African football since the Paris Congress were well received, and it seemed that Africa would continue to benefit from Blatter's patronage for as long as he remained in power. Indeed, in a millennium message to the African football administrators, players, and followers, he unequivocally restated his support for the development of the game on their continent. He declared that Africa could count on the continuing and unwavering help and support of FIFA and its president.[53] Given the principle of reciprocity that has come to dominate FIFA politics, his position at the helm of world football seemed assured. However, in the lead-up to the International Federation's pre-2002 World Cup Congress in Seoul in May, a combination of financial scandal and a challenge from within Africa heralded perhaps the most bitter of all contests for the FIFA presidency.[54]

The tension and poor relations between Blatter and Lennart Johansson, and the former's continuation of Havelange's priority goals, seemed to signal to UEFA and its allies that a challenge to the Swiss was timely. Additional fuel emanated from the bankruptcy of FIFA's media partner, International Sport and Leisure (ISL), in early 2001, and the growing fiscal crisis that it heralded. This sense of urgency of removing Blatter from

---

[51] Maradas, "Meaning of Meridian", 1999, 5.
[52] Ibid.
[53] Blatter, "Message from FIFA President", 2000.
[54] Darby, "Africa, FIFA Presidency and Football", 2003, 1–24.

power culminated in UEFA's leadership seeking out Issa Hayatou, the CAF president, to mount a challenge. In this regard, Lennart Johansson counted on his solid working relationship and personal friendship with his African counterpart and statements of support from CAF's executive as well as Moon-Joon Chung, the influential FIFA vice president and head of the Korean Football Association.[55] Given Hayatou's support for Johansson during the 1998 election campaign, Johansson had little trouble convincing his seven other European colleagues on FIFA's executive that the African would be the type of president who would not seek to undermine European interests in the International Federation in the way Havelange and Blatter had. Thus, on 16 March 2002, at a press conference in Cairo, Johansson stood behind his African ally, passionately believing that Hayatou was the individual to return transparency, solidarity, democracy, and potentially a controlling position for Europe, to FIFA.[56] Given the deep and passionate involvement by UEFA to convince Hayatou to vie against Blatter, many African delegates saw him as a figurehead of dissatisfied Europeans, who desperately wanted to seize power at FIFA's headquarters in Zurich.[57]

This perception of Hayatou as a stooge of the Europeans weighed heavily in his strategy to win FIFA presidency. He, therefore, assumed a defensive posture as he repeatedly dismissed this allegation and pointed out that he was standing as someone who had his own unobstructed vision for the development of the world game.[58] Given that Blatter's philosophy was pro-African football, it was difficult for Hayatou to generate anything distinctively different from that of his opponent. Both promised to continue to fund football development in the developing countries and to improve representation at the World Cup finals for the game's emerging constituencies. To distinguish himself, Hayatou's best chance was to present himself as an individual whose administrative philosophy was fundamentally different from his opponent's and as someone who would preside over FIFA in a more ethical, transparent, and democratic fashion.[59]

Hayatou's anti-Blatter campaign of corruption did not gain much traction with voters.[60] It is interesting that despite Blatter's evident weaknesses

[55] Ibid.
[56] Ibid.
[57] Maradas 2002a.
[58] Sumbuleth 2002.
[59] Darby, "Africa, FIFA Presidency and Football", 2003, 1–24.
[60] BBC Sport Online 2002a, 2002c.

including the collapse of FIFA's media partner, ISL, which coast FIFA between £150 and £200 million, his re-election ambitions remained intact. Blatter's strength lay in the fact that the CAF members, as well as those of UEFA, were not united behind Hayatou despite the pressure from the leadership of the two confederations. Even when Johansson canvassed hard for his African counterpart throughout Europe by highlighting the gradual erosion of UEFA's position within the governance of the world game during the presidencies of Havelange and Blatter, the latter's record for supporting the peripheral countries remained credible.

Hayatou did not help his own cause in UEFA circles by publicly stating that he would facilitate a World Cup berth for Oceania by reducing Europe's allocation by one and a half. This declaration strengthened the resolve of those who were reluctant to follow the official UEFA stance and thereby supported Blatter.[61] For Hayatou to have a chance of winning, he needed near unanimous support from Africa. For some time, it felt like he was on course to master the African vote when he received endorsement of the 11-member east and central African football federations (CECAFA), which had voted for Blatter in the 1998 election. He also received support from Ismael Bamjee, president of the Confederation of Southern African Football Federations (COSAFA). But, despite these statements of support from influential figures and regional groupings within Africa, it soon became clear that the African constituency would not vote uniformly.[62] This lack of unanimous African support was due to Blatter's credible record as an advocate of the African game. The continued reassurance by Blatter on his intentions to support the African game and the launching of several GOAL projects in Southern African countries in spring 2002 served to remind delegates of his commitment to funding football development in the game's poorer regions.[63] Soon after he received endorsements from several African football federations, most notably Liberia, which in late April organized a conference attended by 23 national delegations, under the banner "For the Future of African Football, Let's Support Blatter."[64]

Blatter's campaign also benefitted from support from several high-profile African players, including George Weah and Abedi Pele, and from

[61] Madford 2002.
[62] Darby, "Africa, FIFA Presidency and Football", 2003, 1–24.
[63] Ibid.
[64] Maradas 2002b.

ex-players, most notably Hayatou's compatriot Roger Milla. Milla's comments, which hailed Blatter's record in elevating and strengthening the African presence on FIFA's agenda, were especially poignant given that, like Hayatou, he hailed from Cameroon.[65] With all these African support, Blatter resoundingly beat Hayatou, 139–56 having garnered votes from CONCACAF, Oceania, South American regions and, despite Chung's support for Hayatou, most Asian delegates. The margin of Blatter's victory also revealed that Blatter was viewed by a substantial number of member associations from Africa and Europe as the individual best suited to oversee the world body. And true to those expectations, Sepp Blatter went on to ensure that Africa hosted the World Cup for the first time in 2010, followed by Brazil in 2014, Russia in 2018, and Qatar scheduled to host in 2022, respectively. It was his belief that the world game needed to be taken to the people, hence his policy on rotating the World Cup around all the six Confederations. Incidentally, the elections of 2002 exposed the rot that was taking place in FIFA under the Blatter presidency. It is therefore ironic that he was elected with such a huge margin. His re-election signaled to the world that corruption, unethical practices, and lack of financial transparency were secondary to the vested interests of its affiliated football federations. This could also be a factor in the way FIFA is slow to admonish some of the corrupt and financially inept football association leaders from Africa and elsewhere in the world. His administrative failings notwithstanding, Blatter's commitment to elevating the African game was unrelenting as demonstrated by allocating the hosting rights for the 2010 World Cup to South Africa.

AFRICA'S TURN: SEPP BLATTER, WORLD CUP 2010, AND LEGACY

Sepp Blatter's policy of rotating the hosting of the World Cup around all FIFA's confederations starting off with Africa was designed to reward the African constituency's loyalty. Interviewed on the eve of the 2010 World Cup, Blatter stated thus:

> Just being in South Africa has already made me very happy, "Blatter said."
> It is of course a pioneering move to take the tournament to a continent that has never hosted an event of this size before. So, in some ways, the Africa

[65] BBC Sport Online 2002b.

dream will already have come true when the World Cup trophy is handed over to the winners in Johannesburg. But, of course, it has to be more than that, this World Cup has to be about the legacy that is left behind. Yes, there will be stadiums, roads, airports and all those concrete investments for the future. But what is more important is the activities we are carrying out for football development under our 'Win in Africa with Africa' initiative or for social development with our various Football for Hope programmes and centres."[66]

Blatter also went on to state that "Just bringing boys and girls together, organizing schooling and health education, proving the tools and the incentive to fight against poverty and disease—that is the legacy we want to leave."[67] Indeed, in the wake of South Africa hosting the World Cup, plenty of African Federations now enjoy stadia, offices, training facilities, several trained technical personnel out of the coaching, officiating, administration and sports medicine courses as well as financial support that the previous elitist FIFA of pre-1974 would not have ever dreamt of. In addition, Africa has hosted several age-group competitions, had many health education programs initiated, and has held senior positions within the FIFA Executive, both males and females. Blatter also put in place rules governing transfer of underage players to slow down the massive transfer of talent from Africa to Europe, which he termed, "new slavery."

All these developments have taken place in the African game due to the long struggle that saw their active participation in electing Havelange to the presidency of FIFA to replace Stanley Rous. This ending of the Eurocentric FIFA reign potentially transformed FIFA into a global phenomenon. According to Menon,[68] João Havelange was the first person to truly identify the political potential of siding with the "have-nots," and his defeat of Rous in the 1974 FIFA presidential elections and subsequent 24-year reign laid the blueprint for the phenomenal rise of Joseph "Sepp" Blatter from the tiny town of Visp in Switzerland to the very top of world football. Menon continues to state "The neglected confederations—CAF, CONCACAF, CONMEBOL, Oceania and Asia—were ripe for the picking; starved of funds and recognition, they were crying out for attention.

---

[66] Stewart, R. "Sepp Blatter hopes tournament", 3:39PM BST 08 June 2010.
[67] Stewart, R. "Sepp Blatter hopes tournament", 3:39PM BST 08 June 2010.
[68] Menon, "Sepp Blatter", 2015.

Havelange may have started it—but it was his protégé, Blatter, who mastered it."[69]

Indeed, FIFA is truly democratic as every nation has a say in its functioning as opposed to its earlier history of European elitism. FIFA continues to record phenomenal profits, much of that has been passed on to the member nations (nearly 70% according to FIFA), and strong audit processes have been put in place. The reforms, including an increase of the World Cup slots from 32 to 48 in 2026, will bring more revenue, and together with increased transparency of these transactions, there should be an increase in money share for the smaller nations. Thus, Gianni Infantino's push for a World Cup Tournament comprising of 48 nations promises to cement Blatter's legacy at FIFA, which, which is, the inclusion of the rest of the world into the governing and policy-making process of the world's most popular sport it belongs everyone.[70]

One of the enduring legacies of Sepp Blatter was the successful hosting of the World Cup in South Africa in 2010. Under the stewardship of the then South African president, Thabo Mbeki, the 2010 World Cup became a massive national project designed to enhance the status of the nation-state, as well as the rebranding of the African at the global level. Hosting of the World Cup by South Africa coincided and re-energized the African Renaissance philosophy, which is the belief that modernity and globalization, combined with African cultural heritage, can be harnessed to reinvigorate the continent economically and politically.[71] According to Alegi,[72] "South Africa's hosting of the world cup represents the latest and most ambitious attempt by an African country to use football to showcase its political achievement, accelerate economic growth, and assert the continent's global citizenship." The success of the 2010 World Cup sent a strong signal to the rest of the world that the African continent and its football are likely to continue shaping the culture and history of the global game for many years to come. However, critics of the 2010 World Cup were equally vociferous in complaining about the priority placed on the tournament when there are so many other pressing priorities. But after all the rhetoric and bitter argument, the government said the economic boost to the country (38bn rands) would surpass the outlay. Around 130,000

---

[69] Menon, 2015.
[70] https://in.news.yahoo.com/sepp-blatter-understanding-legacy-man-223440539.html.
[71] Alegi, "Soccerscapes", 2010.
[72] Ibid., p. 132.

jobs were created—but many of those were temporary construction jobs. Additionally, South Africa also succeeded, albeit temporarily about nation-building potential of the World Cup as South Africans came together in a national sense of near-hysteria. There were also significant infrastructure improvements that will serve South African football for a long time. Additionally, successfully delivering the World Cup helped to change perceptions of the country and the continent.[73]

One unique legacy of the 2010 World Cup is the increased stock of knowledge generated on African football through publications. Back in 1986, Versi[74] lamented the absence of literature on the African game. Leading to and after the 2010 World Cup, there was an upsurge of publications[75] on the African game via books, book chapters, peer-reviewed articles in journals, and specific features in the print and electronic media. This shows that the study of football, and African sport in general, is gaining recognition as a critical area of academic inquiry and scholarship. The 2010 World Cup played a pivotal role in eliciting serious academic and scholarly inquiries on the status of football in Africa even though it still lags behind what comes out of Europe and South America.

Infantino, Ahmad Ahmad, Patrice Moetsepe, and African Football's Future

Given the political nature of FIFA, and for as long as Africa continues to constitute such a sizeable political bloc with a sizeable number of members, those seeking powerful administrative positions will find ways to collaborate with or present themselves as advocates of the African game. This trend was evident in Havelange's election manifesto, Johansson's efforts to establish an Afro-European concord, and Blatter's GOAL project and support for a World Cup hosted in Africa and even Gianni Infantino's rise to the presidency in 2016. Indeed, Gianni Infantino' s manifesto emphasized an increase in the number of countries in the World Cup finals,

---

[73] https://www.theguardian.com/football/blog/2010/jul/12/south-africa-world-cup-2010.
[74] Versi, "Football in Africa", 1986, 9.
[75] See Alegi, "Soccerscapes", 2010; Bloomfield, "Africa United", 2010; Cleveland et al., "Sports in Africa", pp. 298; Diop and Fattah, "Sports ecosystem Africa", 2021; Hawkey, "Feet of the Chameleon", 2009; Onwumechili, "Africa's elite football", 2020, pp. 272; Onwumechili and Akindes, "Identity and Nation", 2014, 272; Chari and Mhiripiri, "African Football", 2014, 313.

thereby having better regional representation; continued rotating of the World Cup by having a region host and not just one country; continuing with infrastructural investments and continued financial support to all member states. In this regard, the legacy of Havelange-Blatter on African soccer seems to be safe under Gianni Infantino's stewardship of FIFA. According to Infantino, Africa has "talent, there is passion, and there is an investment that is beginning to come in. All these need to be coordinated. African football needs to work as a unit for the future and FIFA will be at its side for that". To make matters even better, an African woman was appointed as the Secretary-General of FIFA and an African woman headed the women's wing of football. And in 2019, FIFA even seconded the Secretary-General to restore order and ethical leadership in CAF. This shows a solid working relationship between FIFA and CAF. Administratively, therefore, African Football is well represented and making great strides within the higher echelons of political power in FIFA. However, a lot remains to be done to improve the administration and management of the game on the African continent so that performances on the field of play can also be globally visible.

The reigns and exits of Issa Hayatou and that of Ahmad Ahmad as presidents of CAF both left stains of corruption and maladministration that set the continent's quest for progress backward.[76] Ahmad Ahmad ended his reign ignominiously as FIFA suspended him for five years. Upon appealing, the Court of Arbitration for Sport upheld Ahmad's ban from football, though it reduced it from five years to two. The original fine of CHF 200,000 ($213,714) was reduced to CHF 50,000 ($53,429). The three-person CAS panel unanimously found Ahmad guilty of two articles of the FIFA Code of Ethics for "failure to record various financial transactions, acceptance of cash payments, bank transfers of bonuses and indemnities without a contractual or regulatory basis."[77] He became the first Confederation of African Football (CAF) president to be banned from football. Among other accusations, he had breached codes relating to the duty of loyalty, abuse of position, and misappropriation of funds, among others.[78] These accusations are not an isolated occurrence in African football as many national associations experience similar misappropriation of

---

[76] Ibid.

[77] https://www.infobae.com/aroundtherings/federations/2021/07/12/caf-presidents-ban-upheld-by-cas/.

[78] https://www.bbc.com/sport/africa/55809955.

funds and lack of transparency and accountability. Ahmad's reign was characterized by a catalog of administrative fumbles, failures, and ineptitude. It was during his reign that FIFA took over the running of the CAF Secretariat in Cairo, when its Secretary-General was assigned to run it. The move to send a Secretary-General to Africa came on the heels of scandalous reports on and off the field.[79] To further emphasize the inadequacy, unethical and chaotic nature of CAF's leadership, Ahmad's vice president, Constant Omari from Morocco, who served as interim CAF president, failed a FIFA integrity and eligibility check and was barred from running in the CAF elections for a new president.[80] The disqualification of Ahmad and his vice president left the South African billionaire Patrice Motsepe to ascend to CAF's presidency unopposed. The force behind Patrice Motsepe was Gianni Infantino, the FIFA president, who orchestrated and presided over a "ceremony of African unity" where Motsepe's rivals were prevailed upon to step aside and be rewarded with administrative positions in the CAF hierarchy.

President Gianni Infantino's direct involvement in influencing the operations of CAF and even in the electoral process as well as the tinkering of the competition structures comes across as overbearing and a reminder of the neocolonial tendencies of FIFA. His direct role in the election of Patrice Motsepe to replace the disgraced Ahmad Ahmad, who had succeeded Issa Hayatou, raised some eyebrows. Even though he continues to advocate for unity in African football, there is a need for CAF to show levels of autonomy in making decisions rather than being dictated to by FIFA through President Infantino. CAF should be careful not to be seen as a European appendage incapable of resisting external overtures to project an independent African identity.[81] Despite misgivings about Infantino's direct involvement in African football affairs, there is a need for a change of attitude on the part of FIFA's leadership toward the African constituency. Instead of Africa only mattering as a reservoir of presidential votes, there has to be a strategic partnership focusing on the development of the African game.

Despite Africa's enormous potential in football, there are some factors that conspire to hold its development back. One key factor is corruption

[79] Daley, "FIFA's intervention in African football", 2019.
[80] https://www.infobae.com/aroundtherings/federations/2021/07/12/caf-presidents-ban-upheld-by-cas/.
[81] Onwumechili, "CAF Identity", 2014, 201–213.

as FIFA's laissez-faire dispersal of revenues acts as a magnet for the self-interested. Too many FAs lack administrative structures to stem siphoning off the money by administrators rather than the money going toward upgrading facilities. Meanwhile, domestic leagues are underfunded, poorly attended, and home to technically inferior players which then is not attractive to fans who have instead shifted their loyalty to European football widely available via cable television.[82] It is therefore commendable that Infantino's priority upon taking over the FIFA presidency was to unveil a new vision, which is "promote the game of football, protect its integrity, and bring the game to all." The strategic priorities of growing the game, enhancing the experience, and building stronger institutions are timely especially for the African game regarding professionalization of the sport.[83]

One negative legacy of Havelange-Blatter reign that Infantino should address is the need for transparency and accountability of the revenue generously channeled to the African football federations. Thomas[84] quotes Emmanuel Maradas, who stated that African football leaders treated money from FIFA as "piggy banks." They therefore share "the money around instead of using it to develop football." According to Thomas, the inability of many federations to account for their spending and develop a comprehensive plan for grassroots football significantly holds back the development of Africa's listless domestic leagues. He argues that well-resourced youth football academies funded by Europe's elite clubs pick the best talent at a young age before they have a chance to benefit local professional clubs. Similarly, Toesland[85] argued that if the football industry can overcome poor governance issues, stem the migration of talented players, and reignite interest in domestic leagues, the sport can play a significant role in driving Africa's economic and social development. It is imperative that FIFA-CAF relations moving forward should lay premium on instituting measures to promote transparency and accountability for revenue channeled from Zurich to develop the game in Africa.

---

[82] Thomas, "When will Africa Cash in?", 2018, 10–17.
[83] FIFA, "Club Licensing Handbook", 4.
[84] Ibid., 14.
[85] Toesland, "Football Big Business", 2016, 27–28.

Conclusions

African football and its leadership have struggled for recognition and an adequate say in the governance of world football since gaining a foothold in the mid-1950s. Since its first admission on the FIFA Executive Committee in 1954 and the formation of CAF in 1957, African football has played a key role in shaping FIFA's political leadership, strategic priorities, political positions, and administrative structure. Indeed, since 1974, Africa's vote has had a great bearing on FIFA presidency. To achieve their goals, CAF leaders had to adopt a protectionist stance against European domination in advocating for justice and fairness in the global game while at the same time being open to learning from Europe in establishing progressive structures to advance the game in their African constituent members such as the administrative and competition structures of the game. The emergence of Africa and its proactive stance on football issues can, therefore, be understood by drawing on the core-periphery thrust of world system theory and the inter-dependency paradigm, as well as the power that individual leaders play in influencing the fortunes of a people, nations, and regions in a globalized era. Indeed, the role that Havelange, Blatter, Tessema, and Hayatou played vis-à-vis the Eurocentric FIFA presidencies preceding 1974 demonstrates the power that lies in political alliances, relationships within FIFA, and needs together with the ambitions of powerful human agents and clusters of regional groupings all provide a dynamic to understand FIFA and CAF and African Football. This continues to have ramifications for African football and its position within FIFA.

From the look of things, the game will continue to grow. However, the leadership must continue to form strategic alliances with powerful individuals as well as other regional blocks to exert influence on the decisions made by the FIFA executive without surrendering their autonomy in making decisions that are pro-African in nature. If African football administrators are to preserve or build on the strides that they have made within the game's corridors of power, there are key lessons to be learned from the elections of 1974, 1998, 2002, and 2016, some of which were articulated by Darby.[86] These include the following:

1. For effectiveness, CAF should present a politically united front while representing African interests within the governance of the game.

---

[86] Darby, "Africa, FIFA Presidency and Football", 2003, 1–24.

2. CAF's leading figures need to think hard before breaking with the traditional political alliances within FIFA that have done much to facilitate the development of the African game.
3. African football administrators must continue to work toward creating the type of self-sustaining development dynamic that will make them less dependent on individuals or political blocs who seek to realize their ambitions in the International Federation by drawing on African votes.
4. African administrators must put the interests of the African game ahead of their narrow individual interests.
5. African leaders must be continually alive to the pursuit of new opportunities and programs that would affect the growth of professional football on the African continent to minimize the exodus of talent to other regions of the world.
6. African leaders also need to be transparent with the resources that flow through the game so that the real beneficiaries are the players, communities, and the overall growth of the game, nationally, regionally, and globally.
7. African football leadership at CAF and national federations should prioritize investment in the development of sound structures for professional football to develop at all levels, including women and men, if they are to stand any chance of remaining competitive at the global level.

REFERENCES

Alegi, P. (2010). *African Soccerscapes: How a Continent Changed the World's Game*. Athens, OH: Ohio University Press.
Aniche, E. T., and Ukaegbu, V. E. (2016). Structural Dependence, Vertical Integration and Regional Economic Cooperation in Africa: A Study of Southern African Development Community. *Africa Review*, 8 (2): 108–119.
Blatter, S. (2000). Message from the FIFA President. *African Soccer*, 51: 5.
Bloomfield, S. (2010). *Africa United: Soccer, Passion, Politics, and the First World Cup in Africa*. New York: Harper Perennial.
Chari, T., and Mhiripiri, N. A. (eds.). (2014). *African Football, Identity Politics and Global Media Narratives: The Legacy of the FIFA 2010 World Cup*. London: Palgrave Macmillan.
Cleveland, T., Kaur, T., and Akindes, G. (2021). *Sports in Africa*. Athens, OH: Ohio University Press, 299.

Daley, B. (2019, June). FIFA's Intervention in African Football Speaks Volumes About Failed Leadership. *The Conversation*. Retrieved at https://theconversation.com/fifas-intervention-in-african-football-speaks-volumes-about-failed-leadership-119560.
Darby, P. (2000a). Football, Colonial Doctrine and Indigenous Resistance: Mapping the Political Persona of FIFA's African Constituency. *Culture, Sport, Society*, 3 (1): 61–87.
Darby, P. (2000b). Africa's Place in FIFA's Global Order: A Theoretical Frame. *Soccer and Society*, 1 (2): 36–61.
Darby, P. (2002). *Africa, Football and FIFA: Politics, Colonialism and Resistance*. London and Portland, OR: Frank Cass.
Darby, P. (2003). Africa, the FIFA Presidency and the Governance of World Football: 1974, 1998 and 2002. *Africa Today*, 50 (1): 3–24.
Darby, P. (2005). Africa and the World Cup: Politics, Eurocentrism and Resistance. *International Journal of the History of Sport*, 22 (5): 883–905.
Diop, A., and Fattah, M. A. (2021). *The Sports Ecosystem in Africa: A Potential Development Lever*. Mazars and African Sports and Creative Institute.
FIFA. (n.d.). *FIFA Club Licensing Handbook*. Zurich: FIFA.com.
Hawkey, I. (2009). *Feet of the Chameleon: The Story of African Football*. London: Portico.
Maradas, E. (1999). The Meaning of Meridian. *African Soccer*, 42 (March): 10.
Menon, A. (2015). Sepp Blatter—Understanding the Legacy of the Man Who Ruled Football for 17 Years. *Sportskeeda*, 2 June. Retrieved on 23 September 2016 at https://in.news.yahoo.com/sepp-blatter-understanding-legacy-man-223440539.htm.
Murray, B. (1996). *The World's Game: A History of Soccer*. Urbana: University of Illinois Press.
Njororai, W. W. S. (2009). Colonial Legacy, Minorities, and Association Football in Kenya. *Soccer & Society*, 10 (6): 866–882.
Njororai W. W. S. (2014a). South Africa FIFA World Cup 2010: African Players Global Labor Distribution and Legacy. In *African Football, Identity Politics and Global Media Narratives* (pp. 71–90). London: Palgrave Macmillan.
Njororai, W. W. S. (2014b). History and Identity of East African Football Within the African Context. In *Identity and Nation in African Football: Fans, Community, and Clubs* (pp. 67–80). Palgrave Macmillan.
Njororai Simiyu, W. W. (2016). Kenya at 50: Contextualization of Her Post Independence Sporting Success. In *Kenya After Fifty: Education, Gender and Sports* (pp. 125–146). London: Palgrave Macmillan.
Njororai Simiyu, W. W. (2019a). Africa at the Football World Cup Final Tournament, 1934–2018: Defining Moments and Memories on the Field. *Soccer and Society*, 20 (7–8): 973–985, https://doi.org/10.1080/1466097 0.2019.1680497.

Njororai Simiyu, W. W. (2019b). FIFA's Intervention in African Football Speaks Volumes About Failed Leadership. *The Conversation*. Retrieved from https://theconversation.com/fifas-intervention-in-african-football-speaks-volumes-about-failed-leadership-119560.

Onwumechili, C. (ed.). (2014a). *Africa's Elite Football: Structure, Politics, and Everyday Challenges*. New York: Routledge, p. 272.

Onwumechili, C. (2014b). CAF: Perennial Struggle in Crises of Identity. In: C. Onwumechili and G. Akindes (eds.). *Identity and Nation in African Football: Fans, Community and Clubs* (pp. 201–213). London: Palgrave Macmillan.

Onwumechili, C., and Akindes, G. (eds.). (2014). *Identity and Nation in African Football: Fans, Community and Clubs*. London: Palgrave Macmillan. p. 272.

Ramsamy, S. (1988). Keep South African Sports in Isolation. *New York Times*, 11 December.

Schneider, M. (1996, August). Factors Governing Success in International Football: Tradition, Wealth and Size—or Is There More to It. *FIFA Magazine*, pp. 7–11.

Stewart, R. (2010). World Cup 2010: Sepp Blatter Hopes Tournament Leave Lasting Legacy in Africa. Retrieved on 23 September 2016 at http://www.telegraph.co.uk/sport/football/world-cup/7811223/World-Cup-2010-Sepp-Blatter-hopes-tournament-leave-lasting-legacy-in-Africa.html.

Sugden, J., Tomlinson, A., and Darby, P. (1998). FIFA Versus UEFA in the Struggle for the Control of World Football. In A. Brown (ed.), *Fanatics! Power, Identity and Fandom in World Football*. London and New York: Routledge.

Thomas, D. (2018). Football: When will Africa Cash In? *African Business*, August/September, pp. 10–17.

Toesland, F. (2016, October). Could Football Finally Become Big Business in Africa? *Africa Business*, pp. 27–28.

Tomlinson, A. (2000, Spring). FIFA and the Men Who Made It. *Soccer and Society*, 1 (1): 55–71.

Versi, A. (1986). *Football in Africa*. London: Collins.

Wallerstein, I. (1974). *The Modern World System I: Capitalist Agriculture and the Origins of the European World-economy in the Sixteenth Century*. New York: Academic Press.

Wallerstein, I. (2004). *World Systems Analysis*. Durham, NC: Duke University Press.

CHAPTER 3

The Confederation of African Football (CAF): Origins, Accomplishments, and Challenges

Peter Ajongwa Ngwafu and Augustine E. Ayuk

Before the formation of the Confederation of African Football, here and henceforth referred to as CAF in 1957, football operations in the continent were exclusively a colonial venture, directed by colonial governments with support by missionaries. CAF is the dominant football association in Africa, representing fifty-six member associations with Zanzibar and the island of Reunion as new members. CAF is one of the largest of six continental confederations under Fédération Internationale de Football Association (FIFA).

The vision of creating an African football federation emerged at the FIFA Congress in Berne, Switzerland, in 1954. Members at the Congress

P. A. Ngwafu
Albany State University, Albany, GA, USA
e-mail: peter.ngwafu@asurams.edu

A. E. Ayuk (✉)
Clayton State University, Morrow, GA, USA
e-mail: Augustineayuk@clayton.edu

© The Author(s), under exclusive license to Springer Nature Switzerland AG 2022
A. E. Ayuk (ed.), *Football (Soccer) in Africa*, Global Culture and Sport Series, https://doi.org/10.1007/978-3-030-94866-5_3

voted in support of the formation of an African football confederation. However, it would be in Lisbon, Portugal, in 1956, during the FIFA Congress that this dream of an African football federation would be close to realization. Four representatives from Africa at the Congress, Egypt, Ethiopia, South Africa, and Sudan, undertook to meet in the Sudanese capital, Khartoum, in 1957, to draft rules and regulations that would govern the association and discuss modalities for launching of the first African Cup of Nations competition.

On February 8, 1957, the Confederation of African Football (CAF) was formally established, with its headquarters in Cairo, Egypt. CAF was the lone pan-African organization in Africa at the time and was the first sports organization to expel apartheid South Africa from participating in football in 1960.

This governing body of African football represents Africa in international football as well as improves the quality of the sport in the continent.

According to Fletcher, football and CAF membership were "vehicles for pan-Africanism" in postcolonial Africa.[1] Political leaders marked national Independence Day celebrations in Ghana, Uganda, Nigeria, Kenya, and Zambia with football tournament featuring to their new national teams.[2]

This chapter seeks to examine the origins and evolution of the Confederation of African Football, the role the organization has played and continues to play in advancing football management and advancing African football globally. The chapter also explores CAF's role as "activist" in building solidarity among member associations to fighting for equality and against segregation in football in Africa and globally. Furthermore, the chapter will highlight some examples of the association's accomplishments, including expulsion of apartheid South Africa from CAF in 1960, boycott of the 1966 FIFA World Cup in England, and increase in the number of African spots in FIFA tournaments. The chapter will also analyze the contributions of João Havelange and Sepp Blatter, former presidents of FIFA, in solidifying the game in Africa.

Despite its praiseworthy accomplishments, CAF, like other associations in Africa, has been marred by corruption, mismanagement, and

[1] M. Fletcher, M. Confederation of African Football in J. Hugson, K. Moore, R. Spaaij, and J. Maguire, eds., Routledge Handbook of Football Studies, 1st ed. London: Routledge, 2017:423–431.
[2] Ibid.

disorganization. The chapter will explore the challenges faced by CAF and offer some antidotes to reignite enthusiasm and confidence in the confederation.

Aside from the African Union, no other intergovernmental organization in Africa has left an indelible mark on politics, football, and culture as the CAF. This organization has been responsible for managing football, the most popular sporting activity in Africa for over sixty years.

Origins and Evolution of the Confederation of African Football (CAF)

The origin and evolution of the Confederation of African Football are intertwined with the politics of international football in the 1950s and 1960s. Paul Darby divulges that "the rigid Eurocentric stance by FIFA leadership had the advantage of pushing African Associations to coalesce together and therefore fruitfully brought about the formation of Confederation of African Football (CAF) in February 1957, in Khartoum".[3] While the organization was born in the Sudanese capital, it is important to examine how global politics contributed to members' resolve to form Africa's preeminent sporting body. Before the establishment of this body, the global sport of football was dominated by the European Football Federation, under the leadership and influence of England. Paul Darby instructs us that "post-imperial hegemony characterized the governance of the world's game and nowhere was this more aptly demonstrated than in the Eurocentrism that was at FIFA's core, which subsequently generated exasperated reaction by CAF and irritated response from FIFA".[4] In June 1956, African delegates to the 30th FIFA Congress held in Lisbon, Portugal, agreed to form an African football confederation. After the Congress, Egypt, Ethiopia, South Africa, and Sudan were committed to convening again in February 1957 in Khartoum to draft statutes and to discuss staging the first Africa Cup of Nations. At that meeting, the African regional body representing African soccer, the Confederation Africaine de Football (CAF), was formed and its constitutional act was signed in Khartoum, Sudan, on June 8, 1957. Its stated objectives were to develop football throughout Africa, introduce continent-wide competitions, and

---

[3] Paul Darby, *African Football and FIFA: Politics, Colonialism and Resistance*. New York: Frank Cass Publishers, 2002, 35.
[4] Ibid, XIII.

promote African soccer on the international stage. An organizational structure was subsequently established to execute CAF's objectives and Abdel Aziz Salem who had worked tirelessly to secure recognition of football within FIFA was named CAF's first president. Youssef Mohammed became its first Secretary-General, while Fred Tell of South Africa, Ydnekatchew Tessema of Ethiopia, and Abdel Halim Mohamed were elected as members of the executive committee. It was agreed that the General Assembly, which was constituted of delegates from all affiliated national football federations, would meet twice a year. Several standing committees were also created to be responsible for directing and managing various aspects of the organization of the game in Africa. As membership of CAF increased, as many countries gained independence, the organization's initial structure expanded. The number of standing committees increased and in 1963 the executive committee increased to its current size of twelve members. In the same year, six continental subgroups or zones were created to promote and develop football in their geographical regions.[5] Its first headquarters was situated in Khartoum, Sudan, for a few months until a fire outbreak in the offices of the Sudanese Football Association prompted the organization's move to Egypt.

As Paul Darby notes, the creation of the Confederation of African Football in 1957 marked a critical juncture in the development of the game on the continent because it established CAF as the launching pad for what is the most important sport on the continent. The organization became a pan-African sporting body whose membership was limited to independent African nations. The game was used as a vehicle for promoting national and pan-African identity throughout Africa and on the global stage. The organization of the first African Cup of Nations in 1957 was hosted by Sudan and won by Egypt which further aroused a sense of national consciousness throughout the continent. It imbued citizens of newly independent African nations with a sense of nationhood and inspired them to work toward common social, economic, and political goals. However, those African nations still under colonial rule were envious of those that could participate in a historic event as the first African Cup of Nations. When most African nations gained independence in the 1960s, membership in CAF increased and the opportunity to participate in international football became available to newly independent African nations.

---

[5] Ibid, p. 35. For further information about the complete list of all six CAF continental subgroups or zones, see http://www.cafonline.com/en-us/caf/cafzones.aspx.

Besides, membership in the confederation and the opportunity to participate in the Cup of Nations gave them a reason to assert their independence and sense of identity. Issa Hayatou, the sixth president of CAF for nearly years (1988–2017), maintains that "The African Cup of Nations became the symbol of the intense life, of the popularity of football in Africa, the first ground where a new and ambitious nationalism could express itself".[6]

The birth of the Confederation of African Football and the hosting of the first African Cup of Nations not only infused a sense of pride, independence, and nationhood in Africans but also helped to integrate the benefits of the sport into the social, political, and economic thinking of African leaders and citizens. Paul Darby argues that President Nkrumah of Ghana used Ghanaian footballers for the promotion of the pan-African cause beyond Africa. He indicates that in 1962 Nkrumah used the national team as ambassadors during the team's tour of Europe not only as a way of instilling national pride and confidence in Ghanaians, but also as a means of undermining European prejudices about Africans. The integrative mantra of the sport, Darby maintains, has continued to manifest itself in the thinking of contemporary African leaders. To re-affirm Nkrumah's beliefs, Nigeria's Minister of Sports, Sylvanus Williams said, in the early 1980s, that sporting achievements do not only help to integrate people but are also a measure of a nation's greatness. Steve Tshwete, the former South African Minister for Sport and Recreation, argued that football, and sports in general, had a central role to play in the construction of an all-pervasive identity.[7] The construction of stadia all over Africa also reflects the development of a sense of national identity in independent Africa as well as the relationship between the game of football and nationalist sentiments. The construction of the national stadium in Surulere in Nigeria was used in independence celebrations in October 1960. Similarly, Ghana's main soccer venue in Accra is named Independence Stadium as is the national stadium in Lusaka, Zambia. Benin and Senegal have stadia of friendship, and other stadia with nationalistic implications include the stadium of Liberty in Ibadan, Reunification in Douala Cameroon, and Revolution in Brazzaville. The sense of national identity being manifested through football in post-independent Africa was also reflected in the nicknames that were adopted by African national teams.

[6] Ibid, 3.6.
[7] Ibid, 3.7.

The confederation's statutes (the latest version of which was signed by CAF President Issa Hayatou and Secretary-General Hicham El Amrani)[8] require that all African representatives working within FIFA practice their activities "in the spirit of African solidarity".[9]

CAF: ACTIVIST FOR EQUALITY AND AGAINST DISCRIMINATION

Nowhere was CAF's belief in pan-Africanism more visibly demonstrated than in its early policy direction toward South Africa. When South Africa refused to enter a multiracial squad for the first Cup of Nations in keeping with its apartheid policy of racial discrimination against black South Africans, it was exorcized from the competition. During the 1959 Cup of Nations Competition in Cairo, Egypt, South Africa was once again banned due to its decision not to adhere to CAF's policy that it presents a national team that was drawn from all racial groups in country. Finally, at the pre-championship Congress in Ethiopia in 1961, CAF formally expelled South Africa and excluded it from all continental football championships. South Africa's expulsion from CAF sent a message to all aspiring members of the organization that any actions or behavior of any African nation that contravened or jeopardized the spirit of African unity that was evident across the continent at the time would be prohibited from competing in football. In 1964, Ghanaian President Kwame Nkrumah recognized CAF's role in promoting African unity and donated a trophy for CAF's most prestigious club competition at the time, the African Cup of Champion club.[10]

JOÃO HAVELANGE AND SEPP BLATTER, THE MEN WHO CHANGED AFRICA'S FOOTBALL TRAJECTORY

João Havelange and Sepp Blatter are two men who engineered the transition of football from a Eurocentric, foreign inspired game to a global multi-billion-dollar enterprise. They were instrumental in supporting peripheral countries and regions with resources for football to thrive.

---

[8] For detailed information pertaining to all sixty-four statues of CAF, see http://www.cafonline.com/en-us/competitions.aspx.
[9] Paul Darby, 38.
[10] Ibid.

African football experienced significant changes and benefited enormously during their forty-one years at the helm of FIFA.

João Havelange

Brazilian João Havelange is credited with boosting Africa's growing confidence and assuring the African and Asian constituencies of his support to increase the number of spots for Africa and Asia in the FIFA tournament if elected. Before the 1974 FIFA elections, South Africa was in a power struggle for control of football between the Football Association of South Africa (FASA), a white dominated organization, and the South Africa Soccer Federation (SASF), representing all Africans. Havelange's position on this issue was clear, he supported SASF and won the minds and souls of most African constituencies when he promised to exclude FASA from FIFA competitions if he was elected. Indeed, Havelange became an African "champion" who listened to the pleas of Africans for recognition and fight against the apartheid regime in South Africa. Furthermore, Havelange also promised to expand the FIFA World Cup finalists from sixteen to twenty-four, warranting Africa increased automatic place. In addition to fulfilling his pledges, Havelange traveled to many member countries and encouraged his Brazilian national team with superstar, Pele, to travel to Africa and play friendly exposition matches. These actions

Sepp Blatter and CAF: 1998–2015

Sepp Blatter succeeded Havelange, as FIFA's president in 1998. Like his predecessor, Blatter promised and embarked on expanding football throughout the continent, starting with a push for equality. The former FIFA boss supported Africa's bid for the hosting of the World Cup in 2006. Although Morocco was not successful in this bid against Germany, Blatter's support had symbolic importance to African constituencies in FIFA. Blatter's greatest accomplishment in his seventeen-year tenure as FIFA president was the award of the 2010 FIFA World tournament to South Africa. In 1999, Blatter launched the GOAL project, which, according to FIFA, "represented the clearest manifestation of his commitment to the development of the African game".[11] The primary purpose of the GOAL initiative according to Maradas was to "help bridge the gap

[11] FIFA, For the Future of Football. FIFA Newsletter 1999 (May):12–14.

between European and South American football on the one hand, and that in the rest of the world. For Africa, the project holds out great potential benefits".[12] Blatter's commitment to expand football in Africa is captured in his assurance when he uttered the following: "Africa can count on the continuing and unwavering help and support of FIFA and its President to who will leave no stone unturned in ensuring that football continues to benefit everyone, everywhere".[13] Through this initiative, millions of dollars were given to African football federations to improve football facilities—pitches, technical centers, youth academies, education seminars, aggressive marketing, and IT. These accomplishments without a doubt have enhanced football development and growth in Africa and Blatter became a "friend of Africa".

CAF and Women's Football

It was not only men who benefited from the African Cup of Nations under CAF's leadership. A female version of the tournament was also established. Initially known as the Africa Women's Championship, however, it was changed to the African Women's Championship in 2015 by CAF Executives, this international women's football competition was held every two years and was sanctioned by CAF. While it was first contested in 1991, it was not held biennially until 1998. Nigeria is the most successful nation in the tournament's history, having won a record of ten titles, meaning they have won all but two of the previous tournaments. The competition has served as the qualifying event for the FIFA Women's World Cup since it began in 1991.

CAF's development initiatives also include the creation of the African Nations Championship competition, CAF Champions League, the CAF Confederation League, the CAF Super Cup, the U-23 Africa Championship, the U-20 Africa Championship, the U-17 Africa Championship, the Feminine U-20 Africa Championship, the U-17 Africa Feminine Championship, the Africa Futsal Championship, the Africa Beach Soccer Championship, and the All-Africa Games.[14]

[12] Emmanuel Maradas, The Meaning of Meridian. African Soccer 1999, 42(March).
[13] Sepp Blatter, Message from the FIFA President. Africa Soccer 2000, 51:5.
[14] For further information pertaining to the evolution of CAF competitions, see http://www.cafonline.com/en-us./caf/cafcompetitions.aspx.

The creation of the different leagues for different age groups and the establishment of various competitive events by CAF were important milestones in the development of the sport in Africa. It was now left for CAF to manage these different leagues to perform (both in Africa and on the global stage) in a manner that exemplifies the infusion of quality into the sport and respect for African teams and clubs internationally. Perhaps the best means for showcasing and promoting the growth and quality of African football under CAF's leadership was through its collaboration with the various African national soccer federations in preparing and managing the participation of African national teams in the African Nations Cup and the World Cup. While it is true that some Africans nations have done well in the African Nations Cup, with Egypt and Cameroon dominating the competition, the overall development and management of the sport leave much to be desired. For example, African nations have yet to perform beyond the quarterfinals stage of the World Cup let alone win the cup itself. Tamba Nlandu provides compelling reasons undergirding the poor performances of African soccer teams in global competitions. He argues, persuasively, that the lack of economic development in African countries has rendered them incapable of keeping their talented players at home or attracting other talented players from other countries, and political interference in the management of the football federations of African nations, the absence of cohesion between African professionals playing in Europe and home-based players, and the inability of African nations to adopt the concept of multiracial and multinational players in local and national leagues have contributed to the poor performances of African soccer teams in international competitions.[15] It is not clear whether CAF has developed a set of core policies to be used by African football federations to address the challenges constraining the performances of African teams at global competitions highlighted by Tamba Nlandu. Perhaps, a good starting point will be to get the new leadership at CAF to engage in conversations with African football federations regarding the strategic initiatives that can be crafted to examine and improve the performances of African teams at international competitions. The Confederation of African Football has also not been able to absolve itself from the politics and corruption that have tainted the sport at the continental and global levels.

---

[15] For a full discussion of the poor performance of African soccer teams at International competitions, see Tamba Nlandu's "*On some Philosophical foundations of the disappointing performances of African Soccer teams at World Competitions, 2017*" (196–199).

Current scholarship subscribes to the view that these two vices or practices have largely constrained the proper development and management of football in Africa.

Politics and Corruption in African Football Under CAF Leadership

CAF was established against the backdrop of the politics of colonial domination of African countries by Europeans and the desire of African nations to use football as a means of gaining independence and forging pan-Africanism or African unity. Admittedly, while many African nations went on to "adopt nationalistic and ideologist policies which, according to Tamba Nlandu turned out to be incompatible with the development of the game of football",[16] the fact remains that African nations played a role in "democratizing" the management of the sport, amid continental struggles for independence from colonial rule and CAF's campaigns against the South African apartheid policies.[17] One would have thought that African nations would benefit from their experiences in overcoming the politics of marginalization that characterized European control of FIFA (during their quest to establish CAF) and engage in best practices and processes that would truly advance the sport in Africa. Unfortunately, however, politics and corruption which are manifested in all kinds of sporting events around the world have become endemic in the management and development of football in Africa.

Challenges for CAF

CAF and its affiliate associations have been embroiled in corruption and other forms of financial improprieties. Manase Kudzai Chiweshe explains that while corruption in international soccer is characterized by such activities as vote-buying, match-fixing, bribing of officials, sponsorship deals, and even team selections, in Africa, nepotism, tribalism, regionalism, and religion have also become important aspects of corruption in African football. He argues that rampant corruption, maladministration, and lack of accountability have adversely impacted the development (and by

[16] Ibid, 196.
[17] Peter Alegi 2010 African Soccerscapes: How A Continent Changed the World's Game, Athens: Ohio University Press.

extension the management) of football in Africa.[18] It is important to note here that although the political and financial corruption that has undermined the efficient management and development of African football has not been orchestrated by CAF leadership, the various African football federations where such corrupt activities are executed are governed, nonetheless, by CAF. In some sense, the leadership at CAF, until recently, has been the enabler.

In terms of political corruption, numerous examples can be found across Africa where political leaders have interfered in the management of national football federations or the selection of players or coaches for the national team or other elite domestic clubs. In Cameroon, for example, the selection of the coach of the national team and his/her supporting staff members has often been approved by the presidency and not by the Minister of Sports. On some occasions, influential players have been actively involved in the decision to choose or not to choose players for the national team. In many countries in Africa your call to the national team is not entirely based on your skill sets or merits but based on your relationships with some powerful ministers or other political figures with whom they have an ethnic affinity. Similar cases can be found in other African countries. In such situations, Manase Kudzai observes that "political interference provides a context in which football becomes a complex social construct in which space, culture, politics, and economics intersect to produce very little development of the game as a vibrant commercial entity".[19] Although FIFA statutes of non-interference are designed to prohibit political influence or interference in the internal affairs of national football associations, FIFA has had to threaten African governments with suspensions of their national teams from participating in continental and international competitions when evidence of such interference is obvious or blatant. Otherwise, in other circumstances where such political interference has been sophisticated or subtle, corrective action by FIFA has been impossible. Given that football and politics in Africa are inextricably linked, it is not uncommon therefore to find football administrators who are

---

[18] Manase Kudzai provides an extensive narrative of corruption and poor administration in African Football in The Problem with African Football: Corruption and the (Under) Development of the Game on the Continent. See complete details about the paper in the reference section.

[19] Ibid, 27.

selected to fill leadership positions not because of merit but as a result of patronage or tribalism.[20]

Financial corruption in various forms by African football federations under the leadership of CAF over the past several decades has been extensive. Consider the following examples from Cameroon, Nigeria, and Ivory Coast. Mobile phone company MTN pumped in $600,000 of an $800,000 project to renovate several stadiums. The other $200,000 was to come from FECAFOOT, the Cameroonian Football Federation, but instead, $146,000 ended up in the pockets of the then sports minister, Thierry Augustin Edzoa, so that he could "breathe easier", he said after the payment. The work never happened. The $600,000 is unaccounted for. Parliament appropriated more than $24m for another stadium renovation project. No work took place, the country's two main stadiums are more dilapidated than ever and there was nothing to show for the money. FECAFOOT office staff threatened to go on strike after being unpaid for forty-four months. When FIFA sent money for the wages to be paid, officials stumped up sixteen months' back pay and pocketed the rest. A FECAFOOT official took $16,000 expenses for an air ticket after saying his original ticket had been lost. He boarded the plane using the first ticket and kept the $16,000.[21] Under Adamu, Nigerian football has reached a position whereby only 10% of the $7m received from the sponsor reaches the clubs. Television rights for the Nigerian league are worth around $5m, but since this deal was signed no Premier League club has received a share of the money. During the 2010 World Cup in South Africa, the Nigeria Football Federation hired a $100-a-night hotel in the South Africa coastal town of Ballito for their team. However, the federation received $400 per person per night from FIFA for this purpose. Before the tournament, Glenn Hoddle was offered a deal worth $1m to coach the Nigerian national team but claimed an official had told him it would be announced as $1.5m, with the difference shared. Hoddle rejected the offer and made it public. Most recently, $250,000 in cash is understood to have disappeared from the accounts of the Nigerian Football Federation (NFF). Over time the lost money could not be traced.[22] The biggest scandal of recent years was the stadium tragedy of 2009 when twenty died and

[20] Ibid, 31.
[21] Brian, Oliver. 2010 *Making A Killing out of African Football*, http://theguardian.com/football2010/oct24/football-corruption-cameroon-nigeria-ivorycoast.
[22] Ibid.

thirty-five were injured after a World Cup qualifier in Abidjan. The number of tickets sold was 2000 more than the seventy-four-year-old stadium could hold—and many more bought their way in without tickets. Fines were handed out, but Eric Mwamba reported on the continued corruption as the big fish in the Ivorian Football Federation (FIF) escaped sanction. The Ivorian Football Federation received $1.6m a year from the Ivorian Petrol Refinery Company, SIR, but local clubs never got any of the money. The fund's existence only became public when SIR stopped the donations in 2007 on discovering that the money was not being distributed. Sports donations from the corporate sector are now routinely paid directly to the sports minister, to "avoid the money falling into the hands of FIF president and FIFA executive member Jacques Anouma". The problem is exacerbated by the fact he subsequently became the chief financial officer. In 2008 FIF announced a $2.2m surplus, with Anouma saying "Stop accusing us of using taxpayers' money, FIFA gives us money". However, their own 2007 internal report detailed donations from the state-run coffee-cocoa industry of more than $4m and sources suggest a further $6m come directly from the state. Local clubs were angry about claims that players and officials were put up in plush hotels and provided with prostitutes for internationals, paid for by these state funds. Even FIFA recognized the problems at FIF and announced that it would market the Ivory Coast's 2010 World Cup ticket allocation to "minimize the risk of fraud".[23]

The few examples of political and financial corruption within African football federations discussed above have resulted in low player morale, inefficient management practices, lack of accountability, and transparency. The misappropriation of funds allocated for infrastructure development has accounted for the poor state of football stadia in many African countries. Except for countries such as South Africa and Morocco which have world-class stadia and facilities, other African nations such as Angola, Cameroon, Gabon, Ghana, Mali, Burkina Faso, and Egypt have had to build and renovate stadia only because they had to host or are scheduled to host the African Cup of Nations. Political and financial corruption have also adversely impacted the leadership of CAF. The recent FIFA financial scandal (characterized by the bribery of senior FIFA executives by members of nations competing to host the World Cup in exchange for votes), which led to the resignation of FIFA President Sepp Blatter and the

[23] Ibid.

indictment of several FIFA executives also affected former CAF -president, Issa Hayatou, who also served as FIFA vice president until Blatter's removal. In a June 14, 2016, scathing article by the Nigerian Guardian Newspaper, Hayatou was alleged to have accepted bribes from a former Qatar bid employee, Phaedra Almajid, in exchange for his vote for Qatar to host the 2022 World Cup. While Hayatou refuted the allegations, the Guardian argued that the entire executive of CAF (that had been created and nurtured by Hayatou) had to be investigated and replaced because he had orchestrated the amendment of CAF statutes to allow him to contest elections again and add another five years to his twenty-nine-year reign. The paper insisted that Hayatou be "implored to leave and to take along with him all his friends, family members, and all his cronies in the executive committee where once indicted and suspended corrupt officials are celebrated, re-absorbed, recycled and reinstated back into the administration with blatant impunity".[24] On balance though, Issa Hayatou implemented some policy changes as president of CAF to improve the game in Africa. For example, participation in the African Nations Cup was increased from eight to sixteen teams, the number of African teams participating in the World Cup was also increased from two to five teams, while club competitions were restructured and the financing of such competitions was improved. Overall, CAF's budget was increased during his leadership and the first World Cup ever staged in Africa took place in South Africa in 2010, in large part because of his influence. However, because public opinion in most African countries held that Hayatou's long tenure at the helm of CAF had created an atmosphere of corruption, nepotism, lack of accountability, and transparency, it was little wonder that he lost the election for another five-year term to Ahmad Ahmad, President of the Madagascar Football Federation on March 16, 2017, by thirty-four votes to twenty. The election of Ahmad Ahmad, who campaigned on a platform of improved governance with a commitment to increase transparency and accountability, was widely seen as a new dawn for African football because it was not Ahmad Ahmad alone who won but African football.[25]

[24] http://guardian.ng/sport/issa-hayatou-must-also-go-for-the-good-of-African-football/.
[25] https://www.africa.com/caf-confederation-african-football-new-president-new-era/.

CAF Under Ahmad Ahmad: Accomplishments and Challenges

The discussion thus far has depicted CAF, under Issa Hayatou, as an organization that has achieved some measure of success in terms of managing, developing, and promoting football in Africa in its sixty-year history. It has also articulated the many challenges facing this important organization that need to be addressed, in a sustained fashion, if CAF is going to be relied upon to provide the type of transparent and accountable leadership that would increase efficiencies in the management processes that are currently woefully absent within the organization. In March 2017, Ahmad Ahmad of Madagascar, defeated Issa Hayatou, long time CAF president from Cameroon, to become the confederation's seventh president in its sixty-year history. Ahmad Ahmad promised to make CAF more transparent and to introduce a code of ethics that would be characterized by an extension of ethics checks on African football officials. Consequently, under new leadership, CAF must seek first to rid the organization of the systemic corruption that has plagued it for a long and replace it with a culture of good governance characterized by inclusiveness, transparency, and accountability. Ahmad also echoed that CAF needed to establish mechanisms that would monitor the distribution and management of development funds from FIFA and other sponsors, geared toward the development of football from the grassroots, to the youth and national levels within the different African football federations. For quality to be infused in the game, he argued, CAF must ensure that significant investment is directed toward infrastructure development (building and renovation of stadia), training of referees and other football officials, payment of bonuses to players when they participate in continental and international competitions, and development of local talent (within the various football federations) to ensure that they acquire the skills necessary to compete effectively in international competitions. To that end, CAF should ensure that the millions of dollars that FIFA spends on football development projects in Africa (such as constructing offices, training facilities, and building synthetic pitches) should be used for those purposes and not to make friends among African football administrators.[26]

---

[26] Arnold Pannenborg. 2010. Football in Africa: Observations about Political, Financial, Cultural and Religious Influences, NCDO Publication Series Sport & Development, 17.

Barely four months after taking over as CAF president, Ahmad Ahmad began to implement aspects of his vision of CAF's role in advancing African soccer. In July 2017, CAF delegates approved changes to the policy regarding the management of football competitions that included increasing the number of participants in the African Cup of Nations from sixteen to twenty-four teams.[27] The other decisions that were made at the two-day meeting held in Morocco included hosting the African Nations Cup (AFCON) in June–July rather than January–February, moving the CAF Championship League and Confederation Cup competitions to an August–May calendar, rather than inside a single year, paying referees for international assignments instead of host nations or clubs, thus reducing the risk of pressure being placed on match officials to favor one side, organizing zonal Nations Cup qualifiers for the tournament at age grade-levels and improving international partnerships and relations between CAF, its member associations, national governments, and the African Union, and making arrangements to increase the number of women representatives on CAF beyond Isha Johansen of Sierra Leone and Lydia Nsekera of Burundi, currently the only women serving in the confederation. Moving the AFCON competition to a June–July calendar was welcomed by European clubs that had long complained about African players leaving their respective clubs to participate in the Nations Cup. The success of the just-completed AFCON Cup, held in Egypt from June 21–July 19, 2019, is indicative of the fact that this switch has benefited CAF, African players playing for European clubs, and the clubs themselves. The only remaining concern, however, hinges on whether African nations that had struggled to host the sixteen-team tournament would have the infrastructure and the logistical capacity to cope with a twenty-four-team format.[28]

Ahmad's accomplishments, after only two years in office as CAF president, have been undermined by several scandals. In 2014, Cameroon, Ivory Coast, and Guinea were awarded hosting rights for 2019, 2021, and 2023 tournaments, respectively. Unfortunately, CAF had to withdraw hosting rights from Cameroon for AFCON 2019, a little over six months before the commencement of the tournament, over concerns that Cameroon did not have adequate infrastructure and adequate logistical arrangements in place (stadiums and lodging arrangements) to

---

[27] https://www.africanews.com/2019/06/20/highlights-of-ahmad-s-troubled-caf-presidency//.
[28] Ibid.

successfully host the competition. To appease infuriated Cameroonian football officials, CAF then gave Cameroon the hosting rights for AFCON 2021, and this decision was protested by Ivory Coast, which was initially scheduled to host AFCON 2021. In its final decision, CAF gave Egypt the hosting rights for 2019, while Cameroon, Ivory Coast, and Guinea would host 2021, 2023, and 2025 competitions, respectively. The withdrawal and re-awarding of Cameroon's hosting rights and the re-arrangement of the hosting schedule to accommodate Ivory Coast and Guinea exposed CAF's system of awarding hosting rights and prompted repeated accusations from the football associations of various countries which blamed Ahmad for making unilateral decisions.[29] In February 2019, Former Liberian Football Association President Musa Bility resigned from two CAF committees, where he held senior roles, to protest President Ahmad Ahmad's leadership of the organization. In a blistering letter sent to Ahmad and the CAF executive committee, Bility maintained that "Ahmad was leading the noble organization in the wrong direction".[30] Ahmad also came under criticism in June 2019 for revoking the African Champions League victory by Esperance Club of Tunisia. The victory which came following controversy over the Video Assistant Referee (VAR) was not taken kindly by Wyad of Casablanca officials who maintained that their team had leveled the score at 2-2 before the end of the game and should have been allowed to continue had the Gambian referee not disallowed their goal. In a disputed CAF decision, Esperance was ordered to return the trophy and medals and prepare for a replay of the second leg against Morocco's Wyad Casablanca, which appealed the decision. Frustrated and angered by Ahmad's decision, Esperance officials described Ahmad as incompetent and corrupt. The replay of the match was scheduled to take place after AFCON 2019.[31]

In April 2019, media headlines in Africa and Europe were once again dominated by news of another CAF scandal under Ahmad Ahmad, involving the dismissal of the organization's Secretary-General Amr Fahmy of Egypt, who had been appointed to that role in November 2017. Fahmy was sacked because he allegedly submitted a document to a FIFA body that investigates ethics violations, accusing Ahmad of ordering the

---

[29] Ibid.
[30] https://www.insidethegames.biz/articles/1080204/caf-president-ahmad-arrested-over-corruption-allegations.
[31] Ibid.

Secretary-General to pay $20,000 bribes into accounts of African soccer presidents, including Cape Verde and Tanzania. The document also accused Ahmad of misusing funds after canceling a sports equipment contract with the German Sports equipment company PUMA, in favor of an inflated deal with French company Tactical Steel. The deal with PUMA was reportedly worth $351,617 but was dropped in favor of an inflated deal with Tactical Steel worth $1,195,603, costing CAF over $800,000 in extra costs.[32] Furthermore, the report accuses him of harassing unnamed four female staff of CAF, violating statutes to increase Moroccan representation on CAF, and overspending more than $400,000 of CAF money on cars in Egypt and Madagascar where he had overseen the creation of a satellite office for himself.[33] These alleged financial transgressions are said to be in direct violation of the confederation's financial regulations and article 136 of the disciplinary code which states that "Anyone who offers promises or grants an unjustified advantage to a body of CAF, a match official, a player or an official on behalf of himself or a third party in an attempt to incite it or him to violate CAF Regulations will be sanctioned". Those sanctions range from a $25,000 fine to a life ban.[34] More humiliation and pain were inflicted on CAF and FIFA when Ahmad, who was attending a FIFA congress in Paris, was arrested at the Berri Hotel, by French Police on June 7, 2019. Reports of his arrest were widely publicized by several media outlets including the French-based pan-African Magazine and Jeune Afrique. His arrest by the French Central office responsible for investigating corruption, financial, and tax offenses was reportedly in connection with the contract that he terminated with PUMA in favor of an inflated deal with the French equipment Company, Tactical Steel. He is accused of influencing the decision to terminate the contract because he stood to gain over $800,000. While Ahmad was eventually released by French anti-corruption officials without charges, it is clear that the corruption, financial, and sexual misconduct scandals that have dogged Ahmad Ahmad during his two-year reign have greatly tarnished the image of both CAF and FIFA and shocked the football community in Africa. Ahmad won the presidency of CAF on a platform that promised to rid the

[32] Ibid.
[33] https://citizentv.co.ke/news/amr-fahmy-fired-after-accusing-caf-boss-of-corruption-240981/.
[34] https://www.insidethegames.biz/articles/1080204/caf-president-ahmad-arrested-over-corruption-allegations.

organization of corruption and nepotism and render it more transparent and accountable. Thus far, his pledges have been seriously undermined by his actions, decisions, and behavior. He has had to cede the management of CAF to FIFA Secretary-General Fatma Samoura. FIFA, which has also been plagued by corruption and financial scandals over the past several years, is now forced to oversee the management of one of the regional confederations of football under its auspices because of corruption, nepotism, poor management, sexual misconduct, and lack of transparency. While Ahmad was eventually cleared of any wrong doing regarding his business affairs with the French company (Tactical Steel), he was still declared guilty of violating three other FIFA ethical rules. The three-member Court of Arbitration for Sport (CAS) panel partially upheld the initial FIFA suspension of five years imposed on Ahmad by reducing it to two years. However, the panel also decided, unanimously, that he had violated ethical codes concerning the offering and acceptance of gifts or other benefits, abuse of power and misappropriation of funds. CAS's decision paved the way for South African billionaire mining tycoon, Patrice Motsepe, to become the next President of CAF in March 2021, when two rival candidates who had also contested for the position withdrew their candidacy. As the new CAF President, Motsepe will have to address the many challenges facing the organization in order to restore public trust and respect for this pillar of African soccer.

Concluding Remarks

This chapter has attempted to articulate the role that the Confederation of African Football has played in the development and management of football in the continent since its inception in 1957. To that end, it has argued that while the confederation has achieved some degree of success, it has also been stymied by major challenges that have all but obfuscated the organization's hard-won accomplishments during its sixty-year history. As the most popular sport in Africa, the continued growth and management of football or soccer in the continent will continue to impact the history, culture, and politics of African nations in the future as it has done in the past. Without a doubt, CAF was successful in the use of pan-Africanism to forge unity among member states to fight against inequality and discrimination. Furthermore, the organization employed its role as "activist" to expel apartheid South Africa from particularly football in Africa. African solidarity through CAF was unmistakable in 1964, when members of the federation refused to participate in the FIFA World Cup qualifying tournaments leading to the 1966 World Cup. This boycott no doubt sent a powerful message to the rest of the football world about Africa's resolve. If CAF's founding aims of organizing international competitions and advancing the interests of Africa in world football[35] to foster the cross-cultural appeal of the game[36] are to be sustained, credible steps must be taken by CAF to address and correct the root causes of the problems that currently plague the organization.

References

Alegi, P. *African Soccerscapes: How A Continent Changed the World's Game*, Athens: Ohio University Press, 2010
Bounouar, Jalal "CAF-Confederation of African Football: A New President, A New Era" available online https://www.africa.com/caf-confederation-african-football-new-president-new-era/
Cafonline.com "Evolution of CAF competitions" available online at http://www.cafonline.com/en-us./caf/cafcompetitions.aspx
Chiweshe, Manase The Problem with African Football: Corruption and the (Under) Development of the Game on the Continent, African Law and Business Bulletin, 2, 2014
Darby, P. *African Football and FIFA: Politics, Colonialism and Resistance* New York: Frank Cass Publishers, 2002.
Delancey, M. & Neh, R. *Dictionary of the Republic of Cameroon: Historical Dictionaries of Africa, No. 113*, Lanham, MD, The Scarecrow Press, 2010
Encyclopaedia Britannica (2016) African Cup of Nations: Football Competition
Evolution of CAF competitions: available online at http://www.cafonline.com/en-us./caf/cafcompetitions.aspx
Fletcher, M. Confederation of African Football in J. Hugson, K. Moore, R. Spaaij, and J. Maguire, eds., *Routledge Handbook of Football Studies*, 1st ed. London: Routledge, 2017:423–431.
Guilianotti, R. *Football: A Sociology of the Global Game*, Cambridge: Polity Press, 2000

---

[35] Peter Alegi 2010 African Soccerscapes: How a Continent Changed the World's Game, Athens: Ohio University Press.

[36] Richard Giulianotti notes that Football's cross-cultural approach has won followers from its established roots in Europe and South America to mass converts in Australia, Africa, Asia, and even the United States.

Mumbere, Daniel "Highlights of Ahmad's Troubled CAF Presidency" available online at https://www.africanews.com/2019/06/20/highlights-of-ahmad-s-troubled-caf-presidency//

Odegbami Segun "Issa Hayatou Must Go for the Good of African Football" available online at https://guardian.ng/sport/issa-hayatou-must-also-go-for-the-good-of-African-football/

Oliver, B. "Making A Killing out of African Football" available online at http://theguardian.com/football2010/oct24/football-corruption-cameroon-nigeria-IvoryCoast

Olukadoye, T., Bisong, E., Dumisani, N., Mwamba, E., Opala, K., Moyo, P. & Rukini, C. "Arizona Project 2010: Killing Soccer in Africa" *Forum For African Investigative Reporters (FAIR)*, 2010

Pannenberg, A. "Football in Africa: Observations About Political, Financial, Cultural and Religious Influences", *NCDO Publication Series Sport& Development*

Patrick O'Kane "CAF President Ahmad Arrested Over Corruption Allegation" available online https://www.insidethegames.biz/articles/1080204/caf-president-ahmad-arrested-over-corruption-allegations

Six CAF Continental Subgroups or Zones: available online http://www.cafonline.com/en-us/caf/cafzones.aspx

Sixty Four CAF Statues, available online at: see http://www.cafonline.com/en-us/competitions.aspx

The Kenya Drums "Amr Fahmy fired After Accusing CAF Boss of Corruption" available online https://citizentv.co.ke/news/amr-fahmy-fired-after-accusing-caf-boss-of-corruption-240981/

CHAPTER 4

Football in Cameroon, Best of Times, Worst of Times: Exploring the Paradox of Africa's Venerable Football Nation

Augustine E. Ayuk

INTRODUCTION

On December 12, 2009, I traveled to India for a faculty exchange program at Chandibai Himathmal Mansukhani College, referred to simply as (C.H.M.). At the immigration checkpoint at the airport, an attending officer glanced at my passport and greeted me with a broad smile and said "Welcome to India, professor, I see you are a citizen of Cameroon, may I ask if you know 'Roger Milla?'" I responded in the affirmative. He continued, "Milla is a 'football magician,' we in India adore him because he inspires many young players here and around the world. Enjoy your stay in our country."

The story of Roger Milla, Cameroon, and Africa's legendary football superstar, and Africa's footballer of the century, illustrates how football

A. E. Ayuk (✉)
Clayton State University, Morrow, GA, USA
e-mail: Augustineayuk@clayton.edu

© The Author(s), under exclusive license to Springer Nature Switzerland AG 2022
A. E. Ayuk (ed.), *Football (Soccer) in Africa*, Global Culture and Sport Series, https://doi.org/10.1007/978-3-030-94866-5_4

77

can beam light on obscure countries such as Cameroon. At ages 38 and 42, respectively, Roger Milla became the oldest player in the world to score five goals in two separate FIFA World Cup tournaments—four goals in the 1990 World Cup in Italy and one goal in the 1994 World Cup in the USA. His iconic gyration at the corner flag after every goal has made him a world football sensation.

Football is regarded in Cameroon as the popular cultural zone upon which national, ethnic, regional, linguistic, and individual identities integrate and are expressed, revealing what it means to be Cameroonian. The game is the quintessential sport in Cameroon, a cradle of unity, pride, and joy. This national pastime in the country is intensely competitive and touches a deep nerve in Cameroon's psyche. To most Cameroonians, "Christianity is the first religion and football is the second." This statement underpins the significance of the game in the country.

However, it is important that we ask this probing question and seek genuine answers about football and its role in Cameroonian society. Does football serve as an effective tool in breaking down the stereotypes about the "other" and promoting unity and goodwill among all Cameroonians?

For a long time, Cameroonians have postulated that success by the national football team, the Indomitable Lions, serves as the rallying point for all Cameroonians to show their patriotism and devotion to the country. Yet, in the wake of the Anglophone crisis, one has to re-think this heretofore assumption to validate if football truly serves as an effective tool to bring to an end the stereotypes of the "other" and promote goodwill among all Cameroonians.

In Cameroon, the love of football runs across all classes, all ethnic, religious, linguistic, and gender boundaries.[1] Football's unifying power has been a mainstay in Cameroon since the 1960s but was more evident in the post-1990 FIFA World Cup tournament, after the Indomitable Lions' victory over World Cup holders, Argentina. The euphoria among Cameroonians was obvious on the streets, in the bars, and at local "matango" (palm wine) houses. The collective exultation on the surface portrayed Cameroon as a united, peaceful, and stable country, oblivious of any problems between the various multiethnic groups or party differences in the country, such as Francophones versus Anglophones, Cameroon People's Democratic Movement (CPDM) versus the Social Democratic Front (SDF) acrimony, economic crisis, or Biya's anti-democratic

---

[1] J. Lever, *Soccer Madness*, Chicago: University of Chicago Press, 1983.

tendencies. Despite the excitements brought forth by football's victories, it is obvious that the unity and dis-unity binaries are still present in Cameroonian society today. For example, Francophones still perceive their superiority over their Anglophone compatriots in politics, social, economic, and cultural domains, including football. As Martin observes, this "peculiar ability of sport, especially football to unite as well as divide, has allowed fans to forget their differences and to forge a broader sense of identity when regional and international matches were staged."[2] Since independence, football has been a framework for visualizing political contestations among various groups vying for power and dominance in the country. Through soft power dialogues embedded in football, marginalized groups in the country, particularly Anglophones, have been successful in using the game as a platform to expose the inequities perpetuated by their Francophone compatriots.

Football in Cameroon, from the post-independence period, 1960–2020, can best be synopsized by Charles Dickens's masterful line from A Tale of Two Cities, "It was the best of times; it was the worst of times"[3] (Fig. 4.1).

FOOTBALL IN CAMEROON, FROM THE COLONIAL ERA TO 1960

Football was introduced and popularized in Cameroon by Europeans, particularly the French (in East Cameroon or French Cameroon), who wanted to maintain total control of the social and cultural life in the country as well as in other French colonies in Africa.

According to Tsanga, the game began as an unorganized pastime, an exclusive leisure activity of the colonizers.[4] However, as Mfomo[5] and others have argued, the game was promulgated by two African relatives from Sierra Leone—Georges Goethe and his cousin Roman—in the city of Douala in 1923. Mfomo and colleagues argue that the Sierra Leoneans played football with locally fabricated leather balls, which aroused the curiosity of Cameroonians and other Africans in the locality. Goethe's

---

[2] Phyllis Martin M. Leisure and Society in Colonial Braza. Cambridge: Cambridge University Press, 1995.
[3] C. Dickens, C, *A Tale of Two Cities*, London: Chapman & Hall, 1859.
[4] S. Tsanga, "Le Football Camerounais des Origines a L'independance," Yaoundé: 1969.
[5] S. Mfomo, P., Ngbwa, G.-P. et al.; "Indomitable Lions of Cameroon: Roots, Odyssey, and Glory," Yaoundé: Ministry of Communication, 1994.

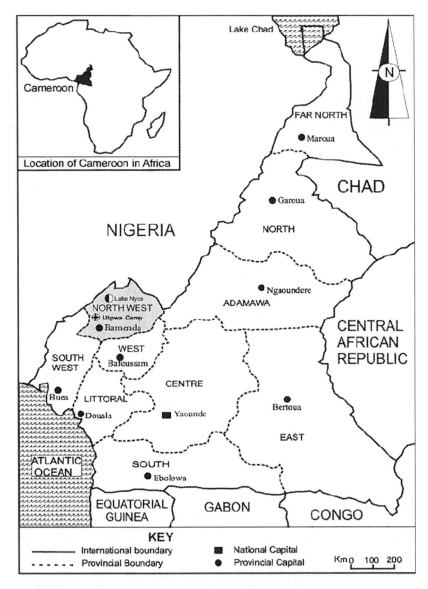

Fig. 4.1 Map of Cameroon showing the ten administrative territories, including the English-speaking areas of the northwest and southwest regions

efforts to diffuse football clubs in Douala were impeded by repressive measures from the French District Assistant Commissioner Guillou, who was determined to maintain tight control over all African voluntary associations and probably limit their numbers.

For now, I will use East Cameroon, French Cameroon, and Francophone interchangeably because this was the territory controlled by the French, under the UN Trusteeship. According to Clignet and Stark,[6] football's development in Cameroon was tied up with European perceptions of superiority over their colonial subjects and its spread was jealously guarded by a French administration that actively discouraged indigenous participation. What resulted was a system of "sporting apartheid" that saw only French and elite African expatriates participate in the game. Despite its massive popularity, football in East Cameroon remained an elite activity and participation was largely contingent upon privileged contacts with the French administration and education system. French administrators according to Clignet and Stark[7] forbid integration of the game in the territory and only allowed competition against Cameroonians and other Africans "when the outcome of the competition confirmed the preeminence of the colonizers, or when their scarcity made their involvement in any social activity dependent upon the participation of the colonized." Tsanga notes that French grip on the game was apparent when the presidency of the emerging national soccer club leagues in French Cameroon was granted to a French high civil servant and later to a man from the French Army.[8]

French preponderance of the game was not limited to the national organization. As Tsanga[9] has observed, it included many regional sections in French Cameroon. Furthermore, French administrators prohibited Cameroonians and African immigrants from participating in the game and refused their involvement in teams such as the Sporting Club of Douala, playing against this or any European clubs. In the city of Yaoundé, for example, two football teams were established, the Etoile Sportive of Yaoundé; one of these teams was strictly for Europeans and the other team

---

[6] R. Clignet, and Stark, M., "Modernization and the Game of Soccer in Cameroon," *International Review of Sport Sociology*, Vol. 9, No. 3–4 (1974): 81–98.
[7] R.Clignet, and Stark, M., "Modernization and the Game of Soccer in Cameroon," *International Review of Sport Sociology*, Vol. 9, No. 3–4 (1974): 81–98.
[8] S. Tsanga, "Le Football Camerounais des Origines a L'independance," Yaoundé: 1969.
[9] Ibid.

mostly made up of a few Cameroonians as well as African expatriates who were considered elites.

The French emboldened the segregation of football in French Cameroon in the following ways:

1. Cameroonians were not allowed to sit in the same space in the football arena as Europeans.
2. The price of admission tickets changed with the perceived differential financial abilities of the local populations. Hence, the ticket prices were much higher in Douala compared to Yaoundé.
3. French authorities prevented clubs in Cameroon from adopting European football club names. Some examples: The Olympic Bonapriso Club of Douala, named after the best French team at the time, Marseille, was forced to change its name to Oryx Bellois Club de Douala. Similarly, the "Diables Noirs" de Deido (Black Devils), nicknamed after one of the most celebrated metropolitan teams in France at that time, the Sporting Club de Fives, was "baptized" and given a new name, Léopard Club de Douala.
4. French authorities also discouraged private firms from actively supporting football clubs in Cameroon.

All teams were organized along occupational lines such as the railroad workers of Bonabéri. It should be emphasized that French authorities were not interested in popularizing football throughout all regions of East Cameroon; they were enthralled, however, in boosting football clubs in specific areas that they administered, particularly in the political and commercial/economic centers. Hence, well-regarded institutions such as the École Supérieure were created and became the supplier of players, trainers, and administrators in the political and economic centers in East Cameroon.

FECAFOOT AND FOOTBALL IN CAMEROON

The Cameroon Football Federation popularly known by its French acronym FECAFOOT was established in 1959 and joined the world football governing body, FIFA, in 1962. FECAFOOT oversees football activities throughout the ten political and administrative regions of the country. Since its founding, the federation has had eighteen presidents, all from the former East or French Cameroon. The first football league after independence consisted of two separate competitions. Clubs in West Cameroon played in one competition, while clubs in East Cameroon played in another according to Pannenborg.[10] Ashuntantang Tanjong maintains that the "winners of the West Cameroon Championship league faced the winners of East Cameroon's La Premiere Division in a confrontation tagged the National League Finals. In a similar disposition, the West Cameroon winners of the Cup of Cameroon knockout series played against the winners of East Cameroon's La Coup at the National Cup finals."[11] Both finals were played in the nation's capital, Yaoundé.

From Inter-Quarter Clash to Division One League

FECAFOOT runs three football league competitions in the country: Division Three (D3), Division Two (D2), and Division One (D1) or Elite leagues. There is, however, a de facto competition not sanctioned by FECAFOOT, popularly known as "the Inter-Quarter Competition." These fierce neighborhood competitions for boys and sometimes girls under the age of 15 usually take place during holidays when kids are out of school and draw lots of crowds in the neighborhoods where the tournaments are played.

In many communities where football facilities are lacking, the kids usually play their game on public roads or trespass on someone's undeveloped property to use as their field. Also, these tournaments are usually played by kids with their bare feet. This bragging rights tournament predictably exposes talented kids to football coaches and managers, who eventually recruit the boys and girls in their clubs. This "holiday football" tournament is also important in that it instills discipline and respect in young boys and girls. Coaches will not allow a child to participate in the competition if he/she does not complete his/her household chores.

The Cameroonian Football Federation has had a blemished history with the world's football governing body, Fédération Internationale de Football Association (FIFA). In 2013, for example, FIFA suspended FECAFOOT from participating in international competitions because of interference by the government in football matters. The suspension was part of a fallout from the re-election of FECAFOOT's former boss, Iya

---

[10] A. Pannenborg, A., *How to Win a Football Match in Cameroon: An Anthropological SAfrica's Most Popular Sport*, Leiden: 2008.

[11] T. Ashuntantang, T., "He Stood Up Against Injustice: Remembering Football Great Joe Ewunkem," *Scribbles from the Den*, 2012.

Mohammed. However, the ban was lifted by FIFA on July 22, 2013, following FIFA's Normalization Committee's ability to access its workspace in FECAFOOT's headquarters in Yaoundé. Modernization and tribalism/regionalism have been and continue to encumber football in Cameroon. Coaches select players for the national team from professional clubs abroad, ignoring talented local footballers who are not given a chance to display their abilities.

FOOTBALL IN FRENCH OR EAST CAMEROON

The game was popularized in East/French Cameroon because of the cultural element introduced by the French. Leisure was remarkably important in this part of Cameroon, and many Cameroonian kids in the cities of Douala and Yaoundé, for example, could spend their entire day playing football instead of attending school, and parents would not admonish the child. However, in the English-speaking sector of the country, it was culturally frowned upon for a child to miss school because of football.

Many football clubs in East Cameroon often reflected the existing social schisms in the towns. The game provided individuals from poor and socially marginalized backgrounds with avenues for achieving status, titles, and positions of authority and a ritualized atmosphere in which they could challenge superiors. Football clubs in East Cameroon, especially in Douala and Yaoundé, underscore the ethnographic divide and struggles in the country. Mfomo and others contend that football in Cameroon "began along ethnic lines and the elite championship competition which started in 1960 was nothing but a stiff tribal competition on the football pitch."[12] They further assert that football clubs were organized along ethnic and tribal lines and that this arrangement was the handiwork of the French, who had propagated segregation of football in the early days in East Cameroon.

In the Douala area of the Littoral region, football clubs such as Oryx, Caiman, and Léopard were established. These clubs recruited players and officials who ran these teams primarily from this ethnic group. Similarly, the Bassas also established clubs such as Dragon Club de Yaoundé and Dynamo de Douala and recruited players and club officials from this ethnic enclave. Not to be left out, the Bamilékés, primarily from the Western

[12] S. Mfomo, S.-P., Ngbwa, G.-P. et al.; "Indomitable Lions of Cameroon: Roots, Odyssey, and Glory," Yaoundé: Ministry of Communication, 1994.

zone of the country, created clubs such as Union Baміléké de Douala, Aigle Royal of Nkongsamba, Racing Club de Baffoussam, and later, Unisport FC de Bafang. The Betis from the Center and South regions established formidable football teams such as Canon Yaoundé, Tonnerre de Yaoundé, Lions Club Yaoundé, and Epervier d'Ebolowa. Canon and Tonnerre dominated Cameroon and African football club tournaments in the mid-1970s to the mid-1980s and are in an area where the ethnic group they represent is dominant.[13]

In the northern stretch of the country, dominated by the Peuls and Hausas, clubs such as Dragon Douala and Soleil of Yaoundé, and later, Coton Sport FC de Garoua were established. Although neither Dragon Douala nor Soleil of Yaoundé won a league championship or cup of Cameroon title, Coton Sport FC of Garoua dominated football in Cameroon from 2001 to 2017. Indeed, Coton Sport FC won fourteen championship tiles in sixteen years and six Cup of Cameroon trophies in the same period.[14]

Football diffusion in East Cameroon was also advanced by sport educational development institutions such as the École Supérieure de Yaoundé. This institution was/is instrumental in recruiting and training football players and referees whose skills reinforced and strengthened clubs in East Cameroon. Furthermore, these football clubs were supported financially by companies, politicians, and business individuals from their respective regions. According to Mfomo and others,[15] approximately 70 percent of elite football club players playing for Unisport de Bafang were former or current students or teachers of the institution. Their corresponding percentage exceeded one-half in the case of teams like the Dragon Club de Yaoundé or Tonnerre Football Club of Yaoundé.

While tribalism was gaining stronghold within football clubs in the country, the government launched a parallel campaign for national unity, and a policy of regional balance was adopted, "to curb ethnic exclusiveness, prevent political conflicts, and promote national unity." On June 12, 1967, the government passed a law banning associations based on ethnic criteria. "This law was to ensure balanced development of all regions of

---

[13] P. Nkwi, N., and Vidacs, B., "Football: Politics and Power in Cameroon," *Entering the Field: New Perspectives on World Football*, Armstrong, G. and Giulianotti, R. eds, Berg Publishers, 1997.

[14] G. Nantz, *Yearbook of African Football 2018*, London: Soccer Books Limited.

[15] S. Mfomo, S.-P., Ngbwa, G.-P. et al.; "Indomitable Lions of Cameroon: Roots, Odyssey, and Glory," Yaoundé: Ministry of Communication, 1994.

the country as well as reducing disparities in the levels of education, regional infrastructure, as well as augmenting participation of all ethnic/linguistic groups in the building of the nation."[16]

With regard to football, the same dogma of regional representation was supposed to apply in the selection of players in the national team. Unfortunately, from 1972 to 1984, the national football team was devoid of players from the English-speaking or former West Cameroon (see Table 4.1). The absence of a West Cameroon player in the 1972 African Cup of Nations selection is of particular significance. At the time of the tournament, the government of Cameroon launched a political ploy which was dubbed by the president of the Republic, Ahmadou Ahidjo, as the "Bloodless Revolution" or "Glorious Revolution," with emphasis on national unity. Regrettably, failure to include a West Cameroon player in the national team for this tournament was interpreted as "failure of the unity test."

Table 4.1 Composition of the national team: foreign, domestic, and regional disposition

Year and tournament	# Foreign players	# Domestic players	# Anglophone players
1972 AFCON	0	17	0
1982 World Cup	6	16	0
1982 AFCON	2	14	0
1984 AFCON (Winners)	6	16	0
1986 AFCON (Runners-up)	6	16	1
1988 AFCON (Winners)	7	10	2
1990 AFCON	8	9	2
1992 AFCON	12	10	2
1996 AFCON	12	10	1
2000 AFCON (Winners)	18	4	1
2002 AFCON (Winners)	22	0	2
2004 AFCON	22	0	1
2006 AFCON	22	0	1
2008 AFCON (Runners-up)	21	1	0
2010 AFCON	23	1	0
2015 AFCON	21	2	2
2017 AFCON (Winners)	21	2	3
2019 AFCON	23	0	2

[16] Ibid.

ATTEMPTS AT DETRIBALIZING AND DEREGIONALIZING FOOTBALL IN CAMEROON

The push to enforce the law of 1967, requiring the detribalization of football, arose at the hills of Cameroon's defeat by "little Congo" in the Eighth Edition of the African Cup of Nations hosted by Cameroon in 1972. The phrase "little Congo" is used here to describe Congo's below-standard performance in football vis-à-vis Cameroon. Before the African Cup of Nations tournament, Cameroon defeated Congo by a score of 7-1. Given this result, Cameroonians were confident that the national team would have an edge over their Congolese opponents in the semi-finals match and would eventually advance to the finals of the competition. Unfortunately, Congo, the supposed "David," defeated Cameroon, the equivalent of "Goliath," to use a biblical analogy. Cameroonians were bewildered by the defeat, and it even caused some Cameroonians to commit suicide. Most Cameroonians blamed the assistant coach of the national team, Atangana Ottou (a Cameroonian), for the national team's defeat. Atangana had fielded a player from his tribe who did not deserve playing time in the game because his skill level was below the other players, and he lacked chemistry with his teammates.

FOOTBALL IN BRITISH SOUTHERN CAMEROON OR WEST CAMEROON

Football culture in the British Southern Cameroons (Southern Cameroon) or West Cameroon was different from the culture in East or French Cameroon. Football, from a British viewpoint, was regarded as part of a statelier agenda brought by Europeans to Africa, and according to Gennaro and Anderinto,[17] the "British wrapped the game into the education system more than other aspects of colonialism." The British believed, according to Baller and Cornelissen (2013), that football had the potential to "discipline people's minds and bodies." Concerned with Africans' morality, the British saw football, and sports in general, as a way to instill European morals on their subjects. West Cameroonians generally did not regard football "as a pathway to success in life" as their East Cameroon compatriots did.

---

[17] Michael Gennaro, J. and Saheed Aderinto., Sports in African History, Politics, and Identity Formation. New York: Routledge Publishers, 2019.

The patterns of diffusion of football in Cameroon, according to Clignet and Stark,[18] are shaped by modes of economic exploitation in the country. In West Cameroon, for example, a major segment of the territory was exploited by huge agro-industrial companies that imported their labor force from other regions throughout the country. Lack of financial resources by West Cameroonians hindered the formation of football teams in the region compared to East Cameroon, whose clubs were financed by African entrepreneurs.[19] Many of the football clubs that emerged in the region were "organized along the lines of occupational solidarity, and many were dependent upon modern administrative or economic organizations." According to Nkwi and Vidacs,[20] what evolved eventually as the West Cameroon (Southern Cameroon) national team was largely made up of young graduates from secondary schools such as St. Joseph's College, Sasse, Buea, an all-boys school. In West Cameroon, children who played football were generally branded as "not bright academically" and less worthy in society. This stigma prevented the growth of football in West Cameroon. Nonetheless, some of the football clubs that emerged, in the region, provided opportunities for bridging class and ethnic cleavages by bringing members of the town's diverse community together as footballers and spectators. Unlike in East or French Cameroon, where football was supported by private businesses, wealthy business individuals, and the government, in West Cameroon, agro-industrial corporations such as the Cameroon Development Corporation (CDC), PAMOL, and the National Produce Marketing Board were crucial in promoting football in the region. Other entities that aided and promoted football in Anglophone Cameroon include the Public Works Department (PWD), Powercam, Pressbook, the Penitentiary Department in Buea, and Post and Telecommunications (P&T).

In the 1980s, new football clubs emerged, supported by state-run corporations like the Oil Refinery Company (SONARA) and the National Electricity Company (SONEL), which served as central pillars promoting football in the English-speaking region. Many football clubs in West Cameroon were supported by "towns" people, including Customs Mamfe,

---

[18] R. Clignet, and Stark, M., "Modernization and the Game of Soccer in Cameroon," *International Review of Sport Sociology*, Vol. 9, No. 3–4 (1974): 81–98.
[19] Ibid.
[20] P. Nkwi, N., and Vidacs, B., "Football: Politics and Power in Cameroon," *Entering the FieNew Perspectives on World Football*, Armstrong, G. and Giulianotti, R. eds, Berg Publishers, 1997.

PWD Kumba, Victoria United, Setracaucam Kumba, Ekumbe Vipers, Ajax Kumba, Heroes Muyuka, Tandon Muea, Tiko United, and Top Tarzan Mutengene. In the Northwest province/region, clubs supported by the "towns" people included Rovers FC Bamenda, Kilo FC Bamenda, COFA Spiders Bamenda, Mankon United, Kom Rangers, Wum Green Eagles, Ndu Tea FC, and Momo Sports FC.

Some of the teams from the former West Cameroon enclave have captured the sought-after Cup of Cameroon, while others have been crowned champions of the Elite Division One competition. In the 2000–01 football season, Kumbo Stickers (Northwest region) won the Cup of Cameroon trophy, the first football team in former West Cameroon to do so. In the 2002 football season, Mount Cameroon FC of Buea (Southwest region) won the Cup of Cameroon. In the 2008–09 football year, Tiko United FC (Southwest region) became the first team in former West Cameroon to win the Elite Division One championship. In 2013, the Young Sports Academy FC (Northwest region) won the Cup of Cameroon. The Public Works Department (PWD) FC of Bamenda, Northwest region, won the Cup of Cameroon trophy in 2019.

These accomplishments by teams in former West Cameroon are important because it helps dismiss stereotypes and myths held by Francophones that Anglophones lack the skills and knowledge in football. It was also a justification for excluding West Cameroonians from the national team.

Cameroon's outstanding performance, however, has been dwarfed by its precipitous failure at the 1994 FIFA World Cup tournament in the USA, its mediocre performance in the 2002 FIFA World Cup in Japan/South Korea, failure to qualify for the 2006 FIFA World Cup in Germany, its appalling and premature exit in the 2010 FIFA World Cup hosted in South Africa, a distressing performance at the 2014 FIFA World Cup hosted by Brazil, and its notorious absence from the 2018 FIFA World Cup in Russia (see Appendix B).

Despite the laudable performance of the Indomitable Lions in these competitions, the national team's feat in AFCON tournaments in any year the team qualified for the FIFA World Cup had always been disappointing. For example, in the CAF tournament in Algeria in 1990, Cameroon lost 0-1 to Zambia, 0-2 to Senegal, then beat Kenya 3-0. In 1994, Cameroon qualified for the World Cup in the USA but failed to qualify for the African Cup of Nations tournament in Tunisia. Predictability and consistency are the two major challenges that the Indomitable Lions of Cameroon face, which are issues other African national teams face as well.

Lack of Consistency

A chief reason why the Indomitable Lions of Cameroon and other African national football teams lack consistency is because of the high turnover rate with the coaches. Since 1965, Cameroon has retained the services of thirty-seven coaches, both domestic and foreign. Most of these managers only serve for two years. The longest-serving national football coach in Cameroon was Dominique Colonna of France, who coached the national team between 1965 and 1970. Other coaches whose contracts lasted three years include Peter Schnittger of Germany, 1970–73; Ivan Ridanović of Yugoslavia, 1976–79; Claude Le Roy of France, 1985–88; Philippe Redon of France, 1990–93; Pierre Lechantre of France, 1998–2001; and Winfred Schäfer of Germany, 2001–04. Jules Nyonga is the only domestic coach whose tenure lasted for two years, 1994–96.

It begs the question, why does the Cameroonian Football Federation rebuff extending the contracts of successful coaches such as Valeri Nepomniachi of Russia, Winfred Schäfer of Germany, Jean-Paul Akono of Cameroon—who won the Olympic Gold Medal in Sydney, Australia, in 2000—or Hugo Broos of Belgium, who revived the Indomitable Lions in 2017, winning the AFCON trophy after a fifteen-year hiatus?

The former General Manager of FECAFOOT, Jean Lambert Nang, underscores the problems blemishing football in Cameroon, particularly the national team. In his book, *Desperate Football House: Six Months in Hell of Fecafoot* (*six mois dans l'enfer de la fécafoot*), Nang[21] undrapes the problems of football in Cameroon as follows: "Cameroon football is a victim of treachery, fraud, financial trafficking, corruption of the actors and personnel, impunity on the part of its main stakeholders, falsification of official documents and the ages of footballers, as well as the indifference of officialdom."

Nang maintains that there is constant dysfunction and scuffles between the Cameroonian Football Federation and the Ministry of Sport and Physical Education over "stolen" money, as well as within FECAFOOT regarding stolen money from football in Cameroon. Nang provides unblemished examples of thievery inside the organization during the 1998 FIFA World Cup tournament in France. He singles out the former Minister of Communication Professor Augustin Kontchou Kuoumrgni, who was in

---

[21] J. Nang, L., *Desperate Football House: Six Months in Hell of Fecafoot*, Édition Inter Press, 2009.

charge of allowances intended for the players, "simply pocketed the money and announced that he had forgotten the bag containing the money in the aircraft."

THE SUCCESS OF FOOTBALL CLUBS

From independence to the late 1980s, the most dominant leagues in Cameroon were in the political capital, Yaoundé, and the economic capital, Douala. The leading football teams in the country at the time were Canon Yaoundé, Tonnerre Yaoundé, and Union Sportive de Douala. These clubs dominated Division One football in Cameroon and Africa in the 1970s and 1980s. Canon Yaoundé, according to Mantz, was champions of Cameroon in 1970, 1974, 1977, 1979, 1980, 1982, 1985, 1986, 1991, 1994, and 2002. The club also won the Cup of Cameroon in 1967, 1973, 1975, 1976, 1977, 1978, 1983, 1986, 1993, 1995, and 1999.

Canon Yaoundé won Cameroon's twin football titles, becoming league champions and cup winners in 1977 and 1986, respectively. At the continental level, Canon Yaoundé emerged as African champions in 1971, 1978, and 1980 and were winners of the African Cup Winners' Cup in 1979.[22] Similarly, Canon's archrivals, Tonnerre football club of Yaoundé, were champions of Cameroon in 1981, 1983, 1984, 1987, and 1988. Tonnerre won the Cup of Cameroon in 1974, 1987, 1989, and 1991 and were league champions and cup winners in 1977.

In 1975, Roger Milla and Tonnerre Yaoundé were continental winners of the African Cup Winners' Cup.

Union Sportive of Douala were league champions of Cameroon in 1969, 1976, 1978, 1990, and 2012 and were Cameroon Cup winners in 1961, 1969, 1980, 1985, 1997, and 2012. Like Canon and Tonnerre, Union Sportive of Douala secured the twin titles, becoming league champions and cup winners in 1969. At the continental level, Union Sportive of Douala were African champions in 1979 and were winners of the African Cup Winners' Cup in 1981.

---

[22] G. Nantz, G., *Yearbook of African Football 2018*, London: Soccer Books Limited.

The Indomitable Lions of Cameroon, Its Meteoric Rise, Setbacks, and Prospects

The moniker "Indomitable Lions of Cameroon" is engraved ineradicably in the psyche of Cameroonian fans and devotees of Africa's most entertaining and much-admired soccer team. In the pantheon of African football, no name outperforms what the late Craig Saga (1990) called "The Cinderella Team." The national team exemplifies and personifies all the values and breakthroughs, the victories, and struggles of football and footballers in Cameroon and Africa.

Christopher Clarey (1994) quotes Maha Daher, President of FECAFOOT, about the Indomitable Lions with the following: "They say that when Cameroon's team does well, the whole country breathes easily, but when the team does poorly, the country catches a cold." Similarly, when the national team is victorious, according to John Bale (1986), it provides "one of those few occasions when large, complex, impersonal and functionally bonded units can unite." The team is admired by fans and opponents alike, because of their incredible athleticism and power, as well as their mental buoyancy in recovery from early setbacks, their swiftness, and deft ball control, as well as fearlessness of their opponents.

The Indomitable Lions made their debut in the FIFA World Cup tournament in Spain in 1982, with a cast of players most of whom played for local clubs like Canon Yaoundé, Tonnerre Yaoundé, and Union Sportif of Douala. Drawn in Group A, with Peru, Poland, and Italy, the Lions gave a proper account of themselves with a scintillating performance. The team drew all three matches, with a 0-0 tie with Peru, a 0-0 tie with Poland, and a 1-1 tie with Italy, the eventual winners of the World Cup. Sadly, despite this impressive performance, the Indomitable Lions failed to advance to the knockout stage of the World Cup tournament.

In 1984, the Lions qualified for the African Cup of Nations tournament hosted by Ivory Coast and defeated their archrivals, the Green Eagles of Nigeria, by a score of 3-1, lifting the sought-after African Cup of Nations (AFCON) trophy for the first time. The Lions reached the finals of AFCON in 1986 against host nation Egypt and lost 5-4 in a penalty shootout after a goalless draw.

The Lions made history in 1990, defeating World Cup holders Argentina in the 1990 FIFA World Cup in Milan, Italy, and reached the quarterfinals, the furthest any African team had accomplished in the history of the game at the time. This victory opened new opportunities for

Africa's participation in international football. The world's football governing body, FIFA, granted the continent of Africa three slots for the 1994 World Cup tournament in the USA.

Cameroon's groundbreaking achievement in 1990 was greeted with exhilaration throughout the world, but especially in Africa. Given Cameroon's extraordinary performance in 1990, many football enthusiasts predicted that "the Cinderella Team" would pull another great trick from the bag, reaching the semi-finals or final in the 1994 tournament. Sadly, this optimism proved to be based on a mirage, as the Indomitable Lions failed to replicate their performance of 1990.

The selection of players for the national team has always been a challenge for coaches, both foreign and domestic. Bureaucratic interference in the selection process is a major hallmark in the national team selection process in Cameroon. Political appointees—ministers, agency directors, officials in FECAFOOT—as well as orders from the presidency have prevented coaches from exercising independence in deciding which players to call up to the national team. A case in point is President Paul Biya's directives in 1990 to the head coach of the national team, Valeri Nepomniachi, to include retired football legend Roger Milla in the 1990 World Cup squad. Biya's decision may have been a blessing for the coach, the team, the country, and globally. Roger Milla's extraordinary performance in Italy in 1990 led the Indomitable Lions to the quarterfinals of the World Cup and propelled him to international stardom.

Other cases of interference by officials have had adverse effects. Superstar striker Patrick M'Boma, frustrated by interference and poor management of the national team by the Ministry of Youth and Sports, decided to leave the national team ahead of Cameroon's preparation and participation in the FIFA Confederations Cup, which kicked off on June 18, 2003, in Paris, France. M'Boma however reversed his decision after talks with the coach and other government officials.

Cameroon's performance in international football has steadily improved as more players have migrated to play professionally in Europe, the USA, Asia, and Latin America. Table 4.1 shows that as the number of Cameroonians playing abroad has expanded, the performance of the national team has also improved measurably. Conversely, as the number of footballers who migrate abroad to play professionally increases, interest in domestic football has decreased and impacts attendance, ticket purchases, and local businesses.

Table 4.1 also reveals the complex make-up of the national team from a geopolitical standpoint. As we indicated in the introductory section of this chapter, Cameroon has a complex cultural and linguistic make-up. Francophones from the East make up most of the country's geography and population. This is reflected in the selection process in the national team. Table 4.1 also shows that from 1972 to 1984, no Cameroonian of English-speaking origin was called to the national team. From 1986 to the present, the number of Anglophone Cameroonians called to the national team did not exceed two, except for 2017. This is not a criticism of the federation, mindful that Cameroon has ten regions. One would equally argue that reliance on professional players has, to some degree, precluded the inclusion of Anglophones in the national team selection in 2008 and 2010, respectively.

Furthermore, Table 4.1 provides a snapshot of the composition of the national team from 1972 to 2019. The data reveals two important facts about the Cameroon national team. (1) The national team recorded more victories as the number of Cameroonians (foreign players) playing professional football in Europe, North America, Latin America, and Asia increased. (2) The number of Anglophone players in the national team has remained steady for a long time and has not exceeded three players at any given tournament. Domestic or local players for the most part have been sidelined, since 1992. This study reveals that an increase in the number of foreign players in the national team has resulted in the success of the Indomitable Lions. The only caveat is that it has negatively impacted domestic football leagues.

The Junior National Team Selection: A Personal Odyssey

My experience in the Junior National team in selection 1985 reflects similar experiences for players from the former West or Southern Cameroons not playing in any of the "big" teams in Cameroon at the time, Canon, Tonnerre, Union Sportif of Douala, or Dynamo of Douala.

Then after the arrival of all twenty-two players, we had a "get to know your" team meeting. Players were to introduce themselves to teammates, providing their names, position(s) club, and the province of origin. My late teammate and friend, Benjamin Massing, volunteered to begin the ritual. "I am Benjamin Massing, Defence, Cammark Bamenda, Northwest

Province. Immediately, someone interjected and whispered in French, "Le Biafra," and a few others followed, "Biafra," "Biafra," to our surprise. The word Biafra is used as a pejorative term in Francophone Cameroon to label someone as Nigerian. The Ibos from Eastern Nigeria decided to secede from Nigeria and form their own country called "The Republic of Biafra." This action led to the civil war that lasted from 1967 to 1970. By implication, these teammates considered Massing as Nigerian because he plays football in the English-speaking region in Cameroon, in the city of Bamenda.

Ironically, Benjamin Massing is not Nigerian, not an Anglophone. Massing is Francophone from the city of Edea. I introduced myself as Augustine E. Ayuk, striker and midfielder, Cammark Mamfe, Southwest Province, another interjection came, and I was labeled " Le Anglo, Anglo," short form of "Anglophone" or from the English-speaking sector of Cameroon. These labels had a profound impact on our interaction in the next two weeks in the political capital of Yaoundé. Most of the time, the players practiced what I describe as "de facto discrimination" in football. The players formed cliques based on their ethnic linage or the teams they are associated with. These players communicated in their dialect all the time, spoke less French, and "no English" at all, not even "broken English" or "pidgin English." I was fortunate, however, to have Benjamin Massing of Cammark Bamenda from the Northwest province as the only person I was able to relate to and communicate within English, at least "Pidgin English." Indeed, Massing freed me from what would have otherwise been a depressingly reclusive venture.

I was the only Anglophone player called to the Junior National team selection in 1985. On paper, however, it showed that two players from West Cameroon or the English-speaking region were called to the Junior National team that year. I, with arrow pointing, played for Cammark, Mamfe, in the Southwest province/region, while Benjamin Massing (top row, the fifth player from left to right) played for Cammark Bamenda, in the Northwest province/region.

The experience in the junior national team can be unnerving for a player from the English-speaking region who has not lived in the Francophone region or is not able to communicate in the French language. Although Cameroon prides itself as a bilingual country, with English and French as official languages, the coaches and the technical staff members of the national team were all Francophones and communicated in the French language all the time.

Later, Ebwelle Bertin (squatting, the fifth player from left to right), of Tonnerre, joined Massing and me, though he had difficulties communicating even in "pidgin English." My mastery of the French language was elementary, and Massing served as our interpreter since he was fluent in French and could communicate well in "pidgin English." My friendship with Benjamin Massing was buttressed by his desire to lure me to join his club, Cammark Bamenda. Massing was overjoyed that he had found a striker and midfielder who could add value to his team.

After our two-week session, I informed both friends that I would not continue with football after our training session. I informed them that I would be traveling to the USA in furtherance of my education.

At the close of our two-week training session, each player was to receive reimbursement for transportation and payment for participating in the selection. Unfortunately, we were not told how much each player received. The two coaches oversaw the cash disbursement to all twenty-two players. Each player received the sum of 30,000 Francs CFA.

The coaches did not factor in transportation costs for players who traveled long distances from the capital Yaoundé. For example, my distance from the city of Mamfe to Yaoundé was 245 miles, Benjamin Massing's distance from the city of Bamenda to Yaoundé was 172.2 miles, the distance from the city of Douala to Yaoundé was 125 miles, one player's distance from Garoua to Yaoundé was 395 miles, and the distance from Bafoussam to Yaoundé was 135.6 miles. After the disbursement of the 30,000 Francs CFA to each of us, I was stunned to see some players give the coaches 5000 Francs from their stipend as a "thank you gift." I later learned from Massing that the gift was a form of a "pay-to-play" strategy to ensure that they would be called up later to participate in tournaments or possibly join the senior team.

One of the Francophone teammates with connections with a FECAFOOT official told us that "the coaches were not truthful with the amount of money they were disbursing to the players." He stated that "The Fecafoot official revealed to him that the actual amount budgeted by Fecafoot for each player, excluding meals, was 75,000 Francs." He added that "This is how the coaches make extra money during the selection in the Junior National team" (Figs. 4.2 and 4.3).

4 FOOTBALL IN CAMEROON, BEST OF TIMES, WORST... 97

Fig. 4.2 Cameroon Junior National team selection (1985)

Fig. 4.3   My time in the Junior National team (1985)

Conclusion

Since the introduction of football in Cameroon, the game has not faced any major challenge for fans' interest. Football rapidly developed and grew in Cameroon, just as the country transformed from a rural to an urban society. The game's future is intertwined with good governance and modern technology—television. Television has generated huge revenues in the game through advertising; unfortunately, there are fears that television will eventually keep fans at home, instead of them continuing to go to the stadium to watch and support their local and national teams.

The success of the national team also revealed the power of football in bringing together citizens with different interests and agendas. In a peculiar twist, however, Cameroon's fifth African Cup of Nations victory in 2017 was not greeted with the same degree of exhilaration as past victories. This accomplishment, by all accounts, was the least celebrated in the country, especially in the two restive Anglophone regions, who were seeking justice and equitable treatment from their Francophone compatriots. Victory in football, therefore, did not erase the realities of thousands of Anglophones Cameroonians who were killed and beaten by forces of law and order, imprisoned, dehumanized, and forced to flee from their domicile to neighboring Nigeria as refugees and as internally displaced persons (IDPs).

It is worth noting that though the game has increased Cameroon's visibility and image globally, the government has not done much to promote football in the country. Football infrastructure in Cameroon, before the construction of three modern facilities in preparation for the hosting of the African Cup of Nations in 2019, was pitiful. Corruption in FECAFOOT is despicable, and a power struggle among federation officials remains high. Issues with player allowances or bonuses remain unresolved, and preference for foreign managers over local coaches has not changed.

On a sanguine note, female football in Cameroon is gaining attention in Africa and globally. The Lionesses of Cameroon advanced to the second round of the FIFA Women's World Cup in Canada and France in 2015 and 2019, respectively.

REFERENCES

Alegi, P.C., "Playing to the Gallery? Sports Cultural Performance and Social Identity in South Africa, 1920–1945," *International Journal of African Historical Studies*, Vol. 35, No. 1 (2002).

Anan, K.A., "United Nations, June 2006, (July 15, 2013) How We Envy the World Cup." http://www.un.org/sport2005/ewsroom/worldcup.pdf.

Ashuntantang, T., "He Stood Up Against Injustice: Remembering Football Great Joe Ewunkem," *Scribbles from the Den*, 2012.

Bailey, K., *The Girls Are the Ones with the Pointy Nail*, London: CAN Althouse Press, 1999.

Baker, W.J., *Sports in the Western World*, Urbana: University of Illinois Press, 1988.

Bale, J., "Sport and National Identity: A Geographical View," *British Journal of Sports History 3*, No. 1 (1986): 8–41.

Baller, S. and Saavedra, M., "La Politique du football en Afrique: Mobilization et Trajectories," *Politique Africaine 118* (2010): 5–21.
Baller, Susan, and Scarlett C. "Introduction: Sport, Leisure, and Consumption in Africa," International Journal of the History of Sport 30, no. 16 (2013):1867–1876.
Beard, A., *The Language of Sport*, New York: Routledge, 1998.
Bowra, M., "Xenophanes and the Olympic Games" in *Problems of Greek Poetry by Author*, Oxford: Clarendon Press, 1953.
Clarey, C., "World Cup 1994: Cameroon Tries to Raise a Dream While All Else is Collapsing," *The New York Times*, May 1994.
Clignet, R. and Stark, M., "Modernization and the Game of Soccer in Cameroon," *International Review of Sport Sociology*, Vol. 9, No. 3–4 (1974): 81–98.
Crompton, J.L., "Economic Impact Analysis of Sports Facilities and Events: Eleven Sources of Misapplication," *Journal of Sport Management*, 9 (1) 1995: 14–35.
Dickens, C, *A Tale of Two Cities*, London: Chapman & Hall, 1859.
Fair, L., "Kicking It: Leisure, Politics, and Football in Colonial Zanzibar, 1900– the 1950s," *Africa: Journal of International African Institute*, Vol. 67, No. 2 (1997): 224–51.
Franken, M., "Anyone Can Dance A Survey and Analysis of Swahili Ngoma Past and Present," Ph.D. Dissertation, Riverside, CA: University of California, 1986.
Gennaro /Michael J. and Saheed Aderinto., Sports in African History, Politics, and Identity Formation. New York: Routledge Publishers, 2019.
Glassman, J., Feasts, and Riot: Revelry, Rebellion, and Popular Consciousness on Swahili Coast, 1856–1888. (Social History of Africa). Portsmouth, N.H.: Heinemann, or James Currey, London, or E.A.E.P., Nairobi, or Mkuki na Nyota, Dar es Salaam. 1995. pp. xvii, 293.
Kiouvulu, N., "Ratings of Gender Appropriateness of Sports Participation," *Sex Roles: A Journal of Research*, Vol. 33, No. 7–8 (1995): 543–57.
Kirk-Green, Anthony., "Imperial Administration and the Atlantic Imperative: The Case of the District Officer in Africa," in Sport in Africa: Essays in Social History, ed. W.S. Baker and J.A. Mangan. New York: Africana Publishing, 1987.
Lever, J., *Soccer Madness*, Chicago: University of Chicago Press, 1983.
Mean, L., "Identity and Discursive Practice: Doing Gender on the Football Pitch," *Discourse and Society*, 12(6), (2001): 789–815.
Martin, Phyllis M. Leisure, and Society in Colonial Braza. Cambridge: Cambridge University Press, 1995.
Mfomo, S.-P., Ngbwa, G.-P. et al.; "Indomitable Lions of Cameroon: Roots, Odyssey, and Glory," Yaoundé: Ministry of Communication, 1994.
Mwanjisi, R.K., *Nduku Abeid amani Karume*, Narobi: East African Publishing House, 1967.

Nang, J.L., *Desperate Football House: Six Months in Hell of Fecafoot*, Édition Inter Press, 2009.
Nantz, G., *Yearbook of African Football 2018*, London: Soccer Books Limited.
Nkwi, P.N., and Vidacs, B., "Football: Politics and Power in Cameroon," *Entering the Field: New Perspectives on World Football*, Armstrong, G. and Giulianotti, R. eds, Berg Publishers, 1997.
Oglesby, C.A., *Women, and Sport: From Myth to Reality*, Philadelphia, PA: Lea & Febiger, 1978.
Pannenborg, A., *How to Win a Football Match in Cameroon: An Anthropological Study of Africa's Most Popular Sport*, Leiden: 2008.
Sager, C., American sports reporter for *CNN* and its sister stations *TNT* and *TBS* (June 8, 1990).
Scraton, S., *Shaping Up to Womanhood: Gender and Girls' Physical Education*, Buckingham, UK: Open University Press, 1992.
Sone, F.B., *This is Sports; This is Football*, 2010.
Strobel, M., *Muslim Women in Mombasa*, New Haven, CT: Yale University Press, 1979.
Suleman, A.A., "The Swahili Singing Star Siti Binti," *Swahili* 39(1), (1969): 87–90.
Tsanga, S., "Le Football Camerounais des Origines a L'independence," Yaoundé: 1969.
Velten, C., *Desturi za Wasuahili*, Göttingen: Vandenhoek & Ruprecht, 1903.
Zenenga, P., "Virtualizing Politics in African Sport: Political and Cultural Construction in Zimbabwean Soccer," *Global Perspectives on Football in Africa: Visualizing the Game* by ed. Baller, S., Meischer, G. and Rassool, C., New York: Routledge Publishers, 2014.

CHAPTER 5

Historicizing Football Nigeria: Disciplinary, Governmentality, and Resistance Within Football Labor's Struggle

Chuka Onwumechili

INTRODUCTION

Few scholars can question the trophy successes of Nigeria's football. Nigeria's trophy-winning is easily identified in Olympic medals of 1996, 2012, and 2016, winning the Cup for African Nations (CAN) in 1980, 1994, and 2013; several African and global championships in youth football, African championships in women football; and winning continental and regional championships at the club level. But there remains a sense that Nigeria could have done more and that its trajectory of growth should be on a continued incline.[1] This sense of unfulfilled potential is amply

---

[1] Nwosu & Ugwuerua, "Nigerian Football Federation." *Intl Jrnl of Physical Education, Sports and Health*, 3(2016): 376–382; Chiweshe, "Problem of African Football." *Africa Sports Law and Business Bulletin*, 2 (2014): 37–33; *UK Telegraph*, "World Cup 2010," www.

C. Onwumechili (✉)
Howard University, Washington, DC, USA
e-mail: conwumechili@Howard.edu

© The Author(s), under exclusive license to Springer Nature Switzerland AG 2022
A. E. Ayuk (ed.), *Football (Soccer) in Africa*, Global Culture and Sport Series, https://doi.org/10.1007/978-3-030-94866-5_5

exhibited in Nigeria media criticism and the frequent disengagement of football technical managers, among other measures. Cates goes as far as to claim that "Nigeria's soccer stands at an important cross roads … if the nation's favorite sports is to survive."[2] Additionally, no less than the country's president, Goodluck Jonathan, announced in 2010 after a poor World Cup tournament performance, that the national team was suspended for two years.[3] These criticisms of Nigeria's football and action by the president may seem rash and unbecoming, particularly when one considers achievements previously listed. The *UK Telegraph* cites a former Nigerian national team player who captures the core reasons for such criticism: "it goes to reveal the pain everybody is feeling including the President for a country with so much talent, so many resources."[4] However, there is value to the criticisms, particularly when one realizes that Nigeria has largely achieved those victories and glories in spite of problems that have existed in the history of the development of its football.

In this chapter, I argue that the oppressive situation in which football labor finds itself in Nigeria has limited, slowed, and at times aborted Nigeria's quest for sustained high performance in football. I use the critical works of Michel Foucault and Antonio Gramsci to frame the criticism of Nigeria's football structure and the ongoing struggle of football labor within such structure. This chapter examines Nigeria's football structure, including any adjustments to it, across history. To do this, it is pertinent to break the history into three periods that are defined by how labor reacted to the situation in which it found itself during each of those periods. Importantly, this work does not abridge history. Instead, it begins by examining the earliest period of football in the country and the condition of labor in those early times. Thus, it is meant to be a historical criticism of Nigerian football structure and its impact on labor.

The ultimate purpose of this chapter is to provide a deep criticism of the game and its structure with four major goals: (1) to illuminate eternal struggle of Nigerian football labor across history, (2) identify instruments of oppression within Nigeria's football structure, (3) identify evolving means of labor reaction and resistance to labor condition, and (4) identify

telegraph.co.uk/sport/football/, 2010; and Cates, "Making the Game Beautiful." *Georgia Jrnl of Intl and Comparative Law*, 39(2010): 365–390.
[2] Cates, "Making the Game Beautiful," 366.
[3] Nigeria's President Goodluck Jonathan rescinded the ban after FIFA threatened severe sanctions against Nigeria for government interference.
[4] *UK Telegraph*, "World Cup 2010."

effects of the eternal struggle on the sustenance of high performance football.

The chapter's discourse begins by analyzing institutional and organizational structures and the mode of power relations within structures. This analysis will be framed through the lens of various critical scholars including Foucault and Gramsci.[5] This analysis will then lead us to an unpacking of power relationships within Nigeria's football structure across history and across three historical periods—early 1950s, 1960s to early 1980s, and then late 1980s to present. The impact of those relationships on football labor and the sustenance of high-level performance of Nigeria's football is then subsequently exposed.

INSTITUTION/ORGANIZATION, STRUCTURE, AND ISSUES OF POWER

Nigeria's football is formally organized with discernible structure, just like any modern organizations. It is within this system that footballers labor for wages. To be sure, wage-earning footballers in Nigeria do not include those that operate at grassroots levels. Thus, it is important to understand that the focus of this chapter is strictly the top-tier levels, the premier league, and national teams where player labor and productivity are compensated with wages.

The above description of Nigeria's football points to the possibility that it is amenable to a critique that uses the frame for criticizing structure and power. Michel Foucault[6] and Antonio Gramsci[7] have developed means for such criticism that are applicable to Nigerian football. Both have studied control mechanisms by elite groups, within nations and states, that oppress the masses and labor. These ideas and conditions can be extended to other systems where the necessities for production require the distribution of power. Here, power refers to the ability to influence activities or behaviors of others or to create conditions that make this influence possible.

---

[5] Foucault, *The Government of Self*. Basingstoke: Palgrave Macmillan, 2011; Foucault, "Governmentality." In *The Foucault Effect*, eds. Gordon & Miller, 87–104. Chicago, IL: University of Chicago Press, 1991; Foucault, *Disciplinary Power*. New York: New York University Press, 1986; and Gramsci, *Prison Notebooks*. International Publishers, 1971.

[6] Foucault, *The Government of Self*; Foucault, "Governmentality." *The Foucault Effect*; and Foucault, *Disciplinary Power*.

[7] Gramsci, *Prison Notebooks*.

Gramsci has argued strongly that power is usually maintained by creating a certain consciousness about what relationships in the world are.[8] This consciousness is not a sudden creation. Instead, it is developed overtime through cultural teaching and learning, and it is largely invisible to most people and, therefore, remains unquestioned even by those oppressed under such relationships. It becomes common sense to most people. It is at this point that Gramsci refers to such consciousness as cultural hegemony. Gramsci argues that such hegemony is practiced and sustained through a variety of tactics including persuasion/dialogue and coercion that are practiced in cultural institutions that may include schools, churches, families, and organizations as well as state apparatuses.[9]

Foucault's ideas are not much different from those of Gramsci. Foucault's modes of power, for instance, mirror the discourse of power from Gramsci's point of view. Foucault identifies three modes of power, which include violence/oppression, disciplinary which essentially reflects the discipline acquired by people via social and cultural training that takes place through life, and governmentality refers to the *mentality* that is derived from persistent and sustained governing. Here, the meaning of governing is far more extended than governance practiced by the state. Instead, governing refers to a relationship between command and control that is intended to regulate behavior at all levels. This may occur within families, within organizations, or within states. In fact, Dean argues that governmentality is not just about the state and its methods of governance but it also includes the governed and how those governed think about how they are governed to the point that they develop the mentality of the governed in ways in which those with power want them to be.[10]

The instrument of the state, or of an institution like Nigerian football administration, is so diverse that it offers several methods for governing the subjects or those subjected to its control. Sokhi-Bulley notes that these methods are not just diverse but they are also creative.[11] For instance, Sokhi-Bulley argues that the state may apply control via policies of health care, asylum, immigration, security, crime, education, among a myriad of control tactics.[12] As we shall see, football administration in Nigeria apply

[8] Ibid.
[9] Ibid.
[10] Dean, *Governmentality: Power and Rule*. London: Sage, 1999.
[11] Sokhi-Bulley, "Governmentality: Notes." http://criticallegalthinking.com/2014/12/02/governmentality-notes-thought-michel-foucault/
[12] Ibid.

similar tactics to control football labor over time. For football, the tactics may revolve around NFA's statutes, wider cultural norms, and sustained patterns of league practices.

The practice of governmentality, according to Foucault, has as a key instrument the gradual imposition of *disciplinary*.[13] By this, Foucault, meant life training that creates the right mentality, which eases the process of governing for the state or the institution. Disciplinary is a process of normalizing the subject socially and culturally. The process of disciplinary occurs through several socializing institutions including schools, churches, organizations, among others, where the goal is to create "docile bodies" amenable to state or elite control. These disciplinary institutions are able to achieve their goals by teaching and training the bodies to internalize and accept state or elite-sanctioned social behavior as a norm. It is this norm that Gramsci referred to as a consciousness or hegemony.[14] It is a stage where the control is total and the power is invisible and hidden such that the majority under this control begins to see the control mechanisms as "common sense" and accept them from a position of docility. Often, this position of hegemony defines control over social behavior intended to protect the economic and political interests of the elite.

The state and institutions that mold the body to internalize certain norms and protect the interest of the elite also have developed a wide range of mechanisms to monitor and impose penalties in order to normalize those bodies that resist or that fail in the process of internalization. This mode of power used in countering those that resist or fail to internalize is what can be described as a sanction, ban, suspension, fine, violence, and/or force. In fact, states have created agencies such as the police, prisons, and the courts to manage this aspect of power. In football, similar mechanisms are used to control labor and its behavior in ways to protect interests of elite administrators.

To summarize, the works of critical theorists like Foucault and Gramsci provide the framework for analyzing the situation of football labor in Nigeria across historical times. I argue that the practices of governmentality, through the apparatuses of Nigerian football administration, provide the process for subjugation and oppression of Nigerian football labor throughout history. In the following section, I gaze at the historical struggle of football labor under the watch of football administrators.

[13] Foucault, *Disciplinary Power*.
[14] Gramsci, *Prison Notes*.

HISTORICIZING STRUGGLE WITHIN NIGERIA'S FOOTBALL

Foucault did not mention sport or football in his extensive critical analyses of power and sociology. However, Foucault's work has been used by several sports sociologists.[15] Here, Foucault's work is invaluable in analyzing and helping expose the power of football elites that player labor has confronted over time in Nigerian football. However, because this work focuses on a long period of time, it is important that we break the periods into meaningful categories in order to account for changes in relationships and modes of resistance over that long period. There are three key periods that I identify: the first is the early period up to the 1950s, which covers the period when amateur football was in a position of primacy and most local players resisted but stayed within elite control inside the country. The second period (1960s to the early 1980s) involved labor resistance through fleeing the control of local football elites but also fleeing from football as career. The third and final period stretches from mid-1980s to date when local Nigerian football is professionalized but yet football labor flees. I now proceed to unpack those three periods.

Early to 1950s

Boer and Onwumechili have documented the history of Nigerian football, tracing its beginnings to early in the twentieth century.[16] Boer noted that the earliest record referred to 1903 when "reference was made to a football game that was played during the festivities celebrating the twenty-fifth anniversary of Wesleyan High School in Lagos ... this mere mention implies that people in Lagos were already playing football."[17] An earlier date is quite possible as missionaries, who used football to convert local youths to Christianity, were already in Nigeria late in the nineteenth century.

---

[15] Ncube, "Interface between Football." *Critical African Studies*, 6 (2014): 192–210; Markula & Pringle, *Foucault, Sport, and Exercise*. London: Routledge, 2006; and Hargreaves, *Sport, Power, and Culture*. Cambridge: Polity Press, 1986.

[16] Boer, "Story of Heroes." In *Football in Africa*, ed. Armstrong & Giulianotti, 59–79. New York: Palgrave Macmillan, 2004; Boer, *A Story of Heroes and Epics*. Ibadan: Bookcraft, 2018; Onwumechili, *Chukastats I*. Bowie, MD: Mechil Publishing, 2010; and Onwumechili, "Nigerian Football." *Critical African Studies*, 6 (2014a): 144–156.

[17] Boer, "Stories of Heroes," 63.

Football beyond youth competition to top-level league competition began in the 1906 in Calabar and culminated into full-blown national competition in 1945 with the Governor-General's Cup. To understand the condition of football labor during this first period in Nigeria's football history is to re-collect and piece together the life of a footballer and football during the period.

Early football competition involved a Calabar competition organized by Captain Beverly of the Southern Nigeria Regiment[18] and the Lagos War Memorial Cup.[19] These competitions were open to schools, military, religious groups, and clubs. The clubs, during that period, were often established government agencies such as the Public Works Department (PWD), the Marines, and the Lagos Town Council (LTC). Football labor at the time was made up of amateurs who spent their off-field time in the classroom or at their daytime jobs. Football was a pastime for them. There was no monetary or other type of consistent compensation for playing football. Players were only compensated based on their daily production in the government agency or other offices. At the games, players were served oranges during halftime even when playing for the national team. According to Onwumechili, "They simply received snacks at halftime for their efforts."[20]

But for the elites,[21] who administered the sport, there were far more tangible outcomes. The sport was not organized solely for recreational purposes at the top level. The earliest period of the games was ruled by Christian missionaries who organized games for the interest of their faith. They used the games to attract recruits from among local youths. This is what scholars refer to as *Muscular Christianity*.[22] Besides the religious elites and their interests, other elites also had interests. These other elite football administrators charged fees to the spectators that came to watch Cup games. Further, there was little concern for player health. Onwumechili

---

[18] Ibid.
[19] Onwumechili, *Chukastats I*.
[20] Ibid., 50.
[21] Elite administrators are the top administrators of the game including Football Association officials and club Chairmen or Presidents. These individuals have extensive power and authority that not only regulate football labor and activities but their continued patterns of practice define the administrative structure of the game.
[22] Darby, "Football, Colonial Doctrine." *Culture, Sport, Society*, 3 (2000): 61–87, and Hokkanen & Mangan, "Further Variations." *Intl Jrnl of the History of Sport*, 23 (2006): 1257–1274.

reports that in 1954, the Port Harcourt team was forced to play in the Governor-General's Cup the next day after arriving the previous night.[23] Elite administrators of the competition refused to reschedule the game citing that the Governor-General was traveling for an exhibition and the game had to be played before his travel. Labor was being presented as exoticism for recreational interest of the Governor-General and political benefits that may accrue to those elites who schedule the game. The Port Harcourt Team Manager, Mr. Anyanwu, was then quoted as claiming the match was akin to Jesus Christ's march to Mount Calvary for crucifixion.[24] In essence, he was troubled that the game's administrators had scheduled the game without concern for the health of his players. It is obvious, therefore, that games were organized in the interest of the elite or the game's administrators.

Why was it easy to co-opt football labor to assist in achieving the interest of these elites? Nigeria, particularly in pre-independence but even long after that, is a high power distance culture. This cultural characteristic is critical in the disciplinary process that created docility among football labor of the time. Onwumechili discussed power distance by arguing that "In Hofstede's study, Nigeria scored 80 (Scale range 0–100), which demonstrates that people expect inequality and largely accept it."[25] This distance is accepted by football labor and created a situation where labor rarely questioned authority of football administrators. Importantly, the power distance norm was and is one that values administrative position over that of football labor. The administrator's place in the social hierarchy is bolstered by educational certification or academic degree that supports the administrator's authority. In the end, Foucault's governmentality is applicable to the power relationship between administrators and football labor and it creates a situation where labor sees administrator's dictates as the way things ought to be.

However, it will be inaccurate to deny the existence of resistance to this power imbalance even in a Nigerian culture where it was much easier and more "laudable" to accept the dictate of football administrators. Here, we use Scott's definition of resistance which describes the concept, in a class struggle, as moments when a member of the subordinated/oppressed class acts to deny claims made by the superordinate or at least advance its

[23] Onwumechili, *Chukastats I*.
[24] Ibid., 58.
[25] Onwumechili, "Nigerian Football," 150.

own claims against that of the superordinate.[26] The denial of claims may be explicit and public but could also be implicit and non-public. Though this definition of resistance by Scott is widely accepted, it appears to neglect other types of resistance that may not be advanced in the way Scott predicts. For instance, resistors may seek freedom and flee from the situation in which they find themselves without an explicit or implied confrontation against superordinate's claims. We will discuss this type of resistance in subsequent sections.

In any case, Onwumechili narrates one example of a rare incidence of resistance to early football administration in Nigeria.[27] As we noted earlier, Nigerian football labor received no monetary compensation in spite of gate taking by football administrators. In 1955, that is six years after the national team's first international game, Godwin Ironkwe met with his teammates including Skipper Peter Anieke and decided to place a claim for financial compensation for a game against Ghana. The administrators were incensed and refused the claim. The team, discouraged, suffered a 0-7 defeat, which remains Nigeria's most lopsided loss to date. The administrators immediately suspended Ironkwe and Anieke from the national team. Though that act of explicit resistance failed, it was the beginning of a struggle that would eventually be successful in ensuring financial compensation for football labor. The move to suspend Ironkwe and Anieke was an attempt to normalize resistors that the elite class believes fail to internalize teachings of a disciplinary system built overtime through culture and its institutions.

1960s to Early 1980s

The second historical period differs from the first in a few ways. This latter period saw the introduction of some compensation for football labor. Instead of players relying on wages earned as office workers, they now received bonus pay from their games. Thus, the resistance mentioned in the first period proved fruitful during this second historical period. However, with football becoming the most popular game in the country, it was regularly watched by large paying crowds, and with introduction of a top-tier nationwide league in 1972, there were even far more competitive matches attracting significant revenue. Bonuses were meager for

[26] Scott, *Domination and Resistance*. New Haven, CT: Yale University Press, 1992.
[27] Onwumechili, *Chukastats I*.

football labor even though the revenue earned through the gates had risen. Also, compensation as office workers remained for football labor. This arrangement was a cheaper way to pay for the labor that was bringing in an increasing amount of revenue. Here, it is important to be clear that football teams were not wealthy enterprises but compensation for players was widely lower compared to payout for top administrators. Several top administrators used their association with football to create fruitful political careers. One such example was Chief Jim Nwobodo, whose Chairmanship of the highly successful Rangers Football Club catapulted him to Governorship of his state. But several of the players whose labor made the club successful retired in penury.

Remarkably, football labor mistakenly believed that what they received as compensation was deserved and adequate. Their baseline for comparison was more likely the earlier era when the likes of Ironkwe and Anieke had led protests for a special football labor pay. However, such comparison is faulty. The earlier era in the 1950s played to crowds that were often less than 10,000 patrons, and Nigerian football labor had no member that was valued beyond the country's borders. In contrast, the latter era played to crowds that at times included over 60,000 paying patrons in bigger arena. This latter football labor produced among them players whose values extended beyond Nigeria including the likes of Muda Lawal, Segun Odegbami, Christian Chukwu, Emmanuel Okala, and Haruna Ilerika. Yet those values were poorly compensated by football administrators who took advantage of the values to make fortunes via estacodes from foreign trips with the team.[28] Earnings from game bonuses barely provided enough compensation for labor. Moreover, with more value attached to labor, administrators easily created and staged events, home and abroad, which provided access to funds for further enrichment of administrators. Such competitions during this era included the All Africa Games and the Sports Festivals, among other sporting events.

Labor's traditional docility prevented major resistance to administrative avarice. Foucault's instruction on the effect of disciplinary and governmentality was notable just as they were in the earlier era. Of great effect is the cultural institution, which establishes the wide power distance between elite administrators and football labor. As Hofstede notes, such power distances are accepted by the oppressed within the system[29] because the

---

[28] Estacodes are daily allowances paid to top administrators during foreign trips.
[29] Hofstede, *Culture's Consequences*. Thousand Oaks, CA: Sage, 2001.

oppressed are taught throughout their lives that such distances are "normal" and to not accept them is to act in "abnormal" sense. Thus, while labor compared itself to labor of an earlier era, the most troubling situation was that the difference between labor of this latter era and the corresponding elite group had in fact widened. Labor's inaction meant that oppression continued because instruments of disciplinary and governmentality were quite effective in maintaining labor docility.

But as is always the case, there exists moments of resistance in each era. In the earlier era, it was protest by Ironkwe and Anieke. In this era, there was also resistance. At the 1982 Cup for African Nations, the captain of the Nigerian national team, Muda Lawal, used his position as a revered player to demand that substitutes receive same amount of bonus as regulars on the team. Hitherto, substitutes received only 50% of bonus paid to regulars. Even though the then Government Minister for Sports, Mike Okwechime, cited this as an example of player "Swollen headedness," today what Lawal demanded is largely the system in use for bonus compensation at the national team level.[30] The increase was not much compared to the loot football elites were able to access from hosting a variety of events and the increased revenue in the era. However, it represented a symbolic moment that demonstrated ability of labor to protest and gain some concession in spite of instruments of "normalization" available to the elite such as sanctions, suspensions, among others.

A second mode of resistance also existed. Instead of confronting the elite and insisting on change as we noted above, a great number of football labor fled from the situation that they found themselves. This is an example of resistance where resistors may seek freedom from a situation without an explicit or implied confrontation against the claims of the oppressor. In this case, an increasing number of football labor quit the local game, escaping control of the Nigerian football administrators and chose to seek higher educational opportunities, mostly outside the country. These educational opportunities were those that the culture considers essential to attainment of higher social hierarchy. Examples of resistors who chose this route include top international-level talents like Tony Igwe, Thompson Usiyan, Godwin Iwelumo, and Godwin Odiye. All those players quit Nigerian football and sought higher education in the United States. Acquisition of higher education psychologically placed them at social hierarchy where they became peers of their erstwhile oppressors, the

[30] Onwumechili, *Chukastats I*.

administrators. In any case, they were no longer within control of powerful football administrators. However, fleeing was not easy as administrators did not always sanction this. Moniedafe, a footballer during that era, mentions in his book that Usiyan had to be smuggled to the airport by team captain Christian Chukwu because administrators would not have approved Usiyan's departure. Moniedafe owned two passports in order to create an opportunity to flee. He used one passport to obtain a United States' visa, while he submitted the other passport to football administrators for use in Nigeria's international games. This tactics by Moniedafe was designed to avoid the disagreeing gaze of football administrators while planning to flee for further studies in the United States.[31]

Mid-1980s to Present

The third and continuing era stretches over three decades. Though it is a much longer period than the previous era, there are characteristics that denote the three decades as a single category for analysis. This period includes eventual professionalization of football in Nigeria marked by the increasing choice of labor to resist by fleeing. However, in fleeing, labor no longer considered education to be the alternative but instead chose to continue or pursue professional football elsewhere. Why? Some Nigerian footballers such as Christian Nwokocha who left in the previous era to earn a college degree had proceeded to play professionally and acquire wealth, which they exhibited in the Nigerian national team camp. For instance, Onwumechili wrote that Nwokocha showed off his luxury car to other players, most of who could not afford a car. Seeing Nwokocha with a car and knowing he played professionally at Sporting Lisbon inspired many others such as Okey Isima and Sylvanus Okpala to pursue professional careers in Portugal. Thus, players began to see professional football outside the country as a way to acquire wealth and climb the social hierarchy.[32]

Locally, players were no longer classified as civil servants. Instead, they were employed strictly as footballers and earned their keep laboring on the football field. Wages were not standardized but based on negotiated contracts and agreed signing fees. These wages, on paper, are much better than the players would have received as civil servants. For instance, an

---

[31] Moniedafe & Onwumechili, *Moniedafe: My Life*. Bowie, MD: Mechil, in press.
[32] Onwumechili, *Chukastats I*.

office clerk which often was the office position for players in the early era earns a little more than N20,000 monthly in present-day Nigeria.[33] The top-tier league players currently are scheduled to receive no less than N150,000 monthly.[34] However, most of the player contracts and agreements are not worth the paper they are written on. Onwumechili noted the following on how football administrators handled such contracts: "(administrators) used their positions to disregard player contracts by withholding wages due to players and forcing players to become beholden to them as they assumed positions of demigods by determining when to pay, who to pay, and what to pay players."[35] Thus, while salaries appear to elevate status of players, in reality player labor continued to be oppressed.

Meanwhile, revenue improved for the national teams because there was increased corporate sponsorship and rights buying. At the club level, revenue from player transfers was on the rise. However, and as noted above, player labor found it difficult to substantively access this revenue. Instead, administrators "captured" transfer fees for personal use by underreporting the fees to club accounts while pocketing the rest. Chiweshe notes that just 10% of $7m received from the league sponsor in Nigeria went to the clubs and no club received money from $5m worth of television rights for the league. This is a meager sum distributed to clubs.[36] So what happened to the rest of the money? The desperation that surrounds competition to win an elected position in administration of Nigeria's football and the sudden wealth amassed by those who serve in those positions give us a clue. There is little doubt that football administration has become an avenue for enrichment. Several scholars write on this phenomenon of administrative avarice.[37] Nwani cites a top-tier player who stated: "We cannot be suffering on the pitch and some people are so happy spending the money that should have been used to take care of the players."[38] The question and the

---

[33] Mustapha, "Niger Messenger Gets." www.Peoplesdailyng.com/

[34] Ogunleye, "Nigeria Premier League." www.premiumtimesng.com/. The official exchange for the Nigerian Naira (N) as of late May 2016 is 1 USD = N199. However, the parallel market rate was as high as 1 USD = N337.

[35] Onwumechili, "Oh Lord you are the Lord." *Identity and Nation*, eds. Onwumechili & Akindes. London, UK: Palgrave Macmillan, 2014b, 149.

[36] Chiweshe, "Problem of African Football."

[37] *Premium Times*, "N1.3 billion Fraud." www.premiumtimesng.com; Cornick, "Corruption, in-fighting." http://sabotagetimes.com/sport/; Onwumechili, "Nigerian Football"; and Nwosu & Ugwuerua, "Nigerian Football Federation."

[38] Nwani, "Nigerian Premier League Players." http://www.goal.com/en-ng/news/, para. 16.

figures provided by Chiweshe give us an idea of the issues of administrative corruption within a system where labor rarely receives due compensation for its on-field production. While stories about corruption in Nigerian football may be sexy in the media, it is what is not often reported that makes corruption possible, endemic, and sustained. What is not often reported is the power imbalance created by the administrators' pattern of control that has made football labor largely impotent and creating a deep-seated erasure.

Scholars have connected Nigerian footballer migration to the poor labor conditions at home.[39] However, the critical incident during this period was the decision of Stephen Keshi, then a national team player and player of the New Nigerian Bank (NNB), to quit Nigeria following a ban for late arrival to the national camp. As argued earlier, the ban is always an instrument used by power elites to normalize behavior of those believed to have stepped out of normality. However, instead of the ban nullifying and docilizing Keshi, Keshi resisted by fleeing abroad. He joined Stade D'Abidjan in the Ivory Coast en route to Belgium where he played most of his professional career. He then, as largely cited, became the conduit for departure of several top Nigerian talents to Europe in quest of a professional career.[40] Keshi was not the first Nigerian player to leave for a professional football career, but he was the one who assisted in the mass migration that followed his departure. Thus, while Nwokocha changed the perception of football as a career, it was Keshi who worked to move significant number of Nigerian and other African footballers to flee to professionalism away from Nigeria.

But not all labor is able to flee during moments of difficulty. To flee successfully means that the receiving locality is able to accept you by offering shelter. This is not always the case as footballers may fail to pass trials, which means that they are not employed at a place they aspire. In such cases, that footballer must stay in Nigeria, no matter how temporarily. This group of footballers is either docile or may also resist. Increasingly, they resist by threatening or carrying out strikes against the oppressive

---

[39] Onwumechili, "Oh Lord, you are the Lord"; Baird, "Watching the Ball." *Turkish Review*, 4 (2014): 370–377; Ngobua, "Clubs Suffocate Players." www.weeklytrust.com.ng/; and Nnabuogor, "Frustrated at Home." www.nationalmirroronline.net/
[40] Hawkey, "Teenaged Prodigy." www.thenational.ae/sport/ and *The Guardian*, Boy Wonder's. www.theguardian.com/

situations in which they find themselves. Onwumechili,[41] Maduewesi,[42] and Oni[43] have all reported the occurrence of such strikes or its threat among football labor in the top tier of Nigerian football league. Onwumechili explained: "This often occurs when management fails to pay, for long periods, agreed remuneration that includes salaries and sign-on fees. Each season, players from several top clubs are involved in this type of resistance."[44] Akpeji[45] and Okpi[46] reported the widely covered violence against football labor involving players of FC Taraba who had gone to the Governor to protest against nonpayment of their salaries. Akpeji wrote: "The rights of Taraba FC players was (sic) yesterday trampled upon, as soldiers numbering over eleven brutalized the players for besieging the government in protest over non payment of their eleven month salaries."[47] Okpi, writing on the same issue, cited an FC Taraba player who said: "Our families are suffering because of this. I have a wife and two children. My children were sent out of school because I could not pay their school fees."[48]

PROBLEMATIZING IMPACT ON SUSTAINED HIGH PERFORMANCE

While Michel Foucault's critical writings, as well as writings of other critical scholars, assist us in understanding the relationship between elite administrators who regulate Nigeria's football and the football labor that they regulate, they do not provide the frame under which we examine the effect of the football labor situation on sustenance of high performance. For that examination, we must look elsewhere. Nwosu & Ugwuerua,[49] Cornick,[50] and Onwumechili[51] provide the logic that helps us understand the impact.

[41] Onwumechili, "Nigerian Football."
[42] Maduewesi, "Players of Heartland." www.allsports.com.ng/2013/
[43] Oni, "Enugu Rangers Players." www.goal.com/
[44] Onwumechili, "Nigerian Football," 151.
[45] Akpeji, "Soldiers Brutalize." http://guardian.ng/sport/, 2015.
[46] Okpi, "Shady Deals." www.TheNews.ng/, 2015.
[47] Akpeji, "Soldiers Brutalize," para. 1.
[48] Okpi, "Shady Deals," para. 9.
[49] Nwosu & Ugwuerua, "Nigerian Football Federation."
[50] Cornick, "Corruption, in-fighting."
[51] Onwumechili, "Nigerian Football."

In Nigeria's case, this goal of high performance is within the African continent and an expectation of a rising trajectory of performance at the world stage. Stagnated football development and the lack of sustained high performance are associated, by several scholars, with corruption and political instability.[52] However, not much has been done in delineating how the power imbalance between football labor and elite administrators has adversely impacted football development or sustained high-level performance. However, there is evidence of impact. There are five areas that impact sustained performance, at a high level, for Nigeria's football. These include weakening of national team performance, increasing loss of control over youth football development, creation of distrust among football labor, widening power distance between elite administrators and football labor, and exposing labor to criminal activities that directly endanger the game. Each of those elements undermine Nigeria's attempt to sustain high performance.

One effect of the struggle between labor and administration is the weakening of Nigeria's national team. As noted earlier, one of the key modes of resistance in the third historical period is fleeing the local football environment for professional football outside the country. This move has increasingly meant that most of Nigeria's top footballers are scattered all over the world, particularly in Europe, instead of being concentrated within the country. This situation, early in the third historical period, may have been a benefit, particularly with Nigeria's rise as a major national team in the mid-1990s, but it now appears as a drawback. The question is why? In the early period, it was clearly the best players that left the country and immediately became affiliated with clubs overseas. These players could easily be monitored and invited to the national team with confidence that they are the country's best. This is not currently the situation. Numerous Nigerian players, some never known by their performance locally, are in disparate clubs in Europe and Asia. Their unknown quality at home, coupled with uneven performance against teams of disparate quality outside the country, make it difficult to claim that the best Nigerian players are now easily monitored and invited to the national team. This doubt about the quality of Nigeria's current national team players coupled with restrictions by FIFA on how long such players may be available to train with the national team impact adversely on team's high performance in a sustained manner.

[52] Nwosu & Ugwuerua, "Nigerian Football Federation."

The migration of football talent from Nigeria to foreign lands do not only affect labor in the top tier of the Nigerian football league. In fact, a growing issue is the departure from Nigeria of players who play at the youth level. These players end up in academies and age-grade teams of clubs in Europe where they are developed for big European clubs or developed for loans to other clubs. The effect on the national team is increasing evident as more and more national team players are Nigerian-born players developed in European academies. The list includes the likes of Obafemi Martins, Ayo Makinwa, Kelechi Iheanacho, Moses Simon, among others. None of those played for a club in the top tier of Nigerian football. This situation is related to the impact mentioned in previous paragraph because it leads to players who have not proved their mettle at home before moving overseas and it is more complex determining their true quality because they perform against varying levels of opposition quality in Europe. Further, this migration reduces the pool of players available to Nigeria's youth teams because migration removes them from easier monitoring. However, this effect on the pool is presently insignificant and has not adversely affected sustained high performance at the national youth teams.

The third impact is the creation of distrust among football labor. This distrust has increased resistance in various ways. Hughes reported that national team players boycotted training for the World Cup in protest over nonpayment of agreed bonuses.[53] As mentioned earlier, the nonpayment of agreed bonuses is a major issue in Nigerian football at both the club and the national team levels. Its frequent occurrence creates cycles of distrust that ultimately affects the team's readiness to perform. According to Cornick: "A complete lack of trust between players and their football association created huge divides culminating in an embarrassing failure to qualify for the 2012 Africa Cup of Nations."[54] Cornick went on to write that "Many questioned where the US$1.25 million of FIFA funds for development were being spent each year."[55] At the 2014 World Cup, players and administrators were engaged in bonus discussions deep into the night on the eve of a crucial World Cup second round game against France, which the team subsequently lost 0-2. More recently, Nigeria's former national coach Sunday Oliseh was quoted as follows: "players

---

[53] Hughes, "World Cup 2014." www.bbc.com/sport/football/
[54] Cornick, "Corruption, in-fighting," para. 11.
[55] Ibid., para. 11.

might reject future call ups to the squad due to their owed (salaries). He said some players are already calling him to ask for their entitlements."[56] In essence, these problems not only create distrust but more likely they also lead to possible future lack of commitment.

In spite of the increasing labor resistance to oppressive acts, there may be evidence that the power imbalance, which precipitates those acts, is widening. For instance, Nigerian clubs' ability to put coaches and players on half salary or withholding their pay has become routinized and has not been successfully pushed back over the years. In essence, club administrators have the power to determine whether to pay labor or not, even when labor has produced or is producing. Ogunleye reported players of Kaduna United as going months without their salaries paid while winning games in the league.[57] But this situation is routine for majority of the clubs in Nigeria's top tier and on an annual basis. It has become normalized and expected. The same situation, albeit to a lesser extent, occurs at the national team level. This is demonstrated in a statement by a top Football Federation official who was responding to complaint made by the then national team coach Sunday Oliseh. The NFF official asked rhetorically: "What about Samson Siasia's team that played all the way to the final and won the Cup without being paid their match bonuses and allowances? What about Emmanuel Amuneke that played till the final and won the World Cup in Chile without being paid?"[58] The official basically insinuates that nonpayment of salaries should be expected, whether the team is producing or not.

The sport itself faces danger with the continued situation where football labor produces without the certainty of compensation. A real and imminent danger is football labor choosing the alternative of criminal activity in order to seek financial payment in lieu of unpaid salaries, bonuses, allowances, and sign-on fees. This option may be to take payment from unscrupulous and shadowy figures to fix results of games. Though reports of such activities in the Nigerian league are rare, it is likely to be on an incline if the current labor situation continues. In 2013, players and coaches from four clubs were banned after being found guilty for fixing results of two critical league games that led to scandalous results of

---

[56] News7Nigeria, "I fear Super Eagles Players." www.news7ng.com, 2016, para. 1.
[57] Ogunleye, "Unpaid Kaduna United." www.premiumtimesng.com/
[58] Inyang, "We owed Amuneke." www.dailypost.ng/, 2016.

79-0 and 67-0.[59] Moreover, coaches are now widely accused of seeking bribes to select players and using them in games. Several of these coaches are owed, like players, for months. AllAfrica.com reported that a Nigerian player, Odion Ighalo, accused Coach Uwua of the Nigerian youth team, at the time, of requesting for ₦100,000 from his (Odion's) agent in order to ensure that he (Ighalo) and a club mate makes the squad.[60]

Conclusion

In this paper, I argue that the oppressive situation in which football labor finds itself in Nigeria has adversely affected Nigeria's quest for sustained achievement in football. I use Michel Foucault's criticism, along with works of other critical scholars, to frame criticism of Nigeria's football structure across three historical times and the ongoing struggle of football labor within such structure.

Ultimately, this chapter critiques structure of football in Nigeria and aims at the following: (1) illuminating eternal struggle of Nigerian football labor across history, (2) identifying instruments of oppression within Nigeria's football structure, (3) identifying evolving means of labor reaction and resistance to labor condition, and (4) identifying effects of the eternal struggle on sustained achievement of football in the country.

* * *

While this chapter has focused on football labor struggles in Nigeria, it is important to note that those Nigerian footballers who have faced this oppressive environment, within the country, eventually contribute to the support of the needy in Nigeria. Therefore, it is important to cite the charity work of two particular footballers, one retired and the other still active. They are both had/have recognizable professional careers outside the country after playing within the suffocating environment in Nigeria. Nwankwo Kanu, perhaps the country's most visible footballer who was instrumental to the winning of the 1996 Olympic football gold medal and also featured for both Arsenal FC in England and Inter Milan in Italy. Nwankwo underwent heart surgery in order to continue his footballing career. This experience led to his establishment and support of The Kanu

[59] Berger, "Nigerian soccer players." www.sportsgrid.com/, 2013.
[60] AllAfrica.com, "Nigeria: Coaches." www.allafrica.com/, 2007.

Nwankwo Heart Foundation in the country. This foundation, created in 2014, supports the treatment of Africa's young underprivileged and young children who suffer from heart ailments. The Foundation has reportedly supported over 500 heart surgeries. Odion Ighalo is another Nigerian international, still active, who established The Ighalo Orphanage Foundation in 2017 to support needy and orphaned children. In 2020, Ighalo drove through the streets in Lagos handing out bags of donations to the street poor.

References

Akpeji, C. (2015, Dec. 5). Soldiers brutalize FC Taraba players for protest over unpaid salaries. *The Guardian*. http://www.guardian.ng/sport/

AllAfrica.com. (2007, Mar 16). Nigeria: Coaches and bribe-taking. www.allafrica.com

Baird, T. (2014). Watching the ball: Deception and exploitation from Nigeria to Turkey. *Turkish Review*, 4(4): 370–377.

Berger, Z. (2013, July 24). Nigerian soccer players and officials involved in most blatant match fixing ever banned for life. http://www.sportsgrid.com/

Boer, W. (2018). *A story of heroes and epics: The history of football in Nigeria*. Ibadan: Bookcraft.

Boer, W. (2004). A story of heroes, of epics: The rise of football in Nigeria. In Armstrong, G., & Giulianotti, R. (eds.), *Football in Africa: Conflict, conciliation, and community* (pp. 59–79). New York: Palgrave Macmillan.

Cates, J. (2010). Making the game beautiful again: Lessons from Brazil provide a roadmap for rebuilding soccer in Nigeria. *Georgia Journal of International and Comparative Law*, 39(1): 365–390.

Chiweshe, M. (2014). The problem with African football: Corruption and the (under)development of the game on the continent. *Africa Sports Law and Business Bulletin*, 2: 27–33.

Cornick, T. (2014, Jan. 2). Corruption, in-fighting and redemption: The return of Nigerian football's Super Eagles. Sabotage Times. http://sabotagetimes.com/sport/

Darby, P. (2000). Football, colonial doctrine and indigenous resistance: Mapping the political persona of FIFA's African constituency. *Culture, Sport, Society*, 3(1): 61–87.

Dean, M. (1999). *Governmentality: Power and rule in modern society*. London: Sage.

Foucault, M. (2011). *The government of self and others: Lectures at the College de France, 1982–1983*. Basingstoke: Palgrave Macmillan.

Foucault, M. (1991). Governmentality (trans. Rosi Braidotti), in Gordon, C., & Miller, P. (eds.), *The Foucault Effect: Studies in Governmentality* (pp. 87–104). Chicago, IL: University of Chicago Press.
Foucault, M. (1986). *Disciplinary power and subjection*. New York: New York University Press.
Gramsci, A. (1971). *Selections from the Prison Notebooks*. International Publishers.
Hargreaves, J. (1986). *Sport, power, and culture*. Cambridge: Polity Press.
Hawkey, I. (2013, Oct. 14). Teenaged prodigy Nii Lamptey exploited and lost his spark. www.thenational.ae/sport/
Hofstede, G. (2001). *Culture's consequences: Comparing values, behaviors, institutions and organizations across nations*. Thousand Oaks, CA: Sage Publications.
Hokkanen, M., & Mangan, J. (2006). Further variations on a theme: The games ethic further adapted-Scottish moral missionaries and muscular Christians in Malawi. *The International Journal of the History of Sport*, 23 (8): 1257–1274.
Hughes, I. (2014, June 27). World Cup 2014: Nigeria assured by President over bonuses. www.bbc.com/sport/football/
Maduewesi, C. (2013, Feb 26). Players of Heartland set to embark on a strike. www.allsports.com.ng/2013/
Markula, P., & Pringle, R. (2006). *Foucault, sport, and exercise*. London: Routledge.
Moniedafe, F., & Onwumechili, C. (2016). *Moniedafe: My life and glory years of Bendel Insurance FC*. Bowie, MD: Mechil Publishing.
Mustapha, Y. (2016, Feb. 5). Niger messenger gets over N.3m monthly pay. www.Peoplesdailyng.com/
Inyang, I. (2016, Feb 3). We owed Amuneke, Siasia but they won trophies – NFF blasts Oliseh. *Daily Post*. www.dailypost.ng/
Ncube, L. (2014). The interface between football and ethnic identity discourses in Zimbabwe. *Critical African Studies*, 6 (2–3): 192–210.
News7 Nigeria. (2016, January 29). 'I fear Super Eagles players might reject call ups because of owed salaries.' www.news7ng.com
Ngobua, D. (2013, July 20). Clubs suffocate players with debts. www.weeklytrust.com.ng/
Nnabuogor, I. (2012, April 19). Frustrated at home, Nigerian footballers seek fame and fortune in India. www.nationalmirroronline.net/
Nwani, E. (2012, Nov 27). Nigerian Premier League players lament the confused state of the game. http://www.goal.com/en-ng/news/
Nwosu, O., & Ugwuerua, E. (2016). Nigerian football federation, corruption and development of football in Nigeria. *International Journal of Physical Education, Sports and Health*, 3(1): 376–382.
Ogunleye, A. (2014a, Sep. 28). Nigerian League: Unpaid Kaduna United players defeat Gombe United. www.premiumtimesng.com/

Ogunleye, A. (2014b, January 20). Nigeria Premier League players to earn N150,000 monthly – Danladi. www.premiumtimesng.cm/
Okpi, A. (2015, Dec. 26). Shady deals: How Nigerian league players lose entitlements to clubs (2). www.TheNews.ng/
Oni, K. (2012, April 25). Enugu Rangers players threaten strike over unpaid sign-on fees. www.goal.com/
Onwumechili, C. (2014a). Nigerian football: Interests, marginalization, and struggle. *Critical African Studies*, 6 (2–3): 144–156.
Onwumechili, C. (2014b). Oh Lord, you are the Lord who remembered John Obi Mikel. In Onwumechili, C., & Akindes, G. (eds.), *Identity and nation in African football: Fans, community, and clubs* (pp. 183–200). London, UK: Palgrave Macmillan.
Onwumechili, C. (2010). *Chukastats 1: History, records, and statistics of Nigerian football*. Bowie, MD: Mechil Publishing.
Premium Times. (2015, Oct. 8). N1.3 billion fraud: Ex-Nigerian football administrators to know fate November 15. http://www.premiumtimesng.com/sports/football/
Scott, J. (1992). *Domination and the arts of resistance: Hidden transcripts*. New Haven, CT: Yale University Press.
Sokhi-Bulley, B. (2014, December 2). Governmentality: Notes on the thought of Michel Foucault. *Critical Legal Thinking*. http://criticallegalthinking.com/2014/12/02/governmentality-notes-thought-michel-foucault/
The Guardian. (2008, Feb. 2). Boy wonder's lost years. www.theguardian.com/
The Telegraph. (2010, June 30). World Cup 2010: Nigerian president bans football team from international competition for two years. http://www.telegraph.co.uk/sport/football/

CHAPTER 6

Football in DR Congo: A Critical Account of "Congolese Football"

Tamba Nlandu

Among the giants of African football, the Democratic Republic of Congo (DRC) has had, since its first participation in continental and world competitions, its moments of glory and demise. The paradox of Congolese football is epitomized by its success during times of political dictatorship, winning two African Cup of Nations (1968 and 1974) under the Mobutu regime, and its decline during times of democratic trials, failing to either qualify for or advance beyond the group stage of Confederation of African Football (CAF) and FIFA competitions. Without any doubt, the DRC has always been blessed with both human and natural resources. However, in football, like many other spheres of Congolese life, these resources have tended to be mismanaged or simply squandered. As a result, fame without fortune appears to be the norm for Congolese football players loyal to their homeland. While football has tended to serve as the "opium of the people," the players have often been left to fend for themselves leading most of them to immigrate to countries with greener football pastures.

T. Nlandu (✉)
John Carroll University, University Heights, OH, USA
e-mail: tnlandu@jcu.edu

© The Author(s), under exclusive license to Springer Nature Switzerland AG 2022
A. E. Ayuk (ed.), *Football (Soccer) in Africa*, Global Culture and Sport Series, https://doi.org/10.1007/978-3-030-94866-5_6

Perhaps the resurgence of the dominance of the Congolese big clubs (especially, Tout Puissant [TP] Mazembe and Association Sportive [AS] Vita Club) in continental competitions coupled with the success of the local-based national team players who have won two of the African Nations Championship titles (2009 and 2016) might be signaling a new era in Congolese football. However, the premature eliminations of TP Mazembe, Maniema Union, and AS Vita Club from the 2021–2022 editions of the CAF Champions League and Confederation Cup coupled with the Leopards' poor performances in their 2019 Cup of Nations, 2020 CHAN, and 2022 World Cup qualifying matches could instead signal the persistence of all the chronic systemic issues inherent in Congolese football.

Introduction

In December 2016 and January 2017, respectively, two events that could be regarded as symptomatic of the contradictions of Congolese football, at the national level, brought to light the immense challenges faced by those who remain optimistic about the future of the sport in DRC. First, on December 14, 2016, Denis Kambayi, the Minister of Sports at that time, unilaterally suspended the 2016–2017 national Super League competition. Among other reasons for his untimely decision, the Minister cited excessive violence in stadiums, lack of sporting civism and adequate fan management, and non-adherence by teams to the league's revenue-sharing policies.[1] One wonders, however, why such a decision had to be taken two days before two of the most anticipated matches of the season: AS Vita Club *versus* Daring Club Motema Pembe in Kinshasa and TP Mazembe *versus* St. Eloi Lupopo in Lubumbashi. Those skeptical of the Minister's decision expressed their suspicion about the fact that that decision had been taken on the eve of the end of what was supposed to be President Joseph Kabila's second and final term. Was this decision motivated by a justified fear of the imminent revolt against President Kabila's refusal to step down on December 19, 2016, as stipulated by the country's constitution? Was it an attempt at avoiding a repeat of the 1959 uprising against the colonial administration, revolt which started after a match played at *Stade Tata Raphael*, in Matonge, Kinshasa, in December 1959,

---

[1] For more concerning this decision, see http://www.radiookapi.net/2017/01/03/actualite/sport/reprise-de-la-division-i-la-linafoot-attend-encore-linstruction-de-la#sthash.apRcJU8z.dpuf, accessed in January 2017.

and culminated in the country gaining its political independence on June 30, 1960? Whatever the motive behind the Minister's untimely decision was, the suspension of the national league competition through a unilateral decision points to the issue of perpetual political interference in Congolese football.

Second, in January of 2017, Florent Ibenge, the coach of the national team, published the list of 24 players selected by his coaching staff for the 2017 African Cup of Nations to be held in Gabon. Striking about Ibenge's list was the fact that it only included five Africa-based players (four from TP Mazembe and one from AS Vita Club). The remaining 19 members of the squad were all based in Europe and the Middle East. Besides, no one among those 19 players based outside the continent played regularly with a top European club. The two head coaches, Christian Nsengi Biembe and Hector Cuper, who have succeeded Florent Ibenge since August 8, 2019, have faced the same selection dilemma. This team selection points to a more serious problem in Congolese, and almost all African, football: *the lack of sport development in Africa and the consequent persistent lack of competition for national team positions.* One could well label this problem the "death of Florent Ibenge's dream" of building a 1972–1974 national team type, wholly composed of DRC-based players who, for two years, dominated teams such as Morocco, Ghana, and Cameroon who often fielded proven Europe-based players in their African Cup of Nations and World Cup qualification matches.

Moreover, like several other African countries, DRC continues to suffer from the persistent brain drain of its soccer talents. Several players born in DRC as well as most of the sons of the Congolese diaspora, who have had successful careers in top European clubs and leagues, have opted to play for their parents' host countries, thus in the process, abandoning the land of their ancestors. The list of these players includes, among others, Steve Mandanda, the Loukaku brothers, Christian Benteke, Steven Nzonzi, and so on.

While these types of stories tend to capture our imagination, especially in books and journals or even news articles, millions of interesting and fascinating experiences of football players, league and team managers, fans, and so on, from all corners of the country, often go unnoticed. As a result, what is referred to as "Congolese football" tends to downplay the important role played by the sport in the lives of the so-called ordinary Congolese people. Therefore, in an attempt to rectify these types of misconceptions, let us begin this chapter with a philosophical disclaimer.

What "Congolese (DRC) Football" Means

There is a tendency to restrict the use of the phrase "Congolese football" to the achievements of a few star players, coaches, or club presidents. It is, thus, customary to encounter through news articles, books, or online chronicles, the stories of the successes and failures of, for example, the 1968 and 1974 national teams or such star players as Paul Bonga, Joseph Loukaka (of Orleans), Julian Kialunda, Kibonge Mafu "Seigneur," as correctly profiled by Ngimbi Kalumvueziko (2015), Pierre Kalala, Mukuna "Trouet," Kakoko Etepe ("Dieu du Ballon"), Muntubile ("Santos"), Ndaye Mulamba, Bwanga Tshimen, and so on. While these players and teams, who may have shaped the national and international image of the sport, deserve to be praised for their contribution to the development of the rich football tradition of the country, it would be a mistake to underestimate the value of the stories of millions of children, high-school and university students, parents, fans, and even uninterested members of society whose lives have been changed, for better or worse, by football. As Leonard Harris correctly notes,

> Valorizing historical figures is as misleading as leaving important historical figures silent. In this tradition, to deny that our decisions are normative choices is as misleading as contending that the voices we select provide a true picture of all the relevant conversations of the past. (Harris 2002, 6)

Therefore, in the ensuing section, an attempt is made to offer, as suggested by Leonard Harris above, a glimpse of the depth of Congolese football construed as a mosaic and progressive tradition.

Also, one wonders whether approaching social and cultural practices, such as football matches, from a nationalistic perspective, would have moral force, particularly if the kind of nationalism which such an approach might call for is not clearly articulated. In other words, one wonders whether it would make sense to evaluate the successes or failures of the entire Congolese nation through the experiences of a few national representatives on the African and world stages of football, especially since such a task might only be achieved through a fairly narrow set of characteristics such as successes or failures in qualifying for the World Cup, reaching the final of the FIFA Club World Cup, or winning the African Cup of Nations.

Hence, perhaps one would be better off arguing that one way to stop the current growing sentiment toward the cultivation of various forms of questionable nationalism is to promote the elevation of cosmopolitanism over patriotism through narratives which would not only de-emphasize but also downplay the value of the successes and failures of a few representatives on the African and world football stages. In so doing, one could avoid the paradox of trying to distinguish between promoting a more pluralistic understanding of the kinds of national football narratives that can be validated and legitimated and the fallacy of attempting to measure the worth of these narratives through the successes and failures of a few national representatives.

Therefore, in the ensuing section, an attempt is made to provide a sample of football narratives from the non-national representative perspective. Here, we plan to show that since any attempt to measure football successes or failures through national team performances or those of the country's representatives in the African and world club competitions is mostly implausible, in principle, Congolese football authorities and investors ought to focus their efforts into building political and socio-economic spaces which would ensure that players, from all corners of the country as well as all walks of life, have the opportunity to forge rewarding football careers within the local, regional, and national competition environments.

Moreover, it is perhaps worth pointing out that Congolese football might well be better off if it were to be judged based on the level of participation achieved by the country's general population. Since football offers a platform for the promotion of such benefits as good health, hardwork, friendship, companionship, respect for teammates and opponents, and so on, DRC football authorities and investors ought to emphasize these benefits by encouraging participation at all age levels. Those familiar with Congolese football are well cognizant of the fact that, unlike several other African countries, stadium spectatorship, for example, especially in major cities such as Kinshasa, Lubumbashi, Kisangani, Mbuji-Mayi, Kananga, and Bukavu, has grown exponentially as the populations of these cities have expanded exponentially over the past few years. On the other hand, the lack of physical exercise facilities or even the sheer absence of empty lots which could, on occasions, be turned into playing spaces continues to hamper participation and physical health activities. Therefore, the promotion of participation through the development of playing fields might, for instance, help address the issues created by, as Peter Alegi correctly points out, "the shared patriarchal assumptions of European and African cultures [which have so far] curtailed sporting opportunities for

African women" (Alegi 2010, 4). Here, the Kabila government's plan to build municipal stadiums across the country seems to be an encouraging starting point.[2]

THE CONGOLESE LIVED FOOTBALL EXPERIENCES[3]

In DRC, football means different things to different individuals and communities. Generally, it has brought happiness to some members of society and sadness to others, wealth to some and poverty to others, temporary mental exhilaration to some and mental anguish to others, peace to some communities, and division to others. Let us imagine a child born and raised in Tsinga-Ngedi, a village in the District of Tsanga-Sud, Bas-Congo, in the late 1960s. The football experience of such a child could be a testament to the healing and educational power of football as well as to its misuse. His first encounter with the beautiful game came to him through the colorful narratives offered by the voices behind the microphones. The national radio was, then, the only window into his magical world of characters who could run faster than Cheetahs, leave their opponents dead on the ground by one simple dribble or fake, score from impossible angles, and so on. The little boy sometimes thought of himself as capable of replicating every move that the charming voices of such sports reporters as Paul Basunga Nzinga, Lucien Tshimpumpu wa Tshimpumpua, and Kabulo Mwana Kabulo (in French), Mosete Mbombo (in Lingala), and Wanani Wanesinda (in Kikongo) had described in their most vivid and colorful language.[4] Hence, he would spend countless hours, on dusty and muddy roads as well as rough and uneven grass-like fields, practicing his craft which he was convinced matched the brilliance of his imaginary characters. As a result, in elementary school, at the Catholic Boarding school in Khesa, Vaku, he attained "fame" under the nickname "Diantela," named after a midfield player from his favorite childhood team: AS Vita Club of Kinshasa. As those with similar experiences could attest, football

---

[2] In the past few years, several municipal stadiums have been built.
[3] See, for example, photos of Demata's students posted by Didem Tali of Al Jazeera in "The healing powers of football in the DRC: Against the backdrop of a brutal civil war, millions of Congolese turn to football to cope with the conflict," published at https://www.aljazeera.com/gallery/2017/2/14/the-healing-powers-of-football-in-the-drc/, retrieved December 20, 2019.
[4] See, for example, the article entitled "Un dimanche de foot a la radio," published by Messager on June 9, 2011, at www.Mbokamosika.com, accessed on March 28, 2017.

playtime became almost the only moment of relaxation and recreation after the grueling daily schedule of the Belgian missionary Catholic education of the time. There were times when the young boy even thought of himself as a "Vclubien," that is, a supporter of AS Vita Club by birth. Such is the experience, and it is a Congolese football experience, of millions of elementary school children who, for example, live in small villages across the countries or even refugee camps spread across East DRC.[5]

Likewise, let us imagine that, some years later, now in middle school at the Catholic Boarding School in Mbata-Siala, located in what some people would characterize as the "middle of nowhere," our young boy had to rely on football for relaxation, recreation, and stressbusting. Having become a goalkeeper, here, he gained "fame" under the nickname "Balonga Bekao," once again named after the goalkeeper of his beloved AS Vita Club. For such a boy and his schoolmates, an afternoon without football almost amounted to the torture inflicted on them by the school administrators. In fact, as middle school students, those young boys were not only required to complete a very rigorous class curriculum, but they were also tasked with helping raise their new classroom building from the foundation up. Among others, their duties included carrying heavy loads of bricks, sand, and cement. Therefore, after hours of extremely demanding curricular and extra-curricular tasks, football time was almost a blessing from the sky. Without football, one could argue, some of those young students could have gone insane. This experience of football as a saving grace has always been an integral part of the Congolese football experience. Here, one could safely claim that those boys' middle school experience might well be consistent with what, for instance, Peter Alegi (2010, 4) has referred to as "the Catholic rendition of muscular Christianity, encapsulated by the Latin phrase *mens sana in corpore sano* (a healthy mind in a healthy body), [which] found a receptive audience among the Belgian [colonial and post-colonial] authorities" and missionaries.

The Congolese football experience appears to be even more complex in the country's major cities. In Kinshasa, for example, as one of the world's football-crazy cities, passion for football often runs wild concerning participation in recreational football as well as spectatorship at the two major

---

[5] See, for illustration, photos included in the article titled "Football fuels friendships in the DRC," published at www.FIFA.com on May 17, 2019, at https://www.fifa.com/who-we-are/news/fri-175-pending-fifa-foundation-piece-cjp-congo-dr-3025293, retrieved on December 20, 2019.

stadiums: *Stade des Martyrs* and *Stade Tata Raphael*. Likewise, in the afternoons and early evenings on weekdays as well as all day long on weekends, the streets of the city often turn into football pitches despite all the inconvenience imposed by these players on drivers and neighbors longing for quietude. From the sandy and dusty walkways of Lemba-Foire to the greenish football fields of the *Institut de la Gombe* (formerly Athénée de la Gombe), children and youth of all ages compete for every inch of space available on streets, back alleys, or school sports fields. The friendships and companionships which often arise out of these structured or unstructured activities have been shown to endure beyond all the challenges brought about, on occasions, by unnecessarily fierce competition. As a matter of fact, several players or even spectators who often took part in those sporting events still bear some residues of the scars borne out of some misconceptions of these street football competitions, which often resulted in broken lips, red eyes, and insult exchanges. However, the players, oftentimes, quickly made peace and were back on the pitch only hours after these types of incidents had occurred. Such was and continues to be the healing power of Congolese football. These are, indeed, Congolese football experiences that, unfortunately, often go unnoticed by the media and sport theorists across the country.

Here, once again, let us imagine a high-school student nicknamed "Technician" or "Lunangu Pélé" who lived and played football in Kinshasa-Livulu, Lemba-Foire, or Limete in the 1970s. Such a young man would face head-on several contradictions typical of Congolese football. Blessed with natural talents, he would have the fortune of being featured as a guest player in several youth teams at multiple youth tournaments across the city. For example, with FC Lisano, an elite youth club based in Kinshasa-Limete, he would witness, from the pitch, the passion of Congolese fans, as his team had been invited to open for two of the most anticipated matches of the mid-1970s at the city main stadium, *Stade Tata Rapheal*, later renamed Stade du 20 Mai by the Mobutu regime. On those occasions, those matches would bring together, on the one hand, two African Cup Champions winners, AS Vita Club and Haffia Conakry, and, on the other hand, the derby of Kinshasa between FC Imana (currently Daring Club Motema Pembe) and FC Dragons (also once renamed FC Bilima). Because those types of matches often featured some of the most celebrated African footballers of the time such as Kibonge "Seigneur Gento," Mayanga Maku "Good Year," Kakoko Etepe "Dieu," Kidumu "Raoul," Ndaye Mulamba, Libilo Boba, Petit Sory, Chérif Souleymane,

"Le Roi" Mokili Saio, and so on, our young player, like most of the Congolese elite young players at that time, would dream of the day he would be entrusted with the responsibility of representing those elite teams in the Congolese or African elite competitions. Such a dream, however, would turn out mostly to be unattainable or even undesirable. Indeed, in the 1970s, most aspiring young players were often discouraged by their parents in their attempt to pursue a career that would, ultimately, have led them to a life of poverty and total dependence on remittances. In fact, despite all their fame, the absence of a professional career path framework in DRC football almost guaranteed that most of the Congolese star players in the 1970s would be left to survive on donations and remittances from club managers, relatives, and politicians.[6] Therefore, the lack of genuine prospects for a better life through football leads most aspiring elite young players to either choose school over football or simply emigrate to Europe or the Middle East despite all the challenges that such a decision would have entailed.[7]

Congolese football has also been instrumental in shaping the destiny of Congolese higher education institutions. For example, in the early 1980s, one could argue that football, perhaps alongside two other equally powerful Congolese institutions, school and music, may have been responsible for keeping the fragile peace and unity forged by President Mobutu's dictatorship on most college and university campuses. To appease the tense political environments of these campuses, higher education administrators had to rely heavily on football. For example, on the campus of the University of Lubumbashi, students were provided with the opportunity to participate in both recreational and competitive football matches. As we indicated above, because many elite young players often chose school over

[6] The most rewarding remittances some Congolese star players may have received for decades came under what was then referred to as "don presidential" (presidential gift).
[7] See, for example, among others, Carl-Gustaf Scott (2015), John Bale (2004), Nlandu (2017, 15), Paul Dietschy (2006), Richard Elliott and John Harris (2014), Richard Giulianotti and Roland Robertson (2009), and Peter Alegi (2010). As Peter Alegi puts it: "The increasing visibility of African players, however, could not mask discrimination against them. Racism in France manifested itself in different ways. For example, wage inequities long affected Africans, especially in the first years of their careers. At stadiums across European fans sometimes heaped racial insults on black players, waving bananas and making monkey sounds—a practice that is still far too common today" (p. 84). In addition, see the article entitled "Foot-Belgique: Matumona Zola dénigré par le président de son club http://www. radiookapi.net/sport/2007/11/01/foot-belgique-matumona-zola-denigre-par-le-president-de-son-club/#sthash.8otdqEjl.dpuf".

the uncertainty of a football career, most higher education competitions often brought together elite players worthy of a national league or national team selection. Hence, at the University of Lubumbashi, for instance, four layers of football competition sought to excite and entertain players and supporters on campus and across the city and Katanga Province during each academic year. First, students could compete in the Residence Halls Cup. Here, team selection was restricted to demonstrated residence hall membership. Second, students had the option of playing with their college or school of registration in the University Cup. In that competition, the Faculty of Natural Sciences, Faculty of Letters, Faculty of Social Sciences, and so on competed against each other, sometimes, in front of thousands of supporters at the *Stade de la Victoire*. Third, the province Governor organized the Higher Education Cup in which various colleges fought mostly for pride and bragging rights. Finally, for the elite players who wished to compete at the highest level of competition in the city but were unable or chose not to join the other elite teams which competed in the *Association de Football de Lubumbashi* (AFLU), which featured such giants of Congolese football as TP Mazembe, St. Eloi Lupopo, and Lubumbshi Sport, the league provided the students with the option of registering a team, under the name FC Kassapards, in either the first or the second division.

Imagine a student who competed under the nickname "Rumm," at each one of those four layers of college football. Besides, he also competed in the AFLU second division with FC SNEL (Société National d'Electricité) and first division with FC Salongo (formerly National Police). Later, after retiring from competitive football, he regularly took part in the Sunday morning adult "friendly" matches, which often preceded a trip to Stade Mobutu Sese Seko for the weekly featured national team or league match. Such a student or university graduate could competently attest to the invaluable health and social benefits as well as, on occasions, the foolishness associated with Congolese football.[8] Amidst growing political tensions which, sometimes, lead to violent on and off-campus battles fought along tribal or regional lines, football often offered an oasis of sanity and respect for human dignity far beyond the reach of almost all the other Congolese institutions (police, army, government, religions, etc.) except for perhaps Congolese Music.

---

[8] The writer of this chapter had both the privilege and misfortune of experiencing Congolese football up close at several levels.

On another plane of Congolese football, spectatorship at stadiums has often generated contradictions. Every major Congolese city has its valued derbies, which, on occasions, have not only brought about joy and excitement to those present at these stadiums but also loss of spectators' lives and the destruction of neighborhoods. In Kinshasa, for example, while no serious sports fan would wish to endure the agony of going through an entire football season without the game between AS Vita Club and Daring Club Motema Pembe (DCMP), this *derby de la Capitale* has always carried with it the potential for loss of life and destruction of either neighboring properties or those belonging to game officials, players, and leagues administrators. Likewise, over the years, the games between TP Mazembe and St Eloi Lupopo, in Lubumbashi, and SM Sanga Balende and AS Bantoue, in Mbuji-Mayi, or those which have pitted these big clubs against each other in the national Super League, have presented the same potential for violence.[9]

For example, on Monday, June 26, 2017, FC Renaissance, a rising club in the DRC Super League at the time, was relegated to the lower division due to its failure to control its coaching staff and fans after the team lost to AS Vita Club by 2-1 following a 90th-minute goal. The club president, coaching staff, and fans were guilty of field invasion which led to a battle between them and the city police. Because of the immense pressure felt by the game officials during most games of the DRC Super League, several Congolese referees, for example, are forced to make incorrect decisions which often lead to their being either suspended or simply banned by the DRC Football Association.

In conclusion, one could argue that, over the decades, Congolese football has, for the most part, successfully played its role as a platform for recreation, relaxation, entertainment, and peacebuilding. Although it still lags far behind many other nations in terms of infrastructure and organization designed primarily for participation, one could argue that it has delivered so far more social goods than almost all the other Congolese institutions, formal or informal.

---

[9] See, for example, the article entitled "DR Congo halts football over fears of political violence," published on December 15, 2016, at http://www.bbc.com/sport/football/38316676, accessed on March 28, 2017; also, "Division I: 15 morts après la rencontre V.club-Mazembe," published at www.radiookapi.net/sport/2014/05/11/division-15-morts-21-blesses-apres-la-rencontre-vclub-mazembe-officiel#sthash.yM9WJuWc.dpuf.

Congolese Football at the Elite Club and National Team Level

The DRC could be regarded as the epitome of the highs and lows of African soccer. It appears that no other country in Africa has lost so much of its resources, both human and natural, to other nations and gained so little from the global community due to political instability, economic mismanagement, and philosophical alienation of its people. One could point to the constant disappointing performances of the national team in the African Cup of Nations and FIFA World Cup competitions as evidence of these shortcomings. These underperformances appear to point to a much deeper challenge involving the crippling dilemma created by the national team coaches' overreliance on professional players based outside Africa. Since the rise of this phenomenon in the late 1970s, many sport theorists have cast doubt about the commitment of national players whose lucrative club contracts appear to be inconsistent with the demanding schedules of CAF and FIFA competitions. Also, political interference in the operations and management of the national team affairs, as well as those of the national and local leagues, continues to prove to be a challenge for success on the pitch. This section seeks to explore some social, political, economic, and cultural complexities of football in the DRC and the pivotal role played by both the public and the private sectors which tend to either enhance or paralyze the beautiful game in this football-crazy country.

Several historians of African football such as Peter Alegi (2010), Laurent Dubois (2010), David Goldblatt (2006) as well as several other scholars from a variety of academic disciplines (see, e.g., Armstrong and Giulianotti 2004) have offered credible accounts of the origins of African football. According to Peter Alegi, in DRC, "a whites-only *Ligue de Football du Katanga* began in May 1911 in the copper-mining town of Elisabethville (today Lubumbashi)" (Alegi 2010, 3). In Leopoldville (today Kinshasa), *La Fédération du Football Association du Pool* was established in 1912.

These scholars of the history of African football have also documented how, in the 1920s, football became an integral part of the physical education curriculum of schools established by European missionaries. Throughout the continent, soccer clubs founded mostly by missionaries, colonial administrators, and the emerging African elites blossomed, culminating in the establishment of some of the current big African clubs. This is also the case for Congolese football. Clubs such as Tout Puissant Mazembe (formerly known as Tout Puissant Englebert) and Association

Sportive Vita Club, Daring Club Motema Pembe (DCMP, formerly FC Imana), and so on, which have dominated Congolese football over the years, can be traced back to colonial Africa. From the 1920s to the late 1950s, Congolese football grew in stature as these big clubs slowly developed their unique playing styles.[10] For better or worse, some of these big clubs incorporated some elements of the African traditional games and rituals in their pre-game and game routines. While some teams opted for entertaining and showboating styles which led to the development and worshipping of a few star players (e.g., in the cases of AS Vita Club and DC Motema Pembe), others became well known for their direct playing styles designed for cohesive and efficient teamwork (e.g., TP Mazembe). Among the rituals of traditional societies which were conserved by most teams and which remain a hindrance to the development of football in DRC, and several other African countries, is *fétichisme*, the belief that one could defeat his or her opponents through recourse to some alleged spiritual, not physical, abilities.[11] As Peter Alegi (2010) correctly notes, "the incorporation of magicians and healers, the rise of different playing styles, the performance of various rituals of spectatorship revealed that football was taking on distinctive indigenous characteristics" (15).

Moreover, after gaining its political independence in 1960, following a bloody revolt against the Belgian colonial administration, new challenges emerged. Several social and political leaders sought to take advantage of the unifying power of football to reshape the new realities created by colonialization and ethnic disunity. While political divisions grew wider, in the years which preceded and followed political independence, football had the potential to serve as a platform for political unification and reconciliation. Unfortunately, as Alegi (2010) accurately points out, Congolese football, like most of African football, continues to be organized along the lines of class and "ethnic divisions" as well as "social cleavages" inherited from colonial times (62–63).

In 1963, having become a member of the Confederation of African Football (CAF), which had been established in 1957 as a forum for

---

[10] For the history of TP Mazembe, founded in 1939, see www.TPmazembe.com; for AS Vita Club, founded in 1935, see www.banavea.com. For the role played by the Belgian Catholic missionary Raphael de la Kethulle (1890–1956) in Kinshasa (formerly Leopoldville) and Father Gregoire Coussement in Lubumbshi (formerly Elisabethville) in the history of Congolese football, see, for example, Peter Alegi (2010, 23).

[11] During the 2016–2017 national league competition, several teams and players were fined for *pratiques fétichistes*.

pan-Africanism and African unity, the newly independent DRC joined other African nations which increasingly sought to distance themselves from their colonial powers. As a result, like those from other nations caught in the "revolutionary" mood of the time, in the late 1960s and early 1970s, DRC political leaders adopted nationalistic and ideologist policies which turned out to be incompatible with the development of football at the world elite level. Among other things, they nationalized most of the football infrastructures and leagues because they argued, privatization, within the capitalistic framework, amounted to a denial of the social good.[12]

As Paul Dietschy remarks in his section entitled "Football according to Mobutu" (87–88), after witnessing the humiliating defeat of his national team against the Black Stars of Ghana by a 3-0 score during a friendly match played in January 1966, in which the Ghanaian players engaged in unnecessary showboating, President Mobutu opted to turn the national team into a prestige fighting unit. Placing the national team under the jurisdiction of the Ministry of Sports and Youth, he ordered the return of all Congolese players stationed in Europe, especially, Belgium. Dispatching representatives to Eastern Europe to recruit "competent" coaches, President Mobutu's policy shift culminated in the Simba's victory over the Black Stars of Ghana (1-0) in the final of the 1968 African Cup of Nations held in Ethiopia. Convinced that his decision to turn the national team into a political tool had been vindicated, President Mobutu brought even more radical reforms by nationalizing, in what became to be known as *Zairianization*, all the football infrastructures and institutions alongside all the major economic and political institutions of the country in 1973.

Thus, among other decisions taken under the guise of the "*Recourse to Authenticity*," the names of the country, currency, and river Congo were changed to Zaire. In football, the national team, formerly known as the Simba (Lions), became the Leopards. The national anthem and flag were redesigned. The two major stadiums in Kinshasa were renamed from *Stade Tata Raphael* (named after the Belgian missionary who built it) to *Stade du 20 Mai* (date of the inauguration of Mobutu's political party, the *Movement Populaire de la Révolution* [MPR]) and Stade Reine-Astrid to *Stade du 24 Novembre* (date of Mobutu's coup d'état in 1965); in

---

[12] See, for example, Peter Alegi (2010), pp. 55–56, for an extended list of sport infrastructures renamed after the dates and names deemed historical by the post-colonial African governments.

Lubumbashi (formerly Elisabethville), the stadium was named after Mobutu himself. Likewise, all the teams with names from pre-colonial times were ordered to find "authentic" African ones. Thus, for example, TP Englebert, FC Dragons, FC Himalaya, and FC St Eloi became, respectively, TP Mazembe, FC Bilima, FC Ruwenzori, and FC Lupopo. As one could predict, after the overthrow of the Mobutu regime, all the stadiums' original names were promptly restored or changed to reflect the Kabila government's view of political independence. In Kinshasa, for example, the *Stade du 20 Mai* regained its original name (*Stade Tata Raphael*), *Stade du 24 Novembre* was named *Stade Cardinal Malula* in honor of the reconciliatory role the Cardinal played in the years of the transition from President Mobutu to President Laurent D. Kabila. In Lubumbashi, *Stade Mobutu Sese Seko* is currently referred to as *Stade Kibassa Maliba*, named after a longtime political leader of the Katanga province.

The catastrophic economic consequences caused by the *Zairianisation* remain so far inestimable. However, one would be foolish to deny the impact of such nationalistic policies on long-term foreign investors. DRC which, alongside many other nations, adopted such disastrous "revolutionary" policies, continues to struggle in the attempt to restore trust and confidence among global investors.

The Glorious Years of Congolese Football

It is well documented that DRC dominated African club and national team football from 1967 to 1974 as TP Mazembe (in 1967 and 1970) and AS Vita Club (in 1973) won the Champions Cup and the national team the African Cup of Nations in 1968 and 1974. TP Mazembe also finished as runner-up in the Champions Cup in 1968 and 1969 as the team reached the final in four successive years. However, the unprecedented mass exodus of players toward Europe and the Middle East which began in the mid-1970s may have led to the persistent weakening of local and national leagues to the point where, today, national team selection has become barely competitive. Perhaps the resurgence of Congolese club soccer in recent years which appears to coincide with the development of a very competitive national league could be a positive step in the right direction.

Despite its dominance of African club and national team football in the late 1960s and early 1970s, DRC has also become infamous due to its poor performances at the 1974 World Cup in Germany. Some football scholars such as Simon Kuper (2006) and Paul Dietschy (2006; 2013) have construed this event as a turning point in African football.[13] In fact, following Morocco who had represented the continent in Mexico in 1970, DRC (formerly known as Zaire) failed to win a single match in Germany in 1974, losing its three group games while conceding 14 goals and scoring none in the process. Many football critics have wondered whether these underperformances could be blamed on the amateur or semi-professional status of the Congolese players who had to compete against European and South American teams which fielded some of the most talented and experienced professional players of the time. One could also raise interesting questions concerning the players' compensation demands which preceded their second and third group games. Could these team underperformances perhaps be attributed to low morale among the players and coaches? Could they be simply the result of poor preparation? Could they have been caused by political interference or unrealistic expectations? While the answers to these questions are, definitely, complicated, it appears that the Zairean FA opted, instead, to promote the exodus of their best talents toward Europe and the Middle East. As a result, since 1976, the Congolese national coaches have mostly selected European and Middle East-based players for continental and world competitions. Was this the right move? Could Congolese football have been better off if the sports authorities had instead invested heavily in local football development?

One would be hard-pressed to deny the fact that, for two years, between 1973 and 1974, DRC (Zaire) dominated every major African competition while fielding only DRC-based players. AS Vita Club of Kinshasa won the club champions' title after defeating Asante Kotoko of Kumasi, Ghana, in the final (2-4 and 3-0). The national team, newly named *The Leopards*, after President Mobutu's legendary hat and cane, and under the guise of the politics of recourse to authenticity, won the African Cup of Nations held in Egypt. They also qualified for Germany in 1974 after eliminating, in the final round, Morocco, which had represented Africa with minimal

---

[13] We regard the Zaire (DRC) experiment of 1973–1974 as a turning point in African soccer. As a matter of fact, the decision to only select DRC-based amateur players was prompted by the performances of its Europe-based professional players during the 1972 African Cup of Nations held in Cameroon. DRC lost to Mali (3-4) in the semifinals after some sloppy defending by its central defenders led by Julian Kialunda of Anderlecht of Belgium. As stated in the paper, the experiment succeeded up until the country poorly performed at Germany 1974. An unprecedented mass exodus of African players toward Europe and the Middle East ensued.

success at Mexico 1970. Relying upon a foundation provided by three of the major clubs in the country, the Congolese national team epitomized the type of cohesive unit necessary for teams competing at the highest levels of African and world soccer competitions.[14] Here, one wonders about the country's failure to replicate such a successful model. Could it, realistically, be replicated in the face of the shift in attitude, from fame for the sake of it to a fortune-first mentality, within the world of elite football, which appears to have occurred over the last four decades? Here, one could characterize the Leopards of those glorious years as firm believers in untainted fame, pride, loyalty, and patriotism at a time when they could have easily sought political asylum anywhere across Europe. Here, one could also argue that, perhaps, those players may have been either naïve or simply ignorant of the social and economic value of their soccer talents. Scholars such as Paul Dietschy (2013) and David Goldblatt (2006) have attributed those Leopards' willingness to stay at home to President Mobutu's intimidation tactics.[15] Notwithstanding their naivety, ignorance, and/or fear of political persecution, however, the Leopards of the late 1960s and early 1970s might deserve praise and recognition for their willingness to embrace the love of the beautiful game as well as the need to foster the internal goods of football over the fortunes they might have obtained through political asylum across Europe. As Nlandu (2017) has suggested, DRC football might be much more competitive on the African and world stages if the country could provide its young talents a path to a football professional career within their natural environments as well as attract the sons and daughters of its diaspora spread across the world. As Nlandu puts it:

> For the sake of argument, let us, for example, envision the prospects of a World Cup Congolese national team featuring, among others, the likes of

---

[14] In the first team, four defenders, including the goalkeeper, came from TP Mazembe, four from AS Vita Club, and three from CS Imana (today's Daring Cub Motema Pembe). As a result, Zaire played as a team, that is, a cohesive unit.

[15] See, for example, Steve Charnock's "The Dark Story of Zaire's 9-Nil Defeat In The 1974 World Cup," published at https://www.history.co.uk/article/the-dark-story-of-zaires-9-nil-defeat-in-the-1974-world-cup, retrieved on December 8, 2020, and Simon Lillicrap's "Exposing The Myth: Why Zaire's Infamous 1974 World Cup Free-Kick Was Far From Comical," published at https://www.thesportsman.com/articles/exposing-the-myth-why-zaire-s-infamous-1974-world-cup-free-kick-was-far-from-comical on June 9, 2019, retrieved on December 8, 2020.

Vincent Kompany, Christian Benteke, Romelu Loukaka, Rio Mavuba, Eliaquim Mangala, Michy Batshuayi, Jason Denayer, Christian Kabasele, Jordan Lukaku, Steve Mandanda alongside Yannick Bolasie, Chancel Mbemba, Serge Bakambu, and their current teammates. In addition, let us imagine the existence of a viable Congolese professional league, which could attract not only the sons of the African diaspora but also some of the best talents from around the world. If these two conditions could obtain, then one might be justified in expecting, at least, a decent quarter-final or even semi-final appearance for such a highly talented team. (Nlandu 2017, 9)

Several questions arise here about Africa's inability to appeal to the sons and daughters of her European diaspora despite the reality that most of them struggle to attain genuine native status in their parents' adoptive countries. In our next section, let us briefly highlight some social contributions made by some of the prominent Congolese players of the national team.

"Football Celebrities and Charity Nexus"

Unlike the well-known social contributions of their basketball compatriots such as Dikembe Mutombo, Bismarck Biyombo, and Serge Ibaka, who have been lucky to play in the NBA (the American National Basketball Association) for huge contracts, Congolese footballers' charitable work remains modest but significant. For example, the Cédric Bakambu Foundation, launched by the former Sochaux (France) and Villareal's (Spain) striker on December 12, 2019, has provided invaluable services aimed at the professional development of young people with the following five specific goals in mind, "namely youth literacy, basic education with the provision of modern educational tools, the promotion of the history of the Democratic Republic of Congo which will allow the rehabilitation of certain historic sites in the country, the promotion of new technologies by providing the beneficiaries with computer tools for learning, and sport with the endowment of sports equipment to youth clubs, as well as training sports supervisors in DRC."[16] In addition, the Foundation has also

---

[16] See Rodolph Tomegah's "RD Congo: Cédric Bakambu Lance Sa Fondation," published on December 14, 2019, at https://www.africatopsports.com/2019/12/14/rd-congo-cedric-bakambu-lance-sa-fondation/, accessed on March 25, 2021.

provided food baskets and school kits to orphanages and areas of Kinshasa where the most vulnerable live.[17]

Another charitable effort worth mentioning is the creation, on June 25, 2020, of the Leopards Foundation under the leadership of their captain Youssouf Mulumbu (former West Bromwich Albion and PSG midfielder) and Marcel Tisserand (Wolfsburg defender). As Taiye Taiwo reported on June 27, 2020, "Faced with the coronavirus pandemic and the resulting food crisis, the Leopards Foundation mobilizes and supports the most disadvantaged population, by directing its first actions aimed at people living with disabilities."[18] In light of the success enjoyed by hundreds of Congolese footballers over the past decades, one wishes there were more substantial charitable efforts of this kind across the DRC.

Concluding Remarks: The Future of Congolese Football

Since Congolese football, one could argue, has achieved most of its success at the local level, that is, in small and large villages, city streets and schools, military barracks, college and university campuses, and so on, a substantial investment which emphasizes participation over elite competition might yield a better aggregate of health and social benefits for all community members. Substantial investment in football infrastructure, if paired with proper educational campaigns about the invaluable health and social benefits of the beautiful game, might perhaps, someday, bring together community members of all ages and from all walks of life. Currently, the few available playing fields are often occupied by young boys and men, and, occasionally on Sunday mornings, by the old generations of men who competed, once upon a time, at some levels of Congolese football. This means that so far, for example, women and other

---

[17] See Alexis Billebault's "L'international de foot Cédric Bakambu vient en aide aux démunis de Kinshasa: Le monde du ballon rond africain multiplie les initiatives de solidarité depuis le début de l'épidémie de Covid-19," published on April 23, 2020, at https://www.lemonde.fr/afrique/article/2020/04/23/l-international-de-foot-cedric-bakambu-vient-en-aide-aux-demunis-de-kinshasa_6037536_3212.html, accessed on March 25, 2021.

[18] See Taiye Taiwo's "Coronavirus: DR Congo players launch Leopards Foundation to help compatriots," published at https://www.goal.com/en-us/news/coronavirus-dr-congo-players-launch-leopards-foundation-to/1avim9kw1c5l71ddhze38zmw2y, accessed on March 25, 2021.

marginalized members of society, such as the physically disabled, have been almost left out of the Congolese football experiences discussed in the chapter.[19]

Notwithstanding the impact of COVID-19 on world football, in general, and Congolese football, in particular, the premature eliminations of TP Mazembe, Maniema Union, and AS Vita Club from the 2021–2022 editions of the CAF Champions League and Confederation Cup coupled with the Leopards' poor performances in their 2019 Cup of Nations, 2020 CHAN, and 2022 World Cup qualifying matches, one could argue that at the elite club and national team levels, Congolese football has exhibited discernable signs of a return to African prominence in the last years. In fact, TP Mazembe has won three Champions League titles (2009, 2010, and 2015), two Confederation Cup titles (2016 and 2017), as well as three Super Cup titles (2010, 2011, and 2016). The team also finished as runners-up in the 2013 Confederation Cup. Also, AS Vita Club finished as runner-up in the Champions League in 2014 and the Confederation Cup in 2018, whereas the Africa-based national team players have won two African Nations Championship (CHAN) titles (in 2009 and 2016). Moreover, after winning the African Champions League title in 2010, TP Mazembe represented the continent with honors at the FIFA Club World Cup. The team reached the final of the competition held in Japan after eliminating the CONCACAF (Confederation of North, Central American, and Caribbean Association Football) and CONMEBOL (South American Football Confederation) Champions. Although the team lost the final game to the European Champions League winner (Internazionale of Milan), it is worth noting here that TP Mazembe became the first team outside Europe and South America to challenge the supremacy of the European and South American teams in this competition.[20] Here, one wonders whether the success achieved by TP Mazembe, AS Vita Club, and the Africa-based national team could be sustained without substantial

---

[19] As a matter of fact, the women's national team has just been disqualified from the 2022 CAN qualification tournament because they failed to travel to Malabo, Equatorial Guinea, for a match scheduled to take place on Wednesday, October 20, 2021.

[20] In 2006, Al Ahly of Egypt defeated Club America (2-1) to finish in third place and, in 2007, Etoile du Sahel of Tunisia finished in fourth place after a 2-2 draw (4-2 on penalties) against Urawa Red Diamonds, the AFC representative. So far no AFC, CONCACAF, or OFC (Oceania Football Confederation) teams have reached the final of the tournament. One could argue, here, that this success story could be a testament to the enormous untapped potential of the African clubs.

investment from global football investors. One also wonders whether DRC could succeed in retaining its young prospects, attract the sons and daughters of its diaspora as well as any interested world stars without substantial private investment which has often been threatened by "revolutionary," nationalistic policies of every new government. As we discussed earlier, such investment does require trust and confidence in the political system. Therefore, the Congolese government might well begin to sow the seeds for such a much-needed trustworthy political system.

Overall, in this chapter, we have argued that, if properly understood as a platform for the display of various Congolese experiences, "Congolese football" has for the most part been quite successful since its inception. This claim is supported throughout the chapter by the wide range of Congolese football experiences one can encounter at grassroots, schools, club, and national team levels. We have, therefore, argued that Congolese football could be even more successful if the Congolese government and sports administrators could work harder to expand the football pie to include the experiences of all members of society.

REFERENCES

Alegi, Peter. 2010. *African Soccerscapes: How a Continent Changed the World's Game* (Ohio Africa in World History). Athens: Ohio University Press.
Armstrong, Gary & Giulianotti, Richard. 2004. *Football in Africa: Conflict, Conciliation, and Community*. New York, NY: Palgrave Macmillan.
Bale, John. 2004. "Three Geographies of African Footballer Migration: Patterns, Problems and Postcoloniality. In Gary Armstrong & Richard Giulianotti. 2004. *Football in Africa: Conflict, Conciliation, and Community*. New York, NY: Palgrave Macmillan.
Dietschy, Paul. 2006. "Football Players' Migration: A Political Stake." *Historical Social Research*, 31(1), 31–41.
Dietschy, Paul. 2013. "Football Imagery and Colonial Legacy: Zaire's Disastrous Campaign During the 1974 World Cup," in Susann Baller et al. 2013. *Global Perspectives on Football in Africa: Visualising the Game* (Sport in the Global Society – Contemporary Perspectives). Routledge, 84–100.
Dubois, Laurent. 2010. *Soccer Empire: The World Cup and the Future of France*. Los Angeles: University of California Press.
Elliott, Richard & Harris, John (Editors). 2014. *Football and Migration: Perspectives, Places, Players* (Routledge Research in Sport, Culture, and Society). New York, NY: Routledge.

Giulianotti, Richard & Robertson, Roland. 2009. *Globalization and Football* (Published in association with Theory, Culture & Society). New York, NY: Routledge.

Goldblatt, David. 2006. *The Ball Is Round: A Global History of Soccer.* New York: Riverhead.

Harris, Leonard (Editor). 2002. *American Philosophies: An Anthology.* Malden, Massachusetts: Blackwell Publishers.

Kalumvueziko, Ngimbi. 2015. *Kibonge, le seigneur du football congolais.* Edilivre.

Kuper, Simon. 2006. *Soccer against the Enemy.* New York: Nation Books.

Nlandu, Tamba. 2017. "Some Philosophical Foundations of the Disappointing Performances of the African Soccer Teams in Word Competitions." *Sport, Ethics, and Philosophy*, Vol. 11, No. 2, 192–206.

Scott, Carl-Gustaf. 2015. *African Footballers in Sweeden: Race, Immigration, and Integration in the Age of Globalization.* Palgrave Macmillan.

CHAPTER 7

Football in Egypt: Between Joy and Politics

Hala Thabet

Football, the beautiful game, is for many supporters a source of joy and happiness and an escape from social and economic challenges. By examining the history of football since its introduction under the British occupation, the study highlights the social and political role played by football in the Egyptian history and discusses the relationship between football and social and political changes. Football managers, players, and even workers in sports media have all welcomed the intervention of political leaders in the game and used it for their own purposes. The major achievements of the Egyptian football were used to raise the spirit of national pride and to glorify the political regime. Social groups, like the Ultras, also used football to fuel opposition against the political system by leading popular demonstrations in the streets against corruption and bad governance and spreading violence, instability, and political unrest in the country.

The Egyptian national football team—the Pharaohs—was ranked ninth in the world in 2010—the highest ranking in the history of Arab teams then. It is also the first African and Arab team to play in the World Cup in 1934, in addition to be the only African Team who won the African Cup

H. Thabet (✉)
Zayed University, Abu Dhabi, United Arab Emirates
e-mail: Hala.Thabet@zu.ac.ae

© The Author(s), under exclusive license to Springer Nature Switzerland AG 2022
A. E. Ayuk (ed.), *Football (Soccer) in Africa*, Global Culture and Sport Series, https://doi.org/10.1007/978-3-030-94866-5_7

147

of Nations for football for seven times, including three consecutive times, and reaching the third place three times. The Egyptian Football Federation was the first Arab and African federation to join the International Football Federation in 1923. And the Alexandria Stadium, built in 1929, is the oldest Arab and African stadium.

Football is considered the most popular game in Egypt, with a popular presence among different age groups, whether children, youth, or elders. It was for many supporters an escape from their real life for 90 minutes, to watch, support, and enjoy the achievements without constraints.

Nevertheless, football in Egypt, as other places in the world, is not just a beautiful game to spread joy and happiness among the people; the relationship between football and politics has always been very close. Political leaders have long used football as a tool to achieve many social and political objectives, to indoctrinate values, to provide role models for the youth, and to maintain social control and contain people's discontent. Football was also used as a tool for political propaganda and to maintain the legitimacy of the ruling system. It was also used by social movements to oppose the political system by spreading violence, instability, and political unrest in the country while also achieving some personal, social, and economic goals.

To examine this relationship, the chapter traces football's history in Egypt since its first introduction under the British occupation. It aims to see how it was perceived as a symbol for national achievement, national pride, and to raise the regime's popularity from the one side and as a tool to oppose the political regime from the other side.

Football and Nationalism

Football was introduced in Egypt in 1882 under the British occupation (1882–1922). It all started in the city of Alexandria. And while Tennis and Polo were the favorite games for British officers and the upper class, football was the popular game for soldiers and the lower class.[1] By building the soldiers' physical capacity through recreation and fun, the British Empire was able to spread its dominance throughout various regions of the world.[2]

---

[1] J.A. Mangan, "Cultural Hegemony and the Institutionalization of British Games", a paper presented at the University of Alberta, Class Edmonton, March 1983.
[2] Colin Veitch, "Play up! Play up! And win the War: The Nation and the First World War 1914–15", Journal of Contemporary History, Vol 20, No. 3, July 1985, p. 366.

Egypt no exception. Soldiers spread the love of the game among young Egyptians who gathered to watch the game for the first time in what is now known as the Alexandria Stadium. From Alexandria, it moved to the streets of Cairo and the Suez Canal cities (where the British forces resided).[3] The spread of the game to the rest of the country came as a result to the official recognition of the game in 1892, when the Egyptian Minister of Education, Mohamed Zaki, introduced sports, including football, in schools. Soon, school teams were formed, and school competitions were organized and held in the backyard of the ministry of finance. However, game rules were not yet developed, and it was left to each school to set its rules depending on the playground available, the type of the goal (wooden, brick, or stone), and the referee.[4]

The introduction of the game in schools had many social and political effects. Although the game remained more popular among the poor who played to gain authority and achieve social prestige, it reached the upper class who afforded to send their children to schools. The sense of belonging to the "team" surpassed any social differences.[5] This also marked the first political use of the game in the country. Zaki used the game to resist foreign dominance over Egyptian sports under the British occupation and to forge a sense of national belonging by forming a national sports federation to represent Egypt in international arenas. Slowly, the game reached state's employees with the government's official permission, such as the Railway club "Al-Sekka Al-Hadid", the oldest sporting club and the first to possess a football field in Egypt, although admitted Egyptians in 1913 after 10 years of its establishment by British and Italian railway engineers. Also, in 1905, the Olympic Club, or the "Red Star" then, was established in Alexandria and admitted workers from the Customs Authority of Alexandria. The admission of Egyptian players in these clubs, although few years late in some cases, accentuated their national feeling as they represented their country in official tournaments (winning the Egyptian League in 1966, Egyptian Cup in 1933, 1934, and in the African

---

[3] Christopher Ferraro, Imperialism, Cultural Identity and Football: How the empire created Egypt's National Sport, Ph.D. Thesis, St. John's University, New York, 2015, pp. 130–133.

[4] Yaser Ayoub, "History of Egyptians with Football (4): Mohamed (Effendy) Nashed" (in Arabic), 14 May 2014, accessed on 15 May 2018 at: http://www.yallakora.com/.

[5] Shaun Lopez, "Sport and Society in the Middle East: An Alternate Narrative of Middle Eastern History for the American College Classroom", Middle East Critique, Vol 18, No. 3, Autumn 2009, pp. 251–260.

Champions League, although Egypt withdrew from the tournament due to the 1967 war).[6]

The establishment of clubs also reflected the divisions between nationals and non-nationals. This is evident in the foundation of the two rival sporting clubs, Al-Ahly and Zamalek. Egyptians' memberships in sporting clubs were banned by the British occupation until Mustafa Kamel, the nationalist movement leader in the nineteenth century, established a national club for high-school students in 1905, the "Students Club" which unified students to practice sport, at the same time led the resistance against the British occupation. At first, as a tactic to avoid direct confrontation with the British administration, the club appointed Mitchell Ince, an English finance ministry official, as president. A year later, the presidency moved to nationals; Ince was replaced by Azziz Ezat, and the club in 1907 changed its name to Al-Ahli club "the National", to become the first club run by Egyptians with Egyptian members and represent Egypt in International tournaments (the Stockholm Olympics in 1912).[7] Soon, the first national team was formed by Mohamed Nashid, an administrative in the garages of the British camp, and also the team captain and coach. The aim was not to resist the British occupation, although opposing it. It was simply to show Egyptian superiority at least on the playground.[8] The team played and won its first match against the British forces in 1895. Local newspapers celebrated the "great achievement against the colonizers". This national feeling was also reflected in the Club's presidents: Saad Zaghloul, the leader of the 1919 revolution, and President Gamal Abdel-Nasser, the leader of 1952 revolution, was its honorary president.[9] On the other side, the Mixed "Al-Mukhtalat" (referring to the Mixed Courts system)[10] was founded in 1913, later after 1952 changed to

---

[6] Yasmin Yehya, "Oldest 10 clubs in Egypt" (in Arabic), El Youm El Sabe3 newspaper (the 7th day), 4 October 2016, accessed on 16 May 2018, at: https://www.youm7.com.

[7] Halim ElMouniry, Essam Badawy, Management in Sport (in Arabic), Academic Bookshop, Part 1, 1991, pp. 154–155.

[8] Hutchison, P. M., "Breaking Boundaries: Football and Colonialism in the British Empire", *Inquiries Journal/Student Pulse*, Vol 1, Issue 11, 2009, last accessed on 13 April 2018, at: www.inquiriesjournal.com/.

[9] Islam Hassan, "When the British occupation caused the birth of the Egyptian Team" (in Arabic), 28 June 2015, accessed on 15 May 2018, at: http://www.dotmsr.com/.

[10] The Mixed Courts of Egypt was an unusual legal institution, founded by the Khedive Ismail, the king of Egypt, in 1875. The Khedive appointed their judges, Egyptians and foreign. By applying a mix of Civil Law and Islamic Law, they tried commercial and civil disputes between nationals and foreigners and between foreigners of different nationalities.

Zamalek, was more open to the foreign community in Egypt, the national elite, the British administrators, and the army leaders. The club was founded in 1911 by George Merzbach, a Belgian British lawyer of Jewish descent, head of the Mixed Courts system, and the legal advisor to the Sultan Hussein Kamel. Merzbach was later followed by the club's famous player, the French Nicolas Bianchi.[11] Other clubs followed Al-Ahly and Zamalek in foundation, and in popularity such as Al-Ittihad (the United), founded in 1914 in Alexandria; Al-Masry, founded in 1920 in Port Said; Tarsana (Maritime Administration), established in 1921; and Ismaili, founded in 1926 after the independence under the name of Al Nahda Club and built by people's donations.[12]

Despite the establishment of football sporting clubs, Egyptians were still excluded from the organizational structure of football. The country's representative in the International Olympic Committee (IOC) was Greek; the members of the newly formed mixed federation of sports were expatriates living in Egypt; and the winner's medal in the national tournament had the face of Alexander the Great engraved on it. That was subject to a wide opposition by the Egyptian clubs who refused to take part in any of the Federation's activities and decided in 1916 to establish the Egyptian Federation of Sports (EFS). The EFS organized the first league between clubs and in 1921 was replaced by the Egyptian Football Association (EFA) as the structured organization for the game. In 1922, after Egypt's independence from British occupation, the championship became national. The EFA set the guidelines for the foundation of Egyptian football clubs and organized the "Cup of Egyptian Excellence" tournament, and in 1923, became member in the International Federation of Football "FIFA". This enabled Egyptian players to participate in FIFA

Many researchers say its establishment aimed to control, not stress, the foreign dominance in Egypt. They were abolished in 1949.
Mark S. W. Hoyle, "The Mixed Courts of Egypt: An Anniversary Assessment", Arab Law Quarterly, Vol. 1, No. 1, November 1985, pp. 60–68.
[11] Amna Zacharias, "Only a game? Not in Egypt", The National, 24 June 2014, accessed on 15 May 2018, at: www.thenational.ae/world/.
[12] Yasmin Yehya, op. cit.
Worth telling that Egyptian sporting clubs were never limited to practicing sports. They are gathering places where members can also socialize, enjoy the day by the pool or hangout, and have lunch with their families. Now, to join the club, members pay extremely high one-time membership fees in addition to an annual subscription. Sporting clubs are affiliated to the government, the Ministry of Youth and Sports (MYS), which allocate their budget and monitor their financial matters.

international tournaments and the Olympics. In 1925, the EFA published the Sports Act and the law of the Egyptian Cup of Excellence. And later, in 1957, became a member of the Confederation of African Football organization.[13]

Sporting clubs were also an expression of the prevailing divisions between rulers and ruled. The following parts discuss how football was used by rulers to increase their popularity and contain people's discontent from one side, whereas social movements used football to express their political opposition to the ruling regime.

Football and Politics

The construction of stadiums reflected the multi-cultural nature of some Egyptian cities, the development imparities in Egypt, and were also used as national projects to gather the populace around the leader. That is evident from a review of stadiums' architecture, locations, and construction under the name of national leaders. Also, some football clubs were founded by Egyptian ministries to reflect their dominance in the Egyptian politics.

First, the construction of the three oldest stadiums in the country, and in Africa, were in Alexandria, Cairo, and Ismailia, Egypt's historically and culturally richest cities. Cairo is the capital; Alexandria is the second largest city in population and the commercial capital of the country. Whereas Ismailia is one of the three Suez Canal cities with its famous national history linked to the establishment of the canal and its international strategic importance. Second, the construction of some stadiums reflected the multi-culture nature of the city such as Alexandria Stadium, built by King Fouad 1 in 1929, which was designed by a Russian architect, inspired by Alexandria's Greco-Roman character, while its walls reflect the Islamic architecture. Third, the construction of the stadiums was used by ruler to gather the population around a national project that holds and glorifies his name. Ismailia stadium was established in 1939 and holds the name of the Khedive Ismail, the Kind of Egypt then. Cairo International Stadium, the official stadium of the national team, was founded in 1958 under the name Nasser, the late president. The Arab Contractors Stadium was built under Sadat's rule by Osman Ahmed Osman, the owner and leader of one of the leading construction companies in Africa and the Middle East, an

---

[13] "History of the Egyptian football game", State Information System, accessed on 15 May 2018 at: www.sis.gov.eg/.

ex-Minister and close friend to President Sadat. Burj Al-Arab International Stadium (the Army's Stadium) was founded by President Mubarak and reflecting the increasing role of the army in Egyptian politics. Other stadiums also existed and reflected the dominance of the military, such as the Military College Stadium and the Border Guard Stadium in Alexandria.[14] Fourth, many Egyptian football clubs were founded by ministries such as Haras El-Hodud (Border Guards club), Talaea El-Geish (Army's Vanguards club), and Al-Intag Alharby (the Military production Club) founded by the ministry of defense; Al-Dakhliya (the interior) by the ministry of Interior; and Enppy and Petrojet by the ministry of Petroleum.[15]

The continuity or banning of the game mirrored the political situation in the country. It was banned in 1967–1970 after the Six Day War, then restored by Anwar Sadat to raise the low national spirit. It was banned again in 1973 because of the war with Israel. It was banned in 2012–2013, after a massive riot in Port Said stadium, leading to the death of 74 fans and the injury of 500.

During times of activity, football teams' achievements raised national pride. Since joining the Confederation of African Football in 1957, the EFA helped launching the African Cup of Nations and hosted the bi-annual championship four times (1959–1974–1986–2006). Egypt's national team "The Pharaohs" broke many records in the Nations Cup (as per the date of writing this manuscript): playing 19 consecutive matches without a defeat in 2010; winning 9 straight games in 2008; playing 24 games without a defeat in 2017. The team also scored the highest participation in the tournament with 23 participations, followed by Côte d'Ivoire 20 and Ghana 18. It is the most to reach the finals (nine times equal with Ghana) and to organize the tournament (four times equal with Ghana). The team won the African Nations Championship seven times (in Sudan 1957, in Egypt 1959 and 1986, in Burkina Faso 1986, in Egypt 2006, in Ghana 2008, and in Equatorial Guinea 2010). Despite their remarkable achievements on the continental level, the Pharaohs only participated in the World Cup three times: in 1934 and in 1990 both in Italy and in 2018 in Russia.[16] Other teams have achievements too, such as the U20

---

[14] Soliman Al-Naqr, "Do you know the official capacity of Egyptian stadiums? Burj Al Arab is in the lead" (in Arabic), El Youm El Sabe3 newspaper (the 7th day), 1 May 2018, accessed on 16 May 2018, at: www.youm7.com.

[15] "Nationalism and violence in Egyptian football culture", The Nordic Africa Institute, January 18, 2017, accessed on 18 April 2018, at: www.nai.uu.se.

[16] EFA official website, http://www.efa.com.eg/.

team who won the bronze medal in the World Youth Cup (later called U-20 Cup) twice: in Argentina 2001 and Australia 1981. And the military team had won the World Military Cup five times (1993–1999–2001–2005–2007) and won the silver and bronze medals three times each.[17] In addition to the national team, the Egyptian clubs are the most qualified for the title of the African Champions League (till date of this manuscript) with 14 titles: Al-Ahli who won eight times and retained the championship cup twice, followed by Zamalek who won five times and retained the championship cup once. Egyptian clubs are also the most crowned with eight African Cup of Nations titles (Al-Ahli four times, the Arab Contractors three times, and Zamalek once) and nine "African Super Cup" titles (Al-Ahli six times and Zamalek three times).[18] Al-Ahly, or the "Century Club" in Africa, participated five times in the Clubs World Cup and achieved the 6th place three times in 2005, 2008, and 2013, the 3rd place in 2006, and the 4th in 2012. It is also the only Egyptian team to win the Confederation Cup in 2014 and the African Cup of Nations Cup. In 2020, it was classified as the 2nd internationally, after Real Madrid, in winning continental championships.[19]

The relationship between football and media have developed tremendously in Egypt over the years. The popularity of football increased after the introduction of Radio in the 1930s and TV in the 1960s. The Radio and TV covered football news, highlighted football achievements, and broadcast matches live. This has also made football players and sports clubs managers more famous and raised their role as source of inspiration to the youth. Mahmoud El Khatib, or "Bibo", the Egyptian legendary player, and the current president of Al-Ahly club. Hani Ramzi, Al-Ahly and German Premier league player (Werder Bremen 1994–1998, Kaiserslautern until 2005, then Saarbrucken), who was ranked 19th in the African Footballer of the Year in the last 50 years and 5th in the African Footballer of the Year by the French Football magazine.[20] Ahmed Hassan, Ismaili player, who won the Turkish Cup in 2006, the Belgian Cup 2008,

---

[17] "History of the Egyptian football game", op. cit.
[18] EFA official website, http://www.efa.com.eg/.
[19] Africa Sports official website, "Al Ahly Will Surpass Real Madrid"—Alessandro Altobelli (africatopsports.com).
[20] "Egypt's Christian Captain", BBC News, 1 December 2001, last accessed on 18 May 2018, at: www.news.bbc.co.uk.

and the African Cup of Nations Cup four times with the Pharaohs.[21] Ahmed Hossam (Mido), Zamalek player, who played in many European clubs (Tottenham, Middlesbrough, Wigan, West Ham United, and Ajax).[22] And Magdi Abdel Ghani who was the first Egyptian player to play in the Portuguese league and nominated as one of the top 20 foreign players in Portugal in the twentieth century.[23] Finally, Mohamed Zidan, Al-Masry player, who started his career in Denmark in 1999 and was named the top scorer of the Danish league in 2004–2005. He moved to the Bundesliga in 2005 (Werder Bremen from 2005 to 2007, Mainz in 2007, and Borussia Dortmund 2008–2012) and won the title as well as the African Championship in 2008 and 2010.[24]

FOOTBALL IN SUPPORT OF THE RULER

The support of Egyptian coaches and players to the ruling regime was crucial to raise the regime's popularity in times of crisis. Hassan Shehata, or "the emperor", is the most successful football trainer in Africa. As a player in Zamalek, he won the Egyptian league top scorer twice (76–77 and 79–80) and the best player in Asia in 1970, in Africa in 1974, and in Egypt in 1976. As a coach, he had many achievements (the Arab Contractors Club won Egypt Cup in 2003–04 and Egypt Super Cup in 2004 for the first time in the club's history; Egypt's U-20 team won the African Championship in 2003 in Burkina Faso; the national team won the African championship three times in a row [2006 in Egypt, 2008 in Ghana, and 2010 in Angola] a record hard to break, and Egypt kept the cup for life) and was the only African team to score three goals against Brazil in one game and beat Italy in the world champion then.[25] Under his coaching, the national team jumped in the FIFA ranking to the 10th place

[21] "30 years on Top" (in Arabic), Eurosport News, 25 June 2011, last accessed on 18 May 2018, at: www.arabia.eurosport.com/.
[22] Adham Al-Badrawy, "Mido ends his football career after 178 local and international goals" (in Arabic), The 7th day (Al-Youm Al-Sabe3), 11 June 2013, last accessed on 15 May 2018, at: www.youm7.com/.
[23] Amro Galal, "Magdi Abdul-Ghani: A history of achievements and glory" (in Arabic), Masr Al-Arabia, 27 July 2016, last accessed on 15 May 2018, at: www.masralarabia.com/.
[24] Asma Omar, "Mohamed Zidan: A brightening start in Europe's stadiums and a dull end in the Egyptian League" (in Arabic), The 7th day (Al-Youm Al-Sabe3), 11 December 2016, last accessed on 15 May 2018, at: www.youm7.com/.
[25] Ibrahim Ramadhan, "The Master 'Shehata': a History of achievements and failures", Tahrir News, 22 November, last accessed on 15 April 2018, at: http://www.tahrirnews.com.

in February 2010 and 9th in July 2010, thus, marking the second-best ranking achieved by an African team in history after Nigeria's 5th place in 1994. Shehata was ranked Africa's best coach for 2008 by the African Football Confederation, the 14th in the Best Coaches chart for 2010 by the International Federation of Football History and Statistics (IFFHS) and was named among the top five coaches in African history.[26] Also, many players won records; both Ahmed Hassan and the goalkeeper Essam Al-Hadari were the first two players in Africa to win the championship four times; Mohammed Naji (Gedo) won the title of "discovery of the tournament" and was top scorer, although he did not participate in the main lineup of the Pharaohs in any match of the tournament. The second national coach to become a source of national pride was Mahmoud El Gohary, the first to win the Confederations Cup title as a player and a coach.

Players were also a tool to fund national projects. In contrast to Mohamed Aboutrika, the former Egyptian top player who was placed on a terror list for ties to the Muslim Brotherhood, and funding their violent opposition against the regime, Mohamed Salah, Liverpool FC player and star striker, became an icon to all Egyptians and Arabs[27] and played an important social role as a financial supporter to various development projects, from youth centers and schools to hospitals and water and sewage stations. But the most important is the image he conveys of a moderate Muslim that not only challenges the dominant stereotypes about Arab youth as terrorists or refugees but also spreads the sense of tolerance and acceptance of the other (as chanted by Liverpool fans: "I'll be Muslim too").[28]

Football achievements were used as a tool to gain legitimacy, for political propaganda and mobilization and to contain political discontent. President Mubarak attended matches played by the national team and supported the players. He has also associated himself with football figures, receiving the national team in the presidential palace after victory, the president's sons were present in all Egypt's matches, building relations

[26] Kent Mensah, "Hassan Shehata: The ups & downs of his tremendous reign with the Pharaohs", Goal last accessed on 15 April 2018 at: www.goal.com/.
[27] Abdel-Fatah Faraji, "The inspiring story of Egypt and Liverpool superstar Mohamed Salah", Arab News, 4 March 2018, last accessed on 20 May 2018, at: www.arabnews.com.
[28] "The 'Mohamed Salah Effect' is real—my research shows how he inspires Egyptian youth", The Conversation, 25 May 2018, last accessed on 20 April 2018, at: www.theconversation.com/.

with the players, and football achievements were used to glorify the regime and the president.

Football players, sports analysts, and workers in the media industry in general publicly supported the regime thus granting it legitimacy. Football TV programs allowed the public to voice their opposition during national crisis and "blow off the steam". Football matches were used to distract people away from national disasters or internal problems or to cover up on the regime's corruption and bad governance. People celebrated Egypt's victory in football, when the seriously defected ferry Al-Salam Boccaccio 98 sank in the Red Sea killing more than a thousand Egyptian workers and pilgrims on their way back from Saudi Arabia. The 90 minutes match is an escape from life difficulties and challenges, even for a moment, into a world of achievements and success.[29] The famous Egyptian film Wahed-Sefr "One-Zero", produced in 2009, shows the suffering of seven different characters from various social and economic classes and captures the moment when they forget their misery to madly celebrate Egypt's winning the African Nations Cup in Ghana 2008 in the streets.[30]

The state also used football to extract large revenues from selling match tickets and broadcasting rights. In this regard, after the national team won the Africa Cup of Nations three times, the price of broadcasting rights for the Egyptian Premier League increased from 1.5 million Egyptian pounds before 2007 to 160 million for the 2011–2012 season. The marketing of media rights and advertisements generated huge income to the sports industry and sporting clubs and managers as well.[31]

Media coverage increased in various ways: newspapers increased the number of sports pages; sports newspapers were launched, such as Al-Ahram Al-Riyadi, Akhbar Al-Riyada, and Al-Hadaf. Sports websites were created like "Filgoal" and "Yallakora", and many sports channels such as Modern Sports, ON sport, Al-Ahly, and Zamalek channels were launched. Sports Radio/TV programs evolved from one weekly program in the 1980s/1990s, to a daily sports programs extending for long hours (some exceeding four hours daily). Hosts like the former goalkeeper of the

---

[29] Ahmed Meshref, "The distracting noise: politicizing football in Egypt", The Gazelle, 16 April 2016, accessed on 20 May 2018, at: www.thegazelle.org.

[30] Mohamed Kassem, "Wahed – Sefr" (One-Zero), Cinema, accessed on 20 April 2018 at: www.elcinema.com/.

[31] Mohamed F.A. Ebrahim, N. David Pifer and others, "Is Egyptian soccer well-positioned for business purposes? Assessing competitive balance in the Egyptian Premier League", International Journal of Sports Marketing and Sponsorship, Vol. 19, Issue 2, pp. 238–240.

Pharaohs, Ahmed Shobeir, and former policeman Medhat Shalaby became national superstars.[32] Many clubs' presidents, football ex-players, and individuals working in the field ran for parliamentary elections seeking parliamentary immunity such as Mortada Mansour, president of Zamalek club; Mohamed Mouselhi, president of Al-Itihad club; and Ahmed Shobeir, former Ahli goalkeeper.[33] Yet, these developments came at the expense of the beautiful game. Sports media instead of attracting qualified individuals relied on famous retired football players, coaches, and analysts. They were soon involved in hate speeches and used their programs or newspaper's columns to verbally fight each other, supported by their parliamentary immunity.[34] In addition, sports media business was not able to compete other regional networks as BeIN Sports Channel which owns all rights to broadcasting all continental and global sports events.[35]

Football was so attached in support of the system that it did not regain the same interest after 2011 revolution. The national team failed to qualify three times for the Africa Cup of Nations since 2010, finally qualified to the Gabon Tournament, and the premier league matches were very years played in empty stadiums, only a limited number of spectators were allowed to attend international games and in distant stadiums.

Despite their achievements, many famous players and coaches were accused of supporting the ruling regime at one point, thus affecting their popularity. For example, Shehata was accused of supporting the deposed president Mubarak and was called to resign from coaching the national team "I supported Mubarak in the demonstrations to calm the sport's atmosphere in Egypt and to let the league come back again, so I wasn't against the protestors".[36] Gohary was an army officer and served with

[32] Inas Mohamed Ali Mazhar, The Edgy Relationship between Sports Media and Sports Organizations in Egypt: The Urgency for an Effective Media Policy, A Thesis of Master of Public Policy, School of Global Affairs and Public Policy, the American University in Cairo, December 2014, pp. 25–27.
[33] Nashwa AbdelTawab, "Politics of Sport", Al-Ahram Weekly newspaper, 15 December 2005, issue No. 773, last accessed on 20 May 2018, at: weekly.ahram.org.eg.
[34] Manal Hamzeh and Heather Sykes, "Egyptian Football Ultras and the January 25th Revolution", Anthropology of the Middle East, Vol. 9, No. 2, Winter 2014, pp. 96–97.
[35] Mohamed Alaa El-Din, Sports media has been neglected in Egypt: Hazem Emam, Daily News Egypt, 05 December 2015, last accessed on 15 May 2018, at: https://dailynewsegypt.com/.
[36] Dorsey, James M. "Egyptian coach under fire for supporting Mubarak", Bleach report online, 17 February 2011 at: Egyptian Coach Under Fire for Supporting Mubarak | Bleacher Report | Latest News, Videos and Highlights.

Mubarak. Zidan was blamed for expressing his love to Mubarak after the revolution, "I kissed Mubarak's hand when he honored Egypt after the 2010 African Cup of Nations as I saw him as a father of all Egyptians".[37]

Football and Political Opposition

As it was a source of national pride to the populace and was used to raise the regime's popularity, football was also a tool to express political discontent and opposition to the ruling system. The rise of football fans groups "Ultras" was the first step to politicize the game, first against the police harassments, then against the ruling regime. The group transformed from following football news and events on the Internet or social media and organizing attractive entrances to cheer their favorite club and players with drums, duffels, and fireworks, to political and social activism against the exiting social and political regimes.

Ultras entered Egypt late. The start came with the establishment of Al-Ahly Club lovers' association on a football blog launched by Egyptians ex-patriots in 1996. But it was the Zamalek fans' association in 2005 that led to the appearance of the first Ultras, the "White Knights" in 2007, followed by "Ultras Ahlawy" in the same year. Soon several Ultras followed: "Ultras Green Magic" of Al-Itihad club, "Ultras Yellow Citadel" of Ismaili Club, and "Ultras Super Green" of Al-Masry club. Their involvement in politics started with the 2011 revolution, when they used the social media and football grounds to lead a political opposition against the corruption and human rights violation of the regime and turn the pitch into a battle over control and power. They started by attacking the police forces in their entrances, songs, and slogans breaking the barriers of silence and fear and encouraging the mass to stand in the face of a dictator regime.[38]

However, they were also partners in two devastating disasters witnessed by the Egyptian stadiums. The first in Port Said Stadium on 11 February 2012 during the Egyptian Premier League's match between Al-Masry and Al-Ahly clubs. According to official statistics, more than 74 were killed

---

[37] Omar, Islam, "Footballer Zidan saw Mubarak as 'Egypt's father'", Al-Ahram newspaper Online, 22 February 2012, at: Footballer Zidan saw Mubarak as 'Egypt's father'—Talents Abroad—Sports—Ahram Online.
[38] "Nationalism and violence in Egyptian football culture", The Nordic Africa Institute, 18 January 2017, accessed on 18 April 2018, at: http://nai.uu.se/.

and hundreds injured. It is the biggest disaster in the history of Egyptian sports.[39] Al-Masry fans attacked Al-Ahly players in the playground during warm-up, between the two halves, and after the end of the match, with white weapons and sticks. The attacks followed a series of provoking social media posts and banners raised in the match by Ultras Ahlawi humiliating the city of Port Said and its team, Al-Masry. This comes after years of Mubarak's neglect of the city after a failed assassination attempt. Many reported the absence of security measures, the reluctance of the police to interfere and stop the tragic accident, closure of many exist doors, thus raising doubts on the intentions of police forces and the government's invisible hands behind the scenes. Ultras Ahlawi left Port Said under police protection in armored vehicles or protected train, while players returned to Cairo in military aircraft. Armed forces were deployed in the city's streets and 21 were found guilty, all from Ultras Masrawy, and they were either sentenced to death or prison. The stadium itself was suspended for five years by the EFA decision, and football activity was suspended for the rest of the season.[40] Ultras of the two major clubs in Egypt, Al-Ahly and Zamalek, continued defying the government and threatening to widespread chaos until the change of the regime. The Ultras Ahlawy attacked the EFA headquarters in 2013 stealing its contents and setting the building on fire, while Ultras Port Said led massive riots resulting in more than 40 killed.[41] The second disaster occurred in 2015, when 22 were killed at the Air Defense Stadium in Cairo. The declared reason was Ultras White Knights' attempt to enter the stadium without tickets, thus exceeding the ten thousands permitted by the security forces, and Police forces irresponsible response by launching gas bombs on the masses. However, the undeclared reason was an attempt from the Ultras to embarrass the governing authority then, the Supreme Council of the Armed Forces that led the country after the resignation of Mubarak. The removal of the council prepares the floor for the Muslim Brotherhood rule. As a result of the two disasters, the court banned the activities of all Ultras fan-groups nationwide,

[39] James M. Dorsey, "Rooted in History: Politics, Identity, and Ultras in North African Soccer", in: Onwumechili C., Akindes G. (eds) Identity and Nation in African Football. Global Culture and Sport. Palgrave Macmillan, London, 2014, pp. 50–51.

[40] Amira Taha, The Ultras in Egypt: Political role before and after 25 January 2011, Thesis in Comparative Politics, The American University in Cairo, 2015, pp. 31–45, 82–88.

[41] Ahmed Rizvi, "Football in times of Crisis: In Egypt, mix of politics, economics and revolution proves combustible", The national, 22 July 2015, accessed on 15 April 2018, at: https://www.thenational.ae/.

enforced empty stadium matches, thus reducing the interest in football, consequently, depriving the regime from a significant source of support.

Conclusion

Since its introduction in 1882, the game of football has become a wide-ranging sports activity. Over time, it has evolved from a mere hobby for recreation and physical training to become a profitable professional industry and developed close with the political regime. The regime seeks achievements to cover its failure on the economic and political levels; workers in the football fields seek economic interests and fame in addition to power and immunity; fans unify with the team's victories to forget their misery and daily difficulties and fall sometimes under the control of the state disguised in media industry. They sometimes leave their comfort zone to rebel against the political system and march in mass demonstrations calling for change and opposing corruption and mismanagement.

Football is not only the beautiful game; it has also become the political tool to support or undermine the ruling political system.

References

"30 Years on Top" (in Arabic), Eurosport News, 25 June 2011, last accessed on 18 May 2018, at: www.arabia.eurosport.com/

"Egypt's Christian Captain", BBC News, 1 December 2001, last accessed on 18 May 2018, at: www.news.bbc.co.uk

"History of the Egyptian football game", State Information System, accessed on 15 May 2018 at: www.sis.gov.eg/

"Nationalism and violence in Egyptian football culture", The Nordic Africa Institute, January 18, 2017, accessed on 18 April 2018, at: www.nai.uu.se

"The 'Mohamed Salah Effect' is real—my research shows how he inspires Egyptian youth", The Conversation, 25 May 2018, last accessed on 20 April 2018 at: www.theconversation.com/

AbdelTawab, Nashwa, "Politics of Sport, Al-Ahram Weekly newspaper, 15 December 2005, issue No. 773, last accessed on 20 May 2018, at: weekly.ahram.org.eg

Alaa El-Din, Mohamed, Sports media has been neglected in Egypt: Hazem Emam, Daily News Egypt, 05 Dec 2015, last accessed on 15 May 2018, at: https://dailynewsegypt.com/

Al-Badrawy, Adham, "Mido ends his football career after 178 local and international goals" (in Arabic), The 7th day (Al-Youm Al-Sabe3), 11 June 2013, last accessed on 15 May 2018, at: www.youm7.com/

Al-Naqr, Soliman, "Do you know the official capacity of Egyptian stadiums? Burj Al Arab is in the lead" (in Arabic), El Youm El Sabe3 newspaper (the 7th day), 1 May 2018, accessed on 16 May 2018, at: www.youm7.com

Ayoub, Yaser, "History of Egyptians with Football (4): Mohamed (Effendy) Nashed" (in Arabic), 14 May 2014, accessed on 15 May 2018 at: http://www.yallakora.com/

Dorsey, James M., "Rooted in History: Politics, Identity, and Ultras in North African Soccer", in: Onwumechili C., Akindes G. (eds) Identity and Nation in African Football. Global Culture and Sport. Palgrave Macmillan, London, 2014.

Ebrahim, Mohamed F.A. & Pifer, N. David and others, "Is Egyptian soccer well-positioned for business purposes? Assessing competitive balance in the Egyptian Premier League", International Journal of Sports Marketing and Sponsorship, Vol. 19, Issue 2.

EFA official website, http://www.efa.com.eg/

ElMouniry, Halim & Badawy, Essam, Management in Sport (in Arabic), Academic Bookshop, Part 1, 1991.

Faraji, Abdel-Fatah, "The inspiring story of Egypt and Liverpool superstar Mohamed Salah", Arab News, 4 March 2018, last accessed on 20 May 2018, at: www.arabnews.com

Ferraro, Christopher, Imperialism, Cultural Identity and Football: How the empire created Egypt's National Sport, Ph.D. Thesis, St. John's University, New York, 2015.

Galal, Amro, "Magdi Abdul-Ghani: A history of achievements and glory" (in Arabic), Masr Al-Arabia, 27 July 2016, last accessed on 15 May 2018, at: www.masralarabia.com/

Hamzeh, Manal and Sykes, Heather, "Egyptian Football Ultras and the January 25th Revolution", Anthropology of the Middle East, Vol. 9, No. 2, Winter 2014.

Hassan, Islam, "When the British occupation caused the birth of the Egyptian Team" (in Arabic), 28 June 2015, accessed on 15 May 2018, at: http://www.dotmsr.com/

Hoyle, Mark S. W., "The Mixed Courts of Egypt: An Anniversary Assessment", Arab Law Quarterly, Vol. 1, No. 1, November 1985.

Hutchison, P. M., "Breaking Boundaries: Football and Colonialism in the British Empire", *Inquiries Journal/Student Pulse*, Vol 1, Issue 11, 2009, last accessed on 13 April 2018, at: www.inquiriesjournal.com/

Kassem, Mohamed, "Wahed – Sefr" (One-Zero), Cinema, accessed on 20 April 2018 at: www.elcinema.com/

Lopez, Shaun, "Sport and Society in the Middle East: An Alternate Narrative of Middle Eastern History for the American College Classroom", Middle East Critique, Vol 18, No. 3, Autumn 2009.

Mangan, J.A., "Cultural Hegemony and the Institutionalization of British Games", a paper presented at the University of Alberta, Class Edmonton, March 1983.

Mensah, Kent, "Hassan Shehata: The ups & downs of his tremendous reign with the Pharaohs", Goal last accessed on 15 April 2018 at: www.goal.com/

Meshref, Ahmed, "The distracting noise: politicizing football in Egypt", The Gazelle, 16 April 2016, accessed on 20 May 2018, at: www.thegazelle.org

Mohamed Ali Mazhar, Inas, The Edgy Relationship between Sports Media and Sports Organizations in Egypt: The Urgency for an Effective Media Policy, A Thesis of Master of Public Policy, School of Global Affairs and Public Policy, the American University in Cairo, December 2014.

Omar, Asma, "Mohamed Zidan: A brightening start in Europe's stadiums and a dull end in the Egyptian League" (in Arabic), The 7th day (Al-Youm Al-Sabe3), 11 December 2016, last accessed on 15 May 2018, at: www.youm7.com/

Ramadhan, Ibrahim, "The Master 'Shehata': a History of achievements and failures", Tahrir News, 22 November, last accessed on 15 April 2018, at: http://www.tahrirnews.com

Rizvi, Ahmed, "Football in times of Crisis: In Egypt, mix of politics, economics and revolution proves combustible", The national, 22 July 2015, accessed on 15 April 2018, at: https://www.thenational.ae/

Taha, Amira, The Ultras in Egypt: Political role before and after 25 January 2011, Thesis in Comparative Politics, The American University in Cairo, 2015.

Veitch, Colin, "Play up! Play up! And win the War: The Nation and the First World War 1914–15", Journal of Contemporary History, Vol 20, No. 3, July 1985.

Yehya, Yasmin, "Oldest 10 clubs in Egypt" (in Arabic), El Youm El Sabe3 newspaper (the 7th day), 4 October 2016, accessed on 16 May 2018, at: https://www.youm7.com

Zacharias, Amna, "Only a game? Not in Egypt", The National, 24 June 2014, accessed on 15 May 2018, at: www.thenational.ae/world/

CHAPTER 8

The History and Development of Football in Ghana

Kwame B. Dankwa

The story of the origins, development, and organization of football in Ghana may not differ from those of other countries of Africa. What perhaps distinguished Ghana's football experience from most African countries was the deliberate and calculated attempt to make the process, organization, and operation of football a powerful instrument to achieve pre-conceived political ends by an astute, and ambitious political actor in his capacity as a founding father of a new nation and a progenitor of his concept of pan-Africanism. Osagyefo Dr. Kwame Nkrumah, Ghana's founding president, charged a group of trusted policy reformers to "come out with bold schemes to make Ghana football a showpiece on the continent of Africa". This was at the official launching of the Football Reformation taskforce soon after independence in 1957, while pledging to the group to be not only its Inspirer and Protective Shield but also the

K. B. Dankwa (✉)
Albany State University, Albany, GA, USA
e-mail: Kwame.dankwa@asurams.edu

© The Author(s), under exclusive license to Springer Nature Switzerland AG 2022
A. E. Ayuk (ed.), *Football (Soccer) in Africa*, Global Culture and Sport Series, https://doi.org/10.1007/978-3-030-94866-5_8

Life Patron.[1] According to Anver Versi,[2] Nkrumah saw sports, especially football, as going hand in hand with the birth of a new nation in Africa. Nkrumah believed, victories by the national team in international competition would endanger patriotic sentiments among the Ghanaian people.[3]

The Origins of Ghana Football

Until March 1957, Ghana was one of the four British colonies on the west coast of Africa. (The others were Nigeria, Sierra Leone, and The Gambia.) Named the Gold Coast around 1498 by the Portuguese, who first settled in Elmina (the mine) because of the abundance of gold nuggets even at the coastline, the colony was not different from any of the other possessions of the European overlords across Africa in terms of governance, trade, and social organization. Precious minerals and other raw materials were shipped to Europe, while finished products also came in aboard European-owned and operated ships.

As football became popular in Europe in the nineteenth century, sailors en route to the Gold Coast ports—and indeed other such outposts—brought with them footballs, boots, and jerseys as a way of keeping themselves engaged athletically while waiting to embark. Cape Coast, a southern city of the Gold Coast colony, had been designated the administrative capital since 1821 and therefore a major port and official residence of the Colonial Governor. It was in Cape Coast that the transient sailors indulged in football matches in make-shift parks among themselves and later with other resident foreign merchants and some colonial officials.

Courtesy of the few foreign newspapers already in circulation in the colony, local high-school students in Cape Coast and the few urbanized natives often read about football in Britain and elsewhere. It, therefore, stands to reason that Cape Coast is still recognized as the birthplace of football in Ghana. Aside from the occasional encounters between the sailors and the few expatriates in the colony that took place on improvised pitches, Gold Coast's first official football match had to wait until Boxing Day.[4]

[1] Djan Ohene, *A Short History of Soccer in Ghana and the Rise of the Black Star Eleven.* Accra, Ghana: Ghana Publishing Corporation, 1965.
[2] Anver Versi, Football in Africa, London: Collins, 1986.
[3] F. Mahjoub, 'Power Games', African Soccer, No. 50 (December 1999):20–23.
[4] Djan Ohene, *A Short History of Soccer in Ghana and the Rise of the Black Star Eleven.* Accra, Ghana: Ghana Publishing Corporation, 1965.

The historical duel between the Gold Coast's first indigenous football team, Excelsior, and a European side drew mainly from sailors of a docked ship, plus some Europeans living in Cape Coast. The Excelsior, on the other hand, comprised twenty-two young students at the Cape Coast Government Boys School under the tutelage of their Jamaican coach, Briton, who was also the headmaster of the school. Having been the beneficiaries of the largesse of some friendly sailors who frequently docked at the Cape Coast port, the students started a secret, nocturnal training regimen in footballing. The enterprising pioneers subsequently ordered equipment like football jerseys, pairs of boots hoses, and caps from Europe.[5]

The venue for this groundbreaking event was the ubiquitous Cape Coast Victoria Park, which had hosted virtually all official events. The colonial governor at the time, Sir Frederic Hodgson, an enthusiastic sportsman, was the special guest of honor. Officiated by European referees, the landmark match was exciting and keenly contested. Although Excelsior played a great game, they lost the duel by a score of 2-1 to their opponents. The spontaneous interest generated by the first official football match was followed by several friendly fixtures, often pitting Excelsior against sailors and subsequently against expatriate civil servants in Cape Coast.

With the popularity of football rapidly spreading throughout the southern towns of the colony, Excelsior responded by arranging out-of-town encounters at Elmina, Saltpond, and Winneba in the subsequent months, and later further west to Sekondi-Takoradi, all on the coast. Quite naturally, Cape Coast became the fortress of football in the Gold Coast, with the formation of the first group of clubs following the success of Excelsior. Everton, Blankson's XI, Swallows, and the Majestics were some of the teams that flourished early. Today, the Cape Coast Vipers and the Mysterious Dwarfs appear to be the only surviving clubs out of the group. Sekondi-Takoradi also witnessed the rise of several clubs around the same time. Clubs like Western Wanderers, Railway Apprentices, and Mosquitoes were among the leaders, although today Sekondi Hasaacas is the only surviving team for the Sekondi-Takoradi area.[6]

This chapter will focus on football in Ghana, from the colonial era to post-independence period. The chapter will probe how Europeans

[5] Ibid., 4.
[6] Ibid., 6.

introduced the game in Ghana and the response by Ghanaians to the new sport. Attention will be paid to the following topics: football administration in Ghana, Central Organization of Sports (COS), the expansion of competitive football across the country, why football prevailed over other sports. The chapter will also analyze Ghanaian football successes, especially the Black Stars' admirable performance in the 2010 FIFA World Cup in South Africa. The chapter will explore challenges faced by the Ghanaian football federation and how it impacts the national team. Other issues that would be explored will include widespread corruption and mismanagement, nepotism, and favoritism.

Football Administration in Ghana

Until the initial moves to organize football at the national level in 1943, the football administration pretty much followed the same path as its introduction and development in the colony: tentative and regional based. Semmer Wilson, the District Commissioner of Sekondi-Takoradi, is on record as having formed the first organizational outfit for football administration in the colony—the Sekondi-Takoradi District Football Association in the year 1925.[7] This purely experimental move for the Sekondi-Takoradi metropolis developed to become the Western Region Football Association, covering about one-third of the coastal colony.

The other "regional football powerhouses" were soon to follow the lead from the west. Mr. Richard Akwei—the man many refer to as the "doyen of football administration" in Ghana—formed the Accra Amateur Football Association (AAFA). However, in 1940, a splinter association calling itself the Ga Football Association (GFA) under the leadership of Kitson-Mills challenged the AAFA under Richard Akwei's leadership.

As a colony of Britain, meanwhile, the Gold Coast could only indirectly be affiliated with the International Federation of Football Administration (FIFA) through the Football Association of England in 1943. By 1947 however, the Gold Coast—having met some basic prerequisites—obtained some affiliation with FIFA, the world's apex organization of football. Determined to use the FIFA affiliation to consolidate its position with the African Football Confederation (AFC), Richard Akwei pushed for a similar recognition from the AFC's Cairo headquarters. Akwei's efforts only made the Gold Coast Football Association eligible for payment of annual

[7] Ibid.

subscriptions. Participation in the African Cup of Nations had to wait until full independence had been attained.[8]
chairman.

CENTRAL ORGANIZATION OF SPORTS IN GHANA

Determined to further develop, promote, encourage, and coordinate sports in Ghana, Nkrumah created a Central Organization of Sports (COS) on July 1, 1960. The outfit was also tasked with directing and facilitating Ghana's sporting commitments with the international community. Structurally, the COS was to be headed by a Director of Sports, who would be assisted by five Senior Schedule Officers responsible for the disciplines of athletics, football, hockey, boxing, and lawn tennis. The unit also included Regional Sports Organizers to help implement policies emanating from Accra in each of Ghana's nine administrative regions. Mr. Ohene Djan—who had performed very creditably as the first Chairman of the new Ghana Amateur Football Association (GAFA) since 1958—would later be promoted to the position of Director of the Sports.

Although the Ministry of Education had oversight responsibility for the operations of the COS, Ohene Djan nevertheless reported directly to the Office of the President. This was so designed to allow the Director to bypass the notorious bureaucratic red tape in sports administration. Among the notable accomplishments of the Central Organization of Sports was its emphasis on the importance of sports in education. Capable former players were sent overseas to be trained as coaches and upon their return were posted to the various regions to help with the development of sports.[9]

THE EXPANSION OF COMPETITIVE FOOTBALL ACROSS THE COUNTRY

In addition to laying the foundations for a national league, the Reformers of Ghana football succeeded in expanding interest in football nation-wide with a series of competitions and tournaments involving other sectors of society. Capitalizing on the prevailing nationalist mood after independence, carefully branded tournaments like Independence Cup and

[8] Ibid., 14–15.
[9] Otoo (2014, 38, 44–46, 50).

Founder's Day Games were established. These competitions were deliberately designed to cover not only the geographical spread of the nation but the manifold occupational divides as well.

Thus, in addition to the registered clubs of the national football league, the Independence Cup involved teams from the newly created administrative regions and other occupational groups like the Farmers' Council, the Workers' Brigade, and the Ghana Army. Separate sporting activities were equally organized for students at all levels of the educational system, with the ubiquitous Osagyefo Trophies at stake. While these nationally choreographed sporting activities were designed to arouse patriotism and the development of a healthy youthful populace, critics charged that it was all part of a grand design by President Nkrumah to build the cult of personality for his selfish motive of power aggrandizement.

Another notable institutional accomplishment during the Football Reformation era was the reconstitution of the Ghana Referees Association. Following the report from the Farrant Committee of Inquiry into the worrisome lapses in the referee's association, Ghana's FA streamlined the performance of the "knights of the whistle" to conform to FIFA standards.[10]

Why Football Prevailed Over Other Sports in Ghana

The prevalence of football in Ghana over the other indigenous sporting activities—and indeed over the other organized, modern sports—continues to arouse interest among many sports enthusiasts. Although considered rather quaint, traditional societies in Africa indulged in several sporting activities for recreational and other purposes. The tendency for traditional societies in pre-colonial Africa to engage in wars for defense and territorial expansion, among other things, resulted in the need for societies to consider their youthful population as a potential fighting force. This was part of the reasons why traditional societies indulged in all kinds of sporting activities, to keep their young men and women in excellent physical condition. Traditional wrestling, boxing, dancing, swimming, and mountain climbing were some of the leisure that also served to keep the youth healthy.[11]

[10] Djan (1965).
[11] Emmanuel Akyeampong, and Charles Ambler. "Leisure in African History: An Introduction" *The International Journal of African Historical Studies 35, No.1* (2002), as quoted by Samuel Eson Otoo. (2014).

While the advent of the first European colonizers to Africa could be traced to the fifteenth century, the introduction of football as a pastime to their colonial possessions had to wait several centuries later. Indeed, it was not until the late nineteenth and the early parts of the twentieth centuries that football made its way onto the continent. The European settler communities invariably built centers where they met on weekends to indulge in sporting activities for purely recreational purposes. With time, their native acquaintances—laborers, mid-level employees, students, and other colonial enablers—developed an interest in these pastimes. Lawn tennis, golf, cricket, hockey, and football resultingly got introduced to the Gold Coast and indeed other European possessions in Africa, depending on geography, climate, and culture. The reasons why football - rather than any of the other sports mentioned above - became popular and successful throughout the Gold Coast, included the fact that it was a team sport which was also affordable, and accessible, compared to golf, lawn tennis, or cricket which were deemed elitist because they were individualized sports which demanded expensive individual gears, facilities, and accessibility.[12]

KWAME NKRUMAH AND FOOTBALL: HOW A LEADER CHANGED AFRICA

Kwame Nkrumah emerged as one of the few mid-twentieth-century African nationalists who espoused a radical pan-Africanist viewpoint. He was of the conviction that history and providence have conspired to thrust Ghana forward to prove to the world that the black man is capable of managing his affairs.[13] Realizing that a united front by the emerging independent African countries was required to complete the decolonization process of Africa, Nkrumah declared, at his now-famous inaugural address at Ghana's Independence Day of March 6, 1957, that "the independence of Ghana is meaningless unless it is linked to the total liberation of the African continent".

Nkrumah was also of the conviction that the diplomatic efforts of Pan-Africanism could use some sub-structural infusion of sports and culture, given the disparate linguistic, ideological, and religious realities of aspiring

---

[12] E. Otoo (2014).
[13] Fiifi Anaman, "The Big Interview": 'We Played Our Part', says Ghana Legend C.K. Gyamfi. http://www.goal.com/en-gh/news/4371/exclusives/2013/08/16/4190482.

states of Africa as the result of colonialism. Determined to use football as a vehicle to unify Africa, Nkrumah was of the conviction that

> By meeting together in the field of sport, the youth of Africa will learn what our elders were prevented from learning—that all Africans are brothers with a common destiny

Furthermore, Nkrumah ssaw football as an opportunity to introduce his perception of the "African Personality" concept. He, therefore, was committed to forming a national football team, well-groomed, equipped, and financed to make an immediate impact on the global scene. Even the name of the team—Ghana Black Stars—had a tinge of nostalgia to the rallying agitation of the legendary Marcus Garvey to blacks in the diaspora eager to return to the motherland aboard a Black Star (Shipping) Line. In the mind of the Nkrumah, the Black Stars were to be an all-conquering team made up of indigenous Ghanaians and to be groomed and managed by a native coach to prove to the world that a new day had dawned on the continent.

Conscious of the emergence of an African Football Federation with a membership of only four countries in the north of Africa, Nkrumah decided to initiate formal competition in football among the West African countries. The tradition of friendly football duels among the emerging West African countries like the Ivory Coast, Ghana, Guinea, Nigeria, Sierra Leone, and Togo was very popular among football fans in the subregion, although these competitions remained intermittent, bilateral, and largely unstructured.

Soon after hosting the All-African People's Conference in Accra in 1958, the Ghanaian leader initiated the formation of the West African Soccer Federation. Consequently, he donated the Nkrumah Gold Cup to be competed for annually, with an amazing prize of 1000 guineas to the winner. The fact that Ghana won the maiden tournament in 1958 and successfully defended it two times probably convinced the Nkrumah that his country was ready to pursue football at continental and global levels.[14]

Again, Ghana under Kwame Nkrumah, proposed and vigorously pushed for the creation of an African Clubs Championship tournament, like the European League Championship (UEFA) tourney. This was to augment Nkrumah's desire to further the greater integration of the

[14] Djan.

peoples of Africa through sports and culture. Consequently, the Osagyefo donated the first trophy for the African Clubs Championship in 1964 to be competed for annually by winners of individual African nations' football leagues. This was to supplement the bi-annual African Cup of Nations (AFCON) competitions established earlier in 1957.[15]

Initial Efforts at Building a National Team

Meanwhile, a Ghana National Team had replaced the Gold Coast XI soon after independence in 1957. Although interest in football was widespread in the new nation, organized international football competitions were limited to the West African subregion. There was the annual Ghana and Nigeria tourney played on a home and away basis. Ghana also had similar series with the fledgling national squads of Sierra Leone and Togo. The last of such bilateral games with neighboring countries was in Lagos, Nigeria, where the Ghana National Team lost to their Nigerian counterparts in October 1960.[16]

Among the epoch-making highlights of the Glorious Reformation was the visit of Stanley Matthews, the legendary British football icon. As a prelude to the crucial role football would play in his administration, Nkrumah approved of the invitation of Stanley Matthews to play exhibition football matches in Ghana as part of the country's independence celebrations in 1957. Matthews, featuring with Accra Hearts of Oak, then one of Ghana's preeminent clubs, played against the other top-tier clubs in several matches across the country. Experienced and young stars like James Adjei, Charles Kumi (C.K.) Gyamfi, and Baba Yara had the chance of their lives playing either with or against the world's greatest footballer. The Ghanaian media also had a field day speculating how the youthful local stars like Baba Yara would measure up against the Blackpool talisman.[17]

The enthusiasm and positive impact Stanley Matthews' visit had on football in Ghana earned him the honorary title of "Soccerhene", meaning "King of Soccer". At the political level, Matthews' visit strengthened Nkrumah's belief in how sports could help forge a national identity out of a heterogeneous nation of manifold ethnic proclivities. The Osagyefo is

[15] Paul Darby (2005, 38).
[16] Djan (1965, 23).
[17] BBC Sport, May 26, 2017.

reported to have used Matthews' visit to emphasize to the Ghanaian youth the endless possibilities of life based on determination and discipline (*Modern Ghana*, September 30, 2016).

The euphoria of Stanley's visit had barely abated when Ohene Djan negotiated for the hiring of another British—George Ainsley—as Ghana's first national football coach. Although George Ainsley lasted only ten months at the helm, he succeeded in instilling "scientific football" among Ghanaian clubs and footballers. A great tactician and a strong believer in keeping the ball on the ground, Coach Ainsley was said to have stated in his farewell speech to the assembled Ghanaian football elite that "Remember the angels don't play football" (Ohene Djan 1964, 20). After Ainsley's abrupt departure, C.K Gyamfi, the captain of the Black Stars, was appointed interim coach until a substantive replacement was hired. Andreas Sjoberg of Sweden signed an eighteen-month contract as Ghana's new coach from 1958 to 1960. If Stanley Matthews was remembered as a master tactician, Andreas Sjoberg is still remembered in the annals of Ghana football history as the guy who insisted on stamina building. This made the Black Stars of 1959–1960 a formidable group that "always excelled in speed and endurance" (Ohene Djan 1964, 20).

In addition to Britain, it will be fair to state that (West) Germany and Hungary were equally impactful in the development of football in Ghana. Ghana's fascination with German football can be traced to the 1960 tour of Fortuna Dusseldorf, a West German first division club to Ghana in 1961. Again, the Ghana Football Association (GFA) later dispatched skipper C.K. Gyamfi to Fortuna in Dusseldorf for a technical upgrade in football. Added to Gyamfi for coaching assignments back home were two other Ghanaian former international stars, James Adjei and Chris Briandt, who had also graduated from the Sports Academy of Cologne in West Germany.

Meanwhile, three other coaches from Hungary were hired by the GFA in 1960 for national and regional coaching duties. While Jozeff Ember was assigned to the national team, Valga and Tibor Kemmeny were deployed to the various regions and schools. Included in the outfit, of course, were an Italian coach Rino Martini and Otto Westphal of West Germany (Ohene Djan 1964, 20).

Determined to extend the game of football all over the country while ensuring the development of local expertise, the Nkrumah government in 1961 sponsored ten former Ghanaian international soccer stars to Czechoslovakia and West Germany to specialize as coaches and trainers. This ensured a gradual replacement of the foreign coaches as the returning foreign-trained local personnel, under the leadership of C.K. Gyamfi, made their presence felt at the schools, districts, and administrative regions all over Ghana (Ohene Djan 1964, 10).

THE BLACK STARS, ONE OF AFRICA'S FOOTBALL GIANTS

In 1982, Ghana was referred to as the "Brazil of Africa". That was because, it was the only country in Africa to have won the African Cup of Nations (AFCON) Cup four times (1963, 1965, 1978, 1982), just as Brazil was the only country to have won the World Cup that many times. In between the first two AFCON trophies, the Black Stars of Ghana ably represented the continent at the Tokyo Olympics in 1964, inspiringly reaching the quarterfinal stage. With a great infusion of centralized planning and governmental support, the Black Stars were determined to become the sole African representative at the 1966 World Cup Finals to be hosted by England. Of course, Ghana's football prowess lost its allure for a good while ceding that enviable sobriquet to Egypt who has—to date—won the AFCON Cup seven times, with Cameroon next with five victories. Other countries like Nigeria and Cote d'Ivoire have also bagged the AFCON trophy three and two times, respectively.

After what seemed like an eternity, football in Ghana began its long journey of recovery, at least at the youth level. In 1992, Ghana's Black Meteors became the first African country to win an Olympics Bronze Medal in football at the Barcelona Olympics. Before the Barcelona feat, Ghana's Under 17 (the Starlets) had twice won their version of the World Cup in 1991 and 1995, respectively. In 2009, Ghana's Black Satellites became the first African country to win the World Cup Under 20 trophy in Cairo, Egypt, defeating their Brazilian counterparts 4-3 on penalties kicks. Before Egypt, the Satellites had been runners up twice in 1983 and 2001.

After several failed attempts, Ghana seemed to have found its winning ways when the Black Stars made it to the World Cup finals on three consecutive occasions—2006, 2010, and 2014. In fact, at the 2010 South African World Cup, Ghana was a penalty kick away from becoming the first African country ever to reach the semi-final stage of the World Cup!

Tensions arising within the aforementioned "regional" football associations continued to undermine the development of the game in the colony. More importantly, with no one national football association, the Gold Coast could not compete in either the Olympic Games or the African Cup competitions.

The Birth of Club Football in Ghana: Real Republikan Sporting Club

One of the recurrent criticisms of Nkrumah then was that he was a man in a hurry. His political opponents in Ghana pilloried him for preoccupying himself with grandiose pan-Africanist policies and their concomitant financial toll on Ghana's economy. Even his post-independence infrastructural outlay for Ghana was equally severely criticized. His blueprint to construct a giant hydro-electric dam on the Volta River at Akosombo, the Kwabenya Atomic Energy Commission, and the Tema Oil Refinery Plant (in a country that produced no oil, then) were all lampooned by critics as white elephants—expensive and prestigious projects that were irrelevant to Ghana's immediate needs.

Equally controversial was Nkrumah's strategy of hurtling the newly formed Black Stars, Ghana's national football team into continental recognition. The traditional method of building a national team is through a national league system. Individual teams—mostly privately or corporate-owned—of up to twenty would participate in a nationally organized league. Depending on the standard of football in a country and its financial and infrastructural wherewithal, there could be two or several football leagues in any year. The competitive nature of the national league system is meant to bring out the best in the players, thereby making it easy for any national coach and his scouts to zero in on the meritorious few to build a national team out of.

Before the last of the annual Ghana-Nigeria football contests, Nkrumah had articulated his intention of forming a model football team to provide inspiration and guide to other clubs in the nation. In a letter to Ohene Djan, he wrote

> *My interest in soccer is so keen that I propose, soon, to encourage the formation of a "model club" which will offer leadership and inspiration to football clubs in the country.*
>
> *The club shall be known as "Ghana Republikans" to commemorate the launch of your a three-year development plan in the year of our Republic.*
> (*Daily Graphic*, March 13, 1961, 14)

Kwame Nkrumah's desire to have a team ready and able to make an immediate impact on the African continent and the global scene must have driven him to buck the time-tested formula of developing a national team.

Instead, he asked Ohene Djan, the Chairman of GAFA, to form an all-star team—out of the players of the participating clubs of the national league—to constitute the nucleus of the new Black Stars. This mega team was also to be registered to compete for the national league trophy. Upon direct orders from the Osagyefo, the national coach and his assistants were to train their eyes on all players of the participating clubs just before the start of the 1961–1962 national league. In a few weeks, they were able to fill each position with at least two top-notch players plucked from the privately owned clubs of the premier league (Ohene Djan 1965, 23).

The formation of the Republikan Sporting Club was the other major policy accomplishment of the Central Organization of Sports (COS). Providing the rationale for the idea—on behalf of the president—in January 1961, Ohene Djan said the new club was to spearhead the acceleration of sports in Ghana. Although initially designed to be a trailblazer in the development of sports in general, it was in football that the model club concept made its greatest impact.

The Ghana Republikans was to also showcase the proper technical and administrative ways of club management to the other football clubs in the country.

> The model club will—through dedicated training, the discipline of the highest order, loyalty, actuated by a genuine sense of patriotism and sound and efficient club administration—set the pattern for club development in Ghana

Real Republikans was the name given to what was soon to be the quasi-national team. Dubbed Osagyefo's Own Club (OOC), membership to the Real Republikans came with incredible perks. Each member was guaranteed a decent-paying job and housing in Accra, the capital city. They were well equipped with training gear and were showered with attractive winning bonuses. Like a reconnaissance squad of an army, members of the OOC not only were always within reach but also were ready, willing, and able to deploy.

In no time at all, young, enterprising local or home-grown stars like Aggrey Fynn and Kofi Pare (Sekondi-Hasaacas); Dodoo Ankrah, E.O. Oblittey, and George Appiah (Accra Great Olympics); Ofei Dodoo and Addo Odametey (Accra Hearts of Oak); Edward Acquah, Ben Acheampong, and Frank Crentsil (Sekondi Eleven Wise); and Salisu, Kwame Adarkwa, and Baba Yara (Kotoko) became the founding members of the Real Republikans. Others included Agyeman Gyau (Brong Ahafo

United). Having experimented in the national league on a non-scoring basis in the first year (1961/1962), the Real Republicans subsequently became a fully accredited team in the league (Ohene Djan 1964, 65).

The impact of the Real Republikans on Ghana football was apparent not only on the national league but also on the Black Stars, Ghana's national team. As referenced above, the team's debut in the local league of 1961–1962 season was on an experimental, non-scoring basis. The season was also unique because, for the first time in Ghana soccer history, the national team embarked on a two-month tour of Europe in the middle of the season. This meant that the entire Real Republican team had to be represented in the league by its reserve outfit. Other teams like Asante Kotoko and Hearts of Oak that had four and three players, respectively, on the touring Black Stars squad endured a rather rough first half of the league season. With the return of the Black Stars from the European tour, the second half of the season eventually became a two-team contest between Kotoko and Hearts of Oak, with the Accra lads overcoming the Kumasi boys by only one point.

The following football season (1962–1963) was when the Real Republikans made history as the first club in Ghana to win the elusive double titles for the regular league and the knock-out (FA) contests. It was also the year that Ghana's young and enigmatic right-winger, Baba Yara, suffered a career-ending injury in a single-vehicle accident. Baba Yara, who was snatched from Kotoko by Ohene Djan to become part of the experimental Republikan club, is arguably considered Ghana's most colorful player of all time. The "King of West African Wingers" sustained a severe spine injury which essentially cut short an otherwise promising football career (Ohene Djan 1964, 58).

The success of the Real Republikan experiment was that, despite widespread public hostility, it was the first club in the country's football history to have won the elusive titles of the regular league and the FA Cup for the 1962–1963 season. The OOC went on to win three more FA Cups before its disbandment in 1966.[18]

Second, according to K.B. Asante, former secretary to the president, Nkrumah believed that sports—particularly football—was an important avenue for the nation to recover its self-esteem deficiencies, after centuries of slavery, colonialism, and deprivation.[19]

[18] Fiifi Anaman (2017).
[19] Otoo (2014, 41).

Consequently, the Republikan Club, as proposed, would foster ethnic integration among not only the players but also the entire Ghanaian society. As has been alluded to earlier, since the introduction of football to Ghana in the late nineteenth century, clubs had been mostly regionally based. In a few instances—like Kumasi Asante Kotoko—ethnic sentiments pretty much underlined the very nom de guerre, official ensigns, and other paraphernalia of the teams. With the creation of the Republikan Club whose members were to be drawn from each of the dozen or so regionally based football teams, the concept of national integration would be showcased, at least at the micro-level.

Kumasi Asante Kotoko FC

A football team that had evolved over the years to symbolize the impregnable Asante Empire of yesteryears spearheaded this protest and even considered boycotting the league altogether. Kotoko's preemptive suspension from the national league by Ohene Djan in 1961—for working "against national interest"—signaled the delicate balance that needed to be maintained between sports and politics in a state emerging out of disparate ethnonational proclivities.

Following direct and timely intervention by the president's cabinet, some palliative measures were announced to stem the frustrations of the other teams. These included the decision to degrade the Republikan Club's participation in the national league on a non-scoring basis. Also, it was decided that players of the Republican Club who wanted to revert to their former clubs would be free to do so.[20]

At its peak, the Real Republicans provided at least eight players for Black Stars for international assignments. In no time, the Black Stars were not only virtually unbeatable and home, but also distinguished themselves on the African continent and in their European tours. Equally phenomenal was the ease with which congenial national team chemistry was realized. In terms of team building, complete understanding among the players and tactical cohesion, the Real Republikans became the veritable "melting pot". As an experimental group put together in a strategic, yet unconventional way, it almost immediately achieved its *raison d'etre* as the nucleus of the national team. As referenced below, in the landmark duel between the Black Star and Real Madrid in 1962, as many as nine players

[20] Ibid.

from the Ghana side were from the Real Republikans team in a match in which the unconquerable Real Madrid were held to a pulsating drawn game of three goals apiece at the Accra Sports Stadium.

GHANA, THE AFRICAN FOOTBALL CONFEDERATION, AND FIFA

Meanwhile, at the African continental level, the four North African countries that were already independent had formed the African Football Association (AFC) and had been admitted to the Federation of International Football Association (FIFA), the world's governing body of football. The founding members of the AFC—Egypt, Tunisia, Morocco, and Sudan—created a biennial African Cup of Nations tournament to be competed for by member nations. The member countries met in Sudan in 1957 for the Cup's maiden tournament in 1957. Ghana joined the AFC as soon as the ink had dried up on its membership application to the United Nations (UN) and FIFA.

Before debuting in the 1963 AFCON tourney, the Black Stars—having been eliminated from the 1962 World Cup Finals by Morocco—embarked upon a historic European tour. Fielding a complete amateur squad, the Black Stars engaged all professional and semi-professional European opponents. Despite a tight schedule of playing twelve matches in forty-two days across Europe straddling West Germany, East Germany, the Soviet Union, and Czechoslovakia, the Black Stars won eight matches, drew one, and lost three (Ohene Djan 1965, 32).

Again, determined to excel in the fourth edition of AFCON, which was to be hosted by Ghana, the handlers of the Black Stars decided to test their strength against other national teams across Africa. As fate would have it, they were invited to a special four-nation tournament in the form of a league knock-out competition featuring Ghana, Kenya, and England (represented by Isthmian league) with the winner to play the Ugandan national team for the Uhuru (Independence) Cup. This was in celebration of Uganda's independence from Great Britain. The Black Stars not only prevailed upon Kenya and England, but they also went ahead to trounce Uganda by a score of 4-1 to lift the Uhuru Cup.

News about the impressive performance of the Ghanaian national in Kampala reverberated across East and Central Africa. Out of the seven invitations from countries in East and Central Africa to the Black Stars to play exhibition football with their fledgling national teams, they accepted only three: Kenya, Tanganyika (Tanzania), and Nyasaland (Malawi). Again, the Black Stars did not disappoint. From Nairobi to Dar-es-Salaam to Blantyre, they came up victorious by incredible goal margins.[21]

REAL MADRID INVITED TO PLAY THE GHANA BLACK STARS

The other event choreographed by the Osagyefo to expose Ghana to global football was the invitation of Spain's Real Madrid to play the Black Stars at the Accra Sports Stadium on August 19, 1962. Coming at the time the Black Stars was still at its formative years, the match-up was dubbed as a "David and Goliath" encounter because of Real Madrid's legendary status of having won five successive European Cups championship. The Real Madrid team against the Black Stars showcased six of their players who started the 1962 European Cup final in Amsterdam, including the incomparable Alfredo Di Stefano (captain) and Ferenc Puskas.

Ghana's team, on the other hand, was made up of local stars. Considered the strongest possible team in the country, the "twinkling shining stars" fielded the following: Dodoo Ankrah, Franklin Crenstil, Addo Odametey, Ben Simmons, E.O. Oblitey, Kwame Adarkwa, C.K. Gyamfi (player-coach), Aggrey Fynn (captain), Baba Yara, Edward Acquah, and Wilberforce Mfum. The final scoreline of 3-3 not only put Ghana on the global football map but also showcased the young patriots as capable of accomplishing anything they would set their eyes on (Fiifi Anaman 2016). Again, this fed into the grand design of Kwame Nkrumah's pan-Africanist agenda which would blend diplomacy with sports.

Glowing with pride by the superlative performance of the Black Stars in their encounter with Real Madrid, Nkrumah decided to use the occasion to further burnish his conception of pan-Africanism beyond Africa. Right after the Real Madrid duel, the Black Stars would embark on a six-week multi-nation tour of Europe to play against professional clubs and a few national teams. Again, Nkrumah's dual intentions were not only to build more confidence in the players but also to challenge European prejudices about Africans.[22]

With their first participation in the African Cup of Nations in their sights, Kwame Nkrumah urged his technical team to swing into

[21] Djan (1965).
[22] Paul Darby (2005, 36, 37).

immediate action. With a carefully balanced national team drawing its core stars from the model Real Republikan Club, Ghana was bent on using the opportunity to make Ghana football "a showpiece on the African continent".

Ohene Djan who had proved himself to be an astute and dynamic football administrator was sent to Moscow for a further brush-up in sports management. His portfolio as Chairman of Ghana Amateur Football Association (GAFA) would soon be elevated to that of Director of Sports. Mr. Djan was charged with raising an all-Ghanaian Black Star team—under the tutelage of an African coach—capable of winning the 1963 edition of the African Cup of Nations. It was in pursuit of this goal that strategic and operational policies like the formation of the Real Republicans Club (1961) and the exposure of the Black Stars to first-class global football—courtesy of the invitation of Real Madrid FC to Ghana to play the Black Stars (1962)—among others, were formulated and executed.

Nkrumah's investment in Ghana's football began to yield dividends. Against all odds, the Black Stars won the AFCON tournament at their first attempt in Accra, Ghana, in 1963. After defeating Sudan by an emphatic 3-0 margin, a foreign sportswriter writing from the Accra Sports Stadium stated, *inter alia*:

> Sporting young and enterprising players, mostly from the Real Republicans Club, the Black Stars went ahead to successfully defend the trophy two years later in Tunis, Tunisia in 1965. Before the Tunisia tournament, however, the Black Stars had been one of the three African countries to have represented Africa in football at the Tokyo Olympics in 1964.

The Ghana Black Stars became a household name all over Africa. Nkrumah reportedly relished occasions when newly independent African countries invited Ghana's national team for anniversary exhibition matches. He would personally fire his boys up to be worthy but modest ambassadors of Ghana.[23]

In addition to timely and effective policy initiatives and financial incentives for players, Nkrumah invested personal time and political capital in the national team. Charles Kumi (C.K.) Gyamfi, the first indigenous African coach to have won the AFCON trophy three times with the Black Stars, recalled when he was summoned to the Flagstaff House

[23] Fiifi Anaman (2016).

(presidential office) together with Ohene Djan after a two-game losing streak in their preparation for an international encounter. After severely lecturing the two with a stern, cold demeanor, he gave the coach his phone number handwritten on a piece of paper, with these reassuring words:

> Call me personally if you need anything you are not getting. It means a lot to me that we've entrusted our football in your hands.

Confronting Domestic and International Turmoil

Having made such an impact on African football in so short a time, the Ghana Black Stars were eager to announce their presence on the world scene. After the Tunisia 1965 victory, preparations were intensified to qualify the Black Stars for the 1966 Mundial in England.

Commenting on Africa's boycott of England 1966 fifty years later, Osei Kofi, the nimble-footed, diminutive right-winger—who was part of the sizzling Black stars of the 1960s that had won the AFCON trophy two consecutive times—still regrets the circumstances that denied the Black Star players the chance of their lives. Osei Kofi, who is now a church minister, told the BBC in Accra that

> We had the Black Stars proper in those days. We had the men, those who were strong, and those who were intelligent. That's why we could have got to the World Cup at any given time. (BBC Sport, July 11, 2016)

Of course, all this preparation for 1966 was underway despite growing threats by domestic league clubs to boycott the national league. This was in response to the growing success of the hybrid experiment of the Real Republicans Club as contrasted with the state of atrophy of the remaining football clubs in the nation.

As stated above, the Real Republicans had been fashioned to become the de facto national team, parading as a regular club in the domestic football league. With all young, enterprising players of the other clubs being lured into the Real Republicans Club, growth in the other teams became dangerously anemic and unsustainable. While opposition to the Real Republican behemoth had been expressed over the years, by the start of the 1965/1966 football season, the threat of a total boycott of the national league by the other clubs appeared real and imminent.

Ironically, the domestic upheaval of the football administration in Ghana was to play second fiddle to the politicization of the beautiful game at the global level. To Kwame Nkrumah, football's instrumentalism was not only to integrate the disparate peoples at the national and continental levels but also as a measure of a nation's (and for that matter a continent's) greatness.

As continental Africa's first intergovernmental organization, the Confederation of African Football (CAF) could, by 1964, pride itself as having laid the foundations for the successful take-off of football on the continent. Membership of the CAF had been on the rise since newly independent African states saw membership of the CAF as a veritable sign of sovereignty, after admission into the United Nations and the Organization of African Unity (now African Union). And with the participation of the African Cup of Nations (AFCON) (and later the African Clubs Championship) having increased from the initial four to almost twenty nations, football on the continent could no longer be ignored.

The CAF's next strategic move was to become part of global football by encouraging newly independent countries to join the International Federation for Football Administration (FIFA), the global governing body of football. Africa was eager to become a constant feature at the World Cup competition to signal improvement upon its only representation by Egypt back in 1934 when Italy hosted it. It was therefore not coincidental that with the rise of the Black Stars of Ghana, they were poised to herald their arrival on the global football arena. And the World Cup of 1966—to be hosted by England—became the logical place and time for this launch.

Kwame Nkrumah's Last Major Football-Related Action on the Global Stage

When in 2004 the International Federation of Football Administration (FIFA), the world's governing body for football, announced that South Africa had been awarded the right to host the 19th edition of the World Cup in the year 2010, the irony of how much progress had been made within the preceding forty years could not have been lost by historians of the world's only "beautiful game". Because it was almost forty years prior that the overlords of global football had ruled that the entire continents of Africa, Asia, and Australia would be entitled to only one representation at the 1966 Mundial to be hosted by England. The furor and consternation triggered by that decision among the governments of these continents resulted in the entire continent of Africa boycotting the England Finals. This forever stigmatized the 1966 World Cup as the only one to have been snubbed by an entire continent. The reality of a new democratic South Africa hosting the World Cup—with the African continent being represented by five countries, therefore—attested to how much progress has been made in football on the continent.

Emerging out of its 1964 special summit over the allocation of participating countries for the 1966 World Cup Finals to be hosted by England, FIFA not only sent shock waves across three continents but also displayed their disdain and utter disrespect for over half of the world's population. FIFA's participation formula stipulated that of the sixteen participating countries, ten slots were given to continental Europe, four were reserved to Latin America, with one slot going to Central America and the Caribbean regions. That meant that the remaining three continents of Africa, Asia, and Australia were to contend for the only one remaining slot.[24]

The outrage displayed by African leaders toward FIFA's 1964 arrangement was palpable, to say the least. Taking direct orders from his president Kwame Nkrumah, Ghana's Director of Sports, Ohene Djan—who was also a member of FIFA's Executive Committee—objected against the FIFA.

Conclusion

Like previous failures, the most recent debacle of the Black Stars has sent journalists, pundits, politicians, and other stakeholders into an apoplectic overdrive in debates over the way forward. To be expected, opinions differ markedly by concerned Ghanaians over reasons for the Stars' hapless performance and how to regain the past glory. Arguments have ranged from unpatriotic, spoiled, and money craven players, who are more committed to their overseas professional teams than national assignments, to lack of tactical effectiveness and team cohesion due to players' disparate backgrounds, as well as coaching effectiveness, among others.

The issue of whether the country should acquire the services of an expatriate coach or continue with Kwasi Appiah assumed serious

[24] Paul Darby (2002, 52–53).

emotional overtones in Ghana right after the Cairo 2019 flop. This issue was put to rest when the reconstituted Ghana Football Association refused to renew Appiah's contract when it expired in December 2019. Instead, Charles Kwabla (CK) Akonnor—who was Coach Appiah's deputy—was tapped to take the place of his former boss. As controversial as the new pick appeared to a section of the Ghanaian population, the choice of an indigenous coach over an expatriate may have been influenced by the historical superior accomplishments of the former over the latter. Given that former Coach Appiah is on record as having been the only indigenous coach to have qualified the Black Stars to a World Cup final (Brazil 2010), coupled with the fact that all Ghana's previous AFCON victories happened under the watchful eyes of Ghanaian coaches, the GFA may have history on its side on the expatriate or native coaches dialectics.

This study also considers player selection and grooming as another prerequisite of successful team building. In the current globalized village syndrome where commodities, services, and ideas are in free circulation, no country can—in good faith—place a ban on their young players from seeking maximum returns for their skills abroad. Because of this, every country must figure out a team-building strategy that can accommodate their overseas-based players, who invariably constitute most of their squads. Many national coaches could prefer more than the one week of "lease time" granted to their players by their professional teams to not only train but also to honor international assignments. This trend, unfortunately, continues to undermine every country's ability to raise a national football team that is stable, cohesive, and effective.

The Ghana Football Federation, and indeed all of Africa's fifty-five FAs, are challenged by this study to come out with a sustainable strategy of keeping players longer together for greater tactical cohesion and efficacy. For instance, did the just concluded AFCON 2019 in Egypt shine any discernible light on any African country's "best practices" to be emulated in this regard? Does the fact that the top four countries were all from North and West Africa reveal anything that the early "drop-outs" may have to learn from, regarding team grooming and cohesion? Does the "model club" format which worked almost perfectly in Kwame Nkrumah's Ghana allow some modifications for twenty-first-century Africa, given the fact that most Africa's national players ply their trade overseas?

Player motivation and management before, during, and after major international assignments also continue to undermine performance. As witnessed by Ghana's team to the Brazil 2010 World Cup finals, issues involving players' traveling, hotel accommodation, and bonuses conspired to sap the energies out of the youthful ambassadors. Lapses in planning due to political patronage and blatant corruption in high places resulted in a ridiculous, spur-of-the-moment policy of chartering an airplane to fly over the Atlantic Ocean to deliver over seven hundred thousand dollars ($700,000) promised bonuses to players in Brazil to forestall their threat of refusal to play.

REFERENCES

Akyeampong, Emmanuel, and Charles Ambler. "Leisure in African History: An Introduction" *The International Journal of African Historical Studies 35, No.1* (2002), as quoted by Samuel Eson Otoo. (2014)
Anaman, Fiifi. "The Big Interview": 'We Played Our Part', says Gnana Legend C.K Gyamfi. 2016. http://www.goal.com/en-gh/news/4371/exclusives/2013/08/16/4190482
Anaman Fiifi, The Last Time: How Ghana Managed an unlikely Ascension unto African Football Throne. Retrieved July 2017.
BBC Sport. "How Africa Boycotted the 1966 World Cup". July 11, 2016, http://www.bbc.com/news/world-africa-36763036
BBC Sport. "The Stanley Matthews Football Revolution Made in Ghana". May 26, 2017, http://www.bbc.com/news/world-40030710
Daily Graphic, January 1960–December 1965
Darby, Paul, *Africa, Football and FIFA: Politics, Colonialism and Resistance*. Londres, Portland: F. Cass. 2002.
Darby, Paul. *Africa Football and FIFA: Politics, Colonialism, and Resistance*. New York, NY: Frank Cass Publishers. 2005
Mahjoub, F., 'Power Games', African Soccer, No. 50 (December 1999):20–23.
Ohene Djan, *A Short History of Soccer in Ghana and the Rise of the Black Star Eleven*. Accra, Ghana: Ghana Publishing Corporation. 1965
Ohene Djan, *A short History of Soccer in Ghana and the rise of the Black Star Eleven*. Accra: Ghana Publishing Company Ltd. 1964.
Otoo, Samuel Eson, *Football and Nation-Building in Ghana Under Kwame Nkrumah, 1951–1966*, June 2014 Thesis (not published)

CHAPTER 9

The Politics of Soccer Management in Kenya: The Rise and Decline of a Popular Sport

Wanjala S. Nasong'o

INTRODUCTION

Soccer, or football as it is known in Kenya, is the country's most popular sport in terms of both the number of participants and volume of supporters. However, although Kenya is internationally known to be a major sporting country, its fame is derived from its prowess in long- and medium-distance running rather than soccer. Arguably, Kenya was at its peak in soccer terms in the 1980s. This is when, at the club level, Kenya's AFC Leopards and Gor dominated the East and Central Africa Club championships, winning all competitions but one during the decade 1977–1987, with AFC Leopards winning the Confederation of East and Central Africa Football Associations (CECAFA) club championships four times between 1979 and 1985. Indeed, the two Kenyan teams ended up playing against each other in the 1985 finals of the CECAFA club championship in Khartoum, Sudan, a duel that Gor won. At the continental level, AFC Leopards reached the semi-finals of the Africa Cup Winners Cup in 1985,

W. S. Nasong'o (✉)
Rhodes College, Memphis, TN, USA
e-mail: nasongos@rhodes.edu

© The Author(s), under exclusive license to Springer Nature Switzerland AG 2022
A. E. Ayuk (ed.), *Football (Soccer) in Africa*, Global Culture and Sport Series, https://doi.org/10.1007/978-3-030-94866-5_9

and in 1987, Gor FC won the same championship. The national team, Harambee Stars, dominated the East and Central Africa Senior Challenge Cup in the early 1980s under Coach Marshall Mulwa and Team Manager Joe Kadenge. Its peak at the continental level came in 1987 when the team narrowly lost 0-1 to Egypt the soccer final of the All-Africa Games. On the other hand, though the national team has qualified six times for the biennial Africa Cup of Nations (in 1972, 1988, 1990, 1992, 2004, and 2019), Harambee Stars has never gone beyond the first round.

This chapter seeks to explore and probe the mixed fortunes of the history of soccer in Kenya to account for the rise and decline of this popular sport in the country. The main argument of the chapter is that the decline of soccer in Kenya is a function of the politics of soccer management since the country's independence in 1963. The chapter begins with a historical exploration of the introduction and development of soccer in Kenya. It then evaluates the mixed fortunes of the sport in the country before focusing on the impact of the politics of soccer management. The chapter concludes with a delineation of remedial measures for reviving soccer in the country back to the competitive edge of its glorious past.

Soccer in Kenya: History and Development

According to available evidence, soccer was introduced in Kenya by the British colonialists in the 1920s (Njororai 2009, 2014). Soon thereafter, it became a national pastime whose popularity grew by leaps and bounds. In 1946, a governing body for soccer, Football Association (FA), was established and charged with organizing the Remington (FA) Cup tournament for which soccer clubs competed. The dominant teams during this time of the 1940s and 1950s included Eastleigh Royal Air Force, Liverpool (of Mombasa), Abaluhyia United, Luo Union, Feisal FC, and Nakuru Railways. During the 1940s and 1950s, soccer teams from Coast Province dominated the Remington Cup competition, especially Mwenge FC (former Liverpool) and Feisal FC (Njororai 2003). These coastal clubs produced notable players such as Ahmed Breik, Kadir Farah, Ali Kadjo, and Ali Sungura. Beyond the Remington, Cup was the Gossage Cup, established in 1926 and ran until 1967 when it was renamed East and Central Africa Senior Challenge Cup. The Gossage Cup was named after its sponsor, the soap manufacturer, Gossage. It involved Kenya, Tanganyika, Uganda, and Zanzibar. Tanganyika and Zanzibar united in 1977 to form today's Tanzania (see Nasong'o 2002, 2012). Among the notable players for the Kenyan national team during the Gossage Cup days were Shem Chimoto, Elijah Lidonde, and Peter Oronge, with Joe Kadenge as perhaps the most accomplished player of the 1960s (see Nene 2015).

A major landmark in the development of soccer in Kenya was the formation of the Kenya Football Association (KFA) in 1960 to govern the management of soccer in the country. This was followed closely by the formation of the Confederation of East and Central Africa Football Associations (CECAFA) to organize regional soccer tournaments. With the KFA in place, an idea was mooted to establish a national league. A committee chaired by Isaac Lugonzo, the founding Chairman of KFA, with Tony Pinto as secretary and including Williams Ngaah and Jimmy McFarnell, was charged with the responsibility of working out the logistical details for this purpose. The national league commenced in April 1963 with ten clubs; seven from Nairobi, two from Coast, and one from the Rift Valley. The Nairobi clubs were Bunyore FC, Kakamega FC, Luo Union, Maragoli United, Marama FC, Nairobi Heroes, and Samia FC. The two Mombasa clubs were Feisal FC and Liverpool FC (later renamed Mwenge FC).

The inaugural league commenced with four matches, two each in Nairobi and Mombasa. Joe Kadenge, who played for Maragoli United, is reported to have scored the fastest goal of the league. However, the first league title was won by the lone team from the Rift Valley, Nakuru All-Stars, coached by then Provincial Sports Officer, Ray Bachelor. Luo Union won the second league title in 1964, inspired by a bevy of talented players including Daniel Nicodemus, James Siang'a, Fred Siranga, and Stephen Yongo. Indeed, Luo Union "capped a glorious season by beating the Ethiopian national team which was then the African Nations Cup winners" (http://kenyapage.net/football/history/60s.html). In 1964, several Luhyia soccer clubs including Bukusu Brotherhood, Bunyore FC, Kakamega FC, Marama FC, and Samia Union, merged to constitute Abaluhyia United FC. Abaluhyia United entered the national league in 1965 finishing fifth with Feisal FC from Coast clinching the title and Luo Union coming in second. Abaluhyia United, fielding many gifted players such as the legendary Joe Kadenge, Jonathan Niva, Daniel Anyanzwa, Livingstone Madegwa, Anthony Mukabwa, Charles Makunda, John Nyawanga, and Moses Wabwayi, won the league title in 1966 and successfully defended it in 1967, becoming the first club in the country to win the league title consecutively.

The political rivalry between Jaramogi Oginga Odinga and Tom Mboya in the mid-1960s seriously impacted the development and constitution of Luo soccer clubs. It saw the Luo Sports Club, sponsored by Mboya, split off from Luo Union, whose patron Odinga was. On account of Mboya's influence in Nairobi, Luo Sports Club was included in the national league and Luo Union, which was much stronger, was left out. To continue playing in the national league, leading Luo Union players decided to join Kisumu Hot Stars—which was problematic because they lived in Nairobi and had thus to travel to Kisumu every Friday for practice. The players included Chris Obure, prolific goal scorer William "Chege" Ouma, long-serving national goalkeeper, James Siang'a, and dependable defender, John "Hatari" Owiti. Through the efforts of some concerned Luo leaders including renowned scholar Bethuel Allan Ogot, Peter Anyumba, and Zack Ramogi, Luo Sports Club and Luo Union merged in 1968 to form Gor Mahia FC. Around this same time, Ramogi FC was formed by the Luo community residing in Mombasa. Gor Mahia FC, with the combined force of the former Luo Sports Club and former Luo Union, won the national league title on their first attempt in 1968. Nakuru All-Stars recaptured the league title in 1969 but folded soon thereafter. Abaluhyia FC made history a second time in 1970 when they won the national league with an unbeaten record.

Perhaps one of the most humiliating moments in the history of soccer in Kenya was in 1965. As part of the celebrations to mark the first anniversary of Kenya's declaration of a republic, Ghana's national team, Black Stars, the African champions at the time, were invited to play against Kenya's national team, Harambee Stars. The lineup for Harambee Stars included Jonathan Niva, Joseph Were, Tom Sabuni, Anthony Mukabwa, Moses Wabwayi, Joseph Okeyo, John Rabuongi, Nicodemus Arudhi, William "Chege" Ouma, James Asibwa, and Moses Ambani. The historic match was graced by the presence of President Jomo Kenyatta. By halftime, the Black Stars were leading by six goals to one for Harambee Stars. A disappointed President Kenyatta left the stadium at halftime and is reported to never have watched another soccer game until his passing in August 1978. It is just as well that the president left at halftime for he saved himself more distress as the game ended with a 13-2 goal difference in favor of the Ghanaian national team (http://kenyapage.net/football/history/60s.html). It should be noted here that the coach in charge of Harambee Stars for the match, then Rift Valley Provincial Sports Officer, Ray Bachelor, had taken charge of the team only four hours to kick off after the substantive national coach, Peter Oronge, mysteriously disappeared, having developed cold feet on learning that President Kenyatta was scheduled to watch the match! (Gachuhi 2012).

Midway through the national league in 1971, the league was scrapped due to serious wrangles within the Kenya Football Association ranks, with Abaluhyia FC atop the league table with one point ahead of Kenya Breweries. It resumed in 1972 and was won by Kenya Breweries FC (later known as Tusker FC). Abaluhyia FC won the title in 1973 and also clinched the Nairobi Provincial League title the same year. In 1973, after losing the contest for Kenya Football Association (KFA) chairmanship to Williams Ngaah, Kenneth Matiba broke ranks and established the Kenya Football Federation (KFF), to which most of the teams subscribed in 1974 (Matiba 2000). Gor Mahia won the first KFF national league in 1974. However, Gor Mahia was hit by leadership wrangles thereafter that resulted in Dan Owino, a former provincial commissioner and ambassador, to reconstitute Luo Union, taking with him critical players such as James Siang'a, William "Chege" Ouma, Fred Siranga, and Stephen Yongo, rated as Kenya's most dependable utility player ever. This new Luo Union FC captured the national league title from Gor Mahia in 1975 and went on to beat Gor Mahia in Mwanza in the finals of the Confederation of East and Central Africa Football Associations (CECAFA) Club competition in 1976 and successfully defended it in 1977 with their striker, Agonda Lukio, emerging top scorer on both occasions.

In 1973, Kenya Breweries FC made history when they became the first Kenyan club to reach the semi-finals of any continental competition. They reached the semi-finals of the Champions Cup after beating Ismailia FC of Egypt in the quarterfinals. At this time, Breweries were a relatively new team on the Kenyan soccer scene. On account of their firm financial base, however, they were able to attract some of the best players in the country such as Elly Adero, Livingstone Madegwa, Binz Mwakolo, Samson Odore, and legendary goalkeeper, Mohamed Magogo. With such stars, Breweries easily won the 1978 national league. Breweries' continental history-making in 1973 was surpassed by Gor Mahia in 1979 when the latter became the first club from East and Central Africa to reach the finals of a continental competition. They beat the defending champions, Horoya Athlétique Club of Guinea, in the semi-finals to reach the finals of the 1979 Cup Winners Cup. According to some commentators, the Gor Mahia team was the best-assembled by a Kenyan club at the time, with quality players in every position:

The defense was marshaled by John Bobby Ogolla and included Peter Otieno Bassanga, Paul Oduwo "Cobra," and Mike Ogolla "Machine." Allan Thigo, quite possibly the best playmaker in Kenya's history, controlled the midfield, ably assisted by Sammy Owino "Kempes" and Tim Ayieko. Schoolboy, wonderboy Nashon Oluoch "Lule" and George Yoga played on the wings supporting center forward Andrew Obunga (http://kenyapage. net/football/history/70s.html)

During the same year (1979), Breweries withdrew from the CECAFA Club Cup held in Somalia and were replaced at the eleventh hour by Abaluhyia FC. Abaluhyia pulled a surprise by winning the tournament. They beat Kampala City Council 1-0 in the finals, with the lone goal scored by Abdul Baraza.

At the national level, Kenya's national soccer team, Harambee Stars, debuted in the Nations Cup finals in Cameroon in 1972 under youthful German Coach Eckard Krautzun, who left before the finals to take up coaching duties of the Canadian national team, leaving Harambee Stars in the hands of Coach Player, Jonathan Niva. Kenya was placed in Group A along with hosts Cameroon, Mali, and Togo. In their opening match, Harambee Stars lost to hosts Cameroon 1-2 with Jean-Baptiste N'Doga scoring for Cameroon twice in the 7th and 20th minutes and Jonathan Niva pulling one back for Harambee Stars in the 44th minute. Kenya drew 1-1 in their second match with Mali, again Niva scoring in the 60th minute. In their final match with Togo, they also drew 1-1 Peter Ouma this time scoring for Harambee Stars. Harambee Stars thus finished third ahead of Togo and were eliminated in the first round, which happened to be the quarterfinal stage since only eight teams qualified for the finals at the time. Nevertheless, the team's striker, Livingstone Madegwa, was named by CAF in an All-African squad selected from the tournament for a friendly match against Brazil, the then world champions. Owing to a breakdown in communications, however, Madegwa missed the trip. Harambee Stars went on to register their first major accomplishment when they won the 1975 Confederation of East and Central Africa Football Associations (CECAFA) Senior Challenge Cup for the first time under English Coach Ray Wood. In 1979, they reached the final of the same tournament under Polish Coach Gregory Polakov.

The hiring of German Bernhard Zgoll as Harambee Stars coach by KFF Chairman, Kenneth Matiba, in 1975 was a major landmark in the development of soccer in Kenya. For the first time in the history of soccer in the country, Coach Zgoll established a series of national youth soccer development centers—the Olympic Youth Program—across Kenya, in Mombasa, Nairobi, Nakuru, and Kisumu. Among notable players to emerge out of these centers were Ambrose "Golden Boy" Ayoyi, Dick Anyanga, Jared Ingutia, Wilberforce "Maradona" Mulamba, Sammy "Kempes" Onyango, Sammy Owino, and Sammy Taabu. It is no wonder that the emergence of these star players from the equivalent of today's soccer academies in the English Premier League coincided with the most achievements of Kenyan soccer. Between 1981 and 1983, Kenya won three successive CECAFA cup titles under Kenyan Coach Marshall Mulwa, arguably the most successful national team coach in Kenyan history. The excellent players under Coach Mulwa and Team Manager Joe Kedenge included, among others, Mahmoud Abbas (popularly known as "Kenya one") in goal, John Bobby Ogolla (the "six-million-dollar-man") and Josephat Murila (the "controller") marshaled the watertight defense, Jared Ingutia and Wilberforce Mulamba ("Maradona") were pivotal in attack, while Joe Masiga ("Bulldozer") and Ambrose Ayoyi ("Golden Boy") formed a formidable strike force. In 1981, Kenya beat hosts Tanzania 1-0 thanks to a free-kick by James Ouma "Jacaranda" to win the first of three successive regional national competitions. The following year, Mahmoud Abbass gave a spectacular display of penalty saving to help Kenya beat Uganda in the final played in Kampala's Nakivubo stadium. In 1983, the tournament was held in Nairobi at the newly constructed Nyayo National Stadium. The home team did not disappoint the home fans. They won all their matches in the run-up to the title, which they won 1-0 against Zimbabwe, thanks to a goal by Joe "Bulldozer" Masiga. Ambrose Ayoyi was the top scorer in the tournament. It was on account of this excellent performance that Ayoyi, from Lanet FC in Nakuru, earned the endearing sobriquet, "Golden Boy."

Arguably, Kenya was at its peak in soccer terms during the decade 1977 to 1987. During this period, Kenyan clubs won all except one of the CECAFA Club Cup championships. Indeed, between 1976 and 1989, Kenyan teams won 11 of 14 (78.5%) of these championships. AFC Leopards (formerly Abaluhyia FC) dominated these championships, winning in 1979, 1982, 1983, and 1984. This was due to AFC's accomplished star players. These included Mahmoud Abbas in goal, legendary for his penalty-saving prowess; the talented playmaker and dribbler, Wilberforce Mulamba; speedy wingers Francis Kadenge and Mike Amwayi; and the indefatigable forward, Joe Masiga. Luo Union won in 1976 and

1979, while Gor Mahia won in 1980, 1981, and 1985, boasting such star players as brilliant winger Nahashon "Lule" Oluoch, Sammy Owino, and great playmaker, Allan Thigo. Kenya Breweries FC won in 1988 and 1989 with their team including stars Paul Onyiera, Douglas Mutua, Aggrey Evayo, and Charles Opondo. That the quality of soccer was at its peak during this period is illustrated by the fact that in 1988, the top two Kenyan teams were AFC Leopards and Gor. However, the two teams withdrew from the CECAFA Club Cup championships held in Khartoum, Sudan. So, third-placed Breweries ended up representing Kenya and won the competition, beating Uganda's Nakivubo Villa 1-0 in the semi-finals and eclipsing the hosts El Merreikh of Sudan 2-0 in the finals.

The year 1987 is reckoned to be Kenya's most successful soccer year. First, the year started with Kenya Breweries clinching the CECAFA Club Cup championship. This was followed by Gor winning the Africa Cup Winners Cup. In so doing, Gor became the first team from East and Central Africa to win a continental title. This was a time when Gor had a formidable team that provided ten players to the national team, Harambee Stars. These included the likes of Peter Dawo, Onyango Fundi, Abbas Hamisi Magongo, George Nyangi, David Ochieng, Austin Oduor, Sammy Onyango, and Charles Otieno. During the same year, Kenya hosted the fourth All-Africa games and, in the soccer tournament, Kenya's national team, Harambee Stars, beat Tunisia 2-1 and drew 3-3 with the Indomitable Lions of Cameroon, a team that included Emmanuel Kunde, Andre Kana Biyik, Jacque Songoo, Benjamin Massing, and Charles Ntamark. Harambee Stars, coached by German Reinhard Fabisch, went on to beat Madagascar 2-1 and, in the semi-finals, beat Malawi 3-2 in a penalty shootout. Quite unfortunately, Kenya lost 0-1 to Egypt in what is described as "a heartbreaking final" (http://kenyapage.net/football/history/80s.html). Ambrose Ayoyi "Golden Boy" played a stellar role in Kenya's performance at the All-Africa games, just as Peter Dawo had played a leading role, scoring ten goals in Gor's victory at the Africa Cup Winners Cup tournament. The great performance by the two Kenyan soccer stars saw them named among the best ten soccer players on the continent. This was the first and only time that two Kenyan players were named among Africa's top ten players in the same year.

The year 1988 could have been another quite successful year for Kenyan soccer at the continental level, but the country seems to have been shortchanged by organizers of the Africa Winners Cup. Both AFC Leopards and Gor participated in the tournament, the former represented Kenya, while the latter were the defending champions. AFC Leopards defeated FC Kalamu of Zaire (DR Congo) 4-1 on aggregate, while Gor defeated Madagascar's BTM both home and away. Both Kenyan teams made the quarterfinals, and the eventuality of an all-Kenyan final was possible. The possibility of an all-Kenyan final was anathema to the continental body who then conspired against the Kenyan teams. When Gor visited Inter Club of Congo, they were denied training facilities for three days before the match. On their part, AFC Leopards seemed destined to eliminate Diamant of Cameroun but their dependable defender, Wycliffe Anyangu, was red-carded under dubious circumstances. Even then, AFC only lost to a penalty kick awarded under questionable circumstances.

Further notable development in the history of soccer in Kenya was the formation of the country's first professional soccer club in 1985—Volcano United. The team included in its ranks national players Nobert Anyira, Hassan Juma, Henry Motego, Vitalis Owuor, and Davis Oyiela with Tanzanian internationals midfielder Hamisi Gaga, striker Zamoyoni Mogella, and defender Lila Shomari. Volcano United soon became a formidable side on the local soccer scene, going on to eliminate giants AFC Leopards 2-0 from the inaugural Moi Golden Cup in 1986 with goals from Zamoyoni Mogella and Davis Oyiela. The professional team, however, was short-lived and disbanded in 1987, only two years after it was established.

Mixed Fortunes: The Decline of Soccer in Kenya

Kenya's national team, Harambee Stars, has performed quite well at the regional level. They have won the CECAFA Senior Challenge Cup six times, in 1975, 1981, 1982, 1983, 2002, and 2013, and have been runners-up seven times, in 1979, 1985, 1991, 1999, 2001, 2008, and 2012. Nevertheless, perhaps nothing better illustrates the mixed fortunes of Kenya's soccer performance than the performance of the national team. Although the team performed wonderfully in the fourth All-Africa games in 1987 as illustrated above and dominated the CECAFA competition in the early 1980s, its record in continental competitions has been dismal. As noted above, the national team qualified for the African Cup of Nations for the first time in 1972 under German Coach Eckard Krautzun and performed respectably well, getting eliminated in the quarterfinals (essentially the first round since only eight teams qualified for the finals). Indeed, Harambee Stars missed the semi-finals narrowly. In the opening game, they lost 1-2 to hosts, Cameroun's Indomitable Lions, though the Kenyans were the first to score through a spot-kick by Jonathan Niva. Harambee Stars drew their subsequent matches 1-1 against Togo and 1-1 against Mali. They missed the semis only because Mali ably held Cameroun to a goalless draw.

After 1972, Kenya next qualified for the African Nations Cup (AFCON) in 1988, 1990, and 1992—the time when, as already mentioned, the quality of soccer in the country was at its peak. Nevertheless, on all three consecutive occasions, Kenya was eliminated in the first round of the competitions. In 1988, the team was under Coach Chris Makokha, but it lacked cohesion even after a tour of Brazil as part of their preparations and the secondment of Brazilian Coach Danilo Alves to the technical bench. The team lost 0-3 to Nigeria and 0-3 to Egypt before drawing 0-0 with Cameroon. At the 1990 AFCON finals, Harambee Stars was under Coach Mohammed Kheri and performed slightly better, drawing 0-0 against Senegal, narrowly losing 0-1 to Zambia, and losing 0-2 to Cameroon's Indomitable Lions that reached the quarterfinals of the FIFA World Cup only two months thereafter. Indeed, after the tournament, Harambee Stars' goalkeeper Washington Muhanji was offered contracts by several European clubs but could not take up any of them because of his standing contract with the Kenya Army. As for the 1992 Kenya participation in AFCON, the Harambee Stars squad deliberately performed poorly (losing both their matches 0-3 to Nigeria and Senegal) on account of their dislike for the national coach, Gerry Saurer, whom they wanted to be dismissed. Saurer was not a qualified soccer coach and only got to be hired to coach Harambee Stars because of his relationship with Adams Karauri, the then caretaker chairman of the Kenya Football Federation. It should be noted, however, that, available evidence indicates that Saurer was a great scout for talent. He traversed the country in search of soccer talent and, in the end, assembled the best national Under-20 in the national soccer history. Among Saurer's recruits, Vincent Kwarula, Allan Odhiambo, Michael Okoth Origi, and Peter Mwololo ended up in Harambee Stars. Following the 1992 AFCON, both Mwololo and Origi were noticed by European scouts and offered contracts, but unfortunately Mwololo had already signed for a Middle East Club just before the AFCON and could not take up the offer. Mike Okoth went on to sign up for KV Ostende of Belgium, where Devok Origi, who now plays for Liverpool in the English Premier League, was born.

After the consecutive qualification for AFCON in 1988, 1990, and 1992, Kenya next qualified for the AFCON competition in 2004 in Tunisia under Coach Jacob Mulee. Again, they got eliminated in the first round, though they registered their first-ever win at AFCON finals when they beat Burkina Faso 3-0 in their final group match, with a goal each from Emanuel Ake, Dennis Oliech, and John Baraza. They were however eliminated despite the decisive victory, having lost 1-3 to Mali and 0-3 to Senegal. Titus Mulama scored Kenya's lone goal against Mali. It took 15 years after 2004 for Kenya to qualify again for AFCON finals. The country qualified for the 32nd edition of AFCON finals in Egypt in 2019 where 24 teams participated instead of the traditional 16 since 1996. In the qualifying round, Kenya was placed in Group F along with Ethiopia, Ghana, and Sierra Leone. Coached by Frenchman Sébastien Migné, Kenya lost their group opening match to Sierra Leone (which was subsequently disqualified from the competition by the Confederation of African Football) but pulled off what is described as a shock victory against Ghana's Black Stars in Nairobi in September 2018 (BBC Sport 2018). The 1-0 victory was through an own goal in the 40th minute by Ghana's Nicholas Opoku. Despite playing ten men for the final half-hour following the sendoff of Joash Onyango in the 60th minute, Kenya successfully held onto the narrow victory. Although Kenya lost 0-1 in the return match in Accra, their 0-0 draw away to Ethiopia and 3-0 victory at home secured them runners-up position to Ghana in Group F and thus secured their ticket to the 2019 AFCON finals in Egypt. Once again, Harambee Stars was eliminated at the group stage having managed only one win of 3-2 against Tanzania and lost to Algeria 0-2 and Senegal 0-3. The victory against Tanzania was hard-fought. Tanzania was first to score in the sixth minute through Simon Msuva. Michael Olunga equalized for Kenya in the 39th minute, but one minute later, Mbwana Samatta put Tanzania ahead again. It was not until the 62nd minute that Johanna Omolo leveled for Kenya and, finally, Olunga struck the winner in the 80th minute.

To compound Kenya's perennial dismal performance at AFCON, the country has not made any major improvements in the campaign to qualify for the FIFA World Cup finals. In the campaign for the 2018 World Cup finals in Russia, Kenya's Harambee Stars was eliminated at the group stages by Cape Verde in 2015! Having won the home match 1-0, Harambee Stars lost to Cape Verde's Blue Sharks 0-2 in Praia. To their credit, Harambee Stars had earlier dislodged Mauritius from the 2018 World Cup on a 5-2 goal aggregate—winning 5-2 away and drawing 0-0 at home in Nairobi. Indeed, the 0-2 loss to Cape Verde was against a background of disorganized travel arrangements for Harambee Stars who arrived in Praia only three hours to kick off after stopovers in Uganda, Nigeria, and Senegal. The closest Harambee Stars have ever come to qualifying for the World Cup was for the 14th edition held in Italy in 1990. The "Italia 1990" campaign remains the only FIFA World Cup competition that Kenya was on the verge of qualifying for up to the last day of qualifying matches. Their last game was an away match with Egypt whom Harambee Stars had held to a goalless draw at home in Nairobi under the successful stewardship of Coach Mohammed Kheri. In the return match in Cairo in 1989, Kenya momentarily celebrated when Austin Oduor's header landed home only to be disallowed by the referee on a claim that the Egyptian goalkeeper had been fouled. Arguably, had the goal been allowed, Harambee Stars could easily have "parked the bus" for the rest of the game and would have qualified for the World Cup finals in Italy. After the goal's cancelation, Egypt put up a spirited fight, edged on by the home crowd, to net two goals and thus eliminate Kenya.

Even at the club level, Kenya has declined in performance since the 1980s when Kenyan clubs were formidable competitors in the regional and continental tourneys. Since the 2000s decade, and even a decade earlier, Kenyan soccer clubs, AFC Leopards, Gor FC, Tusker FC, and Ulinzi FC, have been constantly eliminated during the first rounds of regional and continental competitions—save for 1994 when Kenya Breweries (now Tusker FC) reached the finals of the Africa Cup Winners Cup, coming close to clinching the title a la Gor in 1987. For instance, Gor participated in continental competitions in 2009, 2012, 2013, and 2014 but never made it beyond the preliminary rounds. The only exception is Sofapaka FC whose best performance was in the 2011 CAF Confederations Cup when they eliminated Aviacao of Angola, Ismailia of Egypt, and DR Congo's Lupopo, to reach the round of 16, falling just short of making it to the quarterfinals. This was a great achievement given that Sofapaka was formed in 2004 and was promoted to the top Kenyan soccer league only in 2009.

Several factors help explain the decline of soccer in Kenya at all levels of competition for the last couple of decades. The first major factor is the lack of stability within Kenyan clubs on account of poor pay and terms of service. Because of this, Kenyan clubs have been unable to maintain a playing unit for the requisite amount of the time necessary to make a wholesome team. Player turnover in Kenyan teams is so rapid that the clubs have overtime failed to maintain stability in their playing units. They constantly lose players who seek better fortunes in better-paying clubs in places such as Sudan, Tanzania, Zambia as well as the Middle East, and even far off places such as Vietnam, and of course, Europe. Consequently, Kenyan teams field entirely new players each season who fail to coordinate, work together cohesively as a unit, anticipate each other's strengths and weaknesses, and thus cover up for each other. This factor contributed to Gor's early exit in the preliminary rounds of their participation in continental tourneys in 2009, 2012, 2013, and 2014. In 2009, for instance, Gor had a brand new young team among them schoolboys recently recruited by Gor Coach James Siang'a that lacked experience and cohesion. The team was ignominiously defeated by Rwanda's APR. Gor suffered the same fate in 2012 when they lost 0-4 to Mozambique's Ferroviario on account of lack of coordination and cohesion. Before the competition, Gor had signed a contingent of new players including Ali Apondo, Peter Juma, Yusuf Juma, Wycliff Kasaya, George Midenyo, Ivo Mapunda, Hadji Mwachoki, Hugo Nzangu, Wycliff Ochomo, Moses Otieno, and Rama Salim.

It is noteworthy that the Gor team that won the continental Africa Cup Winners Cup in 1987 had a core group of players who had been together since the early 1980s. These included Peter Otieno "Bassanga," George Otieno "Solo," John Bobby Ogolla, and Austin Oduor in defense. These defenders knew each other well having played together for over six years resulting in a solid defensive unit. The midfield with Abbas Magongo, Charles Otieno, George Onyango, and George Nyangi also had a thorough familiarity with each other. Similarly, AFC Leopards' four times victory in the CECAFA cup between 1979 and 1984 was because of the team's stability resulting from holding onto their best players for long. By 1988, the core group of Wilberforce Mulamba, Michael Amwayi, Francis Kadenge, and Joe Masiga had been together for more than six years. Thanks to the excellent coordination, AFC had a formidable side in 1988. This team, as already noted, would have won a continental diadem in 1988 had the referee been fair in their quarterfinal match. The brilliant coordination between these players also carried over into the national team. When Kenya won the CECAFA Senior Challenge cup three times in a row in 1981, 1982, and 1983, the team had a regular starting lineup that included Mahmoud Abbas, John Bobby Ogolla, Peter Otieno "Bassanga," Hussein Kheri, Josephat "Controller" Murila, Sammy Taabu, Elly Adero,

Jared Ingutia, Joe Masiga, Wilberforce "Maradona" Mulamba, and Ambrose "Golden Boy" Ayoyi.

The second major factor that has contributed to the decline of soccer in Kenya is poor management of the clubs, the national team, and the soccer governing bodies, largely because of corruption and misuse of funds. The regular dissolution of elected soccer governing bodies by the Ministry of Sports and appointment of caretaker committees is ample testimony to the poor management of the sport in the country. Quite often, even when the national team or even club teams are on a winning streak, poor travel and remuneration arrangements kill morale and derail the performance of players. Illustrative of this is the case of Harambee Stars traveling to Cape Verde for a return match in the 2018 FIFA World Cup qualifiers having won 1-0 at home. As Robin Toskin (2015) recounts, after an impressive 1-0 win over Cape Verde in Nairobi, the hope of an unlikely aggregate win swept across Kenya ahead of the return leg in the Atlantic Ocean country. But shambolic travel arrangements that degenerated into a blame game between Football Kenya Federation (FKF) and the Ministry of Sports contrived to ensure the team endured a 15-hour flight with close to an hour of stoppages in Kampala, Uganda; Kano, Nigeria; and Dakar, Senegal, before finally landing in Cape Verde, less than three hours to kick off. Harambee Stars thus lost the match largely on account of this late arrival and the jetlag fatigue. Similar shambolic travel arrangements for Kenya's national Under-23 team saw them bundled out of the 2016 Olympics qualifiers. Pitted against Botswana in their first leg, the team arrived in Lobatse only hours to kick off. A plea by FKF officials Sam Nyamweya and Robert Asembo to their Botswana counterparts to have the match postponed went unheeded. Kenya thus lost 0-3 and, although they won the return match in Nairobi 4-1, they were eliminated on an away-goal advantage. Poor management perhaps is the single most important factor accounting for the decline of soccer in Kenya (see Rintaugu et al 2012) and thus requires special focus in the section below.

The Politics of Soccer Management

Kenya Football Association (KFA), registered in 1946, remained the soccer governing body in Kenya until 1975 when it was replaced by Kenya Football Federation (KFF) formed by Kenneth Matiba. KFF lasted until 2007 when it was replaced by Football Kenya Limited (FKL), which was disbanded in 2011 when it ceased being a limited liability company. It was replaced by the current Football Kenya Federation (FKF). Political rivalry and competition have characterized this constant change of name and the formation of rival bodies. Having been defeated by Williams Ngaah in the KFA elections of 1973, Kenneth Matiba, who had facilitated the formation of Breweries FC, decided to form KFF to which the majority of the teams subscribed and became the governing body in 1975. In 2007, a group of soccer administrators in the country decided to form a rival body to KFF. This is how FKL was formed and was immediately recognized by FIFA as the soccer governing body in Kenya. For some time, the two organizations operated simultaneously with KFF going to court against FKL but lost the case and the courts asked FIFA to continue recognizing FKL, which, as mentioned, was disbanded in 2011 to pave way for the current FKF (see Maliolo 2009).

Following political independence in 1963, the first Chairman of the KFA was Isaac Lugonzo who quit in 1964 to enter politics and became Nairobi mayor. He was replaced by Jonathan Kasyoka from 1964 to 1968. Kasyoka's committee was disbanded in 1968 by the then Minister for Cooperatives and Social Services, Ronald Ngala, who appointed a caretaker committee led by Limuru Member of Parliament, Jonathan Njenga, which remained in charge till 1970. In 1970, Martin Shikuku, an incumbent Member of Parliament for Butere, was elected Chairman of KFA. However, during his tenure, the politics of ethnic rivalry emerged as he was accused of favoring Abaluhyia FC, from his Luhyia ethnic group, and being overly punitive against Gor Mahia, dominated by the Luo. At one point, Shikuku expelled four Gor Mahia players from soccer as well as renown referee, Ben Mwangi. With questions being raised in parliament about Shikuku's alleged favoritism of Abaluhyia FC, the Minister for Cooperatives and Social Services, Masinde Muliro dissolved Shikuku's committee and appointed a caretaker committee led by Bill Martin as Chair, Joab Omino as Secretary, and H.Z. Ramogo as Treasurer (see Table 9.1 for a list of soccer chairmen).

Arguably, Kenneth Matiba remains the best performer as manager of soccer in Kenya. His tenure at the KFF lasted from 1975 to 1978 when he quit joining politics as a Member of Parliament for Kiharu. Matiba was a visionary administrator who sought to inject some professionalism into the running of the sport in the country. He had a lot of resources under his command and when he formed KFF to rival Williams Ngaah's KFA, he would book all soccer stadia in advance, leaving the Ngaah group without venues for their competitions, hence the death of the KFA. As KFF

Table 9.1 List of Kenya's soccer chairmen

Name	Attribute	Period
Isaac Lugonzo	Elected (founding member)	1963–1964
John Kasyoka	Elected	1964–1968
Jonathan Njenga	Appointed (Caretaker)	1968–1970
Martin Shikuku	Elected	1970–1973
Bill Martin	Appointed (Caretaker)	1973
Williams Ngaah	Elected	1973–1974
Dan Owino	Elected	1974–1975
Kenneth Matiba	Elected (KFF not KFA)	1975–1978
Dan Owino	Elected	1978–1979
Chris Obure	Appointed (Caretaker)	1979–1980
Clement Gachanja	Elected	1980–1984
Joab Omino	Elected	1984–1991
Adams Karauri	Appointed (Caretaker)	1992–1993
Joab Omino	Elected	1993–1996
Peter Kenneth	Elected	1996–2000
Maina Kariuki	Elected	2001–2004
Alfred Sambu	Elected	2004–2007
Mohamed Hatimy	FIFA appointed (FKL)	2007–2011
Sam Nyamweya	Elected (FKF)	2011–2015
Nick Mwendwa	Elected	2016–2021

Source: Compiled from various sources by the author

Chairman, Matiba approached the Germans for assistance with youth soccer development. As a result, Coach Bernhard Zgoll was dispatched to Kenya and, as already discussed, helped establish the Olympic Youth Program across the country that saw the development and training of youth soccer. The star Kenyan players that ensured the dominance of Kenyan clubs and the national team in regional competitions in the late 1970s through the 1980s were products of this program.

In his memoir, *Aiming High: The Story of My Life*, Matiba (2000) clearly outlines his vision. He notes that his concern was centered around a major weakness that is always found among people who lack foresight or are unable to think ahead. Until his federation took action, there was no systematic training of young players for the future. To deal with the problem, Matiba approached the German Government to assist Kenya with a coach who would organize youth teams for training players of the future. The German Government not only provided Bernhard Zgoll as a coach for the youth but also agreed to fund the program. Olympic Youth Centers were, therefore, established at Nairobi, Mombasa, Kisumu, and Nakuru, and others were planned elsewhere. Boys aged 12 and 15 years were recruited and received training under Zgoll and his assistant, Jonathan Niva, and other coaches he had selected in every town. The program was so successful that its products formed the backbone of soccer in the years that followed. No less than 80% of the players who won back-to-back East and Central Africa Challenge Cup titles in 1981, 1982, and 1983 were products of these centers. The same players ensured that for 10 years between 1977 and 1987, the East and Central Africa Club championship was won by Kenyan clubs save for one year.

Matiba served at a time when Kenyan soccer was steeped in witchcraft. To help fight it by proving that it doesn't work, Matiba invited Nairobi's AFC Leopards and Gor Mahia and Mombasa's Mwenge FC and Champions FC to use their best witchdoctors against the visiting English team, Norwich City FC in 1975, offering to pay their witchdoctors' budgets for two years if it worked. As was expected, all teams lost against the visitors, and Matiba's point was made (http://kenyapage.net/football/history/chairmen.html). AFC was thrashed 6-1, Gor 4-1, Champions 8-0, and Mwenge 3-1! (Norwich City 2013).

Clement Gachanja's time as KFF Chairman between 1980 and 1984 could rank second to Matiba's. His time at the helm was characterized by the stability that saw Kenya perform well at the club and national levels. However, though Gachanja was a good administrator, he was not as visionary a leader as Matiba. On the other hand, Maina Kariuki's tenure at the KFF between 2001 and 2004 is perhaps the worst in terms of the level of mismanagement. A former executive at Coca-Cola Kenya Limited, Kariuki ran an impressive campaign under the slogan "A New Beginning," promising to bring private sector professionalism to the running of soccer in the country. Elected with him were Hussein Swaleh as Secretary-General and Mohamed Hatimy as Treasurer. Contrary to his promise, Kariuki's tenure was characterized by massive corruption with nothing done to raise the standards of soccer in the country. For instance, in 2001, Kenya played an international match against Swaziland and all the gate collections—Kshs. 8 million ($120,000 at the time) disappeared without a trace. Indeed, it is reported that under Kariuki's stewardship of the KFF, Kenya played eight international matches from which not a single cent was banked by the Treasurer! Taking a cue from the national office, KFF branch officeholders also began misappropriating funds with abandon. Tired of Kariuki's shenanigans, the minister in charge decided to dissolve the KFF committee, but Kariuki went to court and obtained an injunction that nullified the minister's action. Finally, the government got fed up in 2004 and forcefully dissolved the committee. This led FIFA to ban Kenya in April 2004 for "interfering in soccer management" (Wandera 2006). The ban was lifted in August of the same year after an amicable agreement between the government and FIFA (http://kenyapage.net/football/history/chairmen.html).

The epitome of the sorry state of soccer management in Kenya is illustrated particularly well by the rivalry between Mohamed Hatimy and Sam Nyamweya. Hatimy was appointed in 2007 by FIFA to chair a caretaker committee to oversee fresh elections in the troubled KFF whose Secretary-General was Sam Nyamweya. The polls saw the holding of two parallel general meetings by Nyamweya in Nairobi and Hatimy in Mombasa. Nyamweya was appointed Chairman by the government-recognized KFF and, in 2007, obtained a court injunction barring Hatimy from interfering with KFF. Hatimy reacted by forming Football Kenya Limited (FKL) with the blessings of FIFA. Nyamweya appealed to FIFA for arbitration, but FIFA rejected the appeal. He proceeded to the Court of Appeal but also lost to Hatimy. In the interim, between 2008 and 2011, the two organizations purported to run soccer in Kenya, a period when the national team suffered some of the most humiliating defeats (Muganda 2014). It is no wonder that in 2012, FIFA ranked Kenya in position 134 among footballing nations, the worst in the history of soccer in the country. The best ranking was in 2008 and 1998 when the country was placed at number 68.

In 2011, FIFA mandated amalgamation of the two bodies and the holding of fresh elections, which were won by Sam Nyamweya. However, his tenure, 2011–2015, was characterized by shambolic preparations for the national team that saw them regularly arrive at international competitions just hours to kick off. Nevertheless, under Nyamweya, Kenya won the CECAFA Senior Challenge Cup in 2013 for the first time since 2002. But then, held in Kenya, the tournament witnessed the drama of several CECAFA teams locked up in their hotels for non-payment of bills—a testimony to the sheer incompetence of the Nyamweya committee. Some of the teams vowed never to participate in a tournament organized by the FKF again. Hopefully, the new management, under Nick Mwendwa, elected in February 2016 might succeed in turning things around. The downside is that Mwendwa has already been accused of favoritism in sacking national coach, Scottish Bobby Williamson, and appointing Kenyan

Stanley Okumbi as the new Harambee Stars coach. Okumbi previously served as a coach to the second-tier team, Kariobangi Sharks, which is owned by Nick Mwendwa, hence the accusation. Okumbi was subsequently replaced in 2018 by Frenchman Sébastien Migné (see Table 9.2 for a list of Harambee Stars coaches). Nevertheless, with the dismal

Table 9.2   Kenya national team coaches

Name	Nationality	Period
Ray Bachelor	British	1961–1963; 1965
Peter Oronge	Kenyan	1964–1965
Jackie Gibbons	English	1966–1967
Elijah Lidonde	Kenyan	1967–1970
Eckard Krautzun	German	1970–1972
Jonathan Niva	Kenyan	1972; 1978
Bernard Zgoll	German	1974–1975; 1984
Ray Wood	English	1975
Gregory Polakov	Polish	1979
Marshall Mulwa	Kenyan	1980–1986
Reinhard Fabisch	German	1987; 1997; 2001–2002
Chris Makokha	Kenyan	1987–1988
Mohammed Kheri	Kenyan	1988–1990; 1995; 2005
Gerry Saurer	Austrian	1992
Vojo Gardasevic	Montenegrin	1996
Abdul Majid	Kenyan	1998
Christian Chukwu	Nigerian	1998
James Siang'a	Kenyan	1999–2000
Joe Kadenge	Kenyan	2002
Jacob Mulee	Kenyan	2003–2004; 2005; 2005
Bernard Lama	French	2006
Tom Olaba	Kenyan	2006
Francis Kimanzi	Kenyan	2008–2009; 2011–2012
Antoine Hey	German	2009
Twahir Muhiddin	Kenyan	2009–2010
Zedekiah Otieno	Kenyan	2010–2011
Henry Michel	French	2012
James Nandwa	Kenyan	2012–2013
Adel Amrouche	Belgian-Algerian	2013–2014
Bobby Williamson	Scottish	2014–2016
Stanley Okumbi	Kenyan	2016–2018
Sébastien Migné	French	2018–2019

Source: Compiled by author

performance of Harambee Stars in the 2019 AFCON finals in Egypt, it is evident that things are unlikely to change for the better soon.

Conclusion: Back to a Competitive Future

The fact that Kenya has great soccer talent cannot be gainsaid. This is illustrated by the presence of professional Kenyan players in top-flight soccer leagues such as the English Premier League, the French Ligue 1, the Spanish La Liga, and the Italian Serie A among others. Having played for Southampton beginning 2013, Victor Mugubi Wanyama went on to play for Tottenham as a defensive midfielder. Victor was sold to Southampton by the Celtics in 2013 for 12.5 million pounds, thereby making history as the most expensive player ever sold by a Scottish club. He is the first and so far, the only East African soccer player in the English Premier League and the first Kenyan and East African to ever score in the UEFA Champions League, a feat he achieved when he scored the first goal in the 2-1 Celtics win over Barcelona in July 2013. His elder brother, Macdonald Mariga Wanyama joined the Italian side, Parma in 2007 and, in 2010, he became the first Kenyan and first East African to play in the UEFA Champions League when he played for Italy's Inter Milan (Mariga was set to be the first Kenyan and first East African to play for an English Premier League side when his signing for Manchester City failed due to work permit complications that unfortunately were resolved after the 2010 transfer window). Similarly, Dennis Oliech played for the French Ligue 1 side, FC Nantes, between 2005 and 2007 when he joined AJ Auxerre where he remained for six years before joining AC Ajaccio, another Ligue 1 side in 2013. Mike Okoth Origi played professionally in Belgium for ten years between 1996 and 2006 for such clubs as KV Oostende, Genk, Molenbeek, Zeusden Holder, and Tongeren. It was while playing professionally in Belgium that his son, Devok Origi, who currently plays for English Premier League side Liverpool FC, was born. These are just a few examples of many Kenyans playing professional soccer in many countries including the United States, Denmark, Georgia, Norway, Sweden, South Africa, and the Middle East.

The decline of soccer in the country is thus not due to a lack of talent but is explicable in terms of the mismanagement of the sport in the country. To return Kenyan soccer clubs and the national team to their previous competitive edge both regionally and continentally, several measures need to be taken. The first is an investment in youth soccer development. As the

Matiba years at the helm of the KFF amply illustrate, a youth soccer development program across the country would yield great dividends. The focus here should be on identifying talent at an early age, tapping the talent into youth programs, and generally developing soccer at the grassroots. All major soccer-playing nations, and even clubs, have youth soccer development programs, and no country succeeds in soccer without such a program. Indeed, Kenya's domination of regional tournaments in the 1980s at the club and national levels rested squarely on the shoulders of star players that were laureates of the Olympic Youth Program developed by Coach Bernhard Zgoll under the KFF leadership of Kenneth Matiba.

Second and related to the above is the question of corruption. The African Center for Open Governance (Africog 2010, 12) notes that the failure on the part of the national soccer management bodies (in their various names) in Kenya to invest in youth and women's soccer is a consequence of corruption: "Among the many KFF failures, the saddest is the failure to invest in youth and women's football. The funds largely disappeared from the KFF youth and women's football levies at every KFF match as well as the funds sent by FIFA. The KFF officials stole the future of our youth" (see also Stakeholder's Transitional Committee 2004). This problem of corruption needs to be tackled head-on if soccer development in Kenya is to be taken to the next level (see Munro 2005). On account of corruption and misappropriation of both financial and other resources, richly talented players from poor families are unable to exploit their talent and escape poverty because of a lack of investment in youth soccer programs. As a result of corruption, there are many cases where club sponsors withdraw resulting in a collapse of soccer clubs. As Africog (2010, 33) notes, because of corruption and misappropriation of funds, KFF became bankrupt and so indebted that it was no longer a publicly credible organization nor a financially viable entity.

How youth and women's soccer has been mishandled by Kenya's soccer management bodies, especially the KFF, clearly illustrates the problem of corruption. For the duration of its existence, KFF failed to support and enter national girls' and women's teams in CAF and FIFA competitions despite financial allocations from FIFA in support of the same. Africog (2010) cites the case in 2006 when FIFA's Head of Development Management Team, Pascal Torres, wrote to Alfred Wekesa Sambu, Chair of the KFF, informing him that FIFA would make a transfer of USD 113,000 on July the 19th. The finances were to be assigned to youth soccer activities (US$25,000), women's soccer (US$25,000), technical development (US$10,000), refereeing activities (US$10,000), planning and administration (S$33,000), and miscellaneous expenses ($10,000). Despite these clear instructions, youth soccer activities were never funded, women and girls' teams never received allowances nor were they even entered into the FIFA- and CAF-sanctioned competitions. This eventuality led Africog (2010, 33) to conclude that, "at best, women's football is poorly managed. At worst, these [FIFA] funds may not reach the intended recipients." Yet this is not an isolated case, as the comprehensive report by Africog establishes, the KFF officials also misappropriated the youth levy from the gate receipts of all matches including a FIFA Youth Development Program grant of US$250,000 in 2014. Indeed, the chaotic situation in the Kenyan soccer management that pitted Nyamweya against Hatimy between 2007 and 2011 that saw the split between Nyamweya's KFF and the eventual Hatimy's KFL was a contest not between who was most capable of effectively and efficiently running soccer in the country, but essentially a struggle over control of the soccer largesse.

The third critical stage in the quest to return Kenyan soccer to its past competitive edge is to find ways and means for professionalizing its management. As the Clement Gachanja years at the helm of the KFF demonstrate, good administrative leadership is important for the stability of the game both nationally and at the club level. Hence, what is urgently needed in the case of Kenya is a committed, professional, and visionary leadership a la Kenneth Matiba in the latter years of the decade of the 1970s. The frequency with which elected soccer management committees have been dissolved and caretaker committees appointed to run the sport in the country—in 1968–1970, 1973, 1979–1980, 1992–1996, 2007–2011—is ample testimony to the unprofessional manner in which soccer management in the country is handled. It does seem that leadership of the soccer managing body in Kenya is essentially used as a chance to enhance one's profile to parley this into elective political office a la Isaac Lugonzo, Kenneth Matiba, Clement Gachanja, Joab Omino, and Alfred Sambu, among others. Hence the lack of seriousness in managing the sport in the country. This is particularly illustrated by then KFF Chairman (1984–1992) Joab Omino's cavalier attitude toward popular national team Coach, Reinhard Fabisch whom he sacked for lamenting the lack of KFF's effective support for the national team. In sacking Fabisch, Omino argued that after all, coaches "come a dime a dozen"!! As CECAFA Secretary-General, Nicholas Musonye has rightly observed:

Too many national associations are failing African football. We cannot have strong national teams without strong leagues but we do not have strong leagues because too often the associations are run by the wrong people, people who get involved for politics or money, not for football. Until we sort ourselves out, we will have the same old circus. (*The Guardian*, July 11, 2010)

So, at the end of the day, so many good coaches from all over the world have come on board to assist the standards of soccer in Kenya (see Appendix A). However, their efforts have been rendered fruitless thanks to poor management and corruption in the running of the sport in the country. The case of Omino's sacking of German Coach Reinhard Fabisch mentioned above is a good case in point given Fabisch's role in coaching the national team, Harambee Stars, to the finals of the 1987 All-Africa Games.

Fourth and perhaps most important, it is time that FIFA committed to dispassionately serving the global soccer fraternity. There is ample evidence that FIFA has, over time, worked with national soccer management organizations to perpetuate unsavory practices that have resulted in the mediocre management of the sport at many national levels. In the case of Kenya, the contestations between Nyamweya and Hatimy, with FIFA and the Kenya government on either side of the divide, are a critical case in point. FIFA should dispassionately serve the global interest in soccer management, not their entrenched interests, while working in cahoots with national soccer management bodies. It may be time to institute tenure limits for FIFA officials to obviate the development of special interests between them and national soccer management organizations, KFF and otherwise.

References

Africa Center for Open Governance. *Foul Play! The Crisis of Football Management in Kenya*. Nairobi: Africog, 2010.
BBC Sport. "2019 Africa Cup of Nations: Kenya secure shock defeat over Ghana in qualifiers," September 8, 2018.
Gachuhi, Roy. "How Kenya Blew Chance for being Football Power," *Daily Nation*, Nairobi, September 28, 2012.
Maliolo, Michael Agala. "Will the awful football administration in Kenya ever end?" http://www.futaa.com/blog/, September 3, 2009.
Matiba, Kenneth S. *Aiming High: The Story of my Life*. Nairobi: People ltd., 2000.

Muganda, Clay. "Let's face it, Kenyan Football is Going Nowhere," *Standard Digital* (Kenya), July 20, 2014: http://www.standardmedia.co.ke/?articleID=2000128839

Munro, B. "Greed vs. Good Governance: The Fight for Corruption Free Football in Kenya," Report to the Fourth World Communication Conference on Sport and Society," Copenhagen, Denmark, November 6–10, 2005.

Nasong'o, S.W., "Tanzania: Political Culture and Democratization," in Saliba Sarsar and Julius O. Adekunle, eds., *Democracy in Africa: Political Changes and Challenges*. Durham: Carolina Academic Press, 2012, pp. 191–203.

Nasong'o, S.W. "Kenya's Multiparty Elections in an East African Perspective," in Ludeki Chweya, ed. *Electoral Politics in Kenya*. Nairobi: Claripress, 2002, pp. 197–225.

Nene, John. *Joe Kadenge: The Life of a Football Legend*. Nairobi: Phoenix Publishers, 2015.

Njororai, Wycliffe W. Simiyu. "Colonial Legacy, Minorities, and Association Football in Kenya," *Soccer and Society*, vol. 10, no. 6, November 2009, pp. 866–882.

Njororai, Wycliffe W. Simiyu. "The History and Identity of East African Football within the African Context," in Onwumechili, Chuka and Akindes, Gerard., eds. *Identity and Nation in African Football: Fans, Community, and Clubs*. New York: Palgrave Macmillan, 2014, pp. 67–80.

Njororai, Wycliffe W. Simiyu. "The Diversity of Sport in Kenya," in Amusa, L.O., and Toriola, A.L., eds. *Sport in Contemporary African Society: An Anthology*. Mokapane, South Africa: AFAHPER-SD, 2003, pp. 199–229.

"Norwich City Mixed a Potent Punch, but was Witchcraft Involved?" *Daily Nation*, Nairobi, Kenya, September 28, 2013.

Rintaugu, Elijah G., Mwisukha, Andanje, and Onywera, Vincent. "Analysis of Factors that Affect the Standard of Soccer in Africa: The Case of East African Countries," *Journal of Physical Education and Sport* 12(1), 2012, 135–139.

Stakeholders Transitional Committee. "For the Good of the Sport: Good Governance, Financial Transparency and Stakeholder Accountability for Saving and Improving Kenyan Football," Final Report, Nairobi: Stakeholders Transitional Committee, 2004.

The Guardian, London: July 11, 2010.

Toskin, Robin. "Kenya's Harambee Stars Beaten in Cape Verde," *The Standard*, Nairobi, November 18, 2015.

Wandera, Gilbert. "FIFA suspends Kenya Indefinitely," *The East African Standard*, Nairobi: October 25, 2006.

CHAPTER 10

Soccer in Senegal: National Identity, Commercialization, and Acquisition of Wealth

Tamba E. M'bayo

With a long history dating as far back as the early colonial period, soccer or football is by far the most popular sport in Senegal today. Senegalese soccer reached its peak when the national team, *Les Lions de la Teranga* (The Lions of Hospitality), qualified for the FIFA World Cup of 2002 and defeated the former colonial power, France, in the opening match of the tournament hosted by South Korea and Japan. Under a French manager, Bruno Metsu (1954–2013), *Les Lions* advanced to the quarterfinal stage of the tournament (one of only three African countries, together with Cameroon and Ghana, to have done so). Until *Les Lions* qualified again for the 2018 World Cup hosted by Russia, however, Senegalese soccer had experienced a checkered phase since its glorious adventure at the 2002 tournament. Since then, *Les Lions* have performed better and reached the final of the Africa Cup of Nations competition organized by the

---

T. E. M'bayo (✉)
West Virginia University, Morgantown, WV, USA
e-mail: Tamba.Mbayo@mail.wvu.edu

© The Author(s), under exclusive license to Springer Nature Switzerland AG 2022
A. E. Ayuk (ed.), *Football (Soccer) in Africa*, Global Culture and Sport Series, https://doi.org/10.1007/978-3-030-94866-5_10

213

Confederation of African Football (CAF) and hosted by Egypt in 2019. Despite losing to Algeria by a single goal, *Les Lions* reaffirmed their credentials as one of Africa's best soccer teams. And nowadays in Senegal, it is common for various private and corporate commercial enterprises to compete for sponsorship of soccer, expecting to attract its increasing fan base to their products and services. Through the lens of soccer, this chapter engages broader issues about the intersection of national identity/ nationalism and sports, the commercialization of sports, the media and its impact on spectatorship, and the lure of sports vis-à-vis poverty and acquisition of wealth in West Africa. Thus, it argues that sports, in this case soccer, offers a path to illuminate disparities in political, social, and economic capital that exist between various groups in Senegalese society.

As a spectator sport, soccer (football) is the biggest crowd-pulling event in Senegal today.[1] And it arrived in Senegal via France as the latter expanded its colonial holdings in western Africa during the late nineteenth-century European "scramble."[2] Soccer followed a distinctive trajectory in becoming the most popular sport in a country where *laamb* (Senegalese wrestling), athletics, basketball, table tennis, and volleyball have their fair share of enthusiasts among the young and old and men and women alike. In truth, even as French colonial rule was being consolidated in the first half of the twentieth century, soccer spread as a popular pastime in both urban and rural areas. Undeniably the sport has long been part of the fascinating cultural tapestry Senegal represents as a country, where a predominantly Muslim population has coexisted with Christians and practitioners of African traditional religions for extensive periods of its history without

---

[1] Emmanuel Akyeampong and Charles Ambler, "Leisure in African History: An Introduction," *The International Journal of African Historical Studies* 35, No. 1 (2002), 1–16; Martha Saavreda, "Football Feminine – Development of the African Game: Senegal, Nigeria and South Africa," *Soccer & Society* 4, Issue 2–3 (2003), 225–253. https://doi.org/10.1080/14660970512331390925; Jeroen Schokkaert, "Football Clubs' Recruitment Strategies and International Player Migration: Evidence from Senegal and South Africa," *Soccer & Society* 17, Issue 1 (2016), 120–139. https://doi.org/10.1080/14660970.2014.919271.

[2] C. W. Newbury and A. S. Kanya-Forstner, "French Policy and the Origins of the Scramble for West Africa," *The Journal of African History* 10, No. 2 (April 1969), 253–276; Christopher Harrison, *France and Islam in West Africa, 1860–1960* (Cambridge: Cambridge University Press, 1988); A. S. Kanya-Forstner, *The Conquest of the Western Sudan: A Study of French Military Imperialism* (London: Cambridge University Press, 1969).

major religious conflicts.[3] More precisely, soccer has served as a unifier among the diverse ethnic groups of that country despite the local rivalries the sport generates.

This chapter employs the prism of soccer to explore broader issues about national identity/nationalism and sports, the commercialization of sports, the media and its impact on spectatorship, and the lure of sports vis-à-vis poverty and acquiring wealth in Senegal—as in other African countries.[4] It contends that sports, in this case soccer, offer a path for understanding better not only the complex manifestation of national identity, but also the disparities in political, social, and economic capital among various social groups in Senegalese society. A corollary of the main argument is that soccer is experiencing a wave of commercialization in Senegal that influences spectatorship and promotes a "counterculture" embracing sports as a weapon to fight against poverty and obtain wealth.

The first part of the chapter traces the history of soccer to its earliest beginning in Senegal and maps out its route during the colonial period right through the immediate post-independence era of the 1960s. And it continues with a look at contemporary developments in the sport since the 1970s, highlighting the role of soccer in igniting nationalist sentiments. The second part of the chapter then discusses soccer's importance among the youth of Senegal insofar as it serves as a "counter discourse" to articulate the frustrations of ordinary Senegalese against the status quo. In this context, an increasing number of young Senegalese are turning to sports as an escape route out of the vicious circle of poverty that characterizes their lives. Moreover, the increasing commercialization of sports in a global economy allows people in the most remote areas of Senegal (as in other parts of Africa) to follow major sporting events and news—even in the absence of satellite TVs and computers—on mobile devices, especially

---

[3] For more on Islam and Christianity in Senegal and West Africa generally, see, among others, Paul Gifford, "Religion in Contemporary Senegal," *Journal of Contemporary Religion* 31, No. 2 (2016), 255–267; Mamadou Diouf, ed., *Tolerance, Democracy, and Sufis in Senegal* (New York: Columbia University Press, 2013); Lamin Sanneh, *Piety and Power: Muslims and Christians in West Africa* (Maryknoll, NY: Orbis Books, 1996); Benjamin F. Soares, ed., *Muslim-Christian Encounters in Africa* (Leiden: Brill, 2006); David Robinson, *Muslim Societies in African History* (Cambridge: Cambridge University Press, 2004).

[4] Cathal Kilcline, *Sport and Society in Global France: Nations, Migrations, Corporations* (Liverpool: Liverpool University Press, 2019); Manase Kudzai Chiweshe, "Commercialization of Football in Africa: Prospects, Challenges, and Experiences," in Michael J. Gennaro and Saheed Aderinto, eds., *Sports in African History, Politics, and Identity Formation* (New York, NY: Routledge, 2019), 206–219.

cell phones.[5] And with spectatorship for soccer constantly increasing in Senegal, the economic benefits of tapping into the fan base of the sport has not escaped the attention of multinational companies and private entrepreneurs seeking to maximize their profits in the domestic economy.

SENEGALESE SOCCER IN HISTORICAL PERSPECTIVE, THE NATION-STATE, AND NATIONAL PRIDE

French colonial expansion in Africa during the late nineteenth century brought soccer to North Africa, where "French settlers in Oran (Algeria) channeled their sporting passion into the formal creation of a football club," according to soccer historian Peter Alegi.[6] Thereafter, other parts of the sub-region such as Tunisia and Egypt saw the formation of football clubs like Racing Club in Tunis in 1906 and Al Ahly in Cairo in 1924. By then soccer was spreading along the west coast of Africa, where cities such as Dakar in Senegal and Brazzaville in French Equatorial Africa (Congo today) witnessed French and other European soldiers, sailors, traders, and administrative employees play soccer as their leading hobby. Yet, as Alegi points out, unlike the British who introduced sports eagerly after conquest as part of their "civilizing mission," the French were hesitant and slower in spreading a sporting culture in their African colonies.[7] Even so, soccer's popularity in growing urban areas like Dakar was not confined to expatriate Frenchmen and other Europeans. In fact, by the 1920s, the French had embraced the introduction of physical education as part of the curricula for schools in their colonies. In 1923, French policymakers decided to make physical education compulsory in schools.[8] Still, while soccer became an important aspect of students' activities in secular schools such as the École Normal William Ponty in Dakar, the French deferred formal

---

[5] Beth Buggenhagen, *Muslim Families in Global Senegal: Money Takes care of Shame* (Bloomington: Indiana University Press, 2012). On the theme of globalization and its impact on small communities in West Africa, see Charles Piot, *Remotely Global: Village Modernity in West Africa* (Chicago: The University of Chicago Press, 1999).

[6] Peter Alegi, *African Soccerscapes: How a Continent Changed the World's Game* (Athens: Ohio University Press, 2010), 3.

[7] Ibid., 4.

[8] Alegi, *African Soccerscapes*; Bernadette Deville-Danthu, *Le sport en noir et blanc: Du sport colonial au sport africain dans les anciens territoires français d'Afrique occidentale, 1920–1965* (Paris: Harmattan, 1997); Phyllis Martin, *Leisure and Society in Colonial Brazzaville* (Cambridge: Cambridge University Press, 1995).

endorsement of sports as part of their *mission civilisatrice* until the 1930s and 1940s.

During the early colonial period, port cities along the Atlantic coast, among them Dakar, Brazzaville, Cape Coast in the Gold Coast (Ghana), and Calabar and Lagos in Nigeria, facilitated the diffusion of soccer because they were the first sites where European expatriates and indigenous males played together despite the rife racism that typified colonial relations. In Senegal, one of the earliest soccer clubs, Jeanne d'Arc of Dakar, was created in 1921. The name of the club evokes the influence Catholic missionaries had on sporting activities in colonial Senegal, where mission schools in the early twentieth century considered soccer a component of "muscular Christianity"; that is, the idea that sports is good for enriching physical and moral education with emphasis on discipline, endurance, honesty, and fairness, all elements of the Christian ethos. As soccer gained popularity in Dakar, the Union Sportive Indigène was formed in 1929 as local soccer teams began to work together to launch a competitive league.[9] Thus, in 1933, both Union Sportive Gorée and Foyer France Sénégal, which became ASC Diaraf in 1968, the most popular soccer club in the country, were founded.

Far more than any other sporting activity, soccer continued to grow during the colonial period as it spread from urban areas such as Dakar to the interior of the country, especially towns and villages linked to the railway and/or accessible by road transportation. In such places, young boys and men spent their spare time playing soccer, sometimes with makeshift balls made from rags if a proper ball was unavailable. Playing soccer barefooted was a common practice among those who could not afford to buy cheap footwear to use as soccer cleats. For those who played soccer then, it required little to no financial onus to enjoy the thrill of outwitting an opponent, tackling another player, or dribbling past two or three opponents to score a goal. The fact that even those from poor homes without money to spare could play soccer was an appeal that quickly caught on in both urban and rural areas of Senegal during the late colonial period.[10]

---

[9] Ibid.
[10] Susann Baller, "Urban Football Performances: Playing for the Neighborhood in Senegal, 1950s–2000s," *Africa: The Journal of the International African Institute* 84, No. 1 (February 2014), 17–35; see also Tamba E. M'bayo, "The Politics of Football in Post-colonial Sierra Leone," in Brenda Elsey and Stanislao G. Pugliese, eds., *Football and the Boundaries of History: Critical Studies in Soccer* (New York: Palgrave Macmillan, 2017), 267–293.

Indeed, soccer's growing popularity in Senegal and the rest of French West Africa found expression in the inauguration of inter-colony competitions such as the Coupe d'Afrique Occidentale Française (French West Africa Cup) in 1947.[11] Several soccer clubs from Senegal, including Jeanne d'Arc, Union Sportive Indigène, and Union Sportive Gorée, joined others, such as Racing Club from Conakry (Guinea), Jeunesse Club and ASEC from Abidjan (Côte d'Ivoire), and Étoile Filante from Lomé (Togo), in the competition. The competition that started with 16 clubs in 1947 would expand to 302 clubs by 1958, slightly over a decade later.[12] The mass appeal soccer spawned saw hundreds of spectators congregate at matches in Dakar, Abidjan, Bamako, and Lomé to watch their local and favorite teams play against others from different colonies in French West Africa. Such competitions marked the beginning of inter-colonial rivalry in sports that laid the foundations for spectators' support for local soccer teams to take on "nationalist" overtones.

Meanwhile, at the local level in Senegal, soccer gained more popularity in the 1950s, especially in the expanding urban area of Dakar, where neighborhood soccer clubs known as *navétanes* emerged to compete in local competitions. According to Mark Hann,

> The *navétanes* championships take their name from the Wolof "nawet", referring to the rainy season, and it's primarily during these summer months that they take place. Since the 1950s, local teams have competed against one another to defend the honour and pride of the neighbourhood or village, and the *navétanes* matches often attract huge crowds.[13]

Despite their limited organizational structure, such contests at times expanded into regional tournaments that took place after the official national soccer league season ended. By the late 1960s, as Susann Baller recounts, the Ministry of Youth and Sports had endorsed *navétanes* teams as it sought to launch a national soccer body as part of its youth program. While the goal was to organize annual championships, however, the ministry's efforts bred internal conflicts among officials and proprietors of the *navétanes* clubs. And, for sure, this impeded the kind of progress people

---

[11] Alegi, *African Soccerscapes*.
[12] Ibid, 44.
[13] Mark Hann, "Why African Fans Love European Football: A Senegalese Perspective," *The Conversation* (July 2, 2017), 4. http://theconversation.com/why-african-fans-love-european-football-a-senegalese-perspective-79856 (Accessed May 23, 2018).

anticipated.[14] Despite the challenges, however, soccer was a vehicle for building social relations among urbanites in Dakar. And such relations could extend beyond the city, which continued to experience a rapid population increase in the post-World War II period. Bernadette Deville-Danthu observes that the 1950s was a period when West Africa experienced a "sport fever" as soccer emerged as the preferred sport for a significant section of urban dwellers in cities like Dakar.[15]

From this period on, the print media, in the form of newspapers, played a key role in popularizing soccer, an effort complemented in no small measure by radio broadcasts.[16] Especially for soccer fans unable to make it to stadiums or those in remote parts of the country without financial means to travel to Dakar or any other city to watch important matches, the radio became indispensable for listening to live commentaries. Soccer commentators became household celebrities insofar as they could transmit the excitement of matches and the atmosphere in the stadiums via their live commentaries. While newspaper reports could inform readers about soccer matches before and after the events, radio broadcasts had the advantage of streaming live commentaries that kept soccer fans glued to their transistors throughout the matches. Indeed, it was common for dozens of fans including family members, friends, and even strangers to gather around a small radio and enjoy the thrill of a soccer match conveyed via live commentaries. Soccer's popularity in Senegal during the late colonial period meant the French authorities were aware of the important role sporting activities, including the indigenous wrestling known as *laamb*, played in the traditions of various ethnic groups.

By the time of independence in 1960, as Ousseynou Faye explains, sports like soccer and *laamb* had attracted the attention of officials of the new nation-state, who organized competitions under the auspices of the Ministry of Education to promote a sense of nationalism and national

---

[14] Baller, "Urban Football Performances," 17–19. When the *navétanes* organization faded it was not until the late 1980s and early 1990s that is autonomy as an independent association was recognized by the Senegalese Ministry of Interior. Then, in 2008, the association between an affiliate of the Federation Senegalaise de Football (FSF), which was founded in 1960. The federation has been affiliated with FIFA since 1962; and it has been a member of CAF since 1963.

[15] Deville-Danthu, Le sport en noir et blanc, 250–251.

[16] Richard J. Peltz-Steele, "The Sportswriter as Development Journalist: Covering African Football," *Ecquid Novi: African Journalism Studies* 31, No. 2 (2010), 149–173.

identity.[17] At the same time, it is worth noting, as Hann underscores, "The navétanes championships, like wrestling, offer a visceral experience of sporting competition which is rooted in complex local meanings, regional loyalties and historical rivalries."[18] Senegal's independence from France, no doubt, created an opportunity for local loyalties to morph into support for the new nation-state, an aspiration that would cut across both ethnic and regional rifts. In this context, sports, particularly soccer, would take center stage in deploying national pride among all Senegalese as an ethos to drive Senegal forward in its postcolonial life.

Since its formation in 1961, *Les Lions de la Teranga*, the Senegalese national soccer team, has had a checkered history, and this has both infuriated and excited soccer fans in Senegal, across Africa, and around the world. Even when Senegal hosted the African Cup of Nations tournament (CAN) in 1992, *Les Lions* was eliminated by Cameroon's Indomitable Lions in the quarterfinal stage of the competition. Moreover, the zenith of the team's success was in 2002, when *Les Lions* was losing finalists in the CAN tournament in Mali and quarterfinalists in the FIFA World Cup hosted by South Korea and Japan.[19] On their way to the quarterfinals, the Senegalese team defeated the French team, the defending champions at the time, in the opening match of the tournament. That upset was comparable to Cameroon's exploits in the 1990 World Cup, when the Indomitable Lions defeated the then defending champions, Argentina, also in the opening match of the tournament. Like the Indomitable Lions of Cameroon, *Les Lions* of Senegal advanced to the quarterfinal stage, to add more gloss to their defeat of Senegal's former colonial overlord, France. Ironically, the soccer encounter between the former colonizer and colonized country that ended in defeat for France was masterminded by a French manager, Bruno Metsu (1954–2013), who, before taking charge

---

[17] Senegal and The French Sudan gained independence simultaneously on April 4, 1960, as the Federation of Mali. However, the two former colonies decided to form independent nations four months later, and on August 19, the Federation dissolved and Senegal became a separate country on August 20.
[18] Hann, "Why African Fans Love European Football," 4.
[19] Jeff Bradley, "The Rise of African Soccer," *ESPN 2010 World Cup Guide* (May, 2010), 32–35; Alegi, *African Soccerscapes*; Laurent Dubois, *Soccer Empire: The World Cup and the Future of France* (Berkeley and Los Angeles: University of California Press, 2010).

of Senegal in 2000, had managed the national soccer team of Guinea for less than a year.[20]

In hindsight, even before Senegal's arrival on the world soccer stage, soccer's popularity had been increasing in the country during the late colonial period even as its organization left a lot to be desired. Little wonder then that at the time of Senegal's independence in 1960, soccer faced many challenges at the national level. The official soccer league, for example, had to tackle all sorts of problems: poor referees, unruly spectators, violent brawls, and boycotts by soccer clubs, to name but a few. In this scenario, it was common for some officials with vested interests in certain soccer clubs to decide the outcome of matches even before a ball had been kicked. And to compound the aforesaid problems, several soccer clubs seldom treated their players with the kind of civility they (the players) and fans expected. With such problems looming large, the national soccer league struggled to ignite sustained support from spectators despite their obvious passion for the sport. Newspaper accounts of that period allude to erratic refereeing decisions, crowd disruptions at matches, and vicious confrontations involving players, officials, and spectators alike.[21]

This period of crisis in Senegalese soccer, however, did not deter the Ministry of Youth and Sports from pursuing state-sponsored youth programs aimed at instilling a spirit of nationalism in young people and cultivating a distinctive Senegalese identity as part of a wider nation-building agenda. Ironically, though, the ministry was at odds with the popular *navétanes* teams and tournaments organized in various neighborhoods, which by then were not within its official jurisdiction. As Baller explains, despite the state's desire to keep young people in Senegal under control, it had little to nothing to offer the growing population of urban youth. There were hardly any state-funded facilities for sporting activities, not to mention the lack of opportunities for professional career development in soccer and other sports.[22] Thus, while soccer remained vastly popular in Senegal, there was an obvious disconnect between the vision of state officials, who sought more control over sporting activities, and ordinary folks, who gravitated toward *navétanes* teams and their neighborhood competi-

---

[20] Paul Doyle, "Bruno Metsu: The Man who inspired Senegal and all of Africa in 2002," *The Guardian* (October 16, 2013). https://www.theguardian.com/football/blog/2013/oct/16/bruno-metsu-senegal-africa-2002 (Accessed May 26, 2018).

[21] *Dakar-Matin*, August 21, 1964, cited in Baller, "Urban Football Performances," 21.

[22] Balller, "Urban Football Performances," 19–27.

tions. Against this backdrop, the Ministry of Youth and Sports created the ONCAV (Organisme national de coordination des activités des vacances) in 1970, demanding that all *navétanes* teams register with the organization.[23] In its effort to organize national competitions involving the neighborhood teams, the ministry never lost sight of its aspiration to keep Senegalese youth under control, especially after the 1968 student unrests in Dakar.[24]

Commercialization, Spectatorship, and Wealth in Global Senegal

With information technology bridging the communications gap between rich and poor countries around the world, even people in remote parts of Senegal tend to think that they are part of a global community of consumers who share the same products and services with their counterparts in more affluent countries in Europe, North America, and Asia. Through sports, especially soccer, fans in Senegal connect with the media frenzy and idolization of soccer stars such as Lionel Messi of Paris Saint-Germain (formerly of Barcelona FC) and Cristiano Ronaldo of Manchester United (previously of Juventus and Real Madrid), who they watch during soccer matches through satellite TV and cellphones, while also consuming news about the millions of dollars the stars make through advertisements, endorsements, and guest appearances at public events. It is therefore not surprising that Senegalese youngsters, like other young Africans elsewhere, dream of pursuing professional soccer careers in Europe and other wealthier parts of the world.

By the 1980s, an increasing number of European soccer scouts were poaching soccer leagues in Africa in search of talented young players to recruit for clubs in Belgium, France, The Netherlands, Spain, and Sweden, among other countries. The growing interest in African players came at a time when many soccer leagues across Africa were struggling to meet professional standards. With limited financial resources, few commercial sponsorships, and hardly any government investment in the development of soccer, most African national soccer associations lacked the will to cater to the needs of young soccer players. As such, despite the risk of dealing

---

[23] Ibid., 23.
[24] For more on the student uprisings, see A. Bathily, *Mai 68 à Dakar ou la révolte universitaire et la démocratie* (Paris: Chaka, 1992).

with foreign European soccer agents, African players did not hesitate to take chances with the lure of playing in European leagues. Among Senegal's trailblazers was the late dreadlocked Jules François Bertrand Bocandé (1958–2012) who, between 1979 and 1993, played for various clubs in France, most notably Metz, Paris Saint-Germain, and Nice, and gained 73 caps for *Les Lions*, scoring 20 goals.[25] Similarly, the former French international and Arsenal captain, Patrick Viera, who hailed from humble beginnings in Dakar but grew up in France, made a name for himself by winning three English Premier League titles and three FA Cups in England as well as the 1998 FIFA World Cup for France.[26] Such players would gain legendary status in Senegal and serve as an inspiration for younger soccer players aspiring to play professional soccer outside Senegal, preferably in Europe.

Many young Senegalese boys dream of playing for big European clubs. (Photo credit: Mark Hann/GLOBALSPORT, 2017)

---

[25] BBC Sport, "Senegalese Federation Plans Tribute for Bocande" (May 8, 2012) https://www.bbc.com/sport/football/17991406 (Accessed July 7, 2018).
[26] Between 2006 and 2010, Viera also won four Serie A titles with Inter Milan in Italy. Currently, he is the team manager of Crystal Palace in the English Premier League. See Matthew Taylor, "Global Players? Football, Migration and Globalization, c. 1930–2000," *Historical Social Research* 31, No. 1 (115) (2006), 7–30.

Although the financial success of African players was not always guaranteed, the hope of leaving Africa in pursuit of a soccer career abroad was strong enough to convince players about the possibility of escaping from the vicious circle of poverty that typified their lives at home. Thus, from their perspective, entrusting their future soccer careers to foreign scouting agents they hardly ever knew was a risk worth taking. To be sure, the financial lure of a professional contract with a European soccer club, no matter its status, was (and still is) too enticing for Senegalese and other African players to ignore. The ease of watching European soccer games live via satellite TV and mobile devices only increased interest in the global game among African soccer players and enthusiasts.[27] And the financial fortunes (and misfortunes) of soccer stars would become a staple in popular discourse in the same way the successes (and failures) of their careers generate intense debates among soccer fans.

In recent decades, a growing trend in Senegal (and other African countries) has been the formation of youth academies for young soccer players with demonstrated potential to succeed at a professional level. No other academies in Senegal epitomize this orientation than the Diambars Football Academy and Generation Foot, both institutions that combine training in soccer skills and academic study for their students to remain in school.[28] A lot of emphasis is put on studying to get the students to obtain a sound education for a future career besides soccer. Diambars started when four soccer friends conceived the idea between 1990 and 1998: Jimmy Adjovi Boco, a former defender of Benin and RC Lens; Saer Seck, a one-time President of Senegal's soccer league; Patrick Viera, the former Arsenal captain; and Bernard Lama, the ex-goalkeeper of France, Lille, and Paris Saint-Germain. By 2005, the construction of the Diambars complex had been completed in Saly (about three hours' drive south from Dakar), while its youth team was already making a name for itself in

---

[27] John Williams, "The Local and the Global in English Soccer and the Rise of Satellite Television," *Sociology of Sport Journal* 11, Issue 4 (December 1994), 376–397.

[28] Jalal Bounouar, "Africa's Best Football Academies," Africa.com. https://www.africa.com/africas-best-football-academies/ (Accessed July 8, 2018). Académie Génération Foot, or Generation Foot, started life in Dakar in 2000. The academy was the brainchild of former Senegalese soccer player Mady Toure, who played in France in the 1990s before a knee injury forced him to retire. Generation Foot has produced some of Senegal's professional soccer players including Sadio Mane of Liverpool FC, Papiss Cisse, the former Newcastle striker, and Diafra Sakho, who played for West Ham United FC in England. See Generation Foot, http://www.asgenerationfoot.com/ (Accessed July 29, 2018).

tournaments both at home and in Europe.[29] By combining rigorous academic studies with intensive soccer training, Diambars has ensured that its alumni are grounded well enough to embark on both educational and soccer careers. To date, over 50 students from the academy have proceeded to university, while another 45 have become professional soccer players, among them Senegalese internationals Idrissa Gana Gueye of Paris Saint-Germain (formerly of Everton FC) and Papa Ndiaye Souare (previously of Crystal Palace).[30]

The popularity of soccer in Senegal has transformed it into a major enterprise with sponsorship from both private and public companies. Sponsorship deals from various businesses capitalize on soccer's popularity to advertise their products and services. For aspiring Senegalese soccer players who aim to seek their fortune abroad, the sport has become a way of life out of poverty regardless of the challenge of migrating to Europe, North America, or Asia. Despite the harsh reality that only a select few of the players will ever make it to the top and earn the big money they envision, soccer continues to attract a rapidly increasing number of youthful Senegalese. The desire for financial success to take care of themselves and their families motivates Senegalese soccer players in the same way the lure of a professional soccer contract with a European club drives young soccer players to migrate abroad.

In Senegal today, soccer clubs have their fan bases that express their passion for the sport in more ways than one. Besides chanting, screaming, and arguing in favor of their preferred soccer team, fans in Senegal at times display hooligan propensities at different sporting events, just as in other countries around the world. Soccer hooliganism and violence in Senegal, however, tend to be more sporadic than regular. And spontaneity is another feature of soccer violence in the country. It could occur because of perceived unfair refereeing or disappointing results, as was the case in an African Cup of Nations qualifying match in Dakar in 2012, when Senegal lost to Côte d'Ivoire by two goals to nil.[31] This incident

---

[29] Diambars, http://www.diambars.org/bienvenue (Accessed July 29, 2018).
[30] Sophie Eastaugh, "From Sand, to Grass, to Europe? Senegal's Football Dream House," *CNN* (June 8, 2018). https://www.cnn.com/2016/06/07/football/senegal-football-school-diambars/index.html (Accessed July 29, 2018).
[31] Press Association, "Senegal Disqualified from 2013 Africa Cup of Nations after Crowd Trouble," *The Guardian* (October 16, 2012). https://www.theguardian.com/football/2012/oct/16/senegal-disqualified-africa-cup-nations (Accessed July 30, 2018).

compelled CAF to suspend Senegal from participating in the 2013 African Cup of Nations tournament hosted by South Africa.

It is rare, however, to see organized groups of soccer hooligans trooping to matches purposely to fire up violence. Instead, brawls and rioting between rival soccer fans occur when they encounter each other and start trading insults and intimidating other spectators in a stadium.[32] In July 2017, violence erupted between two rival fans of Union Sportive Ouakam and Stade de Mbour during a League Cup Final soccer match at the Demba Diop Stadium in Dakar. As the violence flared and spectators fled from the stands, they got trapped in a stampede when a wall collapsed, leaving at least eight people dead and several others wounded. Indeed, inadequate security and safety standards contributed to the chaotic scenes that ensued as the police fired tear gas to separate the rival fans in a desperate attempt to restore normalcy.[33]

Conclusion

From its beginning as an imported sporting activity introduced by the French around the same time colonial rule was being consolidated in Senegal at the turn of the twentieth century, soccer gained increasing popularity in both urban and rural areas during the colonial period. Soccer clubs in the country started to be created in the early 1900s, leading to the formation of a competitive league in the colony that faced all sorts of challenges while striving to survive. To be sure, soccer's popularity in colonial Francophone West Africa after World War II culminated in the creation of an inter-colony competition in 1947. From only 16 teams when it was inaugurated, the *Coupe d'Afrique Occidentale Française* would grow to include 302 teams by the late 1950s. And by the time Senegal gained independence from France in 1960, soccer had become a sporting tradition through which pride in the new nation-state was being expressed. The creation of the national soccer team, *Les Lions de la Teranga*, in 1961 exemplified a desire by the country's political and sports leaderships to foster a patriotic ethos via sports.

[32] Fernando Duarte, Jonathan Wilson, Shaun Walker, Paolo Bandini and Paul Doyle, "Football Violence: A View from around the World," *The Guardian* (December 19, 3013). https://www.theguardian.com/football/2013/dec/19/football-violence-view-around-world (Accessed July 30, 2018).
[33] BBC Africa, "Senegal Demba Diop: Football Stadium Collapse Kills Eight," https://www.bbc.com/news/world-africa-40621982 (Accessed July 30, 2018).

Today, despite the uneven successes of *Les Lions* since the 1960s, soccer remains not only the most popular sport in Senegal but has also emerged as a booming commercial enterprise backed by private and corporate enterprises seeking to promote their goods and services. Through sponsorship deals, commercials, and guest appearances by famous soccer players on TV shows, various businesses advertise their products while promoting soccer in Senegal on a scale that would not have been imagined when the sport was first introduced in the country in the late 1800s. And with the lure of soccer as a profession to help youths extricate themselves and their families from the vicious cycle of poverty they experience in Senegal, the sport continues to attract increasingly younger players, who hope to one day ply their trade not only in Senegal, but also, perhaps with a little dose of good fortune, in Europe, the Americas, or Asia.

All told, the recent revival of *Les Lions* as a competitive soccer team that went all the way to the final of the 2019 Africa Cup of Nations tournament has generated a lot of optimism in Senegal that the future is bright for the development of soccer in the country. Moreover, as Senegal continues to produce some of the big names in African soccer, among them Sadio Mané (Liverpool FC), Edouard Mendy (Chelsea FC), Kalidou Koulibaly (SSC Napoli), and Idrissa Gueye (Paris Saint-Germain), younger players in the country remain convinced that in soccer anything is possible despite the obvious challenges they face. And with the next CAN tournament in Cameroon scheduled to start in early January 2022, it requires no exaggeration to state that Senegalese soccer fans (and others elsewhere around the world) will be glued to the screens of their TVs and mobile devices to see who will emerge as the next superstars on Senegal's soccerscape, to borrow from Peter Alegi.[34]

References

Akyeampong, Emmanuel, and Charles Ambler. "Leisure in Africa History: An Introduction." *The International Journal of African Historical Studies* 35, No. 1 (2002): 1–16.

Armstrong, Gary, and Richard Guilianotti, eds. *Football in Africa: Conflict, Conciliation, and Community*. Basingstoke, UK: Palgrave Macmillan, 2004.

[34] Alegi, *African Soccerscapes*.

Baller, Susann. "Football and the Representation of History: The Senegalese 2002 'Success Story' in Football Cartoons and Advertisements." *Soccer & Society* 13, No. 2 (March 2012): 309–326.

———. "Transforming Urban Landscapes: Soccer Fields as Sites of Urban Sociability in the Agglomeration of Dakar." *African Identities* 5, No. 2 (2007): 217–230.

———. "Urban Football Performances: Playing for the Neighborhood in Senegal, 1950s–2000s." *Africa: The Journal of the International African Institute* 84, No. 1 (February 2014): 17–35.

Bathily, A. *Mai 68 à Dakar ou la révolte universitaire et la démocratie.* Paris: Chaka, 1992.

BBC Africa. "Senegal Demba Diop: Football Stadium Collapse Kills Eight." (July 16, 2017). https://www.bbc.com/news/world-africa-40621982 (Accessed July 30, 2018).

BBC Sport, "Senegalese Federation Plans Tribute for Bocande" (May 8, 2012). https://www.bbc.com/sport/football/17991406 (Accessed July 7, 2018).

Bounouar, Jalal. "Africa's Best Football Academies." Africa.com. https://www.africa.com/africas-best-football-academies/ (Accessed July 8, 2018).

Bradley, Jeff. "The Rise of African Soccer." *ESPN 2010 World Cup Guide* (May, 2010): 32–35.

Brewer, Benjamin D. "Switching Fields: The World Soccer Economy in an Era of Globalization." PhD Dissertation, The Johns Hopkins University, 2006.

Buggenhagen, Beth. *Muslim Families in Global Senegal: Money Takes care of Shame.* Bloomington: Indiana University Press, 2012.

Chiweshe, Manase Kudzai. "Commercialization of Football in Africa: Prospects, Challenges, and Experiences." In Michael J. Gennaro and Saheed Aderinto, eds. *Sports in African History, Politics, and Identity Formation.* New York, NY: Routledge, 2019, 206–219.

Darby, Paul. *Africa, Football, and FIFA: Politics, Colonialism, and Resistance.* Abingdon, UK: Frank Cass, 2002.

———. "'Let Us Rally around the Flag': Football, Nation-building, and Pan-Africanism in Kwame Nkrumah's Ghana." *The Journal of African History* 54, No. 2 (July 2013): 221–246.

Deville-Danthu, Bernadette. *Le sport en noir et blanc: Du sport colonial au sport africain dans les anciens territoires français d'Afrique occidentale, 1920–1965.* Paris: Harmattan, 1997.

Diambars. http://www.diambars.org/bienvenue (Accessed July 29, 2018).

Diouf, Mamadou, ed. *Tolerance, Democracy, and Sufis in Senegal.* New York: Columbia University Press, 2013.

Doyle, Paul. "Bruno Metsu: The Man who inspired Senegal and all of Africa in 2002." *The Guardian* (October 16, 2013). https://www.theguardian.com/

football/blog/2013/oct/16/bruno-metsu-senegal-africa-2002 (Accessed May 26, 2018).
Duarte, Fernando, Jonathan Wilson, Shaun Walker, Paolo Bandini, and Paul Doyle. "Football Violence: A View from around the World." *The Guardian* (December 19, 2013). https://www.theguardian.com/football/2013/dec/19/football-violence-view-around-world (Accessed July 30, 2018).
Dubois, Laurent. *Soccer Empire: The World Cup and the Future of France*. Berkeley and Los Angeles: University of California Press, 2010.
Eastaugh, Sophie. "From Sand, to Grass, to Europe? Senegal's Football Dream House." *CNN* (June 8, 2018). https://www.cnn.com/2016/06/07/football/senegal-football-school-diambars/index.html (Accessed July 29, 2018).
Faye, Ousseynou. "Sport, argent et politique: la lute libre à Dakar (1800–2000)." In Momar-Coumba Diop, ed. *Le Sénégal contemporain*. Paris: Karthala, 2002, 309–340.
Films for the Humanities & Sciences (Firm). "More Than Just a Game: Competitions and Celebrations in Ethiopia, Ghana, Niger, Senegal, and Sudan." New York, NY: Films Media Group, 2004.
Generation Foot. http://www.asgenerationfoot.com/ (Accessed July 29, 2018).
Gifford, Paul. "Religion in Contemporary Senegal." *Journal of Contemporary Religion* 31, No. 2 (2016): 255–267.
Hann, Mark. "Why African Fans Love European Football: A Senegalese Perspective." *The Conversation* (July 2, 2017). http://theconversation.com/why-african-fans-love-european-football-a-senegalese-perspective-79856 (Accessed May 23, 2018).
Harrison, Christopher. *France and Islam in West Africa, 1860–1960*. Cambridge: Cambridge University Press, 1988.
Kanya-Forstner, A. S. *The Conquest of the Western Sudan: A Study of French Military Imperialism*. London: Cambridge University Press, 1969.
Kilcline, Cathal. *Sport and Society in Global France: Nations, Migrations, Corporations*. Liverpool: Liverpool University Press, 2019.
M'bayo, Tamba E. "The Politics of Football in Post-colonial Sierra Leone." In Brenda Elsey and Stanislao G. Pugliese, eds. *Football and the Boundaries of History: Critical Studies in Soccer*. New York: Palgrave Macmillan, 2017, 267–293.
Martin, Phyllis. *Leisure and Society in Colonial Brazzaville*. Cambridge: Cambridge University Press, 1995.
Newbury, C. W., and A. S. Kanya-Forstner. "French Policy and the Origins of the Scramble for West Africa." *The Journal of African History* 10, No. 2 (April 1969): 253–276.
Peltz-Steele, Richard J. "The Sportswriter as Development Journalist: Covering African Football." *Ecquid Novi: African Journalism Studies* 31, No. 2 (2010): 149–173.

Piot, Charles. *Remotely Global: Village Modernity in West Africa*. Chicago: University of Chicago Press, 1999.

Press Association. "Senegal Disqualified from 2013 Africa Cup of Nations after Crowd Trouble." *The Guardian* (October 16, 2012). https://www.theguardian.com/football/2012/oct/16/senegal-disqualified-africa-cup-nations (Accessed July 30, 2018).

Ralph, Michael. "'Le Sénégal Qui Gagne': Soccer and the Stakes of Neoliberalism in a Postcolonial Port." *Soccer and Society* 7, 2–3 (April–July 2006): 300–317.

Robinson, David. *Muslim Societies in African History*. Cambridge: Cambridge University Press, 2004.

Ross, Eric. *Culture and Customs of Senegal*. Westport, CT: Greenwood Press, 2008.

Saavreda, Martha. "Football Feminine – Development of the African Game: Senegal, Nigeria and South Africa." *Soccer & Society* 4, Issue 2–3 (2003): 225–253. https://doi.org/10.1080/14660970512331390925.

Sanneh, Lamin. *Piety and Power: Muslims and Christians in West Africa*. Maryknoll, NY: Orbis Books, 1996.

Schokkaert, Jeroen. "Football Clubs' Recruitment Strategies and International Player Migration: Evidence from Senegal and South Africa." *Soccer & Society* 17, Issue 1 (2016): 120–139. https://doi.org/10.1080/1466097 0.2014.919271.

Soares, Benjamin F., ed. *Muslim-Christian Encounters in Africa*. Leiden: Brill, 2006.

Taylor, Matthew. "Global Players? Football, Migration and Globalization, c. 1930–2000." *Historical Social Research* 31, No. 1 (115) (2006): 7–30.

Williams, John. "The Local and the Global in English Soccer and the Rise of Satellite Television." *Sociology of Sport Journal* 11, Issue 4 (December 1994): 376–397.

CHAPTER 11

Contradictions and Inconsistencies Facing the South African Football Association and the Premier Soccer League

David L. Bogopa

INTRODUCTION AND HISTORICAL BACKGROUND

This chapter presents a brief historical background of the study and the context of contradictions and inconsistencies within South African soccer. Furthermore, this chapter presents the research objectives as well as the research methodology that was utilized to gather data. Good governance has been used as a conceptual framework to understand the issues of gender inequality, contradictions, and inconsistencies in soccer within the context of South Africa with specific reference to the South African Football Association and the Premier Soccer League. After the abovementioned issues, there is also a critical analysis of the relevant literature that has been consulted which shows that with increases in many communities and social structures, gender is biologically and culturally constructed. Finally, this chapter concludes by outlining the research findings and the

D. L. Bogopa (✉)
Nelson Mandela University, Gqeberha, South Africa
e-mail: David.Bogopa@mandela.ac.za

© The Author(s), under exclusive license to Springer Nature Switzerland AG 2022
A. E. Ayuk (ed.), *Football (Soccer) in Africa*, Global Culture and Sport Series, https://doi.org/10.1007/978-3-030-94866-5_11

recommendations with the view of forging a way forward about gender inequality, contradictions, and inconsistencies encountered within these two soccer structures in South Africa.

It is an open secret that FIFA as a world football body emphasizes the notion of "fair play" meaning that everything in football all over the world must be conducted fairly and equitably. In terms of the FIFA objective number 3, discrimination of any kind against a country, private person, or a group of people on account of ethnic origin, gender, language, religion, politics, or any other reason is strictly prohibited and punishable by suspension or expulsion per FIFA Constitution (2010: 7). There is zero tolerance for any form of discrimination. However, male dominance in football in South Africa continues to be of serious concern including, among others, the South African Football Association (SAFA) and the domestic league known as the Premier Soccer League (PSL).

Furthermore, this chapter presents some of the contradictions and inconsistencies within the South African Football Association and the Premier Soccer League. Some focus of this chapter is on gender inequality and representation which remains a highly contested issue. Moreover, the contradictions and inconsistencies covered in this chapter also include the operational matters and decisions taken by SAFA and PSL authorities.

Problem Statement

Despite SAFA and PSL having policies and rules in place. Increasingly, there are contradictions and inconsistent application and implementation of policies and rules. The above contradictions and inconsistencies are costly, and they are detrimental to the growth of soccer and good governance in South Africa.

Research Questions

What are the challenges faced by the South African Football Association and the Premier Soccer League?

Do PSL and SAFA have effective mechanisms to address issues of contradictions, gender inequality, and inconsistencies within their structures?

Research Objectives

The research objectives of this study include, among others, first, to highlight some of the contradictions and inconsistencies within the South African Football Association and the South African Premier Soccer League. Second, to highlight the gender inequalities in football within the context of the South African Football Association and the Premier Soccer League. Third, to contribute within the anthropology of soccer in South Africa, and lastly, to come up with recommendations with the view to address gender inequality including the contradictions and inconsistencies within the two South African soccer structures.

Research Methodology

This research has followed a mixed method which includes both the qualitative and quantitative approaches. The above mixed methods included individual interviews which include the football-loving spectators in South Africa as well as the current and former football players from both sexes. Furthermore, the researcher also used statistics from the South African Football Association and the Premier Soccer League website to show the gender inequality within these two football structures. An attempt has been made to contact the former professional football players and the South African Football Association officials to voluntarily participate in the interviews, but they failed to respond to emails sent to them.

Maree et al. (2016: 77) state that "qualitative research uses open, exploratory research questions, emphasizes understanding phenomena and uses special strategies for enhancing the credibility of the research design and data analyses". In line with Maree et al. (2016), the researcher used research questions to get the responses from the participants.

Gretchen and Rallis (2017: 79) define observation as "the systematic description of events, behaviors, and artifacts in the social setting chosen for study". Observations have been used as a tool for collecting data about people, processes, and cultures in qualitative research. The researcher observed some of the activities that took place within the SAFA and the PSL.

Sampling is defined by Emmel (2013: 281) as the process of selecting a portion that is representative. Furthermore, Emmel (2013: 289) argued that purposive sampling is a "non-probability sample that is selected based on characteristics of a population and the objective of the study". Purpose sampling was used in this research where 45 interviews were conducted. The original 40 participants include ordinary football enthusiasts in South Africa, and the interviews were conducted before the outbreak of the coronavirus. Additional five interviews were conducted during the COVID-19 period (January 2021 onward). Several attempts were made to interview professional football players and officials of both SAFA and PSL, but due to their busy schedules, the interviews did not materialize. In the light of purpose sampling, I argue that "purpose" represents a location or type of key criteria. Although purposive selection involves quite deliberate choices, this should not suggest any bias like the choices made. It is a matter of identifying subjects that are part of the research question.

Scott defines overt research as "participant observation carried out with the consent of the subjects being studied. This agreement may be tacit or formally expressed" (Scott 2014: 540). In overt research, the researcher reveals their true identity and states the purpose of the study clearly, usually in a form of a general statement (Scott 2014: 540). This research study used the overt research design. Permission to conduct interviews was asked from the research participants before the interviews commenced. The research objectives were clearly explained to each research participant.

De Vos et al. (2011: 68) state that researchers have two basic ethical responsibilities: the responsibility of human and non-human, who take part in a project, and the responsibility to the discipline of science to be accurate and honest in the report of their research. The researcher has complied with the ethics protocol by obtaining permission to conduct interviews as well as maintaining that the names and descriptions of participants are kept confidential.

Good Governance (Conceptual Framework)

I am using good governance as a conceptual framework to understand issues of gender inequality, contradictions, and inconsistencies within football in South Africa. In my view, good governance in sport relies heavily on financial resources and sound administrative skills. Some of the scholars who have contributed to sports governance include, among others, Rondinelli and Shabbir Cheeman (2003), who argued that good governance entails improving government efficiency, accountability, and responsiveness controlling corruption as well as establishing ethical norms. On the other hand, echoing the notion of good governance, Greig et al.

(2007: 7) have touched on some of the factors in the Millennium Development Goals strategy which include, among others, the promotion of gender equality and the empowerment of women as well as the development of a global partnership for development.

Re-iterating the above notion of good governance, Prinsloo (2013) argued that good governance begins with the political will to govern well. Moreover, Prinsloo (2013) mentions that the effectiveness of a political formation in power more often determines whether good governance exists or not. Furthermore, Boya (2016: 75) asserts that good governance in South African sport continues to be a problem. For example, Boya (2016) alluded to the issue of how unethical conduct occurred regarding the 2010 FIFA World Cup which was hosted by South Africa.

In the light of what the above scholars have articulated on good governance, I am, therefore, arguing strongly that both the SAFA and the PSL are far from attaining good governance in terms of running their daily activities. Perhaps, if the leadership of both SAFA and PSL could follow the notion of good governance as described by Rondinelli and Shabbir Cheeman (2003), Greig et al. (2007), Prinsloo (2013), and Boya (2016), they could achieve good governance.

Construction of Gender

Gender is more often constructed differently by many scholars, for example, West and Zimmermann (1987) are some of the scholars who constructed the concept of gender during the late 1980s and early 1990s. These scholars have utilized a socio-cultural point of view in their construct. They argue that gender includes the different traits, roles, behaviors, attitudes, and aptitudes males and females are expected to display (West and Zimmermann 1987). However, Butler (1990), constructed the concept of gender as reinforcement claims of sex membership. Butler (1990) argued that the expressions such as "gendered practices", "gendered language", and "gendered jobs" have been used to emphasize the tenet that gender involves a process of social construction and to make gender a more central explanation of organizational behavior phenomena such as leadership. The above scholars' definitions are based on socio-cultural stereotypes as well as those that are biologically constructed. In almost most of the societies around the world, many people still hold on to the above notions of cultural stereotypes and biological constructions.

Biological Construction of Gender

The scholars who previously contributed research in the area of gender construction on the global scale include Freeman (1983) who challenged Mead's (1935) work on the idea of the cultural construction of gender. Freeman (1983) accused Mead of cultural determinism (that Mead gave priority to culture over biology) and opened a huge debate within the academic and non-academic circles. Freeman (1983) came up with the strength hypothesis that men are physically stronger than women and this gives them superiority.

In the light of the above, Lerner (1994: 4) explains how the metaphors of gender constructed the male as the norm and as the whole and powerful, the female as unfinished, visionary mutilated, and emotionally dependent. Lerner (1994) summarizes the major assumptions about gender and patriarchal society as follows: "Men and women are essentially different creatures not only in their biological equipment but in their needs capacities and functions". Similarly, MacClancy (1996: 75) also contributed to the anthropology of sport within the context of Spain. MacClancy (1996) argued that women in Spain have been previously excluded in Spanish Bull Fighting sport largely because it is believed that only men have qualities such as courage and braveness to play this sport. There is a general belief among Spanish men that a woman's anatomy makes it inappropriate for her to fight bulls (MacClancy 1996: 76).

According to Peach (1997: 20), several arguments have been made over the years to justify the exclusion of women from military combat. It was argued that military effectiveness is often compromised by the women's lack of physical strength and stamina. The exclusion of women in terms of direct ground combat denied them the opportunity for promotion and advancement within and outside the army. Sharing the same sentiment, Driscoll (1998) focused on the male sport model and examines the role played by the media in shaping beliefs and values regarding women and girls in physical activity and sports. Driscoll (1998) argues that some scholars who include, among others, Birrell and Cole (1990) and Kane and Parks (1992), have argued that perhaps more than any other social institution, sport perpetuates male superiority and female inferiority. According to the abovementioned scholars, the Western culture instills these notions from early childhood, and by the time a child enters school, a preconceived idea is formed that males can run faster, jump higher, and throw farther than females. Males are viewed as powerful, dominant, and in control of their bodies and females are weak, submissive, lacking in control, and need of male protection.

Socio-cultural Construction of Gender

Earlier scholars who wrote about the socio-cultural construction of gender, including, among others, Mead (1928, 1935) conducted anthropological research on issues of gender relations. Mead (1928, 1935) researched Samoa and New Guinea and she has utilized her research data to establish the significance of culture in molding the gender differences within the context of Samoa and New Guinea. She wanted to offer an alternative explanation to the idea of the biological construction of gender which dominated the academic literature in the 1920s. Furthermore, Goodman (1996) also argued that gender refers to ways of seeing and representing people and situations based on sex difference; gender is a social or cultural category, influenced by stereotypes about female and male behavior that exists in our attitudes and beliefs. Within the context of sport, Blanchard and Cheska (1985: 234) argued that increasingly, women were deprived of sport competition in the male power-orientated public context. It is only in recent decades that this passive image of femininity has been modified as females become more actively involved in different sporting codes. Blanchard and Cheska (1985: 245) further argued that women's sport in countries such as Mongolia and Tonga previously has not substantially progressed because there were no opportunities at all available for women.

LITERATURE REVIEW

To a large extent, issues of gender inequality have been covered extensively within the context of sport in general and football in particular. Some of the scholars who have written about gender inequality including, among others, Hargreaves (1997: 199) argued about gender inequalities in South Africa within the context of cricket, rugby, and soccer. For example, Hargreaves (1997) argued that out of the three sporting codes above, she cited cricket where an R8 million sponsorship deal was clinched to develop men's cricket in Soweto.

Pelak (2005) focused on the South African Football Association headquartered in Johannesburg, as well as the Western Cape Province headquarters in Cape Town, with semi-structured interviews conducted with 7 soccer players and 11 soccer administrators in Johannesburg and Cape Town. Pelak (2005: 57) found out that South African soccer was still divided along gender lines: for example, men and boys dominated soccer, while women and girls continued to be marginalized.

Reflecting on the contradictions and inconsistent decisions in football administration, Alegi (2007: 35) argues that soccer is still marginalized in Cape Town in terms of sport development. According to Alegi (2007: 36), the construction of Green Point Stadium denied residents from colored areas an opportunity in terms of infrastructural development. Alegi (2007) further argues that it does not make sense to build a soccer stadium in an area where soccer is not popular or not played at all.

Bogopa (2008) highlights the lack of attention and media coverage given to the encounter between the South African Women's National soccer team and their Nigerian counterparts. Furthermore, Bogopa (2010) also comments on issues of gender relations at the FIFA World Cup tournament which was held in South Africa: he points out, for example, that there were no female radio and television commentators, no female match officials, and no female announcers.

McKinley (2010) also contributed to research within the context of South African soccer. McKinley's research (2010: 81) also focused on the historical development of soccer in South Africa during the apartheid and post-apartheid periods. McKinley (2010) examines how huge sponsorships contributed to soccer development programs at both amateur and professional levels. McKinley (2010: 87) argues about how financial assistance from big companies has been utilized incorrectly by soccer authorities in South Africa. For example, Women Soccer Committee received R300,000 out of a huge South African Football Association budget. Clearly, the above allocation on women's soccer shows some inconsistencies in terms of fairly distributing sponsorship between women and men's soccer.

Moreover, Naidoo and Muholi (2010: 106) also contributed to research in gender relations in soccer. Their research focused on the South African National Soccer team also known as *Banyana Banyana*. Naidoo and Muholi (2010) discovered that women were still not fairly represented in the South African football structures. For example, the former South African Women National Soccer coach complained about sexual harassment incidents where some of the male technical team members were sexually involved with female soccer players.

According to Haugaa Engh (2012), despite securing a huge sponsorship of about R20 million from ABSA, one of the leading financial institutions, there are structural inequalities and material constraints. Haugaa Engh (2012: 141) discovered that in Cape Town, the women's soccer team struggled with funds to register their teams into the local football association. Moreover, women's teams in Cape Town struggled to cover their transport costs to travel to different venues to honor their match fixtures.

Contributing to the scholarly work on gender inequality in soccer, Bogopa (2014: 129) argued that the majority of male learners and educators still have the perception that soccer belongs to boys and men and some female learners and educators also believe the same. Bogopa's (2014) findings from his research include issues such as the lack of sponsorship and the availability of space for learners to participate in soccer as well as inadequate soccer fields at the two schools in Tsakane, namely, Reshogofaditswe Secondary School and Khombindlela Primary School.

According to Ogunniyi (2014: 538), even though sports policy documents address issues of gender inequality in soccer, women's soccer continues to be marginalized. Women are still grappling with issues such as poor media coverage and not enough competitive soccer competitions at both local and national levels. Moreover, Ogunniyi (2015: 32) argued that the patriarchal structures and cultural understandings regarding women remain an obstacle in the advancement of women to occupy positions of power within the higher structures of football in South Africa.

Sharing the same sentiments as other scholars regarding gender inequality in soccer, Burnett (2018) has focused on the plight of women and girls in Sub-Saharan Africa who continue to be marginalized. Furthermore, Burnett (2018: 1) argued that gender inequality in soccer in Sub-Saharan Africa has taken a backseat to social transformation. The above notion in Burnett's view (2018) should take a center stage with the view of addressing some of the ills committed in the past.

Re-emphasizing what other scholars have already articulated on the issue of gender inequality in soccer, Sait and Bogopa (2021) further confirm that the scope of gender inequality in soccer within the context of South Africa continues to be of great concern. Moreover, Sait and Bogopa (2021) have discovered how women and girls are still grappling with opportunities to display their soccer talent at Gelvandale in the Eastern Province.

Research Findings

Currently, the executive committees of SAFA and PSL are dominated by male members, while the female continues to be less and that confirms that gender relations within these two soccer structures continue to be a problem. The CEO's positions within SAFA and PSL have been over the years been occupied by males, and it is only currently within the PSL that there is a female acting CEO which is a step in the right direction; however, it remains interesting as to who will be appointed permanently. All PSL teams have employed only male technical staff particularly regarding the coaching department, namely, the head coach, assistant coach, and goalkeeper coach positions and this is of great concern largely because female capable coaches also need exposure at that level. The same trend or pattern of employing the male soccer team managers is witnessed within the PSL teams. None of the PSL teams have and South African National teams have appointed female medical doctors. However, the current head coach of the South African National Soccer team (*Banyana Banyana*) is a female from South Africa and this is a step in the right direction.

The statistics in the above table clearly shows that SAFA structure that the female SAFA Vice President was charged and dismissed from the committee for writing a letter to the South African Sports Minister to intervene within the problems encountered by SAFA. The above unfair dismissal, therefore, means that there are no prospects at this stage to have a female acting president should the current president decide to resign as a member or should the president be away due to business trips overseas or due to illness. Similarly, the unfair dismissal of the female SAFA Vice President close-down the option of having an acting female president should SAFA also charge the president of misconduct and dismiss him. In terms of gender representation, it is evident from Table 11.1 that women are not fairly represented at both national and provincial levels. Moreover, Table 11.2 shows the discrepancy regarding men and women teams with SAFA. Women's soccer national teams are lesser than those of men.

Table 11.3 shows how women's teams are not given more time and exposure in terms of soccer competitions. Furthermore, Tables 11.4 and 11.5 show the imbalances in terms of men's and women's teams as well as skewed competition opportunities.

The PSL system of registration of players is questionable; the PSL office has registered the two Jomo Cosmos and allocated the jersey numbers 86 and 92 without any hassles but the PSL went on to summon or fine Jomo

Table 11.1 SAFA Executive Committee

Position	Representation	Gender
SAFA President	National	Male
SAFA Vice President	National	3 males and 1 female (unfairly dismissed)
SAFA National Executive Committee	National	9 males and 3 females
Provincial Chair and Deputy Chair	Eastern Cape	2 males
Provincial Chair and Deputy Chair	Free State	2 males
Provincial Chair and Deputy Chair	Gauteng	2 males
Provincial Chair and Deputy Chair	KwaZulu/Natal	1 male and 1 female
Provincial Chair and Deputy Chair	Limpopo	2 males
Provincial Chair and Deputy Chair	Mpumalanga	2 males
Provincial Chair and Deputy Chair	Northern Cape	2 males
Provincial Chair and Deputy Chair	North-West	2 males
Provincial Chair and Deputy Chair	Western Cape	1 male and 1 female

https://www.safa.net/safa-national-executive-committee/

Table 11.2 PSL executive committee

Position	Gender
Chairperson	Male
Chief Executive Officer	Female
Members	1 female and 5 males

Cosmos (First National Division) for fielding the two players using the above numbers. The club officials including match officials have transgressed the NSL rules by fielding ineligible players, and yet the rules are stipulated within the NSL book which is made available to every team and this has displayed poor governance.

Table 11.3 PSL teams, owners, coaching staffs, and province

Team name	Owner	Head coach	Province
Amazulu FC	Male	Male	KwaZulu Natal
Baroka FC	Male	Male	Limpopo
Cape Town City	Male	Male	Western Cape
Chippa United	Male	Male	Eastern Cape
Golden Arrows	Female	Male	KwaZulu Natal
Kaizer Chiefs	Male	Male	Gauteng
Mamelodi Sundowns FC	Male	Male	Gauteng
Maritzburg United FC	Male	Male	KwaZulu Natal
Marumo Gallants City FC	Male	Male	Limpopo
Orlando Pirates	Male	Male	Gauteng
Real Kings	Female	Male	KwaZulu Natal
Sekhukhune FC	Male	Male	Limpopo
Stellenbosch	Male	Male	Western Cape
Supersport United FC	Male	Male	Gauteng
Swallows	Male	Male	Gauteng
TS Galaxy	Male	Male	Mpumalanga

Table 11.4 SAFA teams

Men teams	Women teams
Bafana Bafana	Banyana Banyana
Men's Under 23 (aMaglukgluk)	Women's Under 20 (Basetsana)
Men's Under 20 (Majita)	Girl's Under 17
Boy's Under 17 (Majimbos)	
Men's Futsal	
Men's Beach Ball	

Table 11.5 SAFA competitions

Men's competitions	Women's competition
ABC Motsepe League	Sasol Women's League
SAFA Men's Regional League	
Hollywoodbets Super League	

Regarding the registration of Jomo Cosmos FC, one of the participants commented as follows during the interview:

"Ho na le mathata a maholo ko PSL, batho ba sebetsang ko PSL ha ba tsebe ho hlalosetsa dihlopha tsa PSL meloa hantle, ke etsa mohlala, PSL e dumetse jwang ho register dijersey tsa dibapadi tsa Jomo Cosmos tse leng outside number 50? Nna ke sola Jomo Cosmos le PSL kaofela" The above is the Sesotho version arguing that *"there is a big problem within PSL administrators, they do not know how to advise soccer teams on rules. For example, how did PSL agree to register Jomo Cosmos jersey numbers exceeding number 50? I blame both Jomo Cosmos for bringing the wrong application in terms of numbers and similarly blaming the PSL for allowing the incorrect application to go through".*

The PSL Disciplinary Committee has been inconsistent in applying their minds properly regarding the passing of judgment and the case in question is the May 2019 judgment on Mamelodi Sundowns Football Club. The PSL Disciplinary has found Mamelodi Sundowns FC guilty of the charge and imposed an R250,000 fine only. The inconsistency with the abovementioned judgment is that no points were docked from Mamelodi Sundowns FC despite having fielded a player illegally.

More contradictions are that it was reported that the former South African Football Association (SAFA) deputy-president, Mwelo Nonkonyane, who was interviewed after the 29 September 2013 SAFA elections, contradicted himself about the readiness of women to serve within the executive. He was excited about the inclusion of the three top women into the executive committee of SAFA. However, he made a controversial statement that South African football will be ready to have a woman deputy president after the organization's next elections are scheduled for 2017 (The New Age, 30 September 2013: 14). The above controversial statement by the former SAFA deputy clearly shows that gender relations within SAFA structures have a long way to go. The statement above contradicts and is inconsistent with the gender legislative framework by the government that more equal opportunities should be afforded to women.

Further contradiction is that the week starting from 20 to 30 March 2017 was considered as one of the FIFA calendar weeks where football nations utilize the opportunity to organize friendly soccer matches in preparation for the 2018 World Cup Tournament qualifier. Similarly, the acting South African coach called his 23 players to play two friendly games against Guinea Bissau and Angola on the 25 and 28 March, respectively. The above 23 players selected included Kamohelo Mokotjo who was based in the Netherlands for the previous nine years. The major contradiction is that the coach selected Kamohelo Mokotjo fully knowing that he has Dutch citizenship which rules him out to be eligible to play for South Africa. In terms of Section 13(3)(a)(1) of the South African Citizenship Act of 1995 (Act No 88), a South African shall cease to be a citizen if she/he while being not a minor by some voluntary and formal act other than marriage, acquires the citizenship or nationality of a country other than the Republic of South Africa.

When Kamohelo Mokotjo was interviewed by journalists as to what were the reasons for him in the first place to have applied for Dutch citizenship and he responded that he was angry about the treatment he received from the former South African national coach Mr. Shakes Mashaba. He alluded to the fact that the former coach did not afford him game time. The same question was posed to the South African Football Association president Dr. Danny Jordan and his response contradicted that of Mokotjo. The SAFA president argued that Mokotjo has applied for Dutch citizenship for easy European traveling. The above two contradictory statements clearly show that there are no proper communication lines within SAFA. Subsequently, SAFA has approached the Department of Home Affairs for Kamohelo Mokotjo's application to become a South African citizen was approved within less than a week (The Sunday Times Sport 2017: 23). Further contradictions are that in terms of the National Soccer Rules, particularly Rule 30.1 clearly explains that a foreign player is any player who is not eligible to represent South Africa in terms of the FIFA statutes, except for a player who has obtained South African citizenship or who has obtained permanent residence in terms of Section 26 or Section 27 of Immigration Act No 13 of 2002, as amended (NSL Rules 2012: 35). Given the abovementioned NSL rule, it is interesting to note that SAFA and the national coach were fully aware that Kamohelo Mokotjo had Dutch citizenship and he was not eligible to represent South Africa, but the acting coach went ahead to select Kamohelo Mokotjo for the two international friendly games against Guinea Bissau.

In response to the above, one participant uttered these words "Abantu abaphethe idiski lethu okwanamje azange badlale ibola, angeke ibola lasemzantsi liyephambile", above is the Zulu version which says the current soccer administration is dominated by people who have never played soccer at the professional level and as such, progress will not be achieved as long as these people are in charge of managing South African soccer.

On 4 August 2020, PSL has announced the change of rules regarding the player's substitution during the game due to the outbreak of coronavirus. Before the outbreak of coronavirus, only seven players were allowed to be on the list of each soccer team. The new developments announced were that nine players were allowed to be on each team participating in a soccer match. The current new rules are as follows: "Nine (9) substitutes can be named (not 7) in the team list; five substitutions are allowed per club during the game; clubs will get three substitution opportunities during the game (plus half time, which isn't counted as one of the three); if both teams make substitutions at the same time, this counts as a used 'opportunity' for both teams; in a cup game, unused substitutions and opportunities are carried into extra time; teams will get an additional substitute and an additional substitution opportunity in extra time, taking the total of subs to 6 and opportunities to 4; and substitutions made before extra time and during half time of extra time don't count as a lost opportunity" (https://www.kickoff.com/news/articles/south-africa news/categories/news/premiership/PSL-explain-five-substitution-rule-ahead-of-2019-20-season-resumption/682838).

The above new introduction of players substitution seems to have contractions because only five players are allowed to be utilized per match regardless of whether the match game played is a cup or league game. This rule "teams will get an additional substitute and an additional substitution opportunity in extra time, taking the total of subs to 6 and opportunities to 4" creates confusion because it now allows six players instead of the original five players as stated in the earlier rules.

In terms of the COVID-19 government regulations, the following issues are stipulated that the wearing of (a) "a cloth face mask; (b) a homemade item; or (c) another appropriate item, that covers the nose and mouth, is mandatory for every person when in a public place. The above regulations are applied across the board within the borders of South Africa. It has also been announced that people who do not comply with these regulations will face the might of the law. Further, with specific reference to the sport in South Africa, the regulations are stated as follows: (i) sporting activities; inclusive of both professional non-contact and contact sports matches subject to directions for sports matches issued by the Cabinet member responsible for the sport after consultation with the Cabinet member responsible for health; (ii) only journalists, radio, television crew, security personnel, emergency medical services, and the necessary employees employed by the owners of the venue of the sports match, are allowed at the venue of the sports match; (iii) only the required number of players, match officials, support staff and medical crew required for the sports match, are allowed at the venue of the sports match; (iv) no spectators are allowed at the venue or precinct of the sports match; (v) no international sports events are allowed".

The South African government complied effectively with the advice and instructions from the World Health Organization on strategies on how to curb the spread of coronavirus. However, some structures within South Africa did not comply fully with the COVID-19 regulations as prescribed by World Health Organization. For example, the Premier Soccer League did not comply with the required number of 50 persons per event across the board.

The handling of cases by the PSL Disciplinary Committee has displayed clear inconsistencies which made the football fans of South Africa aggrieved. The first case involved Ajax Cape Town which has been relegated to the First Division League at the end of the 2017/2018 soccer season. In terms of FIFA rules, a soccer player cannot play for three football clubs in one soccer season. At the commencement of the 2017/2018 soccer season, a Zimbabwean-born Tendani Ndoro was registered with Orlando Pirates FC. During the window period, Tendai Ndoro was registered with an overseas team. Later within the same 2017/2018 soccer season, Tendai Ndoro came back to South Africa and was registered by Ajax Cape Town. There was nothing wrong with registering Tendai Ndoro; however, the problem was that he was legible to play in the 2018/2019 soccer season. Ajax Cape Town ignored the abovementioned FIFA rule and fielded Tendai Ndoro in several matches. Eventually, the legal battle started over this matter and ultimately Ajax Cape Town lost the court case and was relegated to the lower league because of docked points for fielding Tendai Ndoro.

In the light of the above Ndoro case, the NSL rule 16.1 states that "Member Clubs will duly submit completed team sheet to the referee at least sixty (60) minutes before the start of the match" and 16.2 states that "The team sheet will record the following: the full names of the eleven (11) registered players starting the match, the full names of the seven (7) substitute registered players who may be utilized during the match". Further, the NSL rule 16.3 states that "Changes to the team sheet may be made at any time before the start of the match provided that opposing team captain, the referee and the match commissioner are informed; No player may be added to the team sheet who was not listed on the team sheet that was submitted". The above rules are supposed to apply to every team; however, Mamelodi Sundowns Football Club submitted a team list without their player Wayne Arendse and during the run of play against Bidvest Wits FC, Mamelodi Sundowns FC brought in Wayne Arendse as a substitute. It is strange how the match officials have allowed the substitution to have happened because Wayne Arendse was not appearing on the original team list provided by Mamelodi Sundowns FC. The above matter was brought before the PSL Disciplinary Committee to arbitrate. The outcome of the arbitration was as everyone expected being to find Mamelodi Sundowns FC guilty of transgressing the rules. Mamelodi Sundowns FC was fined R250,000 and Wayne Arendse as a player was fined R50,000. However, what raised eyebrows within the South African football fans is the failure by the PSL DC to dock three points from Mamelodi Sundowns FC for fielding a defaulter. The above decision clearly shows that rules are not applied consistently.

Another extract from interviews reveals the following: *"I-corruption phakathi kwe-PSL is too much and some of the soccer team administrators operates nje ngama-mafia, for example, iAjax Cape Town verstaan ukuthi i-player elidlalele two teams in one year cannot play for the third team in that same year, mara iAjax Cape Town fielded uTendai Ndoro fully knowing this rule"*. The mixed-language version is that *"Corruption is too much within PSL and some of the soccer team administrators operate in a mafia-style, for example, Ajax Cape Town fielded Tendai Ndoro fully knowing that he has played for two teams within the same year"*.

The above two cases clearly show the contradictions and inconsistent application of rules by match officials and clubs as well as the PSL DC. Three points were docked in the case of Ajax Cape Town for fielding a defaulter player (Ndoro), but three points were not docked from Mamelodi Sundowns FC for fielding an eligible player (Arendse).

Recommendations

It is strongly recommended that the South African Football Association and the Professional Soccer League (PSL) in South Africa should fast-track their gender transformation agenda in their next elections by introducing more women to participate in the decision-making committees. Similarly, it is recommended that the PSL executive committee should increase the number of female members to at least three if not equal.

Historically, the positions of Chief Executive Officer (CEOs) within SAFA have been dominated by the occupation of males. It is highly recommended that SAFA should create the CEO's deputy positions with the view of empowering women candidates if there is a lack of capacity in South Africa to get women CEOs.

The South African Football Association is responsible for ensuring that there are female match officials in every PSL soccer match. Currently, match officials are predominantly males; therefore, SAFA must increase the pool of match officials by introducing more female soccer referees, female assistant referees, female fourth officials, including female match commissioners.

Modern soccer requires soccer teams to employ the services of medical personnel. The majority of the PSL teams have male doctors and male physiotherapists, and it is recommended that the PSL teams must start to introduce female team doctors and female physiotherapists because currently the above positions are dominated by males.

The South African Football Association (SAFA) needs to increase the number of female members within its executive in the next elections. It is strongly recommended that the next SAFA president be a female. The above can be achievable by recruiting the current crop of female professional players as well as the retired female players that can make a meaningful contribution to the development of soccer including the protection of soccer players' rights.

There are two females within the PSL's Board of Directors. In terms of the coaching personnel within the 16 PSL teams, there is no female coach or even a female assistant coach and let alone a female goalkeeper coach. Within SAFA, there is improvements, for example, the coaching staff within the South African Women National team are all women. However, there are only three female executive members within SAFA which show that SAFA is trying to address gender representation.

Currently, there are only ball-boys at the PSL soccer matches and there is a need to recruit ball-girls and these will encourage the girls at the tender age to gain knowledge and interest in soccer. The introduction of two ball-girls to work with four soccer ball-boys per PSL soccer match can improve the situation.

The introduction of female commentators within the SABC sports channel is a step in the right direction and it is, therefore, recommended that the SuperSport 4 soccer channel should also learn from the SABC sports channel by at least introducing a female soccer commentator for starters. The above could be achieved in three ways. First, there are currently female soccer commentators and female radio presenters that the abovementioned sport television channels can recruit to address gender inequality within the area of television commentators in South Africa since soccer is watched by millions of soccer spectators. Second, both soccer channels can gradually train the female soccer commentators by making them co-broadcast soccer matches with the experienced male commentators, and by doing that they can have enough pool of female soccer commentators within a year or two years. Third, both soccer channels can go out in communities to search for talent, and surely, it can pay dividends in terms of getting female soccer commentators.

The PSL registration office needs to apply the rules properly and consistently by assisting to interpret the registration rules correctly when the teams are in a process of registering their players. The PSL office could have advised the Jomo Cosmos Football Club accordingly that registering players with numbers 86 and 92 was incorrect in terms of the PSL registration rules which stipulate that the registration numbers should be 1 up until 50.

It is further recommended that all PSL teams should employ employer relations officials within their teams to advise on legal matters and to ensure that the rules are being interpreted properly. The above appointment could minimize unnecessary court cases which bring the PSL into disrepute.

Conclusion

The literature consulted in this study corroborates with the interviews conducted in that similar notion of contradictions, gender inequality, and inconsistent decisions within the PSL and SAFA. For example, the current National Executive Committee of SAFA consists of 15 members and the breakdown is as follows: 12 members are males and 3 members are females. To rub salt into the wound, the president of SAFA is a male and he has three deputies who are all males. The CEO of SAFA is a male. The nine provinces of South Africa are represented by two members each, in which 17 members are males and 1 female member. The current Executive Committee of PSL consist of eight board members and the breakdown is as follows: six members are males and two members are females.

It is evident from newspaper articles, scholarly publications, as well as interviews that contradictions, gender inequality, and inconsistencies within the SAFA and PSL continue to occur. There is a great need for the two soccer structures in South Africa to fast-track the issue of gender representation by introducing a substantial number of women in different positions that contribute to the daily running of soccer. These two soccer structures need to move away from the rhetoric of development and start to implement genuine transformation and development. Sound administration is also key and soccer rules and policies must be applied fairly and consistently without any contradictions.

References

Alegi, P (2007) The Political Economy of Mega-Stadiums and the Underdevelopment of Grassroots Football in South Africa. Politikon. The South African Journal of Political Studies. Volume 34 (3): 315–331.

Birrell, S. J & Cole, C. L (1990) Double fault: Renee Richards and the construction and naturalization of differences. Sociology of Sport Journal, Volume 7, pp 1–21.

Blanchard, K & Cheska, A. T. (1985) *The Anthropology of Sport*. USA: Bergin & Garvey.

Bogopa, D. (2008) The Paradox of Gender and Sports Development: The Case of Nelson Mandela Metropolitan. Impumelelo Interdisciplinary Electronic Journal of African Sports. http://www.ohiou.edu/sportsafrica/journal/Volume3/theparadoxofgender_bogopa.htm

Bogopa, D (2010) Perspectives on the World Cup Tournament in South Africa. Impumelelo The Interdisciplinary Electronic Journal of African Sport. http://www.ohio.edu/sportsafrica/journal/bogopareflections

Bogopa, D (2014) Anthropological Perception of Gender in Soccer: The Case of Tsakane Schools in Gauteng Province. Africa Insight Journal, Volume 43 (4): 121–131.

Boya, K. S (2016) Governance and Social Responsibility Perceptions of the SAFA Affiliated Football Clubs Executives. Corporate Board: Role, Duties, and Composition. Volume 12 (1) pp 75–83.

Burnett, C (2018) The Politics of Gender (In) Equality Relating to Sport and Development Within a Sub-Saharan Context of Poverty. Frontiers in Sociology. Volume 3 (27):1–15.

Butler, J (1990) Post-modern, Queer, Feminist Theories. Oxford: Westview Press.

De Vos, A.S., Strydom, H., Fouche, C.B and Delport, C.S.L. (2011) Research at Grassroots: For the social sciences and human service professions. 4th Edition. Pretoria. Van Schaik.

Driscoll, B. E (1998) Female athletes in the media? http://www.sonoma.edu/users/c/Carltone/ws/driscoll2.htm

Emmel, N. (2013) Sampling and Choosing Cases in Qualitative Research: A Realist Approach. London. Sage.

FIFA Constitution (2010) *Fifa Statuses: Regulations Governing the Application of Statuses Standing Orders of the Congress.* https://resources.fifa.com/mm/document/affederation/generic/01/29/85/71/fifastatuten2010_e.pdf

Freeman, D (1983) Margaret Mead, and Samoa: The Making and Unmaking of an Anthropological Myth. Cambridge. Harvard University Press.

Goodman, L. (1996) Literature and Gender. London: Routledge.

Greig, A, Hulme, D & Turner, M (2007) Challenging Global Inequality: Development Theory and Practice. In the 21st Century. The United Kingdom. Palgrave Macmillan.

Gretchen, B. Rossman & S. F. Rallis (2017). An Introduction to Qualitative Research: Learning in the Field. 4th edition. Sage. London.

Hargreaves, J (1997) Women's Sport, Development and Cultural Diversity: The South African Experience. Women's Studies International Forum, Volume 20 (2) 191–209.

Haugaa Engh, M (2012) *Tackling femininity: The heterosexual paradigm and women's soccer in South Africa.* In S. Cornelissen & A. Grundlingh. Sport Past and Present in South Africa. London: Routledge. Taylor & Francis Group.

Kane, M. J. & Parks, J. B (1992) The social constructs of gender differences and hierarchy in sports journalism: Few new twists in very old themes. Women in Sport and Physical Activity Journal 1, pp 49–83.

Kortjaa, B.B (2017) *I was angry at Mashaba—Mokotjo.* The Sunday Times Sport.

Lerner, G (1994) The Creation of Feminist Consciousness. From the Middle Ages to Eighteen—Seventy. New York: Oxford University Press.

MacClancy, J (1996) Female Bullfighting, Gender Stereotyping, and the State. In J. MacClancy. Sport, Identity, and Ethnicity. Oxford. Berg.

Maree, K., Cresswell, J.W., Ebersohn, L., Eloff, I., Ferreira, R., Ivankova, N.V., Jansen, J.D., Nieuwenhius, J., Pietersen, J and Plano-Clark, V.L. (2016) First Steps in Research. 2nd Edition. Pretoria. Van Schaik.

McKinley, D. T (2010) *Transformation from above: The upside-down state of contemporary South African soccer.* In A. Desai. The Race to Transform: Sport in Post-Apartheid South Africa. Cape Town: HSRC Press

Mead, M (1928) *Coming of Age in Samoa.* New York: Dell.

Mead, M (1935) *Sex and Temperament in Three Primitive Societies.* New York: Dell.

Naidoo, P, and Muholi, Z (2010) *Women's bodies and the world of football in South Africa.* In The Race to Transform Sport in Post-Apartheid South Africa. Ed, A Desai, Cape Town. HSRC Press.

National Soccer League Rules (2012) https://www.yumpu.com/en/document/read/28786220/nsl-rules-supersport

Ogunniyi, C (2014) Perceptions of the African Women's Championships: Female Footballers as Anomalies. Sport in Society, Volume 17 (4) pp 537–549.

Ogunniyi, C (2015) The effects of sport participation on gender relations: Case studies of female footballers in Johannesburg and Cape Town, South Africa. South African Review of Sociology. Volume 46 (1):25–46.
Peach, L. J (1997) Gender and War: Are Women Tough Enough for Military Combat? In C. B Brettell and C. F Sargeant. Gender in Cross-Cultural Perspective. New Jersey: Prentice Hall.
Pelak, C. F (2005) Negotiating Gender/Race/Class Constraints in the New South Africa. International Review for the Sociology of Sport. Volume (40) 1 pp 53–70.
Prinsloo, F.C (2013) Good Governance in South Africa: A Critical Analysis. Technical Report.
Rondinelli, D.A & Shabbir Cheeman, G (2003) Reinventing Government for the Twenty-First Century: State Capacity in a Globalizing Society. United State of America: Kumarian Press, Inc.
Sait, S & Bogopa, D (2021) Anthropological Inquiry on Gender Inequality: The Case of Women Soccer in Gelvandale, Port Elizabeth. Journal of Gender and Behaviour. Volume 19 (2), 17864–17874
Scott, J. (2014) A Dictionary of Sociology. 4th ed. Oxford: Oxford University Press.
The New Age, 30 September 2013: 14.
The PSL Announcement (2020) https://www.kickoff.com/news/articles/south-africa-news/categories/news/premiership/psl-explain-five-substitution-rule-ahead-of-2019-20-season-resumption/682838
West, C, and Zimmermann, D. H (1987) Doing gender. Gender and Society, Volume (1) 2 125–151.

CHAPTER 12

The Origins, Status, Contributions and Contradictions of Association Football in Uganda

Njororai Wycliffe W. Simiyu

Uganda is one of the few African countries that has produced World and Olympic champion athletes in track and field and boxing. However, association football (soccer) is the one that attracts the imagination of the nation as the number one sport. To understand the context of football in Uganda, one should have an idea of the country's history, especially the physical activity-based lifestyle of the youth, legacy of colonization, imperialism and pursuit of national identity. In the late nineteenth and early twentieth centuries, British colonial rule brought with it missionaries and settlers who introduced various European sports—including soccer—in schools and communities. Indeed, the missionaries from the United Kingdom were responsible for introducing football, and other sports, in Uganda in 1897. One avenue that they used to introduce and promote the sport was through schools. Association football became popular with the local youth in schools and soon the indigenous men adopted it around

N. W. W. Simiyu (✉)
University of Texas at Tyler, Tyler, TX, USA
e-mail: Wnjororai@uttyler.edu

© The Author(s), under exclusive license to Springer Nature Switzerland AG 2022
A. E. Ayuk (ed.), *Football (Soccer) in Africa*, Global Culture and Sport Series, https://doi.org/10.1007/978-3-030-94866-5_12

the country. Colonial legacies underpinning the popularity of association football include its culturally neutral nature, royal patronage, regionalism (north and south divide), institutionalization, political upheaval and national patriotism. Indeed, football in Uganda engenders a sense of unity and identity that is remarkable given the major political upheavals that have afflicted the country since gaining independence in 1961 and the more than 40 ethnic groupings. One can, therefore, assert that Ugandan football has been an enduring unifying factor in an otherwise politically unstable and socioeconomically divided country in the years following independence. Despite the passionate following and solidarity at the national level, there is bitter rivalry at the club level. Although this is not unique to Ugandan football alone, it is a phenomenon worth exploring. This chapter therefore analyzes the history, status, contributions and contradictions inherent in Ugandan football.

Physically Active Tradition in Uganda

Before the introduction of western sports such as association football or soccer, the indigenous people engaged in various physical activities for recreational and educational purposes. In Uganda, and many places in East Africa, many ethnic groups used physical activity for fun as well as in their 'initiation schools' to pass on basic societal values to their young, to train boys for warfare and to identify potential leaders.[1] Before the arrival of foreigners, the indigenous people engaged in physical activities to prepare the youth to be responsible adults. The emphasis was on preparing boys to live in society as responsible men who could protect their people at all times and provide them with the necessities of life—food and shelter.[2] On the other hand, they prepared girls to be physically fit, strong and healthy women who could fetch water, cultivate land, cook food for the family and bear and look after children.[3] Preparation for adulthood often entailed some initiation rites that revolved around physical activities.

According to Ndee,[4] the Gisu of Uganda, for example, circumcised their boys after the main harvest, usually between June and September. Leading to the circumcision, the boys went through a series of rituals that

---

[1] Ndee, "Pre-colonial East Africa", 2010b, 780–797.
[2] Ndee, "Sport, Culture and society", 2010c, 733–758.
[3] Ibid.
[4] Ndee, Eastern Africa and Physical Activity", 2010a, 759–779.

prepared them for the initiation ceremony. Ndee[5] cites the personal experiences of J. S. La Fontaine, who divided these preliminary rituals into four main phases structured along the agricultural seasons. The first phase consisted of singing and dancing prior to the main agricultural work of sowing seeds. During this phase, the initiates—all boys—dressed up in traditional costume and danced on the village greens led by an elder, who instructed them in the songs and dances. The duration of this phase normally lasted long enough to allow the initiates to learn the songs and absorb the instruction, to lead themselves—in singing and dancing—in the next phase.[6]

The second phase kicked in immediately after the weeding period. During this phase, the initiates visited all their relatives, both maternal and paternal, and informed them of their imminent circumcision. Led by one of their own, the initiates walked from house to house while singing and dancing, accompanied by their siblings and family friends. After the visitations and invitations were over, the third phase set in. In this phase, which began a few days before the actual circumcision, the initiates engaged in intensive singing and dancing in the presence of the community members drawn from the village and family members invited from afar. In this lead up to the circumcision event, older boys from the family, who had undergone the initiation rite themselves, provided advice and encouragement using teasing, challenging and appealing to family tradition and history of valor and courage. Older people in the community also joined in the ceremony of dancing, singing, drinking and eating that lasted into the night. The final phase consisted of the cleansing of the groves, the rebuilding of the shrines and the offering of sacrifices by the elders. At this stage, the initiates sought blessings and 'formal permission' to be circumcised from their maternal ancestors.[7]

They received two short twigs symbolizing approval and instilling of courage to the initiates who were then ready for the physical circumcision. This phase entailed dancing through the night. A period of convalescence followed the surgical operation of circumcision, after which came the day of 'graduation'. Dancing dominated this important ceremony of admitting the newly circumcised to the status of adulthood. Almost everyone

---

[5] Ibid, 2010a.
[6] Ndee, "Eastern Africa and Physical Activity", 2010a, 759–779.
[7] Ibid, 2010a.

present at the ceremony joined the dancing, which continued for two to three days.

The Gisu people combined dancing and walking exercises in their initiation ceremonies. In the early stages, it was mainly the novices themselves, who danced. Clan elders and others joined the dances at the later stages and on the day of 'graduation', almost everybody danced. The inclusion of dances in all phases of the ceremony accentuates the fact that dance constituted one of the strongest forms of cultural expressions among the Gisu, as was the case in many other ethnic groups in East Africa. Thus, physical activity played an important role in the pre-colonial society of Uganda, just as it did for the whole of eastern Africa. Indeed, physical activity was a means of training for warfare and hunting and was widely used during tribal initiation ceremonies to establish status and to prepare boys and girls for the transition into adulthood.[8]

It is clear that the physical activity lifestyle of the Ugandan people was an ideal foundation for embracing the athletic demands of modern sports especially football. While the preceding account paints a general picture of the pre-colonial life of the indigenous people of Uganda, the next section focusses on how football was introduced and appropriated by the indigenous people.

INTRODUCTION OF FOOTBALL IN UGANDA

The missionaries, administrators, teachers and farmers[9] introduced the game of association football or soccer in Uganda. The game of football, which is simple to follow and easy to play, was a vital instrument used by the British in their efforts to assert imperial hegemony, control and racist discrimination. The British often imposed over-arching constraints on the organization and control of the game in the country and elsewhere in the colonial territories.[10] For Uganda, football arrived after the establishment of railway lines, missionary schools and military bases for the colonial armies. Since Uganda was a colony of the United Kingdom, the pioneer missionaries came from there including Robert Henry Walker, George

---

[8] Ndee, "Eastern Africa and Physical Activity", 2010a, 759–779.
[9] Kanyike, "Tracing Uganda's football history", 2017 at http://www.monitor.co.ug/Magazines/Score/Tracing-Uganda-s-football-history/689854-3827108-lvu7hkz/index.html.
[10] Hokkanen, 'Christ and the Imperial Games Fields'.

Lawrence Pilkington and Alexander Gordon Fraser. One of the prominent pioneers was Rev. Archdeacon R. H. Walker of the Namirembe Church Missionary Society who in 1897 introduced the game of football in Uganda after arranging to bring a ball from England.[11] Walker received able support from G. L. Pilkington, who coached the boys at the Mengo School using a large grass field at Kakeeka in Mengo situated between Kampala and Rubaga.[12] The second playing field established was near Old Kampala hill below Lord Lugard's palace. Another missionary was A. G. Fraser who carried a football to Uganda in 1900 and four years later laid out a soccer field at King's School in Budo, a school established for the sons of Ugandan chiefs. An officer of the British Army, Captain William Pulteney, also played a significant role in the establishment and development of football in Uganda while serving with the Uganda Rifles from February 1895 to September 1897.[13] Apart from the missions and army, the King's School Budo was among the pioneer schools to have football on the curriculum. This led to the formation of the Budo Old Boys in 1909 comprising the alumni of the school. Football practices took place regularly at the Coronation Ground at the Old Kampala, which became the Old Kampala Senior Secondary School Sports Ground. After the move of the Mengo High School from Namirembe to Budo Hill soon after 1927, the Budo Old Boys became the United Old Budonians Club.[14] This team went on to dominate football for several decades as they repeatedly won the Kampala and District League as late as 1949.[15]

Thus, Ugandan boys enthusiastically adapted the game of football. Competitive football, however, started in 1924 with the formation of Uganda Football Association.[16] This marked a major milestone, as the country was able to host Kenya in its first international match in 1924.

[11] Charles Harford-Battersby, ed. (1899). Pilkington of Uganda. London: The Richmond Press.

[12] Alegi, Peter, ed. (2010). African Soccerscapes: How a Continent Changed the World's Game. Athens, Ohio: Ohio University Press. p. 11.

[13] Adrian Harvey, ed. (2005). Football: The First Hundred Years—The untold story. Abingdon, Oxon: Routledge. p. 234.

[14] http://budonian.com/index.php?option=com_content&view=article&id=9&Itemid=11, retrieved on October 13, 2016.

[15] John Iliffe, ed. (2005). Honour in African History. Cambridge, UK: Cambridge University Press. p. 300.

[16] Kanyike, "Tracing Uganda's football history", 2017 at http://www.monitor.co.ug/Magazines/Score/Tracing-Uganda-s-football-history/689854-3827108-lvu7hkz/index.html.

This first international match between Uganda and Kenya set the stage for the inauguration of the Gossage Cup in 1926 involving both countries.[17] This annual competition later expanded to include Tanzania and Zanzibar, who joined in 1945 and 1947, respectively. By 1966, the cup gave way to the East Africa Challenge Cup and eventually in 1973 to the East and Central Africa Senior Challenge Cup.[18] This competition is held on an annual basis involving countries in the East and Central African region comprising Eritrea, Djibouti, Ethiopia, Kenya, Tanzania, Uganda, Rwanda, Sudan, Southern Sudan, Burundi, Somalia and Zanzibar.[19]

From its introduction, football spread rapidly through schools around Kampala and in the hinterland. Some of the competitions that attracted plenty of attention included Masaza cup in Buganda, Madhvani cup and Aspro cup.[20] Indeed, within a very short time, football earned the distinction of being the most popular in Uganda, thereby earning the recognition of being a national sport. Mazrui[21] has argued that football became popular in East Africa, including Uganda, Kenya and Tanzania, because it appealed to people of all socio-economic classes and cultures, unlike sports such as golf, tennis and swimming that were for a long time not as universal in popularity.

COLONIALISM, FOOTBALL AND THE REACTION OF THE INDIGENOUS PEOPLE

It is hard to discuss the popularity of association football in Uganda, and East and Central Africa in general, without referring to colonialism and the reaction of the indigenous people to the sport. The coming of the colonialists in the late nineteenth century greatly influenced the physical activity orientation of the indigenous people in Africa, including Uganda. Prior to colonization, most local African ethnic groups had distinct cultural beliefs and physical activity patterns that they religiously followed. Some of the outstanding and universal cultural activities included dancing, wrestling, hunting, boating and spear throwing.[22] The coming of the

---

[17] Njororai, 'Colonial Legacy and association football", 2009; Njororai, Ph.D. Thesis, 2000.
[18] Ibid.
[19] http://www.cecafafootball.org/about-cecafa/.
[20] Waiswa, "Football Development in Uganda", Master of Science Thesis, 2005.
[21] Mazrui, "The Africans", 1986; see also Ndee 2010a, b, c.
[22] Njororai, "Colonial Legacy", 2009.

white settlers and missionaries discouraged the local dance and physical activities by declaring them pagan. They therefore opened schools and churches where the emphasis shifted to European-approved leisure pursuits including sports. The introduction of European sports in the school curriculum quickened the pace at which foreign sports were adapted including football, volleyball, netball and track and field. However, what attracted the imagination of the local people were football and to some extent boxing as well as track and field. It is worth pointing out that Uganda has won Olympic medals in boxing and track.

Phyllis Martin's Leisure and Society, as quoted extensively by Straker,[23] offers a rich account of football's place in the colonized countries using Congo Brazzaville and Leopoldville. According to Martin, as noted by Straker, the spontaneous positive appraisal of football was because 'Sport as physical, organized, and competitive exercise was not completely foreign to the young workers who watched Europeans play football'.[24] This is because certain values such as courage, endurance and individual skill were also qualities admired in village recreational activities as illustrated by the Gisu initiation rites in eastern Uganda.[25] Thus, the major differences between traditional physical activities and western sports were in the latter's structure, plethora of rules and period which reflected the industrial society in which they were born.[26] Thus, the introduction of football, though a foreign sport, found a willing and enthusiastic African population whose athleticism perfectly fitted the new sport. Peter Mählmann, too, argues on the same line while looking at sport and modernization in Kenya.[27] He examined the role of traditional 'movement culture' in Kenya, which was closely connected to daily life and was differentiated according to age groups and gender. He argued that patterns of movement also differed regionally according to topographical surroundings or climatic conditions. He goes on to argue that the introduction of a 'modern sport

---

[23] Straker, 'Popular Culture', 745.
[24] Straker, 'Popular Culture', 745.
[25] Ndee, "Eastern Africa and Physical Activity", 2010a, 759–779.
[26] Straker, 'Popular Culture'. Also see Martin, 'The Social History'. This paper was part of the project 'African Expressions of the Colonial Experience'. The main focus of this paper is recreational activities and in particular sport in colonial Brazzaville (Congo). The author discusses the origins of football in Brazzaville, its development in the 1930s, individuals and the role sport played in their future life as politicians and the influence sport has on identity.
[27] Mählmann, 'The Role of Sport'. 1992; Mazrui, 1986 and Njororai, "Colonial Legacy", 2009.

culture' in Kenya during the colonial period was superimposed on the traditional movement culture, but in the process, the former was modified to include traditional norms and values. This blending of traditional cultures with the western cultures could apply to Uganda. The Africans were not therefore passive recipients of the new sports. They were active in appropriating the new form of recreation and, with their natural athleticism, were able to turn football into their own.[28]

Paul Darby argues that football developed in a relatively unplanned, haphazard fashion and the indigenous populations in remote African towns and villages embraced it enthusiastically.[29] However, the introduction of the game in urban areas was more deliberate. According to Darby, the European colonialists utilized their hegemonic position to impose football for their own ends. Thus, the settlers and missionaries introduced the game particularly for the 'training of African bodies in pursuit of moral and physical health ... but above all of Christian character'.[30] The missionaries were particularly uneasy with the local traditions rooted in vigorous dancing. They, however, believed strongly in the civilizing and industrial mission of the British Empire. A missionary had to carry both the gospel and modern culture to the Africans, who had an equal right to them. Modern culture entailed modern sport including football, netball, volleyball, cricket and rugby, among others. Some of the missionaries and settlers had a tradition of sporting excellence in their student days and found Africa an ideal place to champion their sports ideology.[31] Thus, the newly arrived athletic missionaries introduced sport, particularly football, as a way of establishing positive contact with the African pupils. Testing of muscle and skill on a football field could, in the words of Hokkanen, 'contribute to or reinforce a notion of physical equality between African and Scottish "Lads", rare during a time when both missionary and imperial propaganda ethnocentrically exaggerated the physical differences between the Europeans and the Africans, to the latter's disadvantage'.[32]

In colonial Uganda, centers of academic excellence such as Mengo, Aggrey memorial secondary school, King's Budo, Ntare school, among others, were also pioneer centers of sports excellence as well as religious

---

[28] Njororai, "Colonial Legacy", 2009.
[29] Darby, 'Africa and the "World" Cup', 2005.
[30] See Hokkanen, 'Christ and the Imperial Games Fields', 748.
[31] Ibid.
[32] Ibid.

discourse. The missionary leaders felt strongly that the civilizing mission include an inculcation of the British passion for sport and discipline.[33] Thus, throughout East Africa, most schools were established with a mandatory provision of sports infrastructure including football, volleyball and netball for girls and track and field. The inclusion of physical education in the curriculum via physical training and gymnastics added to the athletic ideology that characterized British hegemony.[34] Sport in the formal education system was used chiefly as a means to achieve order and discipline. Practicing western sports helped to internalize norms of western superiority and values connected with sports.

Outside the school system, the role of football came to represent a site for generating resistance to colonialism and promoting nationalist aspirations. Overall, therefore, the British introduction of football to indigenous Ugandans was in the words of Darby, 'Eurocentric, patronizing and missionary style'.[35] Nevertheless, regardless of the British motive for introducing football, the indigenous people enthusiastically appropriated the game to promote not only their nationalistic identity but also engendered a regional orientation by the time of independence. One of the characteristic features of modernization, which compelled the indigenous people, especially males, to move from villages to urban centers, was the issue of taxation. The introduction of taxes, especially the poll or hut tax, forced men to migrate in search of jobs in urban areas. While away from their rural homes, the male youth found plenty of free time to engage in the exotic pastime of playing football leading to the formation of teams. Forming teams and participating in football filled a social void that the city dwellers experienced.

According to Straker,[36] football constituted a domain of action where players and referees shared a common knowledge of clear-cut, universal rules. He goes on to say:

> Whereas the daily and seasonal routine of the urban wage-seeker was dictated by fluctuations in investments and initiatives completely beyond his[37] control, football constituted a space where the individual player could

---

[33] Mangan, "The Games Ethic", 1998.
[34] Mangan, "Athleticism in Public School", 1981.
[35] Darby, 'Africa and the "World" Cup', 2005: 885.
[36] Straker, 'Popular Culture', 10.
[37] Note that the writer uses the male reference here to capture the male dominance of football at the time. However, football has now progressed even among the women.

deploy his energies as he saw fit. The sport presented a possibility of reclaiming control over one's body and time. Teamwork and discipline were ineluctable aspects of any game, but what a difference to give and take commands in relation to a goal one has willingly chosen to pursue with fellow African players, rather than according to the externally imposed hierarchies of the workplace. In football, radically unlike the workplace, one willfully directed one's pursuit of the mission at hand at every moment.[38]

Football, therefore, provided a medium that brought out the free expression of the African players. It was a freedom they found curtailed elsewhere including work and in the community where the colonial rules were strict. Straker, who argued that Africans played the game for fun and were unwilling to be regimented by whites in training sessions, captured the difference in approach to the game. The Europeans, on the other hand, emphasized inculcation of values such as team spirit, perseverance and fair play. It is interesting to note that the approach to the game by Africans in the colonial period has persisted to the modern day where African players are perceived as being naive tactically and playing to entertain rather than to win.[39] Looking at football in Uganda, one appreciates the athleticism as well as the entertainment value of the game. One can confidently say that the Ugandan game has produced a fair share of football artists such as Moses Nsereko, Geofrey Katerega and Phillip Omondi, among others.

To the African player, therefore, the joy of the game was, and continues to be, in the self-expression as opposed to the instrumental role of imposing discipline desired by the Europeans. Straker elaborates on this struggle over whether football constituted a vehicle for the extension of colonial power or whether it was a space where that very power would be revised, subverted or altogether suspended. According to him, the more practice of football generated distance and difference from the rhythms and clearly restrictive and more ambiguous laws of the colonial order, the more pleasure it could return to the African players and spectators. This was indeed a fascinating aspect of football in the colonial period and to some extent continues to play out in stadiums where unpopular politicians in government are jeered and opposition leaders given standing ovations. Thus, it is interesting that a rule, which governed sport, created and imported by

---

[38] Straker, 'Popular Culture', 10.
[39] Versi, 'Football in Africa', 1986.

Europeans became a means for Africans to create spaces in which the onerous powers of European imperialism were deflected.[40] The soccer stadium is a vital medium for expressing dissent and displeasure against the political class, administrative control and power. Football is, therefore, the medium and symbol of resistance as well as freedom. The stadium remains the ideal site, as there are no restrictions on self-expression. The large gatherings at the stadium were an alternative to the political rallies, which were subject to intense security restrictions and vetting by agents of the state and the political class.[41]

FUFA, National Competitions and International Football

The free expression against the colonial powers was, however, channeled in a new direction with the onset of international football. As a nation, Uganda had to play against other countries starting with Kenya and later Tanzania and Zanzibar in the East African challenge Cup.[42] The formation of the national team necessitated the pulling together of resources to face a common opponent from a different country. As a nation, Uganda dominates the East African region followed by Kenya,[43] even as shown by the March 2017 Federation International Football Association (FIFA)/Coca Cola rankings, where the former is ranked 74th and the latter 88th in the world.[44] Given the rivalry of the two countries on the soccer field and the free social and economic ties, there were passionate debates and conversations over the outstanding players of the day. Indeed, radio broadcasts of Gossage football and subsequent tournament matches are widely followed to date by the public.

Ugandans follow national and international football in both the print and electronic media with the World Cup serving as the climactic event that is widely monitored by the citizenry. During the World Cup and other major football tournaments, Ugandans flock to their favorite recreational sites in large numbers to root for their favorite teams. It is also clear that

---

[40] Straker, 'Popular Culture'.
[41] Njororai, 'Colonial Legacy', 2009.
[42] Ibid; Njororai, 'The Diversity of Sport', 2003.
[43] The results at http://www.rsssf.com/tablese/eastcentrafr.html show that Uganda has been more dominant followed by Kenya in the East and Central African Regional Senior Challenge Cup.
[44] http://www.fifa.com/fifa-world-ranking/ranking-table/men/index.html.

Ugandan fans are very passionate about their favorite local teams, especially the national team, The Cranes as well as the top three club sides including Express, SC Villa (formerly Nakivubo) and Kampala City Council Authority (formerly KCC). Important matches involving the national team always attract crowds of close to 40,000, with millions more watching on television. In the villages and urban areas, children can be seen playing with bundles of rags, improvised balls and tennis balls, worn out balls and on bare grounds as others walk with radios to monitor the latest football news across the globe.

The Federation of Uganda Football Associations (FUFA) is the governing body of football in Uganda.[45] The association was founded in 1924 as Uganda Football Association, but only affiliated itself with Federation International Football Association (FIFA) in 1960 and Confederation of African Football (CAF) in 1961. However, even before its affiliation to FIFA, the association organized a national team that traveled to England in 1956. This inaugural visit to England was memorable for the fact that the players chose to play barefooted despite the availability of footwear.[46] These players, who were more accustomed to playing barefooted at home in Uganda, felt more comfortable playing bare feet rather than in new footwear. Most of the players, who composed the national team, were selected from Nsambya old times football club (the first soccer team to be formed in Uganda), old Budonian club, Aggrey memorial secondary school and Mengo SSS.[47]

Since FUFA's affiliation to CAF and FIFA, it has managed to organize a number of competitions at the national as well as grassroot levels, making the game of football to be a household sport everywhere in Uganda. FUFA organizes the men and women's national football teams, and the first and second tiers of national football covering the Ugandan Super League and Ugandan Big League, respectively. The third tier (Regional Leagues) is organized by the regional football associations, and the fourth tier (District Leagues/Fourth Division) is administered by the district football associations.[48] The specific competitions organized by FUFA include the following: Azam Uganda Premier League, Ugandan Cup, FUFA Big League, FUFA Women Elite League, FUFA Juniors League

[45] http://www.fufa.co.ug/about-fufa/history/.
[46] http://www.rsssf.com/tableso/oeg-engtour56.html.
[47] Ssekito 2002.
[48] http://www.fufa.co.ug/formation/.

(U-17), Inter Regions Tournament, Mama Becca Women's day cup, FUFA Corporate tournament, Regional Leagues and District Leagues.[49] The Premier league champions and Uganda (Kakungulu) cup winners represent Uganda in the Africa Champions League and Africa Cup Winners' cup, respectively.[50] The Ugandan Cup, popularly called the Kakungulu cup, is the oldest football competition of knockout format having started in 1971.[51] Similarly, the schools and institutions of higher learning sports associations organize their own football tournaments without the direct intervention of FUFA. The district, schools and the institutions of higher learning football associations are responsible for promoting football in their respective areas.[52]

At national level, FUFA is composed of an assembly responsible for policy formulation and election of the National FUFA Executive. After the president is elected, the FUFA constitution gives the winner powers to choose his executive officers to work with for a period of four years. However, as a matter of administrative strategy, the above constitutional mandate has not always been objectively exercised to the benefit of the development of Ugandan football. This is because the FUFA presidents use their prerogative to choose people that are only allied to them, thereby marginalizing and leaving out potentially valuable resource persons with a dissenting voice. This selective privilege even affects the choice of persons to serve in technical positions, which require a certain level of competence. As a result, persons with questionable credentials have ended up serving on the executive committee by virtue of their political activism rather than technical competence.[53]

Contributions and Contradictions of Ugandan Football

During the colonial regime and the years immediately after independence for Uganda, there was fast socio-economic and political development. However, in the 1970s and mid-1980s, retrogression set in affecting all spheres of life especially during the reigns of Milton Obote (twice), Idi

---

[49] Ibid.
[50] Waiswa, Master's Thesis.
[51] http://www.fufa.co.ug/about-fufa/history/.
[52] Waiswa, ibid.
[53] Nsubuga, "Uganda Football at cross roads", 2005 Issue 124, Kampala, Uganda.

Amin, Yusuf Lule, Godfrey Binaisa, Paulo Muwanga, B. O. Okello and Tito Okello.[54] Despite the retrogression in many spheres of life in the 1970s and 1980s, sports activities seemed to thrive. The Uganda national team, The Cranes, qualified for the Africa Cup of Nations in 1962, 1968, 1974, 1976 and 1978. Indeed, the national soccer team made it to the finals of the Africa Cup of Nations in 1978 where they lost to Ghana 0-2 in the finals.[55] This remains the highest achievement of Ugandan football. It is therefore surprising that Uganda's finest moment of football history is within a period that was the most trying and challenging on the political front when Idi Amin was the president. It took Uganda 39 years to qualify for another edition of the African Cup of Nations[56] where they failed to progress beyond the preliminary rounds in January 2017 in Gabon. However, the Cranes managed to qualify again in 2019 where they progressed to the second round before losing to Senegal the eventual losing finalists. At club level, Kampala City Council won the Confederation of East and Central African Football Associations (CECAFA) club championship in 1978. Soccer Club Villa won the East Africa club championship cup in 1987, 2003 and 2005. These successes on the football field came at a time when Uganda was going through a volatile political atmosphere. These successes speak to the contribution of football as a stabilizing force as well as a source of pride and identity of the Ugandan people. All these competitions and activities generated players who rose to prominence both nationally and regionally.

FUFA records further indicate that regional, districts, counties and inter-school football competitions used to be organized throughout Uganda. Tournaments such as Madhvani and Aspro were popular. Similarly, it was compulsory for all schools to participate in football competitions. However, over the years, a negative trend set in that negatively affected the sport. Some of the negative characteristics of Ugandan football include organization of fewer tournaments, poor match attendance and poor sports leadership leading to instability at the national federation level. Despite the administrative and infrastructural inadequacies,[57]

[54] Naiman, R. and Watkins, N., "Structural Adjustment in Africa", 1999.
[55] Kanyike, "Tracing Uganda's football history", 2017 at http://www.monitor.co.ug/Magazines/Score/Tracing-Uganda-s-football-history/689854-3827108-lvu7hkz/index.html.
[56] Njororai, 'Allegiance of African Players', 2017.
[57] Rintaugu, Mwisukha and Onywera, 'East African Football', 2012 and Waiswa, "Master's Thesis", 2005.

Uganda has produced a variety of talented individuals in numerous sports disciplines including athletics, soccer, boxing, basketball, netball, volleyball and rugby, among others. Some of the historic moments of Ugandan sport include Akii Bua, winning a gold medal in world record time in 400 meters hurdles during the 1972 Olympic Games in Munich; Stephen Kiprotich, gold medal in 2012 men's marathon; and Davis Kamoga winning a bronze medal in the 1996 Olympic games in Men's 400 meters. Joshua Cheptegei (5000 mm gold, 10,000 mm silver), Peruth Chemutai (3000 mw steeple chase, gold) and Jacob Kiplimo (10,000 mm bronze) put Uganda's name on the world map by their successful performances at the Tokyo 2020 Olympics held in 2021 due to delays prompted by COVID-19 global pandemic; in boxing, Eridadi Mukwanga (1968 silver medal), Leo Rabwogo (bronze 1968 and silver 1972) and John Mugabi (silver 1980).[58] Also in the 1970s, during a politically charged atmosphere, Uganda produced outstanding players such as Philip Omondi, Jimmy Kirunda, Timothy Ayieko, Moses Nsereko, Mike Kiganda, Denis Obua, Ashe Mukama and many others that propelled the National Team to Africa Cup of Nation's finals in 1978 in Ghana.

One of the enduring contradictions of Ugandan football is that this success of the 1970s, especially the national team, has been elusive ever since and even club football has not made a mark at the African Confederation level. Yet, the Ugandan national team and clubs are dominant within the Confederation of East and Central African Football Associations (CECAFA) tournaments.[59] Overall, therefore, the performances of Ugandan football players have left a lot to be desired, compared to countries such as Senegal, Mali, Nigeria, South Africa, Ghana, Cameroon and others on the African Continent, whose players display their talents in European leagues. It is intriguing that Uganda has not produced outstanding football players that can join top European leagues on a sustained basis. Ugandan footballers are therefore performing below everyone's expectation at international level.

---

[58] https://www.olympic.org/uganda.
[59] http://www.fufa.co.ug/about-fufa/history/.

Background and Status of Club Football

The Ugandan Premier League is the top division of the Federation of Uganda Football Associations. The league assumed a new identity in 2014–15 season from the previous one, the 'Uganda Super League', after new management taking over the running of the nation federation and the fueled by the need to enhance branding and marketing of the league.[60] The league's roots date back to 1966 when a national league was tried out and then in 1968 when the National First Division League was formally established. The genesis of club football in Uganda was an idea copied from England by Balamaze Lwanga and Polycarp Kakooza.[61] The objective was to improve Uganda's performances in the Africa Cup of Nations after disappointing results in the finals in 1962 (fourth place finish) and 1968 (lost all three-group stage matches), both held in Ethiopia. The intention was to start a Uganda National League (the forerunner of the Uganda Super League) to create the foundation for a strong national team. At the same time, forming the national league aimed at identifying potential national team players from the grassroots in an easier and systematic way.[62]

Because there were no clubs to form a league, institutions and districts were contacted to form teams. The 1968 inaugural top-flight league was composed of Prisons, Army, Coffee, Express, Jinja, Masaka, Mbarara and Mbale. There were three institutions, four districts and one club.[63] The league was known as the National First Division League, and the first league champions were Prisons FC Kampala (now known as Maroons FC). After four seasons, the political turbulence in Uganda affected the league. The 1972 and 1973 championships were annulled because of civil unrest. In 1974, the league became known as the National Football League and this title was used until 1982 when the league was trimmed to ten teams and was renamed the Super League (shortened to Super Ten in that inaugural season).[64] The emergence of the Super League in 1982 saw the development of SC Villa (Nakivubo) as the country's leading club. Through the 1980s and a good part of the 1990s, competition between Express, KCC FC and SC Villa lit up the league and fans attended in large

[60] http://www.fufa.co.ug/uganda-premier-league/.
[61] http://www.fufa.co.ug/uganda-premier-league/.
[62] http://www.fufa.co.ug/uganda-premier-league/.
[63] http://www.fufa.co.ug/uganda-premier-league/.
[64] Ibid.

numbers.[65] SC Villa won the league for the first time in 1982 and over the next 22 years won 16 league titles. KCC FC (later renamed KCCA) and Express won the championship title in the intervening years.

Out of 52 seasons that the league has been held, SC Villa (Nakivubo) won 16 (30.77%); Kampala City Council Authority, 13 (25%); Express, 7 (13.46%) and Uganda Revenue Authority, which appeared on the scene in the early part of the twenty-first century, 4 (7.69%). In total 13 different teams have won the title. The variety of winners shows how diversified and unpredictable the league is in some years. However, on the whole, the sheer consistency of the top four teams including SC Villa (Nakivubo), KCCA, Express and URA demonstrate how established teams are resilient and difficult to be displaced from the top.

Despite the consistency with which the league has been organized, it is also evident that there have been enormous challenges. One of the major challenges came in early 1970s when the political turbulence in Uganda affected the league. The turbulence made it impossible for the league to run smoothly in the 1972–73 season. At this time, there was civil unrest in the country.[66] Other challenges include match fixing. For example, during the 2003 season, SC Villa put 22 goals past Akol FC to win the league title edging out Express on goal difference.[67] Additionally, there have been accusations and investigations of match fixing in the Ugandan league in the past four years with Interpol getting involved. This is one of the biggest scandals in Ugandan football.[68] Apart from match fixing, the other challenge was the political interference that for some time caused the decline of Express FC during the dictatorial rule of Idi Amin. Those in Government perceived the Club as being anti-Idi Amin's regime. Finally yet importantly, the continuity and vibrancy of the league continue to experience power struggles in the FUFA and Club leadership levels. Despite all these challenges, Ugandan football continues to thrive. Apart from the National League, FUFA also organizes the men's and women's national football teams, and the first and second tiers of national football covering the Ugandan Super League and Ugandan Big League, respectively.

---

[65] Ibid.
[66] http://www.fufa.co.ug/uganda-premier-league/.
[67] Kavuma "Corruption and bribery in the National League of Uganda", 2003.
[68] http://theugandan.com.ug/new-evidence-points-to-high-level-match-fixing-in-ugandan-football/.

The other high-profile tournament with a long history is the Ugandan Cup (formerly Kakungulu Cup), which is the oldest football competition of knockout format having started in 1971. Even here the dominance of the top three clubs in Uganda including Express (10, 22.73%), SC Villa (9, 20.45%) and Kampala City Council Authority (10, 22.73%) is evident as they won majority of the cup tournaments. These teams have won 29 out of 44 (65.91%) of the editions of the Uganda Cup since its inaugural season in 1971. Just like in the League winners, only 14 teams have had a chance to win the Cup at least once. However, it is interesting to note that despite the dominance by Express, SC Villa and KCCA, a scrutiny of the victories shows that they were in the previous decade and older. However, KCCA has showed resurgence as seen by the latest victories in both the Cup and League. Since 2010, eight different clubs have won the cup and only the Uganda Revenue Authority managed to win in 2012 and 2015. Similarly, KCCA won back to back Cups in 2017 and 2018. Express last won the Cup in 2007, while SC Villa at least managed to lift the Cup in 2015, six years after they had won it in 2009. This unpredictability of the cup winners contributes to the popularity and enduring legacy of the Uganda Cup competition.

Conclusion

This chapter has demonstrated that Ugandan football is very popular despite having under achieved at the continental and global levels. This is despite the country being one of the few African countries that has produced World and Olympic champion athletes in track and field and boxing. Nevertheless, association football (soccer) is the one that dominates the minds and hearts of the Ugandan people as the number one sport in the nation. Although football was introduced from England in the 1890s, it was quickly taken up and appropriated by the indigenous people that were already leading active physical lifestyles. One avenue that they used to introduce and promote the sport was through schools. Association football became popular with the local youth in schools and soon the indigenous men adopted it around the country. Colonial legacies underpinning the popularity of association football include its cultural neutral nature, royal patronage, regionalism (north and south divide), institutionalization, political upheaval and national patriotism.

Indeed, football in Uganda engenders a sense of unity and identity that is remarkable given the major political upheavals that have afflicted the country since gaining independence in 1961 and more than 40 ethnic groupings. One can, therefore, assert that Ugandan football has been an enduring unifying factor in an otherwise politically unstable and socioeconomically divided country in the years following independence. Despite the passionate following and solidarity at the national level, there is bitter rivalry at the club level, which is a sign of a thriving competitive league and knockout competition. The variety of winners of both the Premier League and the national knockout competition shows that Ugandan football is healthy and competitive. Additionally, the national team finally qualified for the 2017 and 2019 African Cup of Nations in a row after a 39-year absence, which shows the resilience and the enduring potential of football to have better times in the coming years.

REFERENCES

Adrian Harvey, ed. Football: The First Hundred Years—The untold story. Abingdon, Oxon: Routledge, 2005: p. 234
Alegi, P. ed. African Soccerscapes: How a Continent Changed the World's Game. Athens, Ohio: Ohio University Press. 2010.
CECAFA. http://www.cecafafootball.org/about-cecafa/
Darby, P. "Africa's Place in FIFA's Global Order: A Theoretical Frame". *Soccer and Society* 1, no. 2 (2000): 36–61.
Darby, P. "Africa and the "World" Cup: FIFA Politics, Eurocentrism and Resistance". *The International Journal of the History of Sport* 22, no. 5 (2005): 883–905.
Harford-Battersby, Charles ed. (1899). Pilkington of Uganda. London: The Richmond Press. http://budonian.com/index.php?option=com_content&vie w=article&id=9&Itemid=11, retrieved on October 13, 2016
Hokkanen, M. "Christ and the Imperial Games Fields in South-Central Africa— Sport and the Scottish Missionaries in Malawi, 1880–1914: Utilitarian Compromise". *The International Journal of the History of Sport* 22, no. 4 (2005): 745–69.
John Iliffe, ed. Honour in African History. Cambridge, UK: Cambridge University Press, 2005: p. 300.
Kanyike, S. R. "Tracing Uganda's football history", retrieved at http://www.monitor.co.ug/Magazines/Score/Tracing-Uganda-s-football-history/689854-3827108-lvu7hkz/index.html on March 30, 2017.
Kavuma S. (2003): "Corruption and bribery in the National League of Uganda". Report to NCS Kampala Uganda.

Mählmann, Peter. "The Role of Sport in the Process of Modernisation: The Kenyan Case". *Journal of Eastern African Research and Development* 22 (1992): 120–31.
Mählmann, Peter. "Sport as a Weapon of Colonialism in Kenya: A Review of the Literature". *Transafrican Journal of History* 17 (1988): 152–71.
Mangan, J.A. *Athleticism in the Victorian and Edwardian Public School*. London: Cambridge, 1981.
Mangan, J.A. *The Games Ethic and Imperialism: Aspects of the Diffusion of an Ideal*. London: Frank Cass, 1998.
Mazrui, A.A. *The Africans: A Triple Heritage*. London: BBC Publications, 1986.
Naiman, R. and Watkins, N. A Survey of the Impacts of IMF Structural Adjustment in Africa: Growth, Social Spending, and Debt Relief. Center for Economic and Policy Research, April 1999 Retrieved at http://cepr.net/documents/publications/debt_1999_04.htm on March 10, 2017.
Ndee, H. S. "Eastern Africa: Geography, Ethnography and Physical Activity", *The International Journal of the History of Sport* 27, no. 5 (April 2010a): 759–779.
Ndee, H. S. "Pre-Colonial East Africa: History, Culture and Physical Activity". *The International Journal of the History of Sport* 27, no. 5 (April 2010b): 780–797
Ndee, H. S. "Prologue: Sport, Culture and Society in Tanzania from an African Perspective". The International Journal of the History of Sport 27, no. 5, (April 2010c): 733–758
Njororai, W. W. S. "African footballers face an allegiance problem: country versus club. The Conversation Africa. Retrieved at https://theconversation.com/african-footballers-face-an-allegiance-problem-country-versus-club-71634 on March 10, 2017.
Njororai, W. The History and Identity of East African Football within the African Context. In Identity and Nation. In African Football: Fans, Community and Clubs, eds. C. Onwumechili and G. Akindes, (67–80). London: Palgrave Macmillan, 2014a.
Njororai, W.W.S. 'Analysis of Technical and Tactical Performance of National Soccer Teams of Kenya, Germany and Argentina.'. PhD diss., Kenyatta University, Nairobi, 2000.
Njororai, W.W.S. 'The Diversity of Sport in Kenya'. In Sport in Contemporary African Society: An Anthology, ed. L. Amusa and A.L. Toriola, 199–229. Mokapane, South Africa: AFAHPER-S.D, 2003.
Njororai, W. W. S. "Colonial legacy, minorities and association football in Kenya". *Soccer & Society* 10, no. 6, (November 2009): 866–882
Njororai, W.W.S. 'Kenya at 50: Contextualization of Post-Independence Sporting Success. In Kenya After 50: Reconfiguring Education, Gender, and Policy. M. M. Koster, M. M. Kithinji and J. P. Rotich ed., 125–146. London: Palgrave Macmillan, 2014b.

Nsubuga, A. Save out soccer. Uganda Football at cross roads. *Monitor publication.* Issue 124, Kampala, Uganda, 2005.

Rintaugu, E. G., A. Mwisukha and V. Onywera. "Analysis of factors that affect the standard of soccer in Africa: the case of East African countries." *Journal of Physical Education and Sport* 12, 1 (2012): 135–139

Sekitto S.P, Football Development in Uganda: (1900–2000). Kampala, Uganda. 2001.

Straker, J. "Popular Culture as Critical Process in Colonial Africa: A Study of Brazzaville Football. Impumelelo". *The Interdisciplinary Electronic Journal of African Sports* 1 (2005). http://www.ohiou.edu/sportafrica/journal.

Versi, A. *Football in Africa.* London: Collins, 1986.

Waiswa K.A. Analysis of factors influencing football development in selected Districts in Uganda Unpublished M.sc Thesis, Kyambogo University Kampala, Uganda, 2005.

CHAPTER 13

Vicious Cycle: Cameroon(ization) and/or Foreign(ization) of the Indomitable Lions' Head Coaching

Alain Lawo-Sukam

The development of soccer and athletic talent in general depends on quality coaching. The importance of coaching practice has been studied for decades by scholars such as B.S Bloom 1985, Côté et al. (1995), P. Bourdieu (1998), Potrac et al. (2002), Rein et al. (2004), Cushion et al. (2006) and Reddy et al. (2013), among others. Soccer head coaches, like trainers in other sports, are "central figures in assigning capital values by the field amongst the players" (Cushion and Jones 152). The development of athletic talent, players' performance and satisfaction depend on quality coaching as well as coaching behaviors in practice, at games and away from sport (Bloom 1985). Nonetheless, more than their relation with players, soccer head coaches also embody symbolically the hope and aspiration of countries such as Cameroon that rely on the performance of the national teams to build unity among their citizens. Needleless to say that the Indomitable Lions are also the torch bearer, the franchise of the nation and ambassador overseer. It is an enormous

A. Lawo-Sukam (✉)
Texas A&M University, College Station, TX, USA
e-mail: Lawosukam@tamu.edu

© The Author(s), under exclusive license to Springer Nature Switzerland AG 2022
A. E. Ayuk (ed.), *Football (Soccer) in Africa*, Global Culture and Sport Series, https://doi.org/10.1007/978-3-030-94866-5_13

275

responsibility which subsequently makes the position of head coach more sensitive and coveted.

Since its creation, the Cameroon national soccer team (the Indomitable Lions) has retained the services of numerous head coaches who were foreigner and white European for the most part. If the selection of European coaches is understandable in the first decade of independence, it becomes questionable after that period when native coaches, well trained and up to the task, were available on the market. This study is not so much about defending or advocating against the choice of foreign head coaches over natives, but to present data on the number of head coaches in Cameroon history and critically analyze the disproportionate imbalance between the natives and the high volume of white Europeans head coaches selected to lead the Indomitable Lions. The paper not only analyzes the validity of the Cameroonization or foreignization of the Indomitable Lions' head coaching, but presents, beyond that, a more complex interpretative argument that involves common sense soccer practice/procedure, politico-ideological and commercial interests/pressure that are intersected. The study considers the position(s) of various stakeholders, which can be contradictory in certain extent. While the official discourse represented by soccer authorities insists on result driven and the application of FIFA regulations in the selection of head coaches, other stakeholders such as native coaches, soccer specialists and fans advocate otherwise, citing discrimination, lack of respect and conflict of interest.

Moreover, I argue that the selection of foreign coaches is a complex process that can be theoretically interpreted from different perspectives: the resurgence of a neo-colonial mentality that favor whites over blacks; a political maneuver by the dominant discourse to avoid ethnic tensions in a very *tribalized* country such as Cameroon; a tactical move to avoid hash scrutiny reserved to native coaches by the population, and lastly the pressure from multinational corporations to secure commercial benefits. It is impossible, therefore, to argue that the selection of the national coach follows due process or not or is guided by practical result driven ideology or not. What remain are multiple hypotheses that have merit and cannot be discarded since the selection decision making is very fluid and more often shrined in mystery.

To strengthen our analysis, we resorted to brief comparative study that involves other African national soccer teams and head coaches' views. This comparative study method is important to better understand the Cameroonian national soccer context since soccer head coaching practices across Africa are interconnected despite each country's specificity. One cannot understand and judge the functioning of the Indomitable Lions' head coaching in isolation. This article is based on a multi-methods approach that includes observational data collected, archives, interviews and Close Reading. Theoretically, it draws upon various frameworks characteristic of postcolonial and cultural studies among others.

Indomitable Lions' Head Coaching: A Burden of Hope Since 1963

After gaining independence in 1960, the Indomitable Lions have been led by 31 different coaches (from 1963 to July 2019). These coaches can be classified in two categories: national/local and foreigners. The national coaches include Raymond Fobété (1969–1970), Leonard Nseke (1993), Jean Manga Onguene (1992–1993, 1997–1998), Jules Nyonga (1994–1996, 2006–2007), Thomas Nkono (2009), Jacques Célestin Songo'o (2010), Jean Paul Akono (2001, 2012–2013) and Alexandre Belinga (2015–2016).[1]

Foreign coaches are all Europeans: Dominique Colonna from France (1963–1965[–1969]), Peter Schnittger from Germany (1970–1973), Vladimir Beara from Yugoslavia (1973–1975), Ivan Ridanovic from Yugoslavia (1976–1979), Zutic Branko from Yugoslavia (1980–1982), Jean Vincent from France (1982), Radivoje Ognjanovic from Yugoslavia (1982–1984), Valeri Nepomniachi from Russia (1988–1990), Philippe Redon from France (1990–1992), Henri Michel from France (1994), Henri Depireux from Belgium (1996–1997), Claude le Roy from France (1985, 1987, 1988, 1998), Pierre Lechantre from France (1998, 1999, 2000, 2001), Winfried Schafer from Germany (2001, 2002, 2003, 2004), Artur Jorge from Portugal (2004, 2005, 2006), Arie Hann from Netherlands (2006), Otto Pfister from Germany (2007, 2008, 2009), Paul Le Guen from France (2009–2010), Javier Clemente Lazarro from Spain (2010–2011), Denis Lavagne from France (2011–2012), Volker Finke from Germany (2013, 2014, 2015), Hugo Broos from Belgium

---

[1] Dominique Colonna was the first professional coach of the Indomitable Lions from 1963 to 1965. He was promoted to technical adviser and later coach of Central African (Inter) States that included Cameroun, Chad, Gabon, R.C.A, Congo Brazzaville and Congo Léopoldville (Kinshasa) from 1965 to 1973.

(2016–2017), Clarence Seedorf from the Netherlands (2018–2019) and Conceiçao Da Silva Oliveira (September 2019–present) from Portugal.

From this data we can classify the coaches in terms of continent, nationality and ethno-racial identity. By continent we have 24 Europeans and 8 Africans. By ethno-racial category we have 23 white European, 8 black African and 1 black European. By nationality we have 8 French, 8 Cameroonians, 4 Germans, 4 Yugoslavians, 2 Belgium, 2 Dutch, 1 Spaniard, 2 Portuguese and 1 Russian.

The Indomitable Lions of Cameroon have frequently qualified for FIFA World Cup in 1982, 1990, 1994, 1998, 2002, 2010 and 2014. They have won five Africa Cup of Nations in 1984, 1988, 2000, 2002 and 2017; four UDEAC Cup in 1984, 1986, 1987 and 1989; three CEMAC Cup in 2003, 2005 and 2008 as well as an Olympic gold medal in 2000 with the Olympic team. This record places the Cameroonian national soccer team among the best in the continent, next to Egypt, Nigeria and Ghana to cite a few. The list of hits also reveals implicitly some failures that has plagued the team since its affiliation with FIFA in 1962 and CAF in 1963. It hasn't won any Africa Cup of Nations from 1988 to 2000 and from 2002 to 2017 and have played poorly in World Cup tournaments after reaching the quarterfinals in 1990 despite having stars' players in the team. The success and failures of the team not only are the result of the behavior and performance of the squad (before and) on the field but also depend on the skill, experience, behavior and record of head coaches.

The vast number of coaches at the helm of the Cameroonian national soccer team is staggering. It not only shows an institutional instability and lack of trust in coaching staff but also exposes complex ideology(ies) behind the decision made by selection committee. From Peter Schnittger to Clarence Seedorf, head coaches don't spend enough time on the technical staff to develop players' skills and build a sustainable relation with the team. Despite their winning or losing record, they often resigned on their own accord, forced to leave or replaced by soccer authorities in a short period of time. Moreover, the clearly overwhelming preference of European head coaches over natives, and white over black, arouse some concern about the *foreignization* and whitening of Cameroonian head coaching position. Many factors are involved in the selection process, from the search of talented coaches to the pervasive neo-colonial mentality ingrained in the psychic of the decision-makers.

Official Discourse: The Voice of the Decision-Makers

The selection of the Indomitable Lions' head coach is the prime responsibility of the Cameroon soccer federation (FECAFOOT).[2] Over the years, soccer authorities have maintained the notion of talent and experience as the credo for selecting head coaches. They have strongly rejected politics, third-party influence and discrimination as part of their decision making, in accordance with the International Federation of Football Association (FIFA) statutes. In fact, as a member of FIFA since 1962, FECAFOOT has the obligation to comply with the principle of good governance dictated by the soccer's world governing body.[3] Among these principles is the independence of member associations and their bodies: "Each member association shall manage its affairs independently and without undue influence from third parties" (FIFA 16). Furthermore, soccer federations should "(b) prohibit all forms of discrimination, (c) be independent and avoid any form of political interference, ... (i) to avoid conflicts of interest in decision-making" (13–14).

By publicly aligning themselves with FIFA mandates and claiming to follow its regulations concerning head coaching selection, Cameroonian soccer authorities not only try to show that they are preserving the integrity of the selection process but also avoid to be punished or suspended for lack of compliance. It is therefore by concern for a job well done that FECAFOOT officially advertises for application and outlines an exhaustive list of requirements that includes soccer coaching certificates, knowledge of African soccer, soccer experience in coaching elite or national soccer clubs, have won trophies, speak the official languages and be willing to permanently reside in the country among other requests. FECAFOOT in partnership with the Ministry of Sports selects the best candidate for the position after reviewing all the applicants' dossiers.

No matter who is selected or fired as head coach, soccer authorities always claim to have followed due process. For example, the dismissal of Volker Finke (October 2015) and the selection of Hugo Bross (February 2016) exemplify the official discourse surrounding the removal and appointment of head coaches.

---

[2] In most cases, the selection is made by Fecafoot in concert with the Ministry of Sports.
[3] Member associations' statutes are listed on FIFA statutes in the April 2016 edition, in force as of April 27, 2016, pages 13–16. http://www.fifa.com/governance/index.html.

The German Volker Finke was appointed head coach of the Indomitable Lions after the removal of the Cameroonian Jean Paul Akono in 2013. His arrival was praised by the soccer federation who saw in him the most qualified coach for the job. After almost three years at the helm of the national soccer team, Finke was sacked in October 2015. Even though the reason for the decision was not available the day of the coach removal, FECAFOOT president Tombi A Roko Sidiki argued that "People have rejected him ... His style of play had become stereotyped, lacking inspiration for the players selected and without any strategy for victory" (*BBC* 2015). In this context, the head coach poor performance and lack of creativity were reasonable causes for dismissal. The Cameroonian Alexandre Belinga was placed in temporary charge of the team until the official selection of a new coach. He was given the mission to win the remaining games and keep the team's hope alive for the Russia 2018 World Cup qualifying campaign. Moreover, the interim coach job could be permanent if he performed well according to Tombi Roko Sidiki: "We would appreciate Belinga's management of the games against Niger in both legs and if he convinces, he can remain there even for ten years" (*BBC* 2015). After the qualification of the team, he was replaced by the Belgium Hugo Bross, who was selected among the 286 candidates.

The choice of the Belgium coach was made public on February 18, 2016, during a speech done by Sidiki while presiding the signing of the contract. The president of FECAFOOT reiterated that the appointment of Hugo Bross aimed at

> doter le banc de touche des Lions Indomptables engagés dans les éliminatoires de la CAN Gabon 2017 et la Coupe du Monde Russie 2018, d'un encadrement technique stable, ambitieux et susceptible de ramener le football camerounais au firmament du football africain et partant de le hisser aux places d'honneur du football mondial. (*Camer.be*)[4]
>
> Providing the Indomitable Lions, who are engaged in the Gabon CAN 2017 and Russia World Cup 2018 play-off round, with a stable, ambitious technical staff that could return Cameroon soccer on the top of African soccer and get the team to a place of honor in worldwide soccer ranking.

---

[4] The entire speech can be found at "Tombi A Roko: 'S'inspirer de cet example belge'." Camer.be 20 February 2016.

The speech of the president was saturated with praises of the new coach experience, talent and awards received during his soccer career. A biographical headline published on the official website of FECAFOOT expresses the satisfaction of the soccer federation about their choice: "Hugo Bross: Un palmarès élogieux pour un entraîneur professionnel" [*Hugo Bross: A Glowing Record for a Professionel Coach*]. The compliment continues in the first sentence of the biography. It reads as follows: "Le nouvel entraîneur des Lions indomptables du Cameroun est un technicien au CV très étoffé et un homme de caractère confirmé" (FECAFOOT)[5] [*The new Indomitable Lions' head coach is an expert with an intensive CV, and an experienced man of character*].

Hugo Bross was fired in December 2017 by the Football Normalization Committee for poor results. His successor Clerence Seerdorf, praised by authorities at FECAFOOT for his talent despite his controversial (poor) performance as coach in his career, was sacked in July 16, 2019, for failing to retaining the Africa Cup of Nations in Egypt. His four years contract signed in August of 2018 was ended abruptly.

The official narrative behind the change of coaches from Volker Finker, Hugo Bross to Clarence Seedorf reflects the discourses that have surrounded most of the dismissals and appointments of head coaches in Cameroonian soccer history. Victory, great performances, trust, or the lack thereof are the mantra that motivates the decision of FECAFOOT and the Ministry of Sport to hire or fire a coach. The accusation of discrimination against native coaches tends to be a nonsense in the eyes of soccer authorities who can point at the trophies of the Indomitable Lions, all won by foreign head coaches (except the gold medal at the Olympics in 2000).[6] In fact, the 2017 Africa Cup of Nations won in Gabon by the Indomitable Lions was used by soccer authorities to vindicate their choice of Hugo Broos as head coach.

---

[5] "Hugo Bross. "Un palmarès élogieux pour un entraîneur professionnel." Fecafoot Web. February 2016. http://fecafoot-officiel.com/?p=5504.

[6] The Indomitable Lions won their five prestigious Africa Cup of Nations (CAN) under the leadership of Hugo Broos in 2017, Winfried Schafer in 2002, Pierre Lechantre in 2000, Claude Le Roy in 1988 and Radivoje Ognjanovic in 1984. They won one Olympic gold medal in 2000 in Sydney with Jean Paul Akono. At a regional level, the four UDEAC Cups were won in 1984 (Radivoje Ognjanovic), 1986 and 1987 (Claude Le Roy) and 1989 (Valeri Nepomniachi). The three CEMAC Cup victories were secured in 2003 (Winfred Schafer), 2005 (Artur Jorge) and 2008 (Otto Pfister).

Considering the short time spent by coaches at the head of the national soccer team in the past decades, the honeymoon between the soccer federation and Hugo Bross didn't last long. The head coach was sacked in December 2017 despite his willingness to stay. The poor performance at the 2017 Confederations cup and the failure to qualify for the 2018 World Cup were among the reasons for the dismissal. Clarence Seedorf only spent less than a year on his four years contract before being dismissed. He was replaced in September 2019 by the Portuguese Conceiçao da Silva Oliveira. With this trend of dismissal of head coaches, it is impossible to predict a sense of stability at the helm of the Indomitable Lions. Despite the controversies surrounding the departure of head coaches, the official discourse on their hiring and dismissal is only the visible tip of the iceberg.

Alternative Voices: The Discourse of (Un)Reason?

The list of Indomitable Lions' head coaches shows a clear preference for foreigners and white Europeans. Even though the official discourse claims talent, experience, fairness and equal opportunity among other indicators of selection, it is hard to fathom that only 9 out of 30 head coaches were Cameroonians. Oddly, those nine coaches were mostly placed temporary in charge of the team without proper contract and received a salary that could be compared to a "bonus" given to their European counterparts. Considering the preference for European coaches over Cameroonians, one could attribute this choice to neo-colonial mentalities that continue to activate the complex of inferiority of Africans over Europeans and blacks over whites.

On the onset, it is quite understandable that, after the independence of the country in 1960, soccer authorities would lean on foreigners and Europeans (nicknamed "sorcier blanc") to lead the Indomitable Lions because of the scarcity of native coaches. In 1963, the selection of Dominique Colonna was needed to develop the team from scratch. After the departure of the French coach, FECAFOOT and the Ministry of Sport banked on foreign nationals to head coaching the team meanwhile trained Cameroonian coaches were left out or just appointed mostly as caretaker despite their good performance. For example, Raymond Fobété was the first Cameroonian head coach of the Indomitable Lions from July 1969 to March 1970. Despite leading the team to its first participation to CAN 1970 in Khartoum, he was only appointed as interim head coach and replaced by the German Peter Schnittger. The Cameroonian Leonard

Nseké also took the headship of the Indomitable Lions as "firefighter" and qualified them for the 1994 World Cup in the United States of America. Unfortunately, he was replaced by Frenchman Henri Michel who led the team to a disastrous campaign in the United States of America. The Cameroonian Jean Manga Onguené replaced the Belgium Henri Depireux as interim head coach and succeeded in qualifying the team to the 1998 World Cup in France. Unfortunately, soccer authorities hired the Frenchman Claude le Roy to lead the team to France where they left the competition in the first round. Like his Cameroonian predecessors, Jules Frédéric Nyongha was called to rescue the Indomitable Lions as caretaker. He successfully qualified the team to the CAN 1996 in South Africa and 2006 in Ghana but left the team frustrated by the lack of support. The story of other native head coaches such as Thomas Nkono, Jacques Célestin Songo'o, Jean Paul Akono and Alexandre Belinga followed almost the same pattern. They were appointed as caretaker and replaced by white Europeans.

If it is true that national soccer team has won their major trophies under white coaches, it is also important to reveal that the team had their worst performance under those foreign coaches as well. Likewise, not all local coaches appointed as interim head coach were very successful in their mission.[7] Nevertheless, the victories and failures of local head coaches came at great expense. They didn't have a permanent contract or no contract at all for some of them. Their salaries were mediocre comparing to their white counterparts and not paid in regular basis. Some coaches like Jules Nyongha had to sue soccer authorities and principally the minister of sports for compensation (Nsigué). Due to their job description as interim coaches, the natives didn't have enough time to develop the team according to their vision and philosophy of soccer.

Are these few interim coaches not talented enough to be permanent head coaches of the national soccer team? Not at all, they are talented and experienced enough to be head coaches and not merely interim or assistant coaches of the Indomitable Lions. For example, Jean Paul Akono led Cameroon Olympic team to its first Olympic gold medal in 2000. He also coached the national team of Chad (2002–2003). Furthermore, certified and experienced coaches abound in Cameroon besides the nine

---

[7] Despite some victories Jean Paul Akono "Magnusson", for example, left the team after a mediocre performance in 2001, and also failed to qualify the country to the CAN 2013 in South Africa.

mentioned earlier. The most visible coaches since the 1970s are Calvin Oyono, Maurice Nanga, Oscar Eyoum, Youdom, Pierroh Amah, Atangana Ottou, Richard Towa, Jean-Michel Njelezek, Jean-Pierre Sadi, Laurent Adoa, Michel Kaham, Nana Salé, Martin Ndtougou Mpilé, Bonaventure Djonkep, François Heya, Pierre Ndjili Ndengue, Emmanuel Maboang Kessack, Aboubakar Souleymanou, Joseph Atangana, Nicolas Tonyè Tonyè, Bertin Ebwellé Ndingué, Siewe Joseph, Francois Oman Biyik, Patrick Mboma and Rigobert Song, to name a few.

The list of Cameroonian coaches is a reservoir of talents that soccer authorities could have utilized to avoid too much dependence on white foreign coaches. (Un)fortunately, most of native coaches are relegated to assistant coaches of the Indomitable Lions or consigned as coaches of less prestigious teams such as "Lions A," "Lions Espoirs," "Lions Juniors," "Lions Cadets" and "Lions Minimes."[8] If the trend continues, the coveted head coach of the Indomitable Lions will still be the panacea of white foreigners. In this context, the preference for European coaches is similar to what Ngugi Wa Thiong'o decried in *Decolonising the Mind*: "Africa is made to believe that it needs Europe to rescue it from poverty" (28).

The neo-colonial notion of dependency complex is pronounced by the lack of African coaches among the selected foreigners as well as the scarcity of black coaches. Clarence Seedorf and Patrick Kluivert hired in 2008 as head and assistant coaches, respectively, are the few exceptions of black European coaches at the helm of the national football team. In general, whiteness becomes a marker of professional privilege. De-Africanization and *de-blackification* turn out to be an imagined dialectics of transformation not only in soccer arena but also in other sectors such as culture, economy and politics. The widespread neo-colonial phenomenon reinforces the Hegelian view "whose premise was that Africa is incapable of producing something good and that therefore Africans have no significant vision for their own futures" (Bongmba 22). African and African diaspora

[8] In 2014, Bonaventure Djonkep, François Heya and Simon Nlend Anjouma were appointed coaches of the Lions A' (Men A); Pierre Ndjili Ndengue, Emmanuel Maboang Kessack and François Toindouba, of the Lions Espoirs (U23); Aboubakar Souleymanou, of the Lions juniors (U20); Joseph Atangana and Nicolas Tonyè Tonyè of the Lions cadets (U17); Bertin Ebwellé Ndingué and Siewe Joseph of the Lions Minimes (U15). In 2016 the coaches of selection A' (Rigobert Song, Ernest Agbor and Simon Nlend Anjouma); Selection U23 (Richard Towa); Selection U20 (Ashu Bessong, Ousmarou Christophe and Hugues Biloa); Selection U17 (Bertin Ebwelle, Thomas Libih and Tadou) and Selection U15 (Joseph Siéwé, Gregoire Antangana and Samuel Some).

scholars such as Frantz Fanon, Ali Mazrui and Ngughi Wa Thiong'o, among others, have criticized the tendency of African leaders and blacks to internalize the complex of superiority of whites and subsequently depreciate the potential and contribution of their fellow countrymen.[9] As Frantz Fanon puts it: "A black man behaves differently with a white man than he does with another black man. There is no doubt whatsoever that this fissiparousness is a direct consequence of the colonial undertaking" (1).

The favoritism bestowed to whites over blacks is manifest in the following statement of Joseph-Antoine Bell, one of Cameroon best goalkeepers:

> Malgré tout ce qui est dit depuis de nombreuses années sur le sujet, le nombre d'entraîneurs étrangers ne cesse d'augmenter en Afrique, ... En Afrique, un Européen remplacera un autre Européen. Eux, ils ont le droit d'être mauvais. Les entraîneurs africains, non. On le vire quand il a été mauvais, et parfois même lorsqu'il a été bon, pour prendre un Européen derrière. C'est donc un problème de mentalité. Et ce n'est pas un problème propre au football. Cette attitude-là, on la retrouve dans beaucoup d'autres domaines ... Ces entraîneurs étrangers viennent de loin, ils ont la couleur de la peau pour eux et il y a toujours quelqu'un pour les engager. (Kalfa)
> *Despite all that is said for many years about the issue, the number of foreign coaches continue to grow in Africa ... In Africa, a European will replace another European. They have the right to perform poorly, but not African coaches. They [natives] are fired when they perform poorly and even when they perform well; and replaced by a European in their back. It is therefore a problem of mentality. It is not a problem only for soccer. That attitude is found in other areas ... These foreign coaches come from far, they are favored because of the color of their skin, and there is always somebody to hire them.*

Joseph-Antoine Bell uses Africa in general to speak implicitly about the case of Cameroon. He criticizes the mentality of African soccer authorities who don't tolerate mistakes made by native coaches. Moreover, African coaches don't have the right to error but not white coaches. The Cameroonian goalkeeper also denounces the fact that despite the talent of native coaches, they are still fired and replaced by Europeans. The white skin color of European coaches is a privilege and a guarantee of employment in Africa.

---

[9] Despite the harsh criticism of de-africanization, Ali Mazrui have also noted a regression of westernization of African societies: "The good news is the slowing down of the process of westernization and of de-africanization in African societies" (200).

The sentiment of "discrimination" that Joseph-Antoine Bell condemned is also shared by the Ghanaian coach James Kwesi Appiah and the late Nigerian coach Stephen Keshi. In an article published on February 6, 2013, by BBC Sport, the Ghanaian coach value the performance of black coaches who are as good as their white counterparts: "Appiah also commented on the issue ahead of his side's last-four clash with the Stallions in Nelspruit, saying he had 'total respect' for foreign white coaches in Africa but that black managers 'can do the same as anybody'" (*BBC*).[10] Additionally, Stephen Keshi, one of the two players who won the Africa Cup of Nations as player and coach, also weigh in on the controversy surrounding the selection of white coaches:

> If you want to bring in a classic, an experienced coach from Europe, I am ready to learn from that coach, because he's better than me, he has more knowledge than me ... Meanwhile, we have quality African players, or ex-African players, [who are] coaches now that can do the same thing, but they're not given the opportunity because they're just black dudes. I don't like it. (*BBC*)

Stephen Keshi made it clear that he was not against the hiring of white coaches but wanted equal opportunity for African coaches. In a BBC Sport's report on January 4, 2013, the Nigerian coach condemned the attitude of soccer federations across the continent for making the job of native coaches tougher than white foreigners' one:

> African coaches—when [federations] employ them, [the federations] want them to win the World Cup, the Africa Cup of Nations and every game, ... Meanwhile, if you give a white person the same job, you tell the white person they need one year to adapt, to know the country and the players—they are told 'don't worry, take your time' ... That is unprofessional and is one thing that is killing African football." (*BBC*)

Kinnah Phiri, the former Malawi national soccer head coach, also weigh in on the controversy of neglecting native coaches in favor of Europeans. Like Joseph-Antoine Bell, he found the source of the problem in the mentality of Africans:

---

[10] "Nations Cup 2013: Keshi criticises 'mediocre' European coaches." BBC Web. 6 February 2013.

Prior to 2010 Fifa World Cup, ... Kinnah Phiri also told BBC World Service that 'it's not fair for us African coaches not to be given a chance to run our own national teams because in the first place most of us are well trained, I trained in Britain; so to me, I think it's just because of our own mentality as Africans that we do not believe in our people'.

The frustration of Joseph-Antoine Bell, James Kwesi Appiah, Stephen Keshi and Kinnah Phiri illustrates the transnationality of the neo-colonial complex of dependency inlayed in the mind of soccer authorities. In this context, the privilege of those racialized as white derived from the erroneous believe of whiteness as "at once development, modernity, intelligence, innovation, technology, cultural and aesthetic superiority" (Pierre 74). Albeit the white positionality and the ideology of whiteness is still strong in the society, Cameroonians are nowadays more inclined to support the candidacy of native coaches and emancipate themselves from the complex of inferiority.

Among the most vocal fans in support of native coaches are sport specialists and sportscasters. They believed that native coaches would be the best at the head of the national soccer team if they received the same financial and logistic support like foreign coaches. For example, in 2015 Jean-René Noubissié, the president of Nousia Sport Academy (a school of soccer based in Douala), argued: "Si les mêmes moyens donnés aux coachs expatriés sont offerts aux entraîneurs nationaux, les résultats n'en seront que meilleurs" (Raoul Mbog) [*If the same financial means that are given to foreign coaches are offered to natives, the results would be better*]. This "nationalistic" idea is reinforced by Emmanuel Jonas Kana, sportscaster and soccer specialist, who plead for the end of the myth of white skin superiority in national consciousness: "Sans être raciste ou xénophobe, il serait judicieux de mettre un terme au mythe de la peau blanche. Les entraîneurs expatriés n'ont rien apporté depuis une décennie" (Raoul Mbog) [*Without being racist nor xenophobic, it should be judicious to end the white skin myth. Foreign coaches have brought nothing for decades*]. The comments of these Cameroonian soccer specialists were in certain way informed by events that took place in other African countries such as Egypt and South Africa among other nations. Both countries have already experienced the Africanization of their national soccer teams by selecting natives as full head coach and not merely caretakers. The mythic Egyptian coach Hassan Shehata has won three Africa Cup of Nations with the "Pharaohs" in 2006, 2008 and 2010. Before him, another Egyptian Mahmoud el Gohary was in charge of the "pharaohs" in the 1990 World

Cup expedition in Italy and won the Africa Cup of Nations' title in 1998. He also coached the national teams of Oman and Jordan. Furthermore, South Africa has more native coaches than foreigners after the collapse of the Apartheid regime in the 1990s. The South African Clive Barker, for example, led the Bafana Bafana to the CAN 1996 title. Ghana's Charles Kumi Gyamfi successfully coached the Black Stars to three African Cup of Nations titles in 1963, 1965 and 1982.

Other soccer federations in Nigeria, Ghana, Ivory Coast, Zimbabwe, Burkina Faso, Bissau-Guinea, Guinea, Senegal, Sudan, Tunisia, Burundi, Algeria, Namibia, Mali, Malawi, Cape Verde, Comoros, Ethiopia, Bissau Guinee, Tanzania and the Democratic Republic of Congo have also hired natives as full head coach and not just interim. Kaba Diawara in Guinea, Augustine Eguavoen in Nigeria, Burhan Tia in Sudan, Kamou Malo in Burkina Faso, Pedro Brito in Cape Verde, Amir Abdou In Comoros, Wubetu Abate in Ethiopia, Aliou Cissé in Senegal, Norman Mapeza, Mondher Kebaier in Tunisia, Kalisto Pasuwa and Sunday Chidzambwa in Zimbabwe, Baciro Candé in Guinea-Bissau, Olivier Niyungeko in Burundi, Djamel Belmadi in Algeria, Ricardo Mannetti in Namibia, Ibrahim Kamara in Ivory Coast, Mohamed Magassouba in Mali, James Kwesi Appiah in Ghana, Emmanuel Amunike in Tanzania and Florent Ibenge in the Democratic Republic of Congo were head coaches of their respective countries either at the 2017 African Cup of Nations in Gabon, at the 2019 CAN in Egypt or at the 2022 CAN in Cameroon. During the 33rd edition of the African Cup of Nations in Cameroon (2022), most head coaches were African.

The Senegalese coach Aliou Cissé recently won the CAN 2022 with the "Lions of Teranga." The Algerian coach Djamel Belmadi won the CAN 2019 with the "Fennec." The Nigerian coach Stephen Keshi won the CAN 2013 with the "Super Eagles." He was replaced by another Nigerian coach Sunday Oliseh. The Ivoirian Francois Zahoui led Ivory Coast to the CAN 2012 final. The Ghanaian James Kwesi Appiah led the Black Stars to the 2014 World Cup in Brazil. He was the first black African coach to take an African national soccer team in the World Cup. Some countries like Chad, Niger, Togo and Central Africa Republic have selected other Africans as head coach.[11] It is unfortunate that despite the success stories

---

[11] Central African Republic hired the Cameroonian François Omam Biyik as head coach in February 2017. Chad selected the Cameroonian Rigobert Song as head coach in October 2015. Niger appointed the Ivoirian Francois Zahoui as head coach in 2015. The Togolese national soccer team was coached by the Nigerian Stephen Keshi in 2011 and, by the Togolese Tchakala Tchanalilé in 2014–2015.

of native head coaches, some soccer federations were still looking abroad (in Europe) to substitute them. That was the case of Francois Zahoui who was replaced by debutant coach Frenchman Sabri Lamouchi and James Appiah by the Israeli and former Chelsea coach Avram Grant.[12]

For African coaches and sport specialists, soccer authorities must value the talent of their own fellow compatriots and select the worthy ones as head coaches instead of relying too much on white Europeans. However, this perspective is not totally shared by Europeans coaches who considered their appointment not as a matter of skin color but as the result of experience and formation that most African coaches lack. This argument was explicitly made by the former Uganda's Scottish coach Bobby Williamson on BBC Sport, reported January 4, 2013. He noted:

> It is not about being black or white, it is about having the qualifications ... I've got them. My UEFA license doesn't expire until until 2016 and I'll be doing what I need to in the meantime to keep it up ... I'm not sure that many African coaches have that qualification and that is the biggest problem. They have Confederation of African Football qualifications, but I don't think they match the level of the European qualifications.

Bobby Williamson's allegations purportedly discard neo-colonial mentality as a reason for hiring white coaches. In this context, his argument is aligned with the official discourse of Cameroonian soccer authorities for whom whiteness apparently has nothing to do with the selection, but qualifications, talent and experience. Nevertheless, accusing African coaches of lacking qualification contrasts with the reality of many African and Cameroonians who are international certified soccer trainers. As coach Kinnah Phiri suggested earlier, most African coaches are well trained and attend the same courses as their European counterparts. Additionally, most Africans play for the same league in which European coaches are products of (Kainja).

---

[12] The number of native head coaches is on the rise since 2015. In the CAN 2018 there were 11 African head coaches among the 24 teams qualified for the competition. In the CAN 2017 there were only four African head coaches among the 16 teams qualified for the competition: Aliou Cissé for Senegal, Kalisto Pasuwa for Zimbabwe, Baciro Kandé for Bissau-Guinea and Florent Ibenge for the Democratic Republic of Congo. In the CAN 2015 there were two African head coaches out of 16: The Zambian Honour Janza for the "Chipolopolo" of Zambia and the South African Ephraim Mashaba for the "Bafana Bafana" of South Africa.

Besides neo-colonial ideologies as a reason behind the selection of foreign head coaches over natives, there are other lesser factors that come into play, namely, political ethnic divisions and strives, pressure from multinational corporations and the hash scrutiny of the public.

As any country beleaguered by tribalism, regionalism and secessionist mentality, the desire to achieve unity in Cameroon is often guided by the principle of ethnic conflict prevention. In certain sensitive administrative position, a way to appease symbolically such strives is through ethnic neutrality that could be achieved by the selection of a personality not affiliated with any of the country tribes. It is important to mention that Cameroon is a land of more than 249 tribes that belong to three main ethnic groups: Sudanese, Bantus and Semi-Bantus. French and English are the two official languages alongside more than 240 national dialects. Two major religions, Christianity and Islam are dominant. This diversity is problematic in terms of power allocation as well as representation in administration, education, security and other high-profile professional occupations. The den of Indomitable Lions is not an exception. As the pride of the nation, the nation soccer team embodies the image of the country. Most of the major ethnic, religion and language groups are represented in one form or another on the team squad. Consequently, the position of the head coach becomes a very important locus of power. At the national level, the tribe of the native head coach turns out to be a contentious issue since the large number of Cameroonian coaches, capable to lead the national soccer team, belong to different tribes. Even as interim coaches, the few natives selected have faced criticism by segments of the population based on their tribal affiliations.

The recent controversial case transpired after the appointment of Alexandre Belinga as interim head coach in 2015. In fact, Bonaventure Djonkep and Alexandre Bélinga were appointed assistant coaches under Volke Finke. After the dismissal of the German coach, Bélinga was selected as caretaker to the detriment of Djonkep who have more international coaching experience. The choice of Belinga was criticized in the press and social media platforms. For example, one of the articles written by Olivier Ndema Epo in Camerpost was titled "Cameroun-Lions Indomptables: Le nouveau sélectionneur pose déjà de nombreux problèmes" [*Cameroon-Indomitable Lions: The New Head Coach Poses a Number of Problems Already*]. The journalist reported that many fans were very critical of the selection of Bélinga. They found inadmissible that Bonaventure Djonkep was named assistant of Bélinga when the latter lacked the coaching experience of the former. A reason for that (mis)fortune was the effect of tribalism: "Tout ceci induit une autre raison, le tribalisme. Un constat défavorable à Bonaventure Djonkep selon ces mêmes internautes" (Epo) [*All this entails another reason, tribalism. A statement unfavorable to Bonaventure Djonkep*]. For some fans, the selection of Bélinga over Djonkep was due to tribalism since Alexandre Djonkep belong to the bamiléké ethnicity, a community that has been oppressed for decades by the dominant discourse. Even though Bélinga had a good performance with the national soccer team, his ethnicity was somehow problematic.

Considering the tribalization of the Cameroonian society, one could conclude that the selection of foreign coaches could implicitly be a solution to transcend ethnic affiliation and conflict. In that regard, ethnic neutrality becomes a political weapon waved by soccer authorities to avoid being accused of ethnic bias. Nevertheless, if soccer authorities wanted to avoid ethnic (de)favoritism, it would have been judicious to select at least an African coach or intend to do so before looking toward Europe. European soccer federations barely hire non-European coaches, and Cameroon soccer authorities could at least experiment the services of African coaches before looking across the Mediterranean Sea.

Another reason for selecting foreign coaches could originate from the hash scrutiny of the public toward native coaches. As Alexis Billebault reported in the magazine *Jeune Afrique* in June 2016: "'Il (le patron technique étranger) sera moins soumis à la pression populaire et médiatique, par rapport à un local qui va vivre tout le temps en Algérie', explique le Cheikh" (Billeault) [*The (foreign coach) will be less subjected to popular and media coverage pressure than a native who will live in Algeria all the time*]. The case of Algeria reflects in certain extent what happens in Cameroon and the rest of Africa. Natives coaches who normally live in the country are more scrutinized by the public and media than foreigners who live abroad and only travel to the country for a short period of time and for specific reasons.

Conflict of interest could also be a motive behind the foreignization of Cameroon national soccer head coach. Players as well as multinational corporations can implicitly contribute to the hiring, retention or dismissal of a coach. For example, the research done by the journalist Raul Mbog for the international journal *Le Monde* revealed that the longevity of Volke Finke as head coach was due to the pressure of Puma:

Pour une partie des médias locaux qui n'ont eu de cesse de demander la démission de l'entraîneur allemand, la longévité de Volker Finke à la tête des Lions malgré ses contre-performances répétées était due aux pressions de l'équipementier Puma qui l'a toujours soutenu. (Mbog)
[*For a number of local media that continuously asked for the dismissal of the German coach, the longevity of Volker Finke at the head of the Lions despite his repeated failures was due to the pressure of the equipment manufacturer Puma that always supported him*]

According to some local news media outlets, the German multinational company pushed for the hiring and retention of the German coach that he sponsored.[13] This pressure purportedly occurred with other national selection before his coming to Cameroon. As the head coach of the Senegalese national soccer team, Volker Finke was openly called by the Senegalese media "Volker Finke, le selectionneur de Puma" [*Volker Fink, Puma's coach*] or "Un choix imposé par Puma" [*A choice imposed by Puma*].[14] It is relevant to mention that Puma is the official supplier of the Indomitable Lions of Cameroon and all its associated teams. The corporation also sponsored around ten African national soccer teams and is the most visible soccer brand in Africa and in the world. This visibility also gives him implicit power and leverage with soccer authorities despite the FIFA rule of noninterference from a third party. In this case, commercial interest and pressure cannot be ruled out when discussing the selection of foreign coaches who additionally have deep ties to multinational corporations.[15]

The conflict of interest at a small scale is also noticeable on the pressure of players to maintain foreign coaches. Talking about the case of Volker Finke and citing local news media, Raoul Mbog stated that, besides the support from Puma, the call to extend the contract of the coach was sustained passionately by Stéphane Mbia. The captain of the team vouched

---

[13] Cameroon newspaper *Le Messager* also mentioned that Volker Finke was sponsored by Puma.

[14] According to Senegalese news media Seneweb and Pressafrik, the German coach's contract was signed by way of the equipment manufacturer Puma, which was ready to support financially the coach by providing 2/3 of his salary. Previous coaches such as Otto Pfister and Peter Schnittger were also financially supported by the German cooperation. "Volker Finke à la tête de l'équipe nationale: Un choix imposé par Puma." Pressafrik Web. 28 December 2012, and "Coach des Lions: Volker Finke, le candidat allemand de Puma en pôle-position?" Seneweb. 26 december 2012.

[15] True or false, the information about the pressure of Puma is substantial enough to be disregarded. There is no smoke without fire says the proverb.

that the German coach was the only one capable of qualifying Cameroon to the CAN 2017: "Le sociétaire de Séville a déclaré à plusieurs reprises que Volker Finke était le seul capable de qualifier le Cameroun pour la Coupe d'Afrique des Nations au Gabon en 2017" (Mbog) [*The player from Seville declared on several occasions that Volker Finke was the only one capable of qualifying Cameroon for the Africa Cup of Nations in 2017 in Gabon*]. The passion of the team's captain was not innocent. It was motivated by personal interest since he wanted to use his good relation with the German coach to get one of his siblings in the national team roster: "D'autres y voient aussi le soutien du capitaine de l'équipe, Stéphane Mbia, lui-même décrié et soupçonné de vouloir imposer son frère cadet en sélection nationale grâce à sa proximité avec l'ex-sélectionneur" (Mbog) [*Others see also the support of the captain of the team, himself slandered and suspected of trying to impose his younger brother in the national team thanks to his close ties to the former head coach*].

The debate surrounding the Cameroonization or foreignization of the Indomitable Lions' head coach continues to be problematic. It is a fact that since the 1960s to 2021, soccer authorities have selected around 30 head coaches among which 9 natives. The overwhelming majority are white Europeans. The interpretation of this fact ultimately depends on the eye of the beholder. It varies from one stakeholder to another. The stakeholders comprise mostly soccer authorities, natives and foreign coaches, fans and commercial enterprises.

This study has shown that soccer authorities as the representative of the official discourse claim fairness and good governance as guidance during the process of selection. Performance and successful results are indicator of retention or sacking of head coaches. Yet other voices contradict those official statements.

The fact that all native coaches were appointed as merely caretakers and replaced, despite their success or failure, shows a lack of respect for local talents who are numerous and as qualified as their foreign counterparts. Moreover, the preference for white Europeans and not even African foreigners could be interpreted as the persistence of neo-colonial mentality. As Jimmy Kainja wrote in *Africa is a Country* (2013): "African football seems to be following the path of its national economies: so many resources and human talent but always looking to the West for help" (Kainja). Even other stakeholders such as sport specialists and the public are progressively encouraging the hiring of native coaches. The call to hire native coaches could fall in the categories of Afrocentrism and nationalism, but it is not an exclusive demand that would mirror reverse racism and discrimination. As Stephen Keshi and other African coaches have stated, they are not against Europeans coaching in Africa. They are against the selection of Europeans who are less experienced or have the same record as the natives. Local coaches demand the opportunity to manage their own national teams. Unfortunately, this plea falls on deaf ears. According to the late Nigerian coach: "they're not given the opportunity because they're just black dudes. I don't like it" (*BBC* 2013).

White foreign coaches like the Scottish Bobby Williamson defends the hiring of Europeans citing the lack of qualifications and coaching license from UEFA which is more valuable than the certification from CAF. This argument contrast with native coaches' assumption and the experience of many Cameroonians and Africans/blacks who are international coaches or have received their coaching licenses in Europe.

Besides official discourse and voices from native and foreign coaches, other forces are implicitly influencing the foreignization of head coaches. As an executive member of FECAFOOT declared to the French news media *Le Monde* on the dismissal of Volker Finke: "Il y a des enjeux qui nous dépassent parfois dans ces affaires" (Raoul Mbog) [*There are issues that go beyond our power in these cases*]. This declaration from an insider and soccer authority summarizes the hidden face of the head coaching selection process. The method of selection might not be as transparent and independent as the official discourse wants the public and FIFA to acknowledge. The intense scrutiny and "utopian" expectation of the public on native coaches as well as the pressure from multinational enterprises eager to impose and protect their protégé for commercial benefit have facilitated the selection of foreigners.

The controversy that surrounds the Cameroonization or foreignization of the Indomitable Lions' head coach is mostly due to the high profile of the team that is the historical pride of the nation as well as the prime image and ambassador of the country. It is also more financially rewarding and valuable than other associated Lions' teams. Contrary to the Indomitable Lions, soccer authorities have Cameroonized the coaching staff of Lions A, U23, U20, U17 and U15. They have even taken a great step to Cameroonize the head coach and staff of the women national soccer team.[16] The Lionesses finished second in 1991, 2004, 2014 and 2016

---

[16] Some of the head coaches of the Lionesses are Enow Ngachu (2004–2017), Joseph Ndoko (2017–2019) and Gabriel Zabo (2019–).

African Women's Championship and 3rd in the 2018 edition. They have participated in the Olympic Games in 2012 and have brilliantly represented the country in their first ever FIFA Women's World Cup in 2015 in Canada. Under the leadership of the Cameroonian coach Enow Ngatchu, the Lionesses reach the 8th finals with a splendid and unexpected performance. The euphoria of their arrival back home was indescribable. The heroic team gave hope to fans disappointed with the debacles of the men national soccer team in international competitions. Enow Ngatchu's talent and experience, combined with players' brilliance during the World Cup 2015, have pushed soccer authorities and the population to have more respect for the women team. The authorities have restored and restructured female soccer clubs and championship that collapsed years ago due to negligence. The Cameroonian coach Alain Djeumfa was appointed national coach in January 2019 and led the team to the 2019 FIFA Women's World Cup in France. He was replaced in June 2021 by another Cameroonian coach Gabriel Zabo.

The trust that soccer authorities bestow on a native coach to lead the women national soccer team contrasts with the men's Lions. The maxims couldn't be more different. If in the case of the selection of Lionesses' head coach the "charity begins at home," in the case of the Lions, it seems that "no prophet is accepted in his own country." The Indomitable Lions head coach selection is a more complex, sensitive and challenging issue where many (conflicting) interests intersect.

The arguments for or against the foreignization or Cameroonization of the Indomitable Lions head coaching job will certainly continue and be passionate. Any choice won't please everybody all the time. Nevertheless, the main stakeholders in the decision making should at least refrain from *negrophobia* and *whitephobia* in order not to be (un)consciously perpetrator of covert racism or reverse racism. It is ultimately up to soccer authorities to make their decision less polemical and explicitly showing the fans that "the black man should no longer have to be faced with the dilemma 'whiten or perish'" (Fanon 80). The Cameroon soccer federation executives have the right to select any head coach as they see fit. They also have the obligation not to ignore without valid reasons the candidacy of native coaches as they do in Europe where the majority of the Indomitable Lions' head coaches originated from.

REFERENCES

Billebault, Alexis. "Football: pourquoi le futur sélectionneur des Fennecs ne sera probablement pas algérien." *Jeune Afrique* Web. 7 June 2016. 10 July 2016. Print.
Bloom, B. S. *Developing talent in young people*. New York, NY: Ballantine, 1985. Print.
Bongmba, Elias K. *The Dialectics of Tranformation in Africa*. New York: Palgrave, 2006. Print.
Bourdieu, Pierre. *Practical reason. On the theory of action*. Cambridge: Polity Press. 1998. Print.
"Cameroon: Volker Finke dismissed from coach role." *BBC* Web. 30 October 2015. 10 June 2016.
Côté, J., J. Salmela, P. Trudel, A. Baria, and S. Russell. "The coaching model: A grounded assessment of expert gymnastic coaches' knowledge." *Journal of Sport and Exercise Psychology*, 17 (1995): 1–17. Print.
Cushion, C. J., K. M Armour, and R.L Jones. "Locating the coaching process in practice: Models 'for' and 'of' coaching." *Physical Education & Sport Pedagogy*, 11(2006): 83–99. Print.
Epo, Olivier N. "Cameroun-Lions Indomptables: Le nouveau selectionneur pose deja denombreux problemes." *Camerpost* Web. 02 November 2015. 25 June 2016.
Fédération Internationale de Football Association. *FIFA Statutes: Regulations Governing the Application of the Statutes*. Zurich: FIFA, 2016. Print.
Kainja, Jimmy. "Why do African countries hire non-African football coaches so much?" *Africa is a country*. Web. 1 February 2013. 28 June 2016.
Kalfa, David. "Vers un record des sélectionneurs étrangers a la CAN 2015." *RFI. Afriquefoot* Web. 27 November 2014. 12 June 2016.
"Keshi raises concerns over white coaches in Africa." *BBC* Web. 4 January 2013. 5 July 2016.
"Nations Cup 2013: Keshi criticises 'mediocre' European coaches." *BBC* Web. 6 February 2013. 11 June 2016.
Nsigué, Guy. "Lions Indomptables: 21 changements d'entraineurs en 22 ans." *Mboafootball* 19 Septembre 2012. 24 June 2016.
Ngugi Wa Thiong'o. *Decolonising the Mind: The Politics of Language in African Literature*. Oxford: James Currey, 1986. Print.
Frantz Fanon. *Black Skin White Masks*. New York: Grove Press, 2008. Print.
Mazrui, Ali and Alamin Mazrui. *The Power of Babel: language and Governance in the African Experience*. Oxford: James Currey, 1998. Print.
"Tombi A Roko: 'S'inspirer de cet example belge'" *Camer.be* 20 February 2016. 17 June 2016

Pierre, Jemina. *The Predicament of Blackness: Postcolonial Ghana and the Politics of Race*. Chicago: Chicago UP, 2013. Print.

Potrac, P., R.L. Jones and K.M. Armour. "'It's all about getting respect': The coaching behaviors of an expert English soccer coach." *Sport, Education and Society*, 7 (2002): 183–202. Print.

Reddy, C., S. M Babu, and W.W Kidane. "The effect of coaching behavior on player's satisfaction in the case of Ethiopian soccer players: review of literature." *International Journal of Social Science and Interdisciplinary Research* 2.1 (2013): 106–117. Print.

Rein, Micheal, Joan Duda and Nikos Ntoumanis. "Dimensions of coaching behavior, need satisfaction, and the psychological and physical welfare of young athletes." *Motivation and Emotion* 28.3 (2004):297–313. Print.

CHAPTER 14

Conclusion

Augustine E. Ayuk

In the introductory chapter, we emphasized that football and politics in the continent are interlaced, that politics influence football, and that football outcomes effect political decisions at the local, national, and international levels. Throughout the volume, contributors provide copious examples of how politics influences the game and how the game contributes to changing political decisions. We argue that football is linked to the lives of most Africans, who regard the game as their "second to religion". Most Africans consider football as a way of displaying their love for country (patriotism). During the colonial period, Africans used football as a uniting tool to fight against colonial rule as well as a symbol of pride. In many African countries, success of the national football team in either continental or international football tournaments is usually interpreted as international or diplomatic victory for the country. In Cameroon, for example, the government usually declares a national holiday after a major victory by the national football team, the Indomitable Lions.

Since the introduction of football in the continent, Europeans have been in charge and dominated the decision-making process including

A. E. Ayuk (✉)
Clayton State University, Morrow, GA, USA
e-mail: Augustineayuk@clayton.edu

© The Author(s), under exclusive license to Springer Nature
Switzerland AG 2022
A. E. Ayuk (ed.), *Football (Soccer) in Africa*, Global Culture and Sport Series, https://doi.org/10.1007/978-3-030-94866-5_14

control of the football governing body, FIFA. From 1934 to 1978, FIFA allocated one place to the African zone for the FIFA World Cup tournament. However, because of protest and an increase in voting power, from CAF, FIFA increased the number of spots for Africa to two in 1982. Currently, the African zone sends 5 representatives to the World Cup, compared to the Europe's 13.

Africans have continued to use their solidarity to push for outcomes they deem important to advancing African football and political interest. Reflecting on solidarity, Armstrong and Giulianotti (2004) maintain that

> Whereas supporters of European national teams care only for their own country, generally decrying the efforts of others, there is a feeling of pride in Africa as a whole for the performance in successive World Cups of the Indomitable Lions, the Super Eagles, and I will add, the Black Stars of Ghana and the Teranga Lions of Senegal.

In Africa, the success of one country in international football is hailed as a success of all in Africa. The cases of Cameroon, Senegal, and Ghana reaching the FIFA World Cup quarterfinals were greeted by all Africans as milestones for the continent.

Solidarity in African football was demonstrated in the 1960 FIFA Congress in Rome, as CAF members lobbied and pushed for anti-racism resolution, demanding that the Football Association of South Africa (FASA) integrate football within one year. FASA's refusal to comply with the resolution impelled CAF members to petition for expulsion of FASA from FIFA. However, FIFA suspended FASA from FIFA organized activities because of FASA's pro-apartheid posture.

Similarly, CAF members demonstrated their solidarity and resolve when they demanded an increase in the number of spots for Africa ahead of the 1966 FIFA World Cup in England. FIFA repudiation of Africa's request led to the boycott of the 1966 World Cup, the first ever in FIFA's history.

African political leaders have capitalized on the successes of their respective national football teams to further their political objectives. Many of these leaders have used football triumphs as inducements to prolong their stay in power. The case of President Paul Biya of Cameroon stands out. Before 1990 World Cup, for example, Cameroon was at the verge of political and economic collapse. However, the success of the national team in the FIFA World Cup competition in Italy saved the day for the president and the country. Indeed, football success by the national team prevented the country from tittering or disintegrating. There are examples throughout the continent, where football has served as the "last solution" to the country's problems (Ivory Coast, Liberia).

Football represents a multiplicity of class, political, social, and cultural interests; at the same time, it serves as the glue that holds together Africa's diverse patchwork of ethnic, religious, language groups together. The game has been used as an instrument to construct national identity in many countries in the continent; at the same time, it has been used as a divisive tool, especially against particular groups based on their religion, ethnicity affinities. As Hobsbawm (1990) rightly puts it, "football is able to seize the popular imagination and arouse both nationalistic and chauvinistic tendencies, more concretely than other realms of cultural and political production".

The cases of Ivory Coast and Liberal stand out, where football stars like Didier Drogbar of Ivory Coast and George Weah of Liberia were able to use their star power as footballers to bring peace to their war-torn countries. These two examples serve as proof that football has the capacity to unite citizens even in war-ravaged countries or communities. On another front, however, citizens in many countries in Africa are denied the opportunity to participate in football clubs, or the national team, because of their ethnic backgrounds, religious affiliation, or gender. In many cases, national team players are chosen not necessarily based on skills but on political pressure on the coach and his/her technical staff by politicians and high-level bureaucrats in the country.

Women and Girls

Many African countries are breaking with tradition by allowing women and girls to participate in football. Today, about a third of African countries have female football national teams that compete at the continental and international levels. The Super Falcons of Nigeria stand out as the best African female national team on the continent. The Lioness of Cameroon have also emerged as credible challengers to the Super Falcons. Both female teams reached the second round of the FIFA World Cup tournament in Canada in 2015 and France in 2019.

In the introductory chapter, we indicated that women's football in Africa was still in its infancy. In most countries in the continent however, women and girls are discouraged from playing football because to most people, it is believed to be a "man's" game. There are of stereotypes associated with women and girls who play football, and the most outlandish is that women and girls who play football are bisexual and will not be able to give birth to a children.

Football is a contested arena with lots of rivalries between national teams in the continent. The most outstanding rivalries include Cameroon and Nigeria, Egypt and Algeria, South Africa and Zambia, Cameroon and Egypt, Morocco and Tunisia, Ghana and Nigeria, Ivory Coast and Senegal, Tunisia and Morocco, DRC and Ghana, and Morocco and Egypt. These rivalries, however, have not resulted in international skirmishes among these countries, as has been the case in some Central American countries. Nevertheless, the case of Egypt and Algeria reminds us that football has the capacity to spark conflict between nations.

Challenges

The success of African national football teams has been undermined by numerous problems and challenges. First, the political windfall associated with victory of the national team emboldens political leaders to interfere in the selection of players in the national team. Hence, political bureaucrats, not football technocrats, decide which players should be called to the national team. Similarly, the diversion of funds earmarked for advancing football in many countries ends up in the pockets of federation officials or members of sports ministries. Corruption has permeated all strata of the football ecosystem in Africa, from CAF to the top officials in the Ministries of Sports, to top guns in the football federations, match officials, as well as ticket vendors. On November 23, 2020, for example, the President of CAF, Ahmad Ahmad, was suspended by an Independent Ethics Committee of FIFA for five years for financial misconduct, and a fine of 200,000 Swiss Franc was levied on the former CAF boss. Later, however, FIFA reduced the suspension to two years.

The players who bring victory and joy to their respective nations do not receive their promised allowances or bonuses. Bonus payments have been an issue of controversy within many African football federations. Many African players have threatened to boycott or refuse to play international football matches as a way to bring attention to their plight. The cases of Cameroon, Nigeria, and Ghana stand out. This problem has persisted for a long time and seems to be going no way. As a result, some players choose to remain and play in their club tournaments than fly home and defend their countries (club versus country conundrum).

African nations have perhaps the poorest football infrastructures in the world. Many governments have not invested enough resources to build or upgrade football facilities in their respective countries. In some cases, such as in Cameroon, monies earmarked for refurbishing of football facilities end up in the pockets of well-connected government officials. Many of the national football infrastructures in Africa do not meet FIFA guidelines. Many children in Africa still play football on the streets with makeshift balls and barefoot.

Football provides enormous economic opportunities for African players, vendors, and local communities. In many countries, throughout the continent, new football academies have been built by African entrepreneurs and foreign capital to train young boys and girls as professional footballers. This initiative has unfortunately led to mass migration of talented African footballers to Western clubs, to the disadvantage of local football. On the flipside, however, the training received by African footballers from these western clubs has enhanced the skills of the footballers, thus improving African national football teams.

The introduction and installation of satellite television throughout the continent have indirectly stifled interest and attendance in local football tournaments. Today, most African football enthusiasts proudly identify with European football clubs such as Arsenal, Manchester United, Manchester City, Liverpool, Chelsea, Barcelona, Real Madrid, PSG, Bayern Munich and so on than identify with a local football club. African fans have their allegiance with European clubs; they purchase memorabilia from these clubs than support local football clubs and footballers.

Africans are deeply divided on the issue of foreign coaches versus local or indigenous coaches. Some argue that Africans can coach their national teams to victory instead of relying on "foreign mercenaries". These critics against foreign coaches further argue that expatriate coaches are too expensive and do not speak the language or understand the culture of the African national team. Opponents, however, counter that local coaches do not have the experience to lead the national teams to victory in international tournaments like the FIFA World Cup competition. Furthermore, opponents argue that foreign coaches will be fair in the selection of players of the national team based on merit not tribal affiliations or linguistic or regional connections. To wrap up, African football has made significant progress within a short period, given all the challenges faced by African nations. Today, Africans are no longer spectators of the game; they are determined participants who have challenged the superiority and monopoly of their former colonial overlords. Africa once again is producing top-quality footballers who are recruited in European, American, and Middle Eastern markets.

This edited volume cannot address all the issues relating to football in Africa. Some areas in need of future research will include:

1. The death of African footballers while playing football for their club and country.
2. Life after football. A handful of African players have not been as successful in their post football lives like their compatriots. Some have been homeless asking for handouts.
3. Should FIFA and CAF be responsible for direct player bonus payments than country federations?

We hope future research on these topics will yield greater understanding of football in Africa.

REFERENCES

Hobsbawm, E. Nationals and Nationalism since 1780: Program, Myth, Reality. Cambridge, UK: Cambridge University Press, 1990.
Armstrong, G., and Giulianotti R. (ed) Football in Africa: Conflict, Conciliation and Community. New York: Palgrave Macmillan 2004.

Index[1]

A
Abdellaziz Abdallah Salem, 34
Abdel Mohamed, 34
Aboutrika, Mohamed, 156
Accra, 169, 172, 177, 178, 183
Accra Amateur Football Association (AAFA), 168
Accra Great Olympics, 177
Accra Hearts of Oak, 173, 177
Acheampong, Ben, 177
African Cup of Nations (AFCON), 86, 87, 89, 90, 92, 99
African Football Association (AFA), 180
African game, 25, 34, 35, 39–41, 43–45, 47, 49, 50, 52
Aggrey Fynn, 177, 181
Aggrey memorial secondary school, 260, 264
Agyeman Gyau, 177
Ahidjo, Amadou, 86
Ahmed Hossam (Mido), 155
Aigle Royal of Nkongsamba, 85

Akii Bua, 267
Akono, Jean Paul, 90, 277, 280, 283
Akpeji, C., 117
Akwei, Richard, 168
Al-Ahly Sporting Club, 150
Alexandria Stadium, 148, 149, 152
All-Africa games, 190, 196, 197, 211
All African People's Conference, 172
Al-Ittihad Club (the United), 151
Al-Masry Club, 159
Al-Salam Boccaccio 98, 157
Amin, Idi, 265–266, 269
Amsterdam, 181
Anglophone crisis, 78
Anglophones, 78, 79, 89, 94, 95, 99
Aniche, E. T., 27
Anieke, Peter, 111–113
Anyumba, Peter, 192
Appiah, James Kwesi, 286–289
The Arab Contractors Stadium, 152
Argentina, 29
Arsenal, 223, 224
Asante Kotoko, 178, 179

[1] Note: Page numbers followed by 'n' refer to notes.

© The Author(s), under exclusive license to Springer Nature Switzerland AG 2022
A. E. Ayuk (ed.), *Football (Soccer) in Africa*, Global Culture and Sport Series, https://doi.org/10.1007/978-3-030-94866-5

ASC Diaraf, 217
ASEC Abidjan, 218
Ashe Mukama, 267
Aspro Tournament, 258, 266
Association, 168, 170
Association de Football de Lubumbashi (AFLU), 134
AS Vita Clubs, 126, 127, 130–132, 135, 137, 137n10, 139, 140, 141n14, 144
Atangana Ottou, 284
Ayo Makinwa, 119

B
Baba Yara, 173, 177, 178, 181
Balamaze Lwanga, 268
Bamako, 218
Bamilékés, 84
Barker, Clive, 288
Beara, Vladimir, 277
Belinga, Alexandre, 277, 280, 283, 290
Bell, Joseph Antione, 285–287
Belmadi, Djamel, 288
Benteke, Christian, 127, 142
Bernadette Deville-Danthu, 219
Binaisa, Godfrey, 266
Biya, Paul, 78, 93
Blackpool, 173
Blantyre, 181
Blatter, Sepp, 29, 37–47, 51
Bloodless Revolution, 86
Boco, Jimmy Adjovi, 224
Bonga, Paul, 128
Boxing Day, 166
Brazil, 175, 186, 187
Brazzaville, 216, 217
British, 87
British colonies, 166
The British occupation, 147–150, 150n9

British Southern Cameroons, 87–89
Brong Ahafo United, 177–178
Broos, Hugo, 277, 281
Budo Hill, 257
Budo Old Boys, 257
Bukavu, 129
Bukusu, 191
Bunyore, 191
Burj Al-Arab International Stadium, 153
Bwanga Tshimen, 128

C
Cairo International Stadium, 152
Cameroon, 77–99
Cameroon Development Corporation (CDC), 88
Cameroonians, 78, 79, 81, 82, 84, 87, 92–94
Cameroon(ization), 275–295
Cameroon's, 78, 91
Cammark Mamfe, 95
CAN, 282, 283, 288, 293
Canon Yaoundé, 85, 91, 92
Cape Coast, 166, 167
Cape Coast Victoria Park, 167
CEMAC Cup, 278
Central African football federations (CECAFA), 43
Central Organization of Sports (COS), 168, 169, 177
Chandibai Himathmal Mansukhani College (CHM), 77
Charles Kwabla, 186
Chief Executive Officer (CEO), 240, 247–249
Chief Jim Nwobodo, 112
Chile, 29
Chris Briandt, 174
Chukwu, Christian, 112, 114
Chung, Moon-Joon, 42, 44

INDEX 307

Cissé, Aliou, 288
Coca-Cola, 38
Colonial governor, 166, 167
Colonization, 13, 253, 258
Conceiçao da Silva Oliveira, 278, 282
Confederation of African Football (CAF), 194, 199, 200, 209
Confederation of East and Central African Football Associations (CECAFA), 189, 191, 193–197, 201, 206, 210
Confederation of North, Central American and Caribbean Association of Football (CONCACAF), 144, 144n20
Confederation of Southern African Football Federation (COSAFA), 43
Congo, 87
Congolese, 125–145
Congolese football, 125–145
Contradictions, 231–250
Core, 26–28
Corruption, 90, 99
Côte d'Ivoire, 218, 225
Coupe d'Afrique Occidentale Française, 218, 226
The Cranes, 264, 266
Crystal Palace, 223n26, 225
Czechoslovakia, 174, 180

D

Dakar, 216–219, 222–226, 224n28
Darby, Paul, 57–59, 260, 261
Dar-es Salaam, 181
David, 87
Davis Kamoga, 267
DC Motema Pembe, 137
De facto discrimination, 95
De-Africanization, 284
De-blackification, 284
Demba Diop Stadium, 226

Denis Obua, 267
Deregionalizing, 87
Detribalization, 87
Diambars Football Academy, 224
Didem Tali, 130n3
Dietschy, Paul, 138, 141
Disciplinary, 103–122
Di Stefano, Alfredo, 181
Djan, Ohene, 169, 174–180, 182, 183, 185
Djeumfa, Alain, 295
Djonkep, Bonaventure, 284, 290
Dodoo Ankrah, 177, 181
Dominique Colonna, 90, 277, 282
Douala, 79, 81, 82, 84, 91, 92, 96
Dragon Douala, 85
Dynamo of Douala, 94

E

École Normale William Ponty, 216
Edward Acquah, 177, 181
Egypt, 56–58, 60, 63, 67, 70–72, 147–161
The Egyptian Football Federation, 148
The Egyptian U20 team, 153
Ekumbe Vipers, 89
England, 168, 175, 180, 183–185
Enow Ngachu, 295
Enow Ngatchu, 295
Epervier d'Ebolowa, 85
Eridadi Mukwanga, 267
Ethiopia, 32, 34, 56–58, 60
Étoile Filante, 218
Etoile Sportive of Yaoundé, 81
Eto'o, Samuel, 2, 9
Eurocentric, 26, 34, 45, 51
European colonizers, 171
Everton, 167
Everton FC, 225
Excelsior, 167
Executive Council, 31, 32

F

Fabisch, Reinhard, 196, 210, 211
Farmers, 256
Farmer's Council, 170
FC Bilima, 132, 139
FC SNEL (Société National d'Electricité), 134
FECAFOOT, 82–84, 90, 92, 93, 96, 99, 279–282, 294
Federation of Uganda Football Association (FUFA), 263–266, 269
Feisal, 190, 191
FIFA Congress, 55–57, 72
FIFA's Normalization Committee, 84
Filgoal, 157
Finke, Volker, 277, 279–281, 290–294
Football, 147–161
Football Kenya Federation (FKF), 202, 203, 206
Football Kenya Limited (FKL), 202, 203, 206
Foreign(ization), 275–295
Fortuna Dusseldorf, 174
Foucault, Michel, 104, 105, 117, 121
Foyer France Senegal, 217
France, 82, 90, 93, 99
Francophone, 78, 79, 81, 89, 94–96, 99
Frank Crentsil, 177
Fraser, Alexander Gordon, 257
FUFA Women's League, 264

G

Gamal Abdel-Nasser, 150
The Gambia, 166
Gender, 231–240, 243, 247–249
Gender inequality, 231–234, 237, 239, 249
George Appiah, 177
Ghana, 56, 59, 67, 165–187
Ghana Amateur Football Association (GAFA), 169, 177, 182
Ghana Army, 170
Ghana Coaches Association (GCA), 186
Ghana National Team, 173
Ghana Referees Association (GRA), 170
Gisu, 254, 256, 259
GOAL project, 41, 43, 47
Goethe, Georges, 79
Gold Coast, 166–168, 171, 175
Gold Coast XI, 173
Gold Medal, 90
Goliath, 87
Gor FC, 190, 200
Gossage Cup, 190, 191
Governmentality, 103–122
Governor-General's Cup, 109, 110
Gramsci, A., 104–107
Guerin, Robert, 29
Guinea Bissau, 243, 244
Gyamfi, C. K., 173–175, 181, 182

H

Al-Hadari, Essam, 156
Hafia Conakry, 132
Hann, Arie, 277
Harambee Stars, 190, 192, 194, 196–200, 202, 207, 208, 211
Hassan, Ahmed, 154, 156
Havelange, João, 29, 36–48, 50, 51, 56, 60–61
Hayatou, Issa, 40, 42–44, 48, 49, 51, 59, 60, 68, 69
Head coaches, 275–295
Heroes Muyuka, 89
Historical perspective, 216–222
Historicizing football, 103–122
Hofstede, G., 110, 112
Hodgson, Frederick, 167
Hungary, 174

INDEX 309

I
Ibenge, Florent, 127
Idrissa Gana Gueye, 225, 227
Iheanacho, Kelechi, 119
Ilerika, Haruna, 112
Inconsistencies, 231–250
India, 77
Indomitable Lions, 78, 89, 90, 92–94, 275–295
Infantinos, Gianni, 46–50
International Olympic Committee (IOC), 36
Ismailia stadium, 152
Italy, 78, 92, 93
Ivan Ridanović, 90
Iwelumo, Godwin, 113

J
James Adjei, 173, 174
Jean-Manga Onguéné, 277, 283
Jeune Afrique, 291
Jimmy Kirunda, 267
Jomo Cosmos, 240–243, 249
Jordan, Dr. Danny, 244
Jorge, Artur, 277
Joys, 147–161
Jozeff Ember, 174
Jules François, 223
Juventus, 222

K
Kabila, Laurent D., 139
Kabulo Mwana Kabulo, 130
Kadenge, Joe, 190, 191, 195, 201
Kaduna, 120
Kakungulu Cup, 265, 270
Kalal, Pierre, 128
Kambayi, Denis, 126
Kampala, 257, 258
Kampala City Authority (KCCA), 269, 270
Kananga, 129
Karauri, Adams, 198
KB Asante, 178
Kemmeny, Tibor, 174
Kenya, 189–211
  Football Federation (KFF), 193, 194, 198, 202, 203, 205, 206, 209–211
Kenya Football Association (KFA), 191, 193, 202, 203
Kenyatta, Jomo, 192, 193
Keshi, Stephen, 116, 286–288, 294
Khartoum, 34, 56–58
Khesa, 130
Kialunda, Julian, 128, 140n13
Kibonge Mafu, 128, 132
King's School in Budo, 257
Kinshasa, 126, 129–132, 135, 136, 137n10, 138–140, 143, 143n17
Kinshasa Limete, 132
Kiprotich, Stephen, 267
Kisangani, 129
Kofi Pare, 177
Kontchou Kuoumrgni, Augustin, 90
Kumasi, 178–180
Kumbo Stickers, 89
Kwabenya Atomic Energy Commission, 176
Kwame Adarkwa, 177, 181

L
Laamb, 214, 219
Lagos, 173
Lagos Town Council (LTC), 109
Lawal, Muda, 112, 113
Lazarro, Javier Clemente, 277
Lechantre, Pierre, 90
Le Guen, Paul, 277
Lemba-Foire, 132
The Leopards, 126, 138, 140, 141, 143, 144
Le Roy, Claude, 90

Les Lions de la Teranga, 213, 220, 226
Lille, 224
Lions Cadet, 284
Lions Espoirs, 284
Lions Junior, 284
Lions Minimes, 284
Lisano, 132
"Little Congo," 87
Lomé, 218
London, 36, 39, 56, 57, 121, 168, 175, 180, 183–185, 223, 257, 264, 268, 270, 300
Loukaku, 127
Lubumbashi, 126, 129, 135, 136, 139
Lugard, Lord, 257
Lugonzo, Isaac, 191, 203, 210
Luo Union, 190–193, 195

M
Madhavani, 258
Maduewesi, C., 117
Magdi Abdel Ghani, 155
Magogo, Mohamed, 193
Mahmoud El Khatib "Bibo," 154
Makuna Trouet, 128
Malawi, 181
Mama Becca Women's day cup, 265
Mandanda, Steve, 127, 142
Maragoli, 191
Marama, 191
Marginalization, 32
Martin, Phyllis, 259
Marxist Feminist Theory, 19
Marzbach, George, 151
Masaza cup, 258
The massacre of Air Defense Stadium, 160
The Massacre of Port Said Stadium, 153, 159
Matiba, Kenneth, 193, 194, 202–205, 209, 210

Matthews, Stanley, 173, 174
Mayanga Maku, 132
Mbata-Siala, 131
M'Boma, Patrick, 93
Mboya, Tom, 192
Mbuji-Mayi, 129, 135
McFarnell, Jimmy, 191
Mentality, 106, 107
Meridian Project, 40
Messi, Lionel, 222
Metsu, Bruno, 213, 220
Metz, 223
Mfum, Wilberforce, 181
Middle East, 127, 133, 139, 140, 140n13
Mike Kiganda, 267
Mike Okwechime, 113
Milla, Roger, 77, 78, 91, 93
Minister of Sports and Physical Education, 90
Ministry of Education, 169
Ministry of Sports, 279, 281, 282
Ministry of Youth, 218, 221, 222
Missionaries, 253, 256, 257, 259–261
Mission civilisatrice, 217
The Mixed Courts system, 150, 151
Mobuto, Sese Seko, 125, 132–134, 138–141
Modern Ghana, 174
Mohammed Naji (Gedo), 156
Mokotjo, Kamohelo, 243, 244
Moniedafe, F., 114
Morocco, 180
Mosete Mbombo, 130
Mosquitoes, 167
Mount Cameroon FC, 89
Mubarak, Mohamed Hosni, 153, 156, 158–160
Mulamba, Etepe, 128, 132
Mugabi, John, 267
Muscular Christianity, 217

INDEX 311

Mustafa Kamel, 150
Muwanga, Paulo, 266
Mwenge FC, 190, 191, 205
Mysterious Dwarfs, 167

N
Namirembe, 257
Nang, Jean Lambert, 90
Nashid, Mohamed, 150
National Executive Committee, 249
National First Division League, 268
National soccer league, 218, 221
National team, 84, 86–90, 92–99
Nation-building, 221
Navétanes, 218, 219n14, 221, 222
Nepomniachi, Valeri, 90, 93
New Nigerian Bank (NNB), 116
Ngaah, Williams, 191, 193, 203
Nice, 223
Nigerian football, 104–108, 111–113, 116, 117, 119, 121
Nigerian Football Federation (NFF), 66
Niva, Jonathan, 191, 192, 194, 198, 205
Nkono, Thomas, 277, 283
Nkrumah, Kwame, 59, 60, 165, 166, 169–174, 176, 178, 181, 182, 184–186
Nkwi, P.N., 88
Nlandu, Tamba, 133n7, 141, 142
Northwest, 80, 89, 95
Northwest region, 89
Nousia Sport Academy, 287
Nseke, Leonard, 277
Nsereko, Moses, 262, 267
Ntare school, 260
Nwokocha, Christian, 114, 116
Nyamweya, Sam, 202, 206, 210, 211
Nyongha, Jules, 283

O
Obafemi Martins, 119
Oblittey, E. O., 177
Obote, Milton, 265
Oceania, 38, 43–45
Odametey, Addo, 177, 181
Odinga, Oginga, 192
Odiye, Godwin, 113
Ofei Dodoo, 177
Ogot, Bethuel Allan, 192
Okala, Emmanuel, 112
Okello, B.O., 266
Okey Isima, 114
Okpi, A., 117
Old Budonian Club, 257, 264
Old Kampala, 257
Olympic Bonapriso Club of Douala, 82
The Olympic Club (the "Red Star"), 149
Omondi, Phillip, 262, 267
Organism Nationale de Coordination des Activités des Vacances (ONCAV), 222
Organization of African Unity (OAU), 184
Oryx of Douala, 84
Osagyefo's Own Club (OOC), 177, 178
Osagyefo Trophies, 170
Ottou, Atangana, 87
Otto Westphal, 174
Ousseynou Faye, 219

P
Pan Africanism, 165, 171, 181
Paris Saint-Germain (PSG), 222–225, 227
Patrick Viera, 223, 224
Péle, 132
Periphery, 27

Peru, 92
The Pharaohs, 147, 153, 155–158, 156n26
Phiri, Kinnah, 286, 287, 289
Pilkington, George Lawrence, 256–257
Poland, 92
Politics, 147–161
Polycarp Kakooza, 268
The Port Said Massacre, 160
Portugal, 114
Post and Telecommunications (P&T), 88
Powercam, 88
President, 29, 31, 35–37, 39–43, 46, 48, 49
Prisons FC Kampala, 268
Professional Soccer League (PSL), 247
Public Works Department (PWD), 109
Pulteney, Captain William, 257
Puskas, Ferenc, 181
PWD Bamenda, 89
PWD Kumba, 89
PWD Victoria, 89

Q
Qatar, 44
Qatar 2022, 68

R
Rabwogo, Leo, 267
Railway Apprentice, 167
The Railway Club (Al-Sekka Al-Hadid), 149
Ramogi, Zack, 192
Ramzi, Hani, 154
Rangers Football Club, 112
Raymond Fobété, 277, 282
Real Madrid, 179–183
Real Republikans, 177–180

Redon, Philippe, 90
Regional Leagues, 264, 265
Remington Cup, 190
Research method, 231, 233–234
Resistance, 103–122
Reunification, 59
Rev Archdeacon, 257
Rimet, Jules, 29, 31–34
Rino Martini, 174
Ronaldo, Cristiano, 222
Rous, Stanley (Sir), 29, 31, 35–38, 45

S
Salah, Mohamed, 156
Samia, 191
Samuel, Otoo E., 170n11
Schäfer, Winfred, 90
Schnittger, Peter, 90, 277, 278, 282
SC Villa, 264, 268–270
Seedorf, Clarence, 278, 281, 282, 284
Segregation, 82, 84
Segun Odegbami, 112
Sekondi Hasaacas, 167, 177
Sekondi Takoradi, 167, 168
Semi-periphery, 27
Senegal, 213–227
Senior Challenge Cup, 194, 197, 201, 206
Shehata, Hassan, 155, 156, 156n26, 158
Shikuku, Martin, 203
Shobeir, Ahmed, 158
Sierra Leone, 166, 172, 173
Simmons, Ben, 181
Simon, Moses, 119
Sjoberg, 174
Soccer hooliganism, 225
Sokhi-Bulley, 106
SONARA, 88
SONEL, 88
Sorcier Blanc, 282

Souare, Papa Ndiaye, 225
South Africa, 168, 184, 185
South African Football Association (SAFA), 231–233, 237, 238, 243, 244, 247, 248
South African Non-Racial Olympic Committee (NROC), 36
South American Football Confederation (CONMEBOL), 144
Southwest, 95
Southwest region, 80, 89
Spectatorship, 214–216, 222–226
Sporting Lisbon, 114
Stade de La Victoire, 134
Stade de Mbour, 226
ST Eloi Lupopo, 126, 134, 135
The "Students Club," 150
Sub-Saharan Africa, 27, 239
Sudan, 56–58, 180, 182
Susann Baller, 218
Swallows, 167
Switzerland, 29, 45

T
Tandon Muea, 89
Tanganyika, 190
Tanzania, 181, 190, 195, 199, 201
Taraba Football Club, 117
Teachers, 256
Tema Oil Refinery Plant, 176
Tessema, Ydnekatchew, 34, 37, 51, 58
Tiko United, 89
Timothy Ayieko, 267
Tito Okello, 266
Togo, 172, 173
Tokyo Olympics, 175, 182
Tombi A Roko Sidiki, 280
Tonnerre Yaoundé, 91, 92
Tony Igwe, 113

Top Tarzan Mutengene, 89
Tout Puissant Mazembe, 126, 127, 134–137, 137n10, 139, 141n14, 144
Tribalism, 84, 85
Tribalized, 276
Trusteeship, 81
Tsanga, S., 79, 81
Tsanga-Sud, 130
Tshimpumpua, 130
Tsinga-Ngedi, 130
Tunisia, 180
2011 Revolution, 158, 159

U
UDEAC Cup, 278
UEFA, 38–43
Uganda, 190, 195, 196, 200, 202, 253–271
Uganda Football Association (UFA), 257, 264
Ugandan Big League (UBL), 264, 269
Ugandan Cup, 264, 265, 270
Ugandan Super League, 264, 269
Uganda Super League, 268
Ukaegbu, V. E., 27
UK Telegraph, 104
Ultras Ahlawy, 159, 160
Union Douala, 85
Union Sportive Indigéne, 217, 218
Union Sportive Ouakam, 226
Unisport Gorée, 217, 218
Unisport of Bafang, 85
United Gold Coast Amateur Football (UGCAF), 18, 166–168, 171, 175, 217
United Nations, 81
United Kingdom, 253, 256
USA, 78, 89, 93, 96

V

Vaku, 130
Victoria United, 89
Vidacs, B., 88
Volta River at Akosombo, 176

W

Wahed-Sefr "One-Zero" film, 157
Walker, Robert Henry, 256
Wallerstein, Immanuel, 27, 28
Wanani Wanesinda, 130
Weah, George, 2, 3, 43, 301
Wesleyan High School, 108
West Africa, 214, 219
West African Soccer Federation (WASF), 172
West African Sub-Region, 173
Western Region Football Association, 168
Western Wanderers, 167
West Germany, 174, 180
White coaches, 283, 285, 286, 289
The White Knights, 159

Woolfall, Daniel, 29
World Economic system, 27
World system theory, 26, 27, 51
The Workers Brigade, 170
Wrestling, 214, 219, 220

Y

Yallakora, 157
Yaoundé, 81–85, 91, 95, 96
Young Sports Academy, 89
Yusuf Lule, 266

Z

Zaghloul, Saad, 150
Zaire, 138, 140, 140n13, 141n14
Zairianization, 138
Zaki, Mohamed, 149
Zamalek sporting club, 150
Zanzibar, 190, 258, 263
Zgoll, Bernhard, 204, 205
Zidan, Mohamed, 155, 159
Zurich, 42, 50

Printed in the United States
by Baker & Taylor Publisher Services